HINTS TOWARD REFORMS,

IN

Lectures, Addresses, and other Writings.

BY HORACE GREELEY.

HASTEN the day, just Heaven!
Accomplish thy design,
And let the blessings Thou hast freely given
Freely on all men shine;
Till Equal Rights be equally enjoyed,
And human power for human good employed;
Till Law, and not the Sovereign, rule sustain,
And Peace and Virtue undisputed reign.

HENRY WARE.

LISTEN not to the everlasting Conservative, who pines and whines at every attempt to drive him from the spot where he has lazily cast his anchor..... Every abuse must be abolished. The whole system must be settled on the right basis. Settle it ten times and settle it wrong, you will have the work to begin again. Be satisfied with nothing but the complete enfranchisement of Humanity, and the restoration of man to the image of his God.

HENRY WARD BEECHER.

ONCE the welcome Light has broken,
Who shall say
What the unimagined glories
Of the day?
What the evil that shall perish
In its ray?
Aid the dawning, Tongue and Pen!
Aid it, hopes of honest men!
Aid it Paper! aid it Type!
Aid it, for the hour is ripe!
And our earnest must not slacken
Into play;
Men of Thought, and Men of Action,
CLEAR THE WAY!

CHARLES MACKAY.

Second Edition, Enlarged.

WITH

THE CRYSTAL PALACE AND ITS LESSONS.

NEW YORK:
FOWLERS AND WELLS, PUBLISHERS,
No. 308 BROADWAY.

BOSTON:
No. 142 Washington St.

1854.

PHILADELPHIA:
No. 231 Arch Street.

TO

THE GENEROUS, THE HOPEFUL, THE LOVING,

WHO,

FIRMLY AND JOYFULLY BELIEVING IN THE IMPARTIAL AND BOUNDLESS GOODNESS OF OUR FATHER,

Trust,

THAT THE ERRORS, THE CRIMES, AND THE MISERIES,
WHICH HAVE LONG RENDERED EARTH A HELL,
SHALL YET BE SWALLOWED UP AND FORGOTTEN,
IN A FAR EXCEEDING AND UNMEASURED REIGN OF

TRUTH, PURITY, AND BLISS,

This Volume

IS RESPECTFULLY AND AFFECTIONATELY INSCRIBED,

BY

THE AUTHOR.

PREFACE.

CARLYLE, if I rightly remember, tells us of an impulsive Frenchman, who, in the very crisis of the great Revolution, when the frenzied public mind was intent on nothing short of the world's regeneration, and the due and ample feeding of the Guillotine as essential thereto, rose in the National Convention, full to bursting with an idea which he could no longer stifle, and vociferated, "Mr. President, I move that *all* the knaves and dastards be arrested!"—the very thing, you see, that the whole People were intent on, expressed in one very compact sentence. Where prisons could be found to hold the arrested, or jailers to guard them,—much more, provisions to subsist them—the mover had never stopped to calculate. He saw clearly that the fundamental evil, parent and fountain of all others, was the impunity allowed, the favor manifestly shown, to Knavery and Cowardice, and he was bent on a Radical Reform. A right good fellow, he was, too, at heart, I am sure, though not, perhaps, so practically sagacious, so readily cognizant of the relations of means to ends, as he might have been. As he grew older, he doubtless became cooler, sager, more considerate, more conservative; yet one may well doubt whether he ever rose above the moral altitude of his single recorded inspiration.

This apprehension of *all* the knaves and dastards, if you but consider, is one of the chief ends of Man's existence and effort on earth. A very arduous and tedious work, you may well pronounce it, especially when you observe that they who should combine to do it, including many of those who think they *are* doing it, with those who make a show of doing it, in the hope of imposing on their cotemporaries if not on themselves, are personally of the very class on whom the operation needs to be performed. It were a study to see the work really effected, and note how many who at the outset were flourishing handcuffs and trying to fit them to their neighbors' wrists, holding up ponderous jail-keys and calling out, 'This way, brother officers! Here's where the culprits are to be secured till further orders!' would find themselves wearing the ruffles and tenanting cells at the close, with eyes of blank amazement and visages of yard measure Not entirely a novel spectacle would this be, and yet deeply interesting and instructive.

Yes, 'the arrest of *all* the knaves and dastards'—or rather their thorough cure of knavery and cowardice—is a task given us to perform, and each must strive to do his part of it, even though with painful distrust that he himself is not wholly free from the vices he is laboring to eradicate. The more evil he discerns or suspects in himself, the harder he should labor for the general abolition and extinction of evil, beginning with his own faults but not forgetting that others also deserve and require effort for their eradication. Perchance in the general warfare against injustice, meanness and wrong, the sincere soul finds the best attainable discipline and corrective for its own faults and errors.

The volume herewith presented is mainly composed of Lectures prompted by invitations to address Popular Lyceums and Young Men's Associations, generally those of the humbler class, existing in country villages and rural townships. These Lectures were written in the years from 1842 to 1848 inclusive, each in haste, to fulfil some engagement already made, for which preparation had been delayed, under the pressure of seeming necessities, to the latest moment allowable. A calling whose exactions are seldom intermitted for a day, never for a longer period, and whose requirements, already excessive, seem perpetually to expand and increase, may well excuse the distraction of thought and rapidity of composition which it renders inevitable. At no time has it seemed practicable to devote a whole day, seldom a full half day, to the production of any of the essays contained in this volume. Not until months after the last of them was written did the idea of collecting and printing them in this shape suggest itself, and a hurried perusal is all that has since been given them. The Lecture here entitled 'The Organization of Labor' has been recast in part, to conform it to the existing state of facts; the others are printed as they were delivered. Some of them are more florid in style than my present mood would dictate—that entitled 'Human Life' especially—but they were faithful transcripts of the mind whence they emanated at the time they were written, and I could not now change without destroying them. Should their diction provoke the critic's sneer, so be it:

I am tolerably case-hardened to the shafts of periodical wit, and shall receive any that may be in store for me with fortitude if not with complacency. I am quite aware that the Literary merits of this volume are inconsiderable indeed.

But this work has a loftier and worthier aim than that of fine writing. It aspires to be a mediator, an interpreter, a reconciler, between Conservatism and Radicalism—to bring the two into such connection and relation that the good in each may obey the law of chemical affinity, and abandon whatever portion of either is false, mistaken or outworn, to sink down and perish. It endeavors so to elucidate and commend what is just and practical in the pervading demands of our time for a Social Renovation that the humane and philanthropic can no longer misrepresent and malign them as destructive, demoralizing or infidel in their tendencies, but must joyfully recognize in them the fruits of past and the seeds of future Progress in the history of our Race. Defective and faulty as these 'Hints' may be found or judged, I feel confident that their tendency is to practical beneficence, and that their influence, however circumscribed, can not be otherwise than wholesome. In the absence of any reasonable ground of hope for personal gain or popularity, this trust must justify my intrusion upon the public, for the first and perhaps for the last time, as the author of a book.

The great truths that every human being is morally bound, by a law of our Social condition, to leave the world somewhat better for his having lived in it—that no one able to earn bread has any moral right to eat *without* earning it—that the obligation to be industrious and useful is not invalidated by the possession of wealth nor by the generosity of wealthy relatives—that useful doing in any capacity or vocation is honorable and noble, while idleness and prodigality in whatever station of life are base and contemptible—that every one willing to work has a clear social and moral right to Opportunity to Labor and to secure the fair recompense of such Labor, which Society can not deny him without injustice—and that these truths demand and predict a comprehensive Social Reform based upon and molded by their dictates—these will be found faithfully if not forcibly set forth and elucidated in the following pages. Of course, as the Lectures were written independently of each other, and with intervals of months and often years between them, the reader can hardly fail to find the same proposition restated, the same arguments adduced, the same illustrations employed, in two or more instances. Each Lecture is a separate thesis, deriving (I trust) confirmation and support from others, but not maintaining connection therewith. And in the arrangement of the volume, so far as any plan was kept in view, diversity and variety rather than continuity and consecutiveness were deemed desirable. I know how easily the public mind grows weary of dry discussion.

—Of the briefer Essays which conclude the volume, two only—that on 'Death by Human Law' and that on 'Flogging in the Navy'—have been recast expressly for this work, and these but to give a more compact and methodical expression to views already submitted in other forms to the ordeal of public judgment. Four or five of these essays (mainly of a religious cast) were written from year to year for 'The Rose of Sharon' Annual, while the residue have in good part appeared at various times in the columns of The Tribune. These were generally suggested by some recent event, some apparent public necessity, but I hope they will not be found antiquated nor out of place now and here.

—I trust this explanation of the impulse and character of these 'Hints' will not be mistaken for an apology. I make none, and solicit no lenity. I inculpate no partial friend, no delighted auditor, as instigating this volume. If there be no true worth in it, let the serious guilt of adding another to the deplorable multitude of books unfit to be read rest on my shoulders alone. But if it shall be found to utter any word calculated to irradiate, however faintly or transiently, the on ward pathway of our Race, then it will stand fully justified, though all the critics should unite to blast it by their fiercest maledictions or their more fatal silence. H. G.

NEW-YORK, April 20, 1850.

CONTENTS.

HINTS TOWARD REFORMS.

I.

THE EMANCIPATION OF LABOR:

A LECTURE.

WORK stands in no need of eulogium. From olden times Priests and Poets have vied with Orators and Statesmen in heaping praises and flatteries on the man of honest, independent, useful toil. Not merely have these resonantly proclaimed that he *ought to be*, but that he *is* the most blessed among mortals. Indeed, an unsophisticated listener or reader might well imbibe the notion that all these honeyed eulogists, earth's great and glorious, had been thrust out, by some harsh decree of inexorable Fate, from the plow-field and the work-bench—sent sorrowing exiles into forums or senates—and there compelled to witness afar off the felicities they too might have enjoyed had they been born under kindlier stars, and to be content, in their sublime self-denial, with but depicting the delights of digging and delving, which only the more fortunate millions must enjoy.

Yet, in the midst of all this deluge of flattery and felicitation, the Worker of the Nineteenth Century stands a sad and care-worn man. Once in a while a particularly flowery Fourth-of-July Oration, Political harangue, or Thanksgiving

Sermon, catching him well-filled with creature-comforts and a little inclined to soar starward, will take him off his feet, and for an hour or two he will wonder if ever human lot was so blest as that of the free-born American laborer. He hurrahs, cavorts, and is ready to knock any man down who will not readily and heartily agree that this is a great country, and our industrious classes the happiest people on earth. The hallucination passes off, however, with the silvery tones of the orator, the exhilarating fumes of the liquor which inspired it. The inhaler of the bewildering gas bends his slow steps at length to his sorry domicile, or wakes therein on the morrow, in a sober and practical mood. His very exaltation, now past, has rendered him more keenly susceptible to the deficiencies and impediments which hem him in: his house seems narrow; his food coarse; his furniture scanty; his prospects gloomy, and those of his children more sombre, if possible; and as he hurries off to the day's task which he has too long neglected and for which he has little heart, he too falls into that train of thought which is beginning to encircle the globe, and of which the burden may be freely rendered thus—"*Why should those by whose toil* ALL *comforts and luxuries are produced or made available enjoy so scanty a share of them? Why should a man able and eager to work ever stand idle for want of employment in a world where so much needful work impatiently awaits the doing? Why should a man be required to surrender something of his independence in accepting the employment which will enable him to earn by honest effort the bread of his family? Why should the man who faithfully labors for another and receives therefor less than the product of his labor be currently held the obliged party, rather than he who buys the work and makes a good bargain of it?* In short, Why should Speculation and Scheming ride so jauntily in their carriages, splashing honest Work as it trudges humbly and wearily by on foot?"—Such, as I interpret it, is the problem which occupies and puzzles the knotted brain of Toil in our day. Let us ponder it.

But first, let us look at the whole matter in the light in which it presents itself to Conservatism, or the champions of the established order of things. We can lose nothing, we may gain something of insight, by so regarding it, which will reward a few moments' attention. Inestimable is the value of a Fact, if we do but rightly apprehend it; and very strong is the inherent presumption that the shape things have actually, and as we say naturally, taken is the very best they *could* have taken, all things considered, including the nature of Man. Let us look, then, at this whole matter of Labor, its Condition and Recompense, as it must appear to the men of substance and of thrift all around us.

All extreme statements begin and end in error, and nothing can be more mistaken than the vulgar presumption that Wealth goes by luck, or in fact that, searchingly regarded, there is any such thing as luck in the Universe. The man of respectability and property, whose blocks of houses adorn the busiest streets of our towns, and whose note goes unquestioned in bank, can you think him distinguished by no substantial qualities from those who were his playmates and schoolmates, and who are now his tenants and hirelings? O rely on it, there is no such instance of results without a cause in Nature! The man may be no better, I readily grant you, than those around him—perhaps in the truest sense no wiser—but very different he must be, and for that one purpose of accumulating property, a vastly superior being. Tried in History or Geography, in Psalmody or the Catechism, he might prove of small account; but in that wisdom which coins dollars from rocks and extracts fertility from marshes and miasms, he must be an adept. Nay, I go farther, and insist that a keen eye would have readily picked him out from among his schoolmates, and said, 'Here is the lad who will die a Bank President, owning factories and blocks of stores!' Now let us see how the questions we meditate must appear to this thrifty, practical man:

Trace his history closely, and you will find that in his boyhood he was provident and frugal—that he shunned expense and dissipation—that he feasted and quaffed seldom, unless at others' cost—that he was rarely seen at balls or frolics—that he was diligent in study and in business—that he did not hesitate to do an uncomfortable job, if it bade fair to be profitable—that he husbanded his hours and made each count one, either in earning or in preparing to work efficiently. He rarely or never stood idle because the business offered him was esteemed ungenteel or disagreeable—he laid up a few dollars during his minority, which proved a sensible help to him on going into business for himself—he married seasonably, prudently, respectably—he lived frugally and delved steadily until it clearly became him to live better, and until he could employ his time to better advantage than at the plow or over the bench. Thus his first thousand dollars came slowly but surely; the next more easily and readily by the help of the former; the next, of course, more easily still; until now he adds thousands to his hoard with little apparent effort or care. But the germ of all this spreading oak was in the tough acorn whence it sprang. Given the original qualities of the lad, all beyond was plainly deducible therefrom, unless prevented by death or some extreme calamity.

Now we shall but waste our breath in attempting to convince this man that the world is not a very good world as it stands, and labor rewarded exactly as it should be. Talk to him of the wants and woes of the Poor, and he will answer you that their sons can afford to smoke and drink freely, which he at their age could not; and that he now meets many of these poor in the market, buying luxuries that he can not afford. Dwell on the miseries occasioned by a dearth of employment, and he will reply that *he* never encountered any such obstacle when poor; for when he could find nothing better, he cleaned streets or stables, and when he could not command twenty dollars a month, he fell to work as heartily and cheerfully for ten or five. In vain will you seek to explain to him that his rare faculty both of doing and of finding to do—his wise adaptation of means to ends in all circumstances, his frugality and others' improvidence—are a part of your case—that it is precisely because all are not created so handy, so thrifty, so worldly-wise, as himself, that you seek so to modify the laws and usages of Society that a man may still labor steadily, efficiently, and live comfortably, although his youth was not improved to the utmost, and though his can never be the hand that transmutes all it touches to gold. Failing here, you urge that at least his children should be guarantied an unfailing opportunity to learn and to earn, and that they, surely, should not suffer nor be stifled in ignorance because of their parent's imperfections. Still you talk in Greek to the man of substance, unless he be one of the few who have, in acquiring wealth, outgrown the idolatry of it, and learned to regard it truly as a means of doing good, and not as an end of earthly effort. If he be a man of wealth merely, still cherishing the spirit which impelled him to his life-long endeavor, the world appears to him a vast battle-field, on which some must win victory and glory while to others are accorded shattered joints and discomfiture, and the former could not be, or would lose their zest, without the latter.

It seems to him quite plain that all might become as rich as he is if they would make the needful sacrifices of ease and mortifications of appetite; and if they won't, what can *he* do for them? To dissipate his fortune in prodigal beneficence would injure thousands and bring lasting good to few; to reduce mankind to some sort of Agrarian level would, if practicable, render life a tame, plodding, humdrum affair, hardly worth taking as a gift. In fine, the world appears to him the best that could be for the men and women who inhabit it,—its usages and laws the plain dictates of Divine benignity contemplating human depravity; and to all your suggestions of radical improvement he simply shakes his head and turns away to inquire the price of Cotton or the chances of an alteration in the Tariff.

Him we will leave for a season to his more congenial pursuits, while we inquire and consider in our own way what changes are necessary to the Emancipation and Social elevation of the laborer. I affirm, then, that there are three important respects in which the condition of the Laboring Mass, even of our own countrymen, may be improved, ought to be improved, and in regard to which it is the duty of the rich and powerful, of the Church and the State, to cowork for the required melioration. Of these I would place first in order, though perhaps not in practical importance,

Their relation to the Soil. I place this first, because I think Society and Government have been guilty of a *positive*, not a negative, wrong in regard to it—a wrong of usurpation and misdoing, and not merely of neglect and short-coming. God created the earth for the use and subsistence of mankind, and not primarily of a part, and of the rest in subordination to these. By Nature's law, use and improvement can alone vest in any individual a right to call some spot of earth his own, and exclude all others from the enjoyment and benefit thereof. Nothing can well be a more palpable subversion of the order of Providence than the assumption by Governments of a right to grant a province or county of virgin soil to some favorite, whether with or without consideration, to be held by him and his heirs for their own use and benefit, and to be cultivated and improved by others on terms which make the landlord class rich without labor or useful doing, and keep the tenant class mainly poor and subservient, though they do their best. If there ever was or can be a monstrous subversion of the order of Providence, it is here. Man has a natural right to such a portion of the earth not already improved by others as he can cultivate and make fruitful; the act of Government is simply officious and impertinent which assumes to give him this, and it is a gross usurpation and moral nullity to undertake to give him more. As well might it attempt to farm out the rain or sunshine, giving to one man all that falls on his own land and several of his neighbors', and directing these to buy so much as they need of him. What Government rightfully may and ought to do in the premises is simply to determine and declare the area of the earth's surface which one man may justly, and therefore legally, appropriate to himself and transmit to his posterity without encroaching on the equal natural rights of others. In a young and thinly-peopled community, this area may be larger; as population increases and arts are perfected, it should be gradually reduced and the freehold left vacant to-day by death be divided among the heirs, so as to leave no one in possession of more than the public good prescribes as the maximum for any one man. At first, a mile square might be allowable, there being so much or more for each family in the community; and we see that this allotment has been decided upon in the settlement of Oregon. I can not doubt that this is far too much, whether we regard individual or general good; that the settlers, thus held apart by their mutual grasping, will lose vastly more in education, social intercourse, neighborly kindnesses, than they can possibly gain in ultimate wealth. If the principle of Limitation had been early adopted and maintained, I presume a much smaller area would have been deemed ample. As it is, the emigrant to Oregon grasps not for himself and his children, his flocks and herds only, but with a view to his future aggrandizement by selling off or renting to others. But let a colony on a territory, say of 50,000 arable square miles, begin by allotting to each pioneer a square mile, if he be unwisely greedy enough to desire so much, with the express understanding, however, that this area is to be diminished to future occupants so soon and so fast as the increase of population shall demand it, and that meantime no person shall be allowed upon any pretext to acquire more than the maximum prescribed by law.

'What!' says an objector, 'would you take away a part 'of a man's land, honestly acquired by inheritance, gift or 'purchase, and give it to some one else who needs it?' No, sir! there is no call for this. Let every man keep through life what the law has once decided to be his. But when the landlord of thousands of acres shall die, it is perfectly just, it is urgently expedient, that the Law which has assured and guarded his ample possessions shall say with regard to Land aggregation, as it has long said with regard to Usury, 'Thus far and no farther!' Let the dying rich man leave all his wealth to his heirs, but let him not perpetuate the Land Monopoly which reason conspires with experience in pronouncing, prejudicial to the dearest interests of mankind. The law may say, and should say, 'Take the property, Messrs. heirs, and share it as you shall agree, or as the ministers of justice shall decide; only it is decreed that none of you shall take and retain beyond a certain limit, say 320 acres, of arable soil: whatever falls to any one in excess of that must be sold within a year to some person who will still have less than the legal maximum.' After a few years, this will have been entirely adjusted, and, no man having more than the maximum quantity, none will be restricted in disposing of what he has; only the man who has already as much as the law allows him will be required, on coming into possession of more, to choose what portions of the whole, not exceeding the legal maximum, he will retain, selling the residue to some one who has no land, or less than the legal allowance, within the term specified by law. When population shall have grown considerably more dense, a narrower limit may justly be enacted, to which possessions shall be required gradually to conform, as we have already seen.

I might well despair of impressing on any mind which has not hitherto reflected on this subject the vital importance and vast beneficence of the principle of Land Limitation. To me it seems the very key of the arch which is destined to upbear the unportioned millions from their measureless degradation and abounding misery. I trace the frequent lack of employment, the scanty reward, and the meager subsistence, often accorded to Labor, directly to the resistless influence of Land Monopoly. Here, for example, is a new community, just emerging from barbarism or just planted on a virgin soil. For a season all goes well with it; no man stands idle for want of employment, and Industry reaps what it has sown. But population gradually increases; the land is all appropriated; and good arable soil gradually rises in market value from ten to one hundred dollars per acre, and perhaps higher. Is it not inevitable that it is now far more difficult than formerly for the portionless young man to buy a farm and become his own employer? and that he who cultivates as the tenant or hireling of another must now receive for his labor a far smaller share of its product than of old? Suppose the crop be Corn, and the average yield thirty bushels to the acre, worth fifteen dollars; one dollar of this, or a fifteenth part of the product, would have paid the rent when the land was valued at ten dollars; but now it takes six dollars, or two fifths of the entire product. But population still increases, and its increase steadily carries up the market value of land, until at length the corn-field becomes worth three hundred dollars per acre, from sheer force of competition and necessity acting upon those who have no land and yet must live. Now the tenant can no longer afford to grow Corn, unless he can immensely increase the product, or unless he is willing to perform all the labor and run all the risks of blight, hail, drouth, frost, &c.,

and give the entire avails of a full harvest for the privilege of cultivation. It seems to me impossible, with Land stationary and incapable of increase, Ownership naturally tending to fewer and fewer hands, and population illimitably increasing, that the subsistence of the Laboring Mass should not become more and more meager and precarious, and their condition more and more depressed and hopeless.

For the last half-century, this tendency has been partially counteracted by the invention of Labor-saving Machinery and the immense development of natural and mechanical resources. Thus it is computed that the labor now annually performed in England would have required the best efforts of at least twenty times the present population of that island two centuries ago. Yet such is the evil influence of the Land Monopoly so fearfully prevalent there that, though the present Laboring Class of England accomplish twenty times as much as did their ancestors two centuries back, they yet receive a more scanty reward, (computed not in money, but in the necessaries of life,) are worse fed, lodged, more severely worked, and hardly better clad nor taught, than those ancestors were. Capital, monopolizing Land and Machinery, takes all the profit of Labor to itself. The recompense of Toil has not increased, but the rent and valuation of Land have immensely. And the number of substantial proprietors, inconsiderable since the fatal Norman Conquest, is still sensibly diminishing. A Scotch Duke owns a tract 100 miles by 70, while twenty-nine thirtieths of the whole People remain on the island at the good pleasure and sufferance of the other thirtieth, and might be legally driven into exile by that inconsiderable fraction at any time it chose.

In this country, things have come to no such pass as yet, thanks to our Republican institutions and to the Republican spirit which generally pervaded and directed the first settlers on these shores. There are portions of our continent where a vicious system of granting vast tracts of wilderness to some favorite of the British crown or of some provincial governor, or the sale of millions of acres at a nominal price by some step-mother State to one or more speculators, has engendered some portion of the evils whereof unhappy Ireland affords the most conspicuous example; but, in the main, land has been comparatively easy of acquirement, and the vast stretch of still untamed forest has operated as a perpetual check on the cupidity of forestallers. Yet this exemption has been comparative only. I am personally acquainted with extensive regions which, having fallen within the grasp of monopoly, have been parceled out in small allotments to indigent pioneers on credit at two or three dollars per acre; and these pioneers, after wrestling from ten to twenty years with privation, hardship, fevers, the giant forest and the prowling wild beast, until fertility and beauty were beginning to smile on their little openings, found themselves utterly unable to pay the stipulated price and accumulated interest while maintaining their families, and thus were compelled to abandon their hard-won homes and plunge afresh into the wilderness, often with broken constitutions and in the evening of their days. Some are now hard at work on their third or fourth experiment of this kind in Wisconsin or Iowa. I do not say that all of them have been as industrious, frugal, temperate, as they should have been. I know well that many have not, and that others are justly termed bad managers. I give full force to all this, and still say that the State should have secured to these poor men, for their families' sake if not for their own, the homesteads which they first wrested from the wilderness, so that no clutch of speculator or whisky-seller could have torn those homes from under them. And I cannot doubt that the errors of the past, once detected and vividly portrayed, will be guarded against in future.

A limitation of the area of arable land which any man may acquire and hold, and an exemption of a far more restricted

Homestead of a family from involuntary transfer by mortgage or execution, are twin measures which, after a few years of denunciation and abuse, will be understood, approved, and enduringly engrafted upon our Constitutions and statutes. That these will do much to secure employment and adequate reward to labor, wherever adopted, I can not doubt. Few have any idea of the extent to which Labor is now obstructed by Land Monopoly. The starving poor of Great Britain and Ireland might be abundantly employed and subsisted on the rich soil now uselessly, ostentatiously devoted to immense Parks, Forests, and Game-Preserves. I was, in 1845, discussing with an eminent Western Statesman the effects of Protection and Manufacturing on the welfare of the country, when he casually observed that he owned twelve hundred acres of the finest river bottom land in Ohio, richly worth fifty dollars per acre, yet which he could find nobody to purchase and improve because the floating capital of the country was all attracted to and locked up in Eastern factories. It seemed to me, and I could not help telling him, that the obstacle and the wrong in the case was his attempting to exact fifty dollars per acre for land to which nothing had been done except possibly to divest it of some of its most valuable timber since it was purchased of the Nation for a dollar and a quarter per acre. Yet the Great West is covered with such reservations, to the serious obstruction of settlements and detriment of settlers. One or two such may deprive a school district of any fit school for twenty years; three or four will keep a township destitute of the preaching of the gospel, miserably provided with roads and bridges, scantily supplied with mechanics and artisans. Such a reservation is by no means a mere blank—it is a positive blight and discouragement. It has usually been selected as soon as the lands of that district were offered for sale, and comprises some of the very best in its vicinity. Often two long prairies, each twenty or thirty miles wide, are separated by a small river or mill-stream with a fringe of timber half a mile wide. Speculation early fastens its grasp upon this belt of timber, including all the water-power, fencing and fuel of one or more counties. Soon settlers begin to arrive, and find good prairie abundant and likely to remain so at the Government price, ten York shillings per acre. But this is utterly unavailable, uninhabitable, without timber and water, which can only be had by paying the speculators their ten to twenty dollars per acre, with a thousand or two dollars for a mill-site, which must ultimately be had at whatever price. There are other sections wherein Speculation kindly disposes of the land to settlers who have no money, only asking a liberal share of the first four or five crops in payment. Millions of acres are now occupied by the preëmption claimants, under articles binding the speculators who have bid them off at the Government sales to convey them to the occupants upon the payment of the principal cost with twenty-five to fifty per cent. interest. It is a moderate estimate that every dollar put into the Treasury by public land-sales has taken three to four dollars from the pockets of the actual settler and cultivator.

Still, the remedy required is not so much the substitution of gift for sale as the limitation of the quantity which one man may acquire. Reduce the Government price to ten cents per acre, and you but facilitate the operations of Monopoly, and hasten the day when the great mass shall be beggars for the privilege of cultivating God's earth, and general scarcity of employment shall lead surely to penury of reward and scantiness of food. But establish the principle that no man shall acquire but a limited area of the land yet public, and whether that land be still sold at a moderate price or allotted for the bare cost of survey and transfer to the settler, the Nation's chief peril will have been averted, and a broad and strong foundation laid for the edifice of Social Justice and Industrial Emancipation.

I urge the application of this salutary, vital principle first to the Public Lands, because there it can not be parried by any pretence than its adoption will interfere with Vested Rights. He who does not choose to settle on Public Lands on such terms as the Nation shall see fit to impose has all the world before him; he may hire or work on shares or buy wherever else he pleases. If he does see fit to remove from lands made private to those yet public, he can not reasonably object to the conditions which the Public Will shall impose. He must assent to them and prepare to obey them in good faith. But in truth there is not a township so old nor so new that the principle of Land Limitation therein would not prove a great blessing to its whole people. Into the midst of a sluggish or careless community is born a stirring and sharp-dealing man, possessed by the twin demons Avarice and Ambition. He betakes himself to Trade or Speculation, or Usury; or possibly he makes large annual gains by sheer industry, sharp bargains, and good management. The spirit of territorial aggrandizement soon awakes within him; he finds his patrimony too narrow to afford scope for his energies. And the same Providence which gave being to foxes ordained geese also. Here a family has encountered a succession of calamities, finding their climax in the death of its head; heavy debts hang over it, and the Homestead must be sacrificed just when it has become vitally necessary to save the mother and her babes from dispersion and servitude. The next farm is held by a drunkard or prodigal, and this is soon brought to the hammer. In the next house lives a foolish father and mother, whose darling son must be sent to College, which in the end sends them to the Poor-House. All these, and more, fall successively into the hands of the general devourer of widows' houses, who goes on expanding and amassing till death stops him. In the course of one or two generations, all will very probably be dissipated, but the evil already done is not thereby remedied. The displaced families are very rarely restored. A new accumulator starts up, perhaps in the same school district, perhaps in the next; and runs the old race over again. Thus the children of the poor and the prodigal are constantly falling into homelessness, and more generally as the community grows older; while the ability and energy which, properly directed, would have made one farm a model and a spur to the whole township—which could hardly have failed to do this if the law had not proffered to the possessor the fatal facility of adding broad acres to a domain already too extensive—are worse than wasted in acquiring the farms of others instead of rendering fruitful and beauteous his own. One hundred acres might have been rendered as valuable and as productive as the many hundreds now are, and been made to give employment to as much Labor; but the larger territory sounds louder in the public ear, and to own the most land of any man in the County is, unfortunately, a greater distinction than to work a moderate farm the best. All this must be amended, and it *will* be. Land Reform is the natural and sure basis of all Social and Industrial Melioration.

Next in order to Land Reform stands the question of Labor Reform, or the regulation of the hours of daily manual toil. I am not aware that any noted writer on Social Economy, or on the sanitary and moral condition of the Laboring Classes, has failed to condemn the exaction of twelve to thirteen hours' labor per day as excessive and pernicious—an offence against general well-being, and even against the self-interest of the Employers. One* of the most eminent British manufacturers of the last generation, who retired from business twenty years ago with a large fortune, the fruit of thirty years' faithful assiduity and exertion, and who still lives to enjoy the competence he so fairly won, informs me that he for twenty years neither exacted nor

* Robert Owen.

allowed more than ten hours' labor per day of any one in his employment, and that he prospered as well and amassed property quite as fast as any of his competitors or rivals, who kept their mills running from twelve to sixteen hours per day. It is his deliberate judgment that even less than ten hours per day will ultimately be found better for all parties. In Scotland, it is the rule in some counties to work twelve hours per day at Farming, in others but ten; and impartial testimony establishes the fact that the shorter term is fully as effective as the longer. But I do not propose here to discuss, much less to settle, the precise number of hours which should be held as constituting a usual or regular day's work. That question will properly come up after we have settled the prior and more important point that there *shall be* some definite and uniform meaning to the term 'day's work,' so that an agreement to work a month or week shall imply some precise and well-known term, and not remain subject to be stretched or contracted at the mere pleasure, convenience, or fancied interest of one of the parties. This is a Reform which seems to me not only important but inevitable. It would be as sensible and just to prescribe that a pound of meat, of sugar, or of coffee, should consist of just so many ounces as the buyer should see fit, after the price had been settled, to exact, or that a bushel of grain should consist of an indefinite number of quarts, as that a day's work should consist of ten, eleven, twelve, or thirteen hours' faithful labor, just as the purchaser of that labor should think proper to require. Labor in our day has become so extensively a commodity—a marketable product, like cheese or chocolate—that it is most essential to all fair dealing that it be measured as definitely and equally as possible. And, when it is settled that it shall be so measured, I understand it to be the uniform testimony of impartial men who have investigated the subject, that, at least in all employments not liable to interruption by the elements, the number of hours constituting a day's work must be reduced as well as defined and equalized, so as to afford opportunity not merely for deliberate meals and ample rest, but for study, reading, and relaxation, also. Man was not made merely to eat, to work, to sleep. He has faculties which such a routine does not develop—wants and aspirations which it does not satisfy. Especially where the fixed attention of the mind as well as a constrained attitude of the body is exacted by the nature of his labor, and where that labor is continued from day to day, week in and week out, without interruption by storm or frost, it seems manifest that the regulation of the hours of labor should respect the mental no less than the physical demands of his nature, and that the day's toil should be broken off before the body has been so wearied and exhausted as to leave no strength nor spirit for mental improvement or exertion. Such I understand to be the essence of the demand for a general Reform in the hours and conditions of Labor.

I am encouraged to hope for an early and favorable action on this subject by recent action in England. It is sometimes made a reproach to our influential and wealthy class that they pattern closely after England, and copy her fashions, her laws, habits, and thoughts, with servile alacrity. I will not here stop to consider how far this ought to be esteemed a reproach if it were admitted to be a truth. It seems to me that we might learn much from that same England, both by way of example and of warning. Be this as it may, the fact that the British Parliament has passed a law decreeing a reduction of the Hours of Factory Labor to eleven, and after one year to ten per day, will doubtless do much to pave the way for and hasten the adoption of some kindred measure here. Such action on the other side of the Atlantic will be effectual not merely as an example, but by removing the dangers, real or fancied, of unequal Foreign competition, in case of a reduction of hours on this side. And I may fairly presume that the most ferocious hater of British laws and precedents will make little objection to our imitating this.

Yet a Limitation of the Hours of Labor seems to me a secondary though most important Reform. So long as unemployed Labor crowds the market and the street, eagerly chaffering and underbidding for opportunity to earn a bare subsistence, I fear any stringent legislation on this point could not be enforced. Indeed, the difficulties environing the subject are by no means few nor trivial. The evil resembles in character the 'compound fracture' of the physical man. We can all agree at the outset that ten hours' faithful, skillful labor per day *ought* to enable any man to support his family comfortably and respectably. But here are men whose personal burdens are excessive—who owe debts incurred by past sickness or misfortune in business; who have sick or disabled relatives cast upon their hands, and who choose to labor excessively in order to meet manfully the demands made upon them. Can the law wisely interfere to say that such men shall not work twelve or fourteen hours if they choose? Again: a dam gives way, the machinery of a mill breaks, and five hundred workers must stand idle and incur expense until a few can make all right again. Would it be wise and just to prescribe that these few shall be inflexibly restricted to ten hours' labor per day? These instances might be multiplied, but enough. Since it is confessedly impolitic and indeed impossible to fix by law the *price* of any service or commodity, it is not without reason that some have honestly doubted that any law prescribing arbitrarily the boundaries of a day's work would be effective or useful. The end aimed at is at last to be reached, in my judgment, from the other side—by such a change in the Social Condition of the mass of Laborers and in their relation to the Soil, as will leave them *really* free to accept an offer of employment, in view of all its conditions, or decline it. Secure to them this, and they will enforce a suitable limitation of the Hours of Labor without the aid of positive, peremptory statutes; but so long as this is not, I apprehend that no law can surely and uniformly accomplish the desired end.

But, now that we have considered the natural difficulties and limitations to be encountered, I think we are prepared to state clearly what the law can and may do in the premises. All must allow that there should be *some* definite limit to an ordinary day's work, and that that limit should not be fixed and changed as the mere pleasure or interest of the Employing Class shall dictate. I intend by this no reflection on the character of that Class. That would ill become me, since to that Class I at present belong. I do not believe it less wise, humane, or considerate, in the average, than the Employed, nor less likely to do right where the interests of the two may seem to conflict. But the sound general rule that no man is a proper judge in his own case applies here as well as elsewhere. There should always be two parties to a bargain, and to every part of it, otherwise it is apt to prove a hard one. And while I hold that the State can not properly prescribe that no man shall in any case work more for another than ten hours in any one day—still less can it in my view, make one law for Corporations and another for Individuals—it may yet, as the general Protector of the Weak against the Strong, do much, and ought to do much, to mitigate the evils of excessive hours of daily toil. The action I would recommend, and which in one State* has already in part received the sanction of the Legislature, is substantially as follows:

1. An act forbidding absolutely the employment of children or minors, whether Apprentices or Hired, for more than ten hours per day. The State has a right to see, and ought to see, that the frames of the rising generations are not shattered nor their constitutions undermined by excessive labor. She should do this for her own sake as well as

* New Hampshire.

Humanity's. She has a vital interest in the strength and vigor of those who are to be her future fathers and mothers, her defenders in war, her cultivators and artisans in peace. She may safely make this limitation imperative, since for whatever service it may be necessary to employ labor for a longer term per day there will always be found an abundance of adults, if proper inducements are offered.

2. A simply declaratory act that in all cases where no other term is specified, the Law shall presume and decide that an agreement to work a week, a month, a year, or any other term, implies ten hours' faithful work on each secular day, and no more. It may be expedient to vary this term in certain out-door employments, especially Farming, making it nine hours between October and March, and eleven between April and September, the four months named standing at ten hours; but this would be in perfect consistency with the general principle that ten hours should constitute a legal day's work, wherever the parties, being responsible and independent adults, do not see fit to vary this by express agreement. The moral effect of such an act, in inducing a very general conformity to its dictates, would be great, and I can not believe that much hired labor would ultimately be performed otherwise than in accordance with the rule it prescribed, save in pressing emergencies.

To the ardent and dogmatic Reformer, who holds the Ten-Hour Rule the chief and sufficient means for the Emancipation of Labor from thraldom and depression, this suggestion will seem tame and halting; but I confidently believe such an act as it contemplates would effect more enduring good than would one that took the more arbitrary and inflexible form. Yet I would see with pleasure the two tried side by side, in sister States, by way of experiment.

—A Limitation of the Hours of Labor, once accomplished, will be valuable mainly for the Opportunity it proffers—the prospect it opens. 'The end is not yet'—very far from it. If the worker, released from excessive drudgery in the mill or the shop, shall misimprove his new-found leisure in the groggery, the cigar-store, the gambling den, or some other haunt of vileness, it were well for him if he had remained a patient, abject drudge for life. And herein is the discouragement of many from all effort to improve the physical and temporal condition of the less fortunate Laboring Class. They can only see that more wages give more liquor, and more leisure incites to more dissipation. Alas! let us confess in deep humility and sorrow that there is a deplorable truth at the bottom of this. Yet no—I think it is *not* at the bottom, but nearer the surface. Fearfully true it is that many of those whose lives are mechanical merely—whose days are consecrated to drudgery, and the gloom of whose narrow tenements is rarely softened by the sun of Hope—*do* usually spend their hours snatched from toil in degrading, brutalizing sensualities, so as to give plausibility to the conclusion that they would be better if they had no leisure at all and no resources beyond the means of supplying the barest necessaries of life. But the logic which thence infers that the victim of inccssant toil and meager recompense ought ever to remain such is that which exalts Slavery into a Divine and beneficent institution, and proves War a general blessing by demonstrating the average worthlessness or worse of those it employs and consumes. We must stop this arguing from existing evils in support of the abuses and wrongs which created them. Let us give Human Nature a fair trial, and see if it utterly lack sense as well as any glimmering of virtue, before we pronounce it a hopeless failure, to be managed only with the strait-jacket and the halter. Let us have a fair and full trial of a Laboring Class thoroughly educated, not overworked, fairly remunerated, with ample leisure, and adequate opportunities for Social, Moral, and Intellectual culture and enjoyment, and then, if the hard-handed multitude shall still persist in squandering their leisure and their means in riot and dissipation, we must sadly, reluctantly, but utterly, abandon all hope of a better day coming for the Toiling Millions, and leave them to the tender mercies of the miser, the forestaller, the pawnbroker, the grog-seller, as fair game. Whether the land-pirate strip the wreck or the sea swallow it, what matter? But I can not doubt that a better Social condition, enlarged opportunities of good, an atmosphere of Humanity and Hope, would insure a nobler and truer Character, and that the dens of dissipation will cease to lure those whom a proper Education has qualified, and whom excessive Toil has not disqualified, for the improvement of Liberty and Leisure. At all events, the momentous consequences depending should impel a speedy trial of the experiment, and insure a fair trial.

I should be most unfaithful to my own convictions, and leave room for false inferences and misstatements which I claim the right here to repel, if I omitted to rank War among the scourges which a pure Christianity, a true Civilization, must banish from off the face of the earth, before the Emancipation of Labor from depressing want and unmerited suffering can be permanently effected. War, indeed, elevates as well as depresses, expands as well as crushes; but those refreshed and gladdened by its golden showers are never the humble workers—the men whose bread is moistened by their own daily sweat, and won by the peaceful might of sturdy sinews—for these, War has showers of grape and canister only, not of eagles and doubloons. Their bodies serve passably to fill trenches, shrouded in their own blood—but their names are rarely deemed good enough to fill half a line in the most inflated and deceitful bulletin. War destroys in a day the fruits of many years' peaceful effort, fills the world with destitute cripples, widows and orphans; it ravages provinces to fertilize a single battle-field, and leaves barbarism instead of refinement, idleness in place of industry, weeds in place of gardens; blood, ashes, and tears, instead of fertility, beauty, and joy. Not till the Laboring Millions shall have become wise enough to loathe the glory which wreathes the brow of Carnage, and admire one Franklin or Clarkson more than twenty Napoleons or Wellingtons, may we reasonably look for the Elevation of Labor to its proper condition and dignity. Hopeless is the degradation of the slave who idolizes the chains and trappings which hold him in perpetual bondage.

So on a kindred though apparently opposite point. To me it seems indispensable to the just recompense, steady employment and sure elevation of Labor, that the Industry of each community or People be rendered as various and diverse as is consistent with efficiency in production—that everywhere Agriculture, Manufactures, Mechanic Arts, &c., should intermingle and blend with each other, so as to afford employment for the greatest possible diversity of tastes and capacities in regard to industrial pursuits. You may agree with me that it is the proper duty of Government to strive for and as far as possible secure such diversity, by fostering and upholding the introduction of such departments of Useful Labor as are yet unestablished or in their infancy—or you may incline to the opposite theory, that this matter will better take care of itself, and that Government can not act more wisely, beneficently, than to let it entirely alone. I will not here discuss the relative soundness of these antagonist theories: but I insist that the condition of the Laboring Class can never be independent and comfortable while a Nation buys its bread, or its clothing, its wares or its fabrics, mainly from abroad. I know well that National landmarks are, in the eye of Philanthropy, as if they were not: I look only to the inevitable consequences of carrying Grain across half a continent and an ocean, and bringing back Cloths in return; and I say that this is, in general, at deadly war with the permanent interests of Labor, which unerringly demand that the exchanges of products should be in the main as direct and simple as possible, and as nearly as may be between producer and produced, with but one or two intermediates at most. So long as the Grain grown in the great Valley of the Mississippi is in good part exchanged for the Cloths of England, the Linens of Ireland, the silks and wines of France, the glass, the toys, the knick-knacks of Germany—all which, if needed, might as well be produced in our own country as elsewhere—so long will the bulk of American Labor be deprived of more than half its just reward through the depression of its great staples at the point of production and the exactions of a superfluous Traffic. At this moment,* Corn sells abundantly for twenty cents per bushel in the most productive sections of our Great West, though famished Ireland eagerly pays for it two dollars per bushel; and so with other things. The shipper charges twice to thrice as much for conveying each bushel from New York to Liverpool as the farmer receives for growing it. The ultimate remedy for this—effect it as you will—is the naturalization of the arts, and if need be the artisans, of the Old World along-side of the fertile prairies of our boundless West, thereby securing them twice as much grain for the product of each day's labor as they now receive, while benefiting in equal measure our farmers, and diverting the non-productive labor now employed in needless transportation into the channels of productive Industry. Call this, if you please, a digression—to me it seems unavoidable if misapprehensions are to be prevented. I proceed with my general statement.

Unquestionably the Emancipation of Labor is to be effected through or in conjunction with the mental and moral improvement of the Laboring Class. So far, all are of one mind. But whoever argues thence that nothing is to be done, nor even attempted, in the way of physical or circum-

* December, 1846.

stantial melioration, until the Laboring Class shall have wrought out its own thorough spiritual development and moral renovation, might as well declare himself a champion of the Slave-Trade at once. The internal and external renovation are each necessary to the completeness of the other. Merely lightening his tasks and enlarging his comforts will not raise a groveling, sensual, ignorant boor to the dignity of true manhood; but no more can just and luminous ideas of his own nature, relations, duties, and destiny, be expected often to irradiate the mind of one doomed to a life of abject drudgery, penury, and privation. "Tom," said a Colonel on the Rio Grande to one of his command, "how can so brave and good a soldier as you are so demean himself as to get drunk at every opportunity?"—"Colonel!" replied the private, "how can you expect all the virtues that adorn the human character for seven dollars a month?" The answer, however faulty in morals, involves a grave truth. Self-respect is the shield of Virtue; Comfort and Hope are the hostages we proffer the world for our good behavior in it; take these away, and Temptation is left without counteracting force or influence. 'Without *hope* and without *God* in the world,' says an inspired Apostle; let not the sequence or its significance be forgotten. Show me a community, a class, a calling, wherein poverty, discomfort, and excessive, unrewarded toil have come to be regarded as an inexorable destiny, and I will tell you that there the laws of God and man are sullenly defied or stupidly disregarded.

The Industrial Education of the Poor is a matter of the very highest and most pressing Social concern. Here are hundreds on every side of us toiling their lives out for some beggarly four to six shillings per day, and barely existing in want and wretchedness thereon, when others, intrinsically no wiser and better than they, earn thrice as much, and live in ease and comfort. This immense disparity has its origin in the slight and unregarded circumstance that the one class were in youth so fortunate or so provident as to be enabled to acquire trades or callings in which labor is well rewarded, while the others have grown up at random, doing what came handiest, or rather that which in the general scramble was left to them; and now they are qualified only for such employment as none beside them will take. Nothing can be more culpably thoughtless in a parent than to let his son or daughter grow up unfitted for some sphere of decided and fairly-rewarded usefulness. A good trade is an estate out of which the most confiding can not be swindled, and which is almost beyond the reach of adverse fortune.

But it is not merely desirable that each child should be trained to decided efficiency in some branch of Industry—it is essential also that each should be incited to a constant exertion of all his faculties in devising and perfecting improvements therein. The son should not be satisfied with doing as well as his father did—he should begin there, resolved to do better and better. Herein is the radical difference between Free and Slave Labor, which is already rendering Slavery unprofitable, and is destined to blot it out of existence. Slavery controls the sinews and the limbs only; the brain and the will are beyond its power. The world has as yet hardly known what Free Labor is—it has had few or no full and fair specimens of it, such as it must and shall have. And it seems to me that one great means toward the promotion of a more intellectual and efficient Laboring Class than the world has yet seen is the adoption of a law of Proportion or rateable dividend to Capital and Labor in place of the present system of fixed and arbitrary wages. I know that no such change can be effected suddenly, but I believe some approximation might immediately be made to it with decided benefit to all. Let us suppose, for instance, that a manufacturing company, in addition to the payment of the usual wages, were to set apart a small proportion of its net earnings—say five or ten per cent. to begin with—to be divided among *all* its permanent workmen on some predetermined scale at the close and settlement of each year's business. Does any man believe that such company would be a cent the poorer for this, in view of all the probable consequences? I am confident it would be richer; and that the dividend of profits to Labor would, after a few years, be increased, to the signal advantage of all parties. And the effect of this system upon the industry, fidelity, and skill of the workmen, it would hardly be possible to exaggerate.

The difficulties which impede any plan of Radical and thorough Reform are never slight, and can not be surmounted at a breath. And, unfortunately, when our machinery fails to work out the desired result, we are usually too imperfectly acquainted with the subject of our high emprise to detect the real cause of our disappointment. The shortness of vision which caused our failure disables us for correcting it. Here a fond father of small intellectual attainment, having been often rendered painfully conscious of his own deficiencies, resolves to lavish his hard-earned coin to give his son the very best—that is, the most expensive—Education. He pushes him sturdily through school, academy, and university, qualifies him (so far as money can) for a profession; and after all, young Hopeful turns out a blockhead or a blackguard, a drunkard or a swindler. Forthwith the sorely disappointed parent rushes to the conclusion that *Education* is a curse and a cheat—that an honest man is better without it than with it. He does not consider that his failure has proved, not that Education is worthless, but that his son has not been educated—that the training he has paid so much for was not true education, or that it has been counteracted and overborne by the false and pernicious teaching of the street, the bar-room, the revel—very possibly of the paternal fireside itself. So we, when we affirm that this or that change would be beneficial, can not say that *other* influences may not take simultaneous effect, and more than counterbalance all the good effects of this. Nay, more: That which is good in itself has often fallen upon evil ground, and been turned to evil by the baleful conjunction. From no partial data can we predict the formation of a true and genial character. It must be the product of the whole circle of influences surrounding the individual from birth to intellectual and physical maturity.

Here, then, is the basis of our demand for that integral and all-pervading reform in the circumstances and conditions of human existence which we term Association, and in which rests my hope of a better day at hand for the down-trodden millions. Association affirms that every child born into the world has a rightful claim upon the community around him for Subsistence until able to earn for himself; for an Education which shall enable him to earn efficiently as well as rightly to improve and enjoy; and for Opportunity to earn at all times by honest Industry steadily employed and justly remunerated. These it affirms as the common Rights of Humanity, denied or subverted as to many by our present Social arrangements, but which Society ought to be and must be so recast as to establish and secure. It wars upon no Rights of Property, would take nothing from the Rich to bestow on the Poor, nor does it ask that any shall abandon his elegant private mansion and Social exclusiveness until and unless he shall see fit of his own motion to do so; but it does solicit the Wealthy, the Refined, the Philanthropic, the Religious, to invest something of their pecuniary means in and give something of their countenance and good wishes to all earnest efforts of the Laboring Class to emancipate and elevate themselves. The endeavor will be resolutely and perseveringly made, even though Wealth coldly frown and Theology mistakenly denounce; and it will ultimately succeed, though a thousand failures should be encountered, and the present generation of its advocates be long previously laid in obscure, unhonored graves. To short-sighted human impatience, it now seems deplorable that Philanthropy and Christianity do not instantly rally the influential and the affluent to our aid, and enable us to demonstrate the feasibility of a vast and beneficent Social Reform forthwith; but I doubt not that those who shall ultimately reap where we have sown will clearly perceive that the Providential direction was far wiser than our haste, and that our rebuffs and disappointments were a part of the necessary agencies whereby their success was rendered perfect and enduring.

Every manufacturing village, every extensive manufactory, is a striking evidence of the immensely increased efficiency which ORGANIZATION imparts to Human Labor. A population of Thirty Thousand, whose efforts are controlled and directed by a few superior minds, accomplish results which One Hundred Thousand laboring separately, and thus capriciously, ineffectively, fail to achieve. In like manner, we see an ably commanded Army of Two Hundred Thousand veterans overrun and subdue with ease a Kingdom of Ten Millions of People, as brave perhaps and as robust individually as their conquerors, but lacking unity, discipline, and competent leading. Thus, too, the manufacturing city or village usually accumulates wealth faster than the surrounding country, its command of natural forces being much greater, and its labor being far better organized and therefore more efficient. Hence the appearance of one of our manufacturing villages, standing like some magical exhalation on a plat of ground perhaps familiar to my boyhood as a waste of rock or sand, is to me a cheering spectacle, not so much for what it actually is, as for what it suggests and foreshadows. I reflect by whose labor and toil all this aggregation of wealth, this immense capacity of producing more wealth, have been called into existence; and I say, If these rugged toilers are able to accomplish so much for *others,* why may they not ultimately do even more for *themselves?* Why may not they who cut the timber, and burn the brick, and mix the mortar, and shape the ponderous machinery, ultimately build something like this of their own? Why may not their sisters and daughters in time spin and weave as the partners rather than the hirelings of the mill-owners? Why may we not give to Labor a republican organization, as we have, in defiance of a croaking world, given one to Government, so that the workers shall freely choose their own chiefs or overlookers, regulate their own hours of daily toil, and divide the general product according to a preconcerted scale whose sole end shall be mutual and universal justice? Is Labor so intractable, so senseless, that it can never run its appointed race without a rider? Let us at least hope not.

Let me rudely sketch you a village, township, school district, or whatever you may term it, organized as we would have it, and as we hope many ultimately will be. The basis is a faith among the associates or members that they can live harmoniously with and deal justly by each other, treating any casual imperfections which may be developed with forbearance and kindness. One hundred families, animated by this spirit, resolve to make an attempt toward a more trustful and genial life, and to that end sell off as they can their immovable possessions and resolve to seek a new home together; we will say in Michigan or Wisconsin. They send out two or three chosen leaders, who, after careful examination, select and purchase a tract of one to five thousand acres, as their means will warrant, embracing the largest circle of advantages—Timber, Prairie, Water-Power, convenience for Transportation, &c., &c. They have carefully foreseen that proper building-materials, including brick or stone, lime and timber, are to be obtained with facility. Mills are erected and various branches of Manufacturing established as fast as they are needed, or as there is any labor which can be spared for and advantageously employed therein. New members who bid fair to be desirable accessions are received, on due probation, as fast as there may be accommodations for them, and so they can be profitably employed. If a blacksmith, a carpenter, a brickmaker, or glazier, is wanted, he is obtained by hiring until, among the wide circle of friends or acquaintances of the members, one is found who would like to unite his fortunes with the Phalanx, and who is deemed a worthy associate. Thus they go on, producing abundant food and other raw staples, steadily extending the bounds of their cultivated area, and increasing its product; enjoying at least the necessaries of life and doing without the superfluities until they are enabled to obtain them without running in debt. Soon an edifice, intended for the permanent home of them all, is commenced and finished piecemeal in the most substantial manner—fireproof so nearly that fire could not spread from one section to another, and so planned that the whole may be warmed, lighted, supplied with water, and cleared of refuse by arrangements answering as well for a thousand persons as for one. Three or four large and spacious kitchens, barns, granaries &c., &c., supplied with every convenience, would answer the purpose of three or four hundred under our present economy, saving vast amounts now lost by waste, vermin, the elements, &c. &c. A tenth part of the labor now required for Household service, procuring Fuel, &c., would suffice, while that now consumed in journeys to the mill, the store, the blacksmith, the shoemaker, and the like, would be saved entirely. There would be abundant employment in the various branches of Industry pursued for all ages, capacities, tastes, and all that would be saved in the kitchen and the woods could be advantageously and agreeably employed in the gardens and nurseries, the mills and factories. The productive force of this population would be vastly greater than under existing arrangements, while its economies in other respects would be immense. For a brief season, admit that these advantages would be counterbalanced by inexperience and perverseness —that some would refuse to work where they were needed, and insist on working where they would be comparatively inefficient, or nowhere—that bickerings and jealousies would arise, and that some would feel that their work was not adequately credited and remunerated—I foresee all these difficulties, and more. Yet I see also, the *end* being kept steadily in view—that of having no unproductive labor or as little as possible, rewarding all work done according to its absolute worth, and charging each head of a family the simple cost of what he had—the rent of his exclusive rooms and the actual outlay for the subsistence and education of his family—in short, establishing Social Justice throughout—there would be a constant tendency and approximation toward the state of things desired and the harmony which must result from it. The defects of one year would suggest the remedies of the next, and each year's adjustment of accounts would be more satisfactory than the last.

The immense advantages of such an arrangement with reference to Universal Education need hardly be pointed out. I am not accustomed to take desponding views of Human Progress and Destiny, yet I confess that the existing condition of the children of destitution and vice with regard to Education is most appalling. Grant that the means of Education be rendered ever so abundant and accessible, how are the denizens of cellars and garrets, subsisting precariously on the products of chance employment and beggary, ever to be truly and thoroughly instructed? The angel may trouble the waters incessantly, but who shall guaranty that these cripples get down to the pool? They are unclad, uncouth, with the manners and feelings which befit the Pariahs of Society—nay, they must devote to their poor ways of getting a living the time demanded by the school, or sink into still deeper misery. Make schools as free and abundant as possible, and there will still be a class — I fear, increasing in number — who will be withheld by extreme poverty and consequent shabbiness — by the stolid ignorance or brutal drunkenness of their parents — by infirmities which forbid their attendance on a school located at some distance from their homes — by the thousand consequences of Want, Uncertainty, Disease, and Vice — from the acquirement of a proper Education. But in an Association such as we contemplate, the thorough Intellectual, Moral, and Physical Education of each will be the direct and palpable *interest* of all — a matter of the highest and most intimate concern. The cost of the books now thinly scattered in five hundred dwellings will procure one ample and comprehensive Library, with the apparatus and materials required to demonstrate the truths of Chemistry and the whole range of Natural Science. The best teachers in every branch will in time be selected — those who unite a natural capacity for teaching with the fullest attainments, and who do not need the stimulus of high salaries to induce them to devote some hours of each day to the inculcation of Knowledge, Industry, and Virtue. Frequent and agreeable alternations from the school-room to the garden, the factory, the halls and grounds set apart for exercise and recreation, will benefit alike teachers and scholars, giving a zest to learning as well as industry unknown to our monotonous drudgery, whether of work or study. In short, I see no reason why the wildest dreams of the fanatical believer in Human Progress and Perfectibility may not ultimately be realized, and each child so trained as to shun every vice, aspire to every virtue, attain the highest practicable skill in Art and efficiency in Industry, loving and pursuing honest, untasked Labor for the health, vigor, and peace of mind, thence resulting as well as for its more palpable rewards, and joyfully recognising in universal the only assurance of individual good.

Doubtless, the realization of such visions is yet afar off, for the Actual and the Possible of Human Character are still immensely separated. We can not wonder that Heaven seems so distant while Hell is so near. To the slave dancing to the music of the lash in some Carolina rice-swamp, idleness with abundance of victual is the highest ideal of existence ; not so to Oberlin or Wilberforce. The dingy, back-bent hireling in some gloomy, unwholesome den of Mammon, whither he is summoned from his sleep by a bell while his bones yet ache with yesterday's protracted toil, will have most difficulty in realizing that he, too, might, under different auspices, take delight and pride in the very task he now performs so grudgingly. But give him a true Education, an unfailing Home, a direct interest in the product of his labor, and thus in its excellence, an equal voice in choosing his superiors and an equal chance to be chosen if found worthy; workshops planned and constructed with express reference to his health and comfort; let him realize that himself and family are the Social equals of all around them, and his children as well educated as any, with equal chances of attaining distinction and honor, and you will find him an entirely different being. Idleness and dissipation are the paradise of the overtaxed body and the vacant mind; for the rightly trained and developed they have no fascinations.

Whenever the class of Hired Laborers shall be brought to realize that a beneficently Radical Reform in its condition and its relations is practicable, then that Reform will be on the high road to its accomplishment. It is the desperate character and complication of the disease that renders its cure so difficult. So long as the mass of those who must live as hirelings by rude manual toil have no minds above their lot—no aspirations beyond Blue Monday,—it will be difficult indeed to achieve any substantial improvement in their condition. It is a melancholy fact that while it has hitherto required comparatively no effort to rally the Millions in behalf of an effort to rend and destroy—to tear down and scatter abroad—it has been difficult to bring them to realize that the work to be done in their behalf is one of patience not of wrath; of construction, not destruction; of elevation not abasement; and that the absolute extinction of the Capitalist class would avail them nothing for good, very much for evil, so long as the *principles* which exalt the few and depress the many are left in unchecked operation. Marat was sure there was no other way to make good *Sans Culottes* of the Rich but to strip them to their shirts. But stripping them could avail little for good without clothing those already naked; and then these have become proper subjects for the stripping operation in turn. You thus wear out what clothes there are, while restraining every one from making more, yet nobody is permanently clad. All is confusion, violence, unthrift, uncertainty; until by-and-by some strong-armed soldier throws his sword into the scale, and Anarchy is supplanted by Despotism. Such is the unvarying history of revolutions impelled by hatred and the envious passion for tearing down—the same anciently, recently, now and evermore.

True Reform has its origin in a different spirit and contemplates a different end. It recognizes all men as brethren, and desires the emancipation of the miser and monopolist no less than of the hireling and drudge—the slave of his own money-bags no less than the slave of another's water-wheel. It recognizes the truth that the Social evils which afflict mankind have their origin in the errors not of a part but of all, and that by the coöperation of all should they be overcome. It compassionates not more the weary servitor of the loom or the hod than the plethoric victim of dyspepsia or hypochondria, dying by inches for the want of that healthful exercise of body and mind which nothing but the consciousness of sinews usefully employed and time laudably spent can really give. It wars with no existing Rights—it would deal gently even with established Wrongs, where it can do so without treason to Human Well-being. Its aims are not narrow, nor envious, nor vindictive, and it would be led to distrust itself if those from time to time won to its standard were not elevated and purified thereby. When the strong arms and stout hearts of the men of rugged toil shall have rallied round its standard, it hopes that, however long deferred may be *its* triumph, *their* gain will be immediate and certain; for it will have commenced in themselves.

But—sad necessity!—Esau must have pottage. Priceless is his birthright, but its use seems distant, while Hunger is sorely pinching him now. We must not be surprised nor provoked that those who most palpably need a true Social Reform seem most indifferent to its accomplishment, and least willing to make the efforts and sacrifices essential thereto. The hopeless infidelity of the most depressed as to any real improvement in their Social condition is one of the strongest demonstrations of its necessity, and of the duty of those a little less unfortunate to struggle manfully and ungrudgingly in the cause of Universal Reform.

Let us take courage from the evidences of Progress all around us. It is not half a century since the Slave-Trade was in its glory, and men eminent in Church and State made fortunes by engaging in it without reproach or scruple. We have yet Doctors of Divinity who justify laws which authorize the buying and selling of mothers from their children; but this is evidently dying out; and, in a few years, Sermons proving Slavery a Bible institution will be advertised as antique curiosities. So of Privateering, War, and the traffic in Intoxicating Liquors. To our impatient spirits, the march of improvement often seems mournfully slow; but when we consider where the world is and where it has been—how recently, for instance, a man could only speak against Slavery, however temperately and guardedly, at the hazard of personal violence and defilement, while press after press, on bare suspicion that it *would* be used to disseminate Anti-Slavery, was destroyed by mob violence, and in one instance the life of its heroic owner and defender along with it—and now, the strolling Abolition lecturer is more likely to be mobbed for asserting that any body in the Free States justifies or palliates Slavery than for condemning it himself—we ought to be assured that the age which has given us Railroads and Locomotives, Steam Presses and Electric Telegraphs, will not pass away without having effected or witnessed a vast change for the better, alike in the moral and the physical condition of mankind.

For that change let us faithfully labor and undoubtingly hope. Whether its consummation shall take the precise form which you or I now anticipate or prefer, who shall say? Nay, who need seriously care? Enough that we know well that all things are wisely ordered by One whose observation no sparrow's fall can escape: in whose providence no generous effort can fail of its reward. It can not be that the vastly-increased Intelligence, Philanthropy, Productive Capacity, and Industrial energy of our age shall fail to leave their impress upon the condition of even the most abject and least fortunate of our Race. We could not retard the great forward movement of Humanity if we would; but each of us may decide for himself whether to share in the glory of promoting it or incur the shame of having looked coldly and indifferently on, preferring present ease and pleasure to the stern calls of Duty, the soft pleadings of Human Brotherhood, bidding us 'remember those in bonds as bound with them.' Each age summons its own heroes; ours demands those who will labor and if need be suffer reproach in behalf of a Social Order based on Universal Justice, not the dominion of Power over Need; on the spirit of Christianity, not the supremacy of Mammon. The struggle may be long, but the issue can not be doubtful. Fortunate shall they be esteemed hy future generations who are privileged to stand in Earth's noblest Thermopylæ and battle for the rights, for the hopes, for the enduring good, of Humanity in all time to come It is a distinction to which the loftiest might well aspire, but which proffers opportunity alike to the humblest. Who would slumber through life ingloriously when such crowns are to be won?

II.

LIFE — THE IDEAL AND THE ACTUAL

A LECTURE.

THIS dry, old mummy Life, so weird and withered, so parched and blackened, so hackneyed and threadbare, shall I be able to draw from it a single idea or thought worthy of your patient regard? Doubtless, there is warm blood yet lingering within the worn tenement, despite the incessant phlebotomy to which it has been subjected; now and then by skillful leech, but always by swarms — ay, clouds — of minute, but indefatigable musquitoes. Should I fail utterly in my attempt, blame the operator, not the subject.

Human Life — unlike what we know of the lower creation, unlike what we fairly presume of the higher — is twofold, the Actual and the Ideal. Our daily deeds, our daily aspirations, clash with each other — are the positive and negative poles of our being. Desire and Duty are the centrifugal and centripetal forces whose counterbalancing attractions hold us firm to our appointed orbit in the grand career of existence. A lofty discontent with the Actual is the main impulse to whatever is noble and heroic, as a mean dissatisfaction with physical conditions — a pining for richer food, or dress, or ampler service — is the incentive to the ignobler efforts of the million. A thoroughly contented man, could such be found, might have his uses. He would tend to moderate the fierceness of Aspiration and soothe the pangs of Disquiet, so prevalent in the human breast; but a thoroughly contented community would be a blank, a failure, a practical nonentity. China affords us some idea of it, by approximation; and to what purpose those Three Hundred Millions of Chinese have lived these forty centuries, who beneath Omniscience can say? The divergence of the Ideal from the Actual liberates the electricity of life.

This discrepancy pervades alike the cottage and the palace. The swart laborer discerns the conditions of happiness only in the luxuries and dainties of the man of millions; while Crœsus, though he hugs his possessions, finds them a heavy and thorny burden. Ease, the grand desideratum, visits neither the rude pallet on which the one rests his toil-worn, aching limbs, nor the downy couch whereon the other nightly struggles with the twin demons Dyspepsia and Hypochondria, to whom his sumptuous fare and exemption from physical labor have rendered him a helpless prey. "O that I were a man!" cries the impatient child, "then I should no more be tyrannized over, and treated as a helpless idiot! Childhood is allowed no scope —no respect; its joys are few and trifling: haste, haste! hour of my emancipation!" "O that I were a child again!" responds the man; "that this load of consuming cares and duties were lifted from my burning, boiling, half-distracted brain! Childhood! glad season of innocence and bliss! when simple life was pleasure, and any casual grief was quickly chased from the mind's dial by whole troops of dancing joys!" The king often looks on the beggar with something akin to envy—he would not exchange conditions, as a whole; but he would give much, very much, to be rid, for a few days, of his tiresome, never-ending round of dull formalities, and absurd, exacting ceremonies, and unloved but inevitable associates, and harassing councils, and state dinners to be eaten with a headache instead of an appetite, and turbulent provinces, and unreasonable yet tenacious suitors, and murmuring ministers or allies, with death-warrants, demagogues, and a thousand shifting causes of life-long disquiet. He would not be a beggar—pride and fear forbid—the beggar might do very well as a king, while the king would starve as a beggar—but, oh, what would he not give for a week's free roving through forest and heather, plucking the fruits fresh and juicy from the branches, instead of having them handed him, dead and tasteless, in golden vessels borne by supple slaves. Food they may still be, but that the palled appetite rejects; fruits they ceased to be when God's sky no longer bent unobstructedly above them, and the ripple of the brook and sighing of the winds through the branches blent no longer with the blithe carol of the birds all around. Not even for a king will nature be defrauded; and the truant boy, who, by long watching, has found the goldfinch's nest, shall vainly consent to sell his prize to another. The nest and its twittering tenants may be carried to my lady's window and made fast there, but that which made their charm remains with the wood and its urchin ranger.*

It was no hyperbole, therefore, no windy pretense of 'Macedonia's madman,' when he said of the cynic of the tub, "If I were not Alexander, I would be Diogenes." It was *his* impulse to illustrate Manhood thoroughly in a particular direction; lacking this impulse, he would have been driven to that different sphere illustrated with equal thoroughness by his stoical cotemporary. Perchance he dimly apprehended, through all the pomp and glitter and physical power and fulsome adulation surrounding him, that the philosopher who needed nothing, wished nothing, but his personal share of God's sunshine, was truly mightier than the lord of continents who could weep for more kingdoms to conquer. Possibly he discerned that, after a score or so of centuries,

* Of course, this idea must have been suggested by a passage in Emerson's fine poem, "Each in All," though unconsciously.

the truth should be made apparent even to the common understanding, so that the era which witnessed the overthrow of Darius and Persia, should come to be regarded as the age, not of Alexander, but of Diogenes. But, even if this be exalting too far the prescience of the son of Philip, let us never distrust his sincerity. He, too, was a veritable man in his perverse, bad way, and knew how to reverence simple Manhood. In a world of Alexanders, a Diogenes would never lack sunshine.

Have we not here an explanation of the charm which Literature exercises even over the most simple, unlettered, and prosaic? The Arab circle gathered around the evening fire, hang breathless on the lips of the narrator, as he recounts the wondrous adventures of some Haroun, Saladin, or Rustam, because each listener is engrossed in the development of qualities which he feels stirring within him, and which propitious circumstances might have ripened into deeds like those which challenge his admiration. In the wildest flight of imagination, the least credible adventure of paladin or genii-aided hero, we recognise some before undiscerned possibility of our own nature. The wonder-worker has not yet vaulted far above our heads; he has ascended, indeed, but has drawn us up with him. I think the ultimate lesson of History is not dissimilar. What do we read with more delight, even in the polished, glittering pages of Gibbon or Robertson, than their narratives of the resignation of empire, the glad exchange of unrivaled power for powerless retirement and seclusion, by Dioclesian and Charles V.? These are true heroes, because recognised by our hearts as brethren, and brethren of all mankind. Of narrow, one-sided persons — mere plowmen, pedagogues, generals or kings — the world is full enough; but the True Man is universal — includes all these and more, and he it is we would have brought palpably before us — him we would grapple to our hearts with hooks of steel. "Equal to either fortune," was the talismanic expression of a mighty though erring spirit; the thought would almost redeem a life of crime. It is this sentiment which has made, and will long make, Byron's gloomy heroes popular, in defiance of their misanthropy and utter want of conscience. Childe Harold and Lara have great faults—their lives have "little relish of salvation" in them—but they display a wide range of capacities, and are at home in any environment of circumstances—they are men, and regard all around them with searching, manly gaze, looking straight through gauds and trappings to the unclothed heart, and testing all things by absolute standards. Misanthropic themselves, they yet inspire in us a deeper confidence and a loftier pride in humanity. We see their error, and avoid it if we choose; the trust they inspire in the yet unfathomed capacities of our nature endures. The military leader who, having won by his ability a mighty and conclusive victory, shuns the parade of triumph, the roads strewn with flowers, and lined with grateful, adoring thousands, the civic banquets and the munificence of rescued kings, choosing rather to commune with himself in the deep forest, or retire to the dim cloister, there to ponder over Man's career and destiny—this is the hero our hearts yearn to, for by him they are chastened and exalted. He has added something, by exploration at least, to the common domain of our race. And thus our Washington, achieving no brilliant or astonishing success as a General or Statesman, vaulted at once to the topmost round of greatness by sincerely, steadfastly refusing a continuance of power, exalting himself above all conquerors and autocrats by simply declining their company, and refusing to be accounted more or other than a man.

Rare indeed are the individuals who live exactly the life they would—whose Ideal and Actual exist in congenial, blended harmony. The son but seldom finds the conditions he seeks beneath the kindly, paternal roof; as Manhood opens to his gaze, he quits its warm shelter, and strikes off into the bleak world without, to find or make his future sphere and home. Art, Trade, Adventure, Professional Life, present their varied attractions, and each wins some; while to others, the stormy, heaving Ocean wears a winning smile, and even grim and horrid War finds votaries. A discontent with the Actual is pouring Europe's surplus millions on the Western shore of the Atlantic, and thence over the whole surface of our continent. It is dotting the prairies of Illinois with the cabins of the sons of New-England, and year by year the smoke of the squatter's lodge rises nearer and nearer the Rocky Mountains, while hardy bands have already passed those formidable barriers, and are lining with their tents the shores of the mighty Pacific. Torrid heats and Arctic snows are lightly braved by thousands at all times, eagerly courting any change from the wearisome inanity of their past existence. Daily the city's crowded streets are pressed by thousands fresh from the plow and the rural workshop, who mind not how thronged the course on which they are entering, so that they can but secure a foothold upon it, and Hope beckons to them from the distant goal. But intermingled with that host of eager, sanguine strivers, I see another, it seems an older, thinner, feebler band, who also have their trunks and portmanteaus beside them: they are the sated or oftener disappointed seekers of Wealth or Fame, who, having sped their arrow and spent their strength in the rugged rivalry of the mart, are seeking once more the country's green lanes and shady quiet—for health, perchance, or peace, or space to breathe, and time to think or pray—at all events for grassy graves. Not theirs the firm, elastic step, the gallant, sturdy bearing; the soul intent on stern encounter and high achievement. No more is 'Excelsior' their motto, but 'Implora pace;'—their youth's Ideal, whether realized or not, has faded, flickered, disappeared, giving place to one less lofty, more readily attainable. A snug cottage and a few pliant acres would now be happiness to him whose ambition once clutched at mines, or squares, or kingdoms. Who shall say that career has been a failure which, though it has won no golden store, has wrought this change of spirit?

A discontent with the Actual is the mainspring of most that is noble in human endeavor. It spurs the traveler into the darkest dens of African barbarism or Tartar cruelty, and sends the Missionary to spend his life rapidly in sickly Burmese huts or frozen Esquimaux lodges—joyfully dying that those he never saw till now may live for ever. The same spirit is now lighting the dens of loathsomest vice with the unwonted presence of angel purity and pity, and braving the filth and noisomeness of prisons, heedless of aught save the human hearts there shackled and pining for sympathy and freedom. Not even the scaffold's grim appointments can repel its fearless approaches, for wherever it sees Humanity, however scarred and ulcerated, however defiled or blasted by sin's ravages, it recognises the lineaments of a brother.

But a revolt against the tame insipidity of common life impels to evil as well as good—hurls the warrior, the slaver, the pirate, on his fell career, and blackens earth with carnage and ruin. It is not enough that man, as he is, should act up to the standard of his aspirations, for these also need to be corrected and exalted.

Two antagonist thoughts—Self and All—lie at the bottom of the many warring tendencies in the breasts of mankind. Their symbols may be found in the geocentric and heliocentric theories of planetary motion. The advocates of the former appeal with success to the human senses uninstructed by Science—to our eyes to bear witness that the Sun *does* truly move around the earth—to our position and that of all unfixed, gravitating bodies, to prove that the Earth is a vast plane and does *not* turn over day by day.

The evidence for this theory is such that its truth may be said to be intuitively perceived by every infant. But by-and-by comes along the Astronomer with his telescope, the Mathematician with his Geometry and Algebra, and reverses this conviction, enlarging the bounds of the visible Universe, and developing Laws of which the child knew nothing. Yet by far the larger part of mankind still live and die, as *all* formerly lived and died, in the undoubting belief that the Earth is daily circled by the Sun and Stars.

So with human character and effort. The child is born a citizen of the great Commonwealth of Man, but his entrance to it is through the narrow gate of the Family. His practical education there, during the most impressible and important period of his life, stamps into his mind three cardinal maxims, namely:

1st. To take special good care of himself in all cases, and shape everything he can control to his own enjoyment or uses;

2d. To bestow whatever he does not thus need, or can not make available to his personal ends, on the narrow circle by which he is surrounded;

3d. To give all beyond this—his blessing, for instance—to the general good of mankind.

Who can fail to see that the soul is distorted, shriveled, dwarfed, by this schooling?—that the boy becomes a selfish, sensual, grasping man—in fact, only a politer beast of prey? The influences most immediately surrounding him from the cradle have all tended to this. *Mine* and *Thine*—the former to be prized and treasured—the latter to be acquired or left to take care of itself—are the first distinctions impressed on his unfolding intellect. All within this narrow tenement, within these encircling fences, is *ours*, to be guarded, toiled for, beautified; all without is others', to be obtained, envied, or disregarded. The stranger child who oversteps that magic ring in search of some fruit or herb, which, though enjoyed to satiety by us, would be luxury to him, is to be saluted with a stone or mastiff for his depraved temerity, and driven back to sate his gnawing hunger on the nettles of the highway. Now I am not quarreling with this as a fault of the individual, or a wanton exhibition of churlishness. On the contrary, I recognise it as a necessary feature of a system—necessary while the system shall endure. I am but regarding it in the light of its influence on the molding of Human Character. And in this light I do not hesitate to say that the Family and Social influences surrounding our youth are most unfavorable to the development of manly, generous, sympathizing natures. These influences tend to educate the human race into two classes, thieves and constables—to foster an eternal antagonism between Wealth and Want—and throw every one into the attitude of a scout in an enemy's country, pressing cautiously forward with eyes piercing the thickets around him and rifle in the hollow of his arm. Here and there an individual triumphs over all these influences, by the force of rare qualities or a singularly happy training, and shows us what Mankind might be, give them but fair play. But a *race* of Heroes of Humanity—a People elevated to Love and Universal Blessing—such we have not and can not expect until the influences which overshadow Childhood, our modes of training youth for Manhood, are radically changed.

And a race of Heroes was never more needed on earth than now. The old manifestations of Heroism have become effete or abhorrent, but the Nineteenth Century has need of many a Hercules, a Hector, an Achilles, who shall be all its own. Its Patriotism demands relief from the vain boasters, the self-seekers, the noisy braggarts, who, reckless of general misery and ruin, would fain involve nations wantonly in butchery and deadly hate, that they may chance to riot in the spoils of the universal devastation. Its religion pleads for release from the stifling bondages of Cant and Formalism

—from sour asceticism and a pestilent wrangling on points of non-practical belief. It protests against laying emphasis on any article of a creed which can not be embodied and evinced in a life. Its Philanthropy, pointing to new, vast, slightly-explored fields inviting effort for Human Well-being, calls on the generous, the hopeful, the ardent, to engage heartily in the work of securing to the next generation a better world than that which we received from the last.

Ah! if we had but a few regiments of life-enlisted volunteers in the service of Humanity, who, having first graduated their own physical wants to the standard of real necessity, should consecrate all their powers, mental and physical, to the persistent, unwearied, unshackled increase of Human Happiness and diminution of the causes of Suffering, the world could not remain where it is, but must move forward swiftly to that fairer future which can not be merely a Poet's dream. The history of Lot's sojourn in and escape from Sodom is not without its enduring lesson. States, cities, communities, are preserved from destruction, so long as preserved at all, by so much virtue as they embody; when that wanes to insufficiency, the remnant may escape or linger, but the destruction of the depraved mass is inevitable. And, as the absolute lack of moral good is inexorable ruin, so is its unusual prevalence the sure occasion of strength and prosperity. There is no habitable portion of our globe where a thoroughly virtuous population might not reconstitute the Garden of Eden.

But to the formation of such a people, few influences conduce, while those which forbid it are incessant and innumerable. There has been little systematic training to heroism of any sort since the days of the Spartans. Our children are steeped in selfishness from their cradles, and nine-tenths of them are practically taught to dread Useful Labor as odious and degrading, and to regard idleness, with sensuality and ostentation, as the *summum bonum* of life. I know that something different from this is stolidly dealt out, though never pointedly, consistently taught, from the Catechisms; but I am speaking of the every-day lessons, and not those which are inculcated only on Sunday, if ever. How many children in a thousand, whether rich or poor, are taught to regard virtuous poverty in humble garb as *really* more to be honored and desired than wealth undistinguished by worth? How many are taught to heed God's appointment, "Six days shalt thou labor," as plainly directed to them, and by them to be joyfully and faithfully obeyed, irrespective of riches or station? How many are early taught that they can have no right to squander on their own appetites or pride that which the law of the land says is theirs, but for want of which another suffers? What reverend monitor now says, habitually and earnestly, and not unheededly, to the child of affluence and luxury, 'Sell *all* thou hast, and give to the Poor, *then* follow Him, whose only personal disciples *were* the poor?' Alas! the flower of life is cankered in the bud, and what should be beauty and fragrance is turned to deformity and death!

Next to the lessons of infancy come those of the School, with its constant bickerings and ardent, envious rivalries for advancement and honors. All is intensely individual—egotistic. The school-boy's triumphs are won *over* and not *for* his comrades. His glory is their mortification and shame; his disasters the theme of their undisguised, unchecked exultation. Thence he passes into some sphere of active life, and finds the same law everywhere prevailing, and producing its natural results. The brilliant leader at the bar makes a rapid fortune, but the unknown hundreds of middling counselors are left to starve; and the popular physician who is supposed to cure everybody dooms his fellow practitioners to that consumption for which Falstaff could 'get no remedy.' Everywhere the victor in the grand battle of Life advances to grasp the laurel over piles of unheeded corpses. He can not afford to calculate too nicely the moral nature and consequences of each act—he must live; and the more flagrant and palpable the guilt of the felon whom the lawyer's skill saves from justice, the more brilliant is that lawyer's triumph, the more extravagant his fee,—the more rapid his march to fame and fortune.

But perhaps the most imperative of the influences of practical life to narrow and distort the man is that exercised by Traffic. To obtain More for Less—this is the aim and the impulse of Trade. The game of the counter, like that of the boxing-ring, places two persons opposite each other at proper distance, and bids them shake hands and begin. That each *may* be a gainer by the bargain is of course practicable; (though which of them naturally cares for this?) that both may be honest men is freely conceded. The criticism impeaches not the men but the attitude in which they are pitted against each other. Where Wealth is the object of general and eager desire, where Labor is loathed and Luxury coveted—it is too hard on frail Human Nature to place it where a slight departure from rectitude may win its thousands. The temptation *may* be resisted—it doubtless often is; for Trade has furnished its full quota of the upright and more than its share of the benevolent of our race; but while these may probably have owed to Commerce the *means* of being liberal, I doubt whether any have been indebted to it for their *integrity*. Of that, a man must carry all into a life of buying and selling that he expects to bring out again, and he can hardly afford to commence business on a small capital either. If a man of unsettled or weak principles ever trafficked five years without becoming a rogue, he must present a striking evidence of the sustaining, saving mercy of an overruling Providence.

The position and sphere of the independent, virtuous, contented Farmer has from earliest time been pointed at as one of the most fortunate and healthful, mentally as well as physically, that earth can afford. Living in the immediate and visible presence of the all-embracing Heavens, directly dependent on the Author of all for whatever blesses him, he would seem to be marked out for integrity and elevation of sentiment. Nature will not be cheated ; whoever shall undertake to palm upon her a single bushel of chalk for lime, for instance, will find her incapable of relishing his ingenuity. So much for so much, is her invariable law ; no shams nor appearances avail anything with her—even her children the crows are not half so often taken in by them as the contrivers imagine. With unequaled advantages for the maintenance or attainment of health and vigor, with a thousand silent preachers of the blessedness of Temperance, Exercise, Justice, and Truth, constantly attending him, the Farmer's character would seem insensibly, irresistibly moulded to probity and honor. In his vocation, a bow and a smirk avail not; that which comes not from the core is nothing and passes for nothing. Only where he ceases to be a worker and begins to be a trader in other men's labor or the fruits of his own, does the temptation to injustice and insincerity begin. Living ever in the presence of Heaven, and in direct, visible dependence on its free bounties, we should say that the Farmer's bearing should ever tell of the free, bland breezes, and his countenance reflect the stars.

And yet, on practical acquaintance, we find him quite often another being—narrow, prejudiced, and selfish ; perverse, sensual, and depraved; a foe to other men's good and his own. And not this merely, but his sons have no love for his vocation ; they too generally escape it when they can, or embrace it only because they have not the ability or detest the study necessary to make them anything else. From the noblest and richest rural homestead, you will see the youthful heir eagerly hieing to the distant city, there to consecrate years to the exhibition of sarsnets to simpering, shopping misses, or to the service of some six-by-eight subterranean money-changer's den, which a hedgehog would disdain to inhabit. Where one youth is heartily seeking the Farmer's life from choice, there are forty striving or pining to escape it. Thus are our cities overgrown and bloated with a redundant, thriftless population, who, having no legitimate sphere of exertion, underbid each other for employment, and are too often driven by want and despair into depraved and forbidden courses. Talent, knowledge, and skill, which are greatly needed in the sphere of rural life, crowd and jostle each other on the city's pavements, and often sell to Capital for a month's livelihood some happy invention or combination which should have insured a competence for life. Alas for human frailty, beset by ravening hunger or pinching frost!—full-pursed depravity is enabled oft to drive still harder bargains than these!

Facts abundantly indicate that the actual position of the cultivator is not what it might and should be. He ought to be, by science and wisdom, the master of the elements, yet is, through ignorance and imperfection, their slave. The floods which should fertilize his soil, often wash it away, and with it the fruits of his labor. The winds, which should drive the plow through his naked fields, or spend their force on smoothing away any undesired irregularities of surface, do far oftener prostrate his granaries and fences. The electric currents, which should push forward his vegetation with a rapidity and vigor unimagined save by the initiated few, are left to shatter his house or barn, perhaps only destroying therewith his annual harvest, perhaps finishing himself and his labors. Instead of being, as in Manufactures or Navigation, the director and controller of the blind forces of Nature to his own use and profit, the Farmer allows these to escape him in uselessness or mischief, and feebly, inefficiently supplies their place by overtaxing his own sinews. Hence weariness, disgust, and meager recompense; hence the accomplished or longed-for escape of countless thousands from the paltry drudgery of the hoe and spade to the larger hopes and more intellectual sphere of effort elsewhere afforded.

It is the mission of our age to regenerate and dignify Agriculture, by rendering it practically an intellectual and expansive vocation. Within its sphere lie yet enfolded the germs of future conquests far mightier and nobler than those of any Cæsar or Napoleon. These petty, cramped enclosures, these deforming, dwarfing fences, which render the landscape so insipid and characterless, shall yet be swept away by the genius of Improvement, through the application of the truths of Science to the daily economies of life. Then the brook shall no more brawl idly down the declivity while the laborer delves wearily yet ineffectively by its side, and Man will no more stoop doggedly to burdens which the free breezes would gladly bear to their appointed destination. We stand but on the threshold of the world of Science made practical, and our vision rests on and is bounded by its application to Manufactures alone. Wondrous as is the progress which half a century has witnessed in this direction, it is as nothing to what remains to be accomplished for the whole circle of Human Industry, and especially in the department of Agriculture, to which nearly all the Natural Sciences, as well as Mechanical forces, shall yet advantageously minister. The farmer of the coming age — master and manager of steam rather than tyrant of enslaved, toil-worn, hungry beasts, — shall not need painfully to heave the ponderous rock from its base, but will rather, by some simple chemical solvent, pulverize it to fertile dust where it lies. To his informed, observant mind, the changes of temperature, the succession of calm and storm, shall bring no surprise, no disaster, being unerringly foreseen and profited by like the rotation of the seasons. For his behoof the plow shall pursue its unguided, resistless course across the spacious landscape, and the following seed shall fall regularly into its appointed place, without need of special oversight or guidance. The inequalities of surface and of soil shall disappear before the steady, unexpensive action of natural forces thereon; steam giants shall loosen and deepen the soil to any extent desirable, sweeping down forests as a fire does the dry grass of the prairies, and extracting roots like a tornado. There is no practical limit to the powers at all times presenting themselves to do the bidding of Man, had he but the talent and genius to adapt and apply them. Nature wills that the plow, the sythe, the axe, the harvest-wain, shall move forward on their proper errands, as irresistibly, inexpensively as the saw, the throstle, the shuttle, and with equally beneficent results. Actually, the capacity of human labor to produce fabrics has been increased some twenty-fold within the last century, while in its application to rural pursuits it has not been more than doubled, if so much. This disparity is not necessary, but factitious, and must be overcome. Half a century will suffice to bring forward Agriculture to the point which Manufacture has now reached, banishing for ever the still lingering fears of occasional famine, and rendering food as abundant and accessible as the common elements.

Yet the Farmer's vocation needs something more than increased efficiency and mastery of Nature to reconcile it with a lofty and generous ideal. We need a change in the man himself, and in those circumstances which *vitally* affect his character. He is now too nearly an isolated being. His world is a narrow circle of material objects he calls *his own*, within which he is an autocrat, though out of it little more than a cipher. His associates are few, and these mainly rude dependents and inferiors. His daily discourse savors of beeves and swine, and the death of a sheep on his farm creates more sensation in his circle than the fall of a hero elsewhere. Of the refining, harmonizing, expanding influences of general society, he has little experience. For extensive travel or intercourse with minds which have profited by a large comparison of nations, climates, customs, he has but rare opportunities. The family circle, precious as are its enjoyments, and healthful as are its proper influences, is not alone sufficient to form the noblest character or satisfy all the aspirations of the human heart. The lofty, ingenuous soul revolts at the idea of wearing out its earthly career mainly in the rearing of brutes and the composting of manures, shut out from all free range of congenial associates and obedience to nobler impulses. It feels that a human life is ill spent in the mere production of corn and cattle. Hence our youth of largest promise too generally escape from the drudgery of their paternal acres to court the equally repulsive slavery of the office or the counter—not because it is preferable in itself, but because it gives scope to larger hopes, suggests larger possibilities, and at all events is supposed to afford larger opportunities for observation, for intellectual development, and choice of companions. Here is one cause of the inferior development and progress in Agriculture, as compared with other departments of industrial effort. The genius and intellect which should have taught us to 'speed the plow' with Titanic energy has been attracted to other vocations, leaving that of the old patriarchs as sterile as some bald mountain on which every rain levies tribute to fertilize the surrounding valleys. Not till the solitary farm-house, with its half-dozen denizens, its mottled array of mere patches of auxiliary acres, its petty flock and herd, its external decorations of piggery, stable-yard, etc., making it the focus of all noisome and villainous odors, shall have been replaced by some arrangement more genial, more expansive, more social in its aspects, affording larger scope to aspiration and a wider field for the infinite capacities of man's nature, may we hope to arrest the tendencies which make the farmer too often a boor or a clod, and the cultivation of the earth a mindless, repugnant drudgery, when it should be the noblest, the most intellectual and the most desired of human employments.

But in truth the whole atmosphere of our better education, the influence of our higher seminaries, tends to unfit our noblest youth for lives of peaceful industry, and win away their affections therefrom. The young man acquires or is given an education, as it is technically called, in order that he may be something else and better than a farmer. The mother's darling, the hope and pride of the family, must be fitted for some career less insignificant and slavish than that of his progenitors. So the cracked sugar-bowl is relieved of its slowly-gathered dollars, and the budding genius is sent to the academy and thence to college, not with a view to his becoming a larger, better man in any abstract sense—still less with the remotest notion of making him a better farmer—but purely that he may escape his father's groveling, despised vocation, and become something nobler and more exalted than a tiller of the soil. His first lessons of contempt for all the ways of manual industry are therefore taken by the paternal fireside; and these are quickly reinforced by those of the University, with its courtly airs and lily fingers. With all the wisdom hoarded in and dispensed from those classic halls, the wisdom of God in making Man dependent for the satisfaction of his most inevitable wants on his habitual toil—the wisdom which decrees, 'In the *sweat of thy face* shalt thou eat bread'—is not perceived and acknowledged. Under the auspices of a President and Faculty, whose lives have almost necessarily been given to books, to ideas and words, to the exclusion of manual exertion—with whom the extraction of roots has uniformly been a mathematical, never a horticultural process—half of whom are paying, through dyspepsia, gout, or nervous derangement, the penalty of violating the law aforesaid—the youth enters upon his new career. Should he cherish some lingering regard for that wise ordinance which demands labor of all as the *inexorable* condition of health and vigor, he speedily succumbs to the *genus loci*—the atmosphere and the sentiment which surround him. The student in one of our popular colleges must be daring and wilful who would venture even to saw or carry up his own wood, however convinced of the wholesomeness or necessity of such occupation. But instead of work he is admonished to avail himself of that vague, illegitimate something—or more commonly nothing—termed (after the similitude of Bottom's dream) Exercise, which, to a prisoner chained to a dungeon wall, is very commendable. And thus, giving some ten hours per day to study, as many to food and rest, and the balance to recreations which are recreations only and hardly, the divorce of Learning from Labor—of Science from Practice—of Man the Thinker from Man the Worker—is rendered complete, and the educated youth goes out into the world to preach, or plead, or physic, with such success as may attend him, but with an implanted, usually inveterate repugnance to regular Manual Labor in all its departments—a feeling that his position is above it, and that he would be degraded by descending to it—a fixed resolution to avoid it evermore if possible. The evil consequences of this mistake are more numerous than could be compressed into a volume. The young physician or attorney who has spent his last shilling, and perhaps incurred onerous debts, in pursuing his studies, must not devote his leisure hours, while awaiting the slow approaches of business, to downright, practical labor in the fields or workshops around him, where other men work and earn, although his circumstances pressingly require and his health might be re-established by such a course. Should he do so, he would be adjudged sordid or mean-spirited, and his attempt to establish himself professionally a conceded failure. But far worse than this are the jealousy and aversion aroused in the breasts of the working class by the visible repugnance to and disdain of their pursuits by the educated, and the desire evinced to keep the intellectual distinction of caste as broad and rigid as possible. Hence, in part, the failure of the liberally educated to exert their due influence over the opinions and course of the more numerous classes —the want of any quick and cordial sympathy between the learned and the unlearned, as members of the same social body. In fact, the common impulse of the larger mass is to oppose rather than support whatever the more fortunate and better informed appear to favor—a most deplorable and calamitous impulse, especially in a Republic. We must learn to vanquish this, and the removal of its cause is its only effectual remedy.

Bear with one more illustration of the pernicious contrast created in the unfolding mind between the ideas awakened by our present or indeed any thorough course of Intellectual Culture, and the pursuits of gainful Industry, as they appear and are carried on around us. An ardent, ingenuous, impressible youth, leaves his parental fireside for the academy and college, where he is made master of the Dead Languages and their rich treasures—becomes acquainted with Classical Antiquity, and imbued with its spirit. But of that Antiquity, History has borne down to us only or mainly the bloody aspect—it delights in and expatiates upon the doings of daring and violent men. The victory of Marathon —the defence of Thermopylæ—the passage of the Granicus —the exploits of Achilles, Alexander, Hannibal, and Cæsar—these and the like are the staple of the student's daily contemplations and nightly dreams. Regarding the *really* great events in man's annals—the first use of Iron, the Invention of the Plow, the Spindle, the Loom, the Mariner's Compass, History is almost if not entirely silent. Archimedes is rescued from oblivion by the accident of his connection with the defence of Syracuse—while the invention even of Printing, so recent and so mighty a transformer of the mental world, is claimed by different nations for different and still obscure men, though we know well who first compounded Gunpowder, where Cannon were first used, and where the Bayonet was invented. The most peaceful and gentle youth is thus insensibly taught, by the influences surrounding him in school and college, to regard Fame with a passionate longing, from observing that the heroes of History have been and still are the theme of study and admiration in every seminary throughout the civilized world, and that upon their lives as models the characters of the educated class in all time are molded. Not merely the love of Fame, for itself, is thus taught, but that Fame is a child of Courts, and Camps, and Cabinets, visiting rarely or never the humble dwellings wherein unselfish Philanthropy labors to soften anguish and remove from lowly souls the stains of Vice and Sin. At length, from years of fascinating familiarity with whatever is most dazzling and theatrical in human annals, the young man is at once recalled to the practical realities of life—he has finished his education—at least, his studies. He reënters the work-day world a very different being from that which he left it. He has now to choose a pursuit and a sphere of life-long effort. The range for selection is wide; for, if his education has been real and thorough, he is by it better qualified for any useful vocation. But how tame, how monotonous, how frivolous, seem the common ways of mere productive labor, to a mind so trained and occupied! How insipid, after years of battling and conquering with Scipio or Marlborough, to come down to mere mowing and gardening with Jones and Jenkins! The impatient, aspiring soul revolts at it—not so much that the work itself is fatiguing and repugnant, as that it seems unworthy to engross a lifetime—a glaring misuse and waste of its capacious, sharpened faculties. Nor is this feeling confined to the graduates of our universities. From every country village, every rural hamlet, the better class of youth are fleeing, they care not whither, to escape the insupportable exactions of a life of toil which has ceased to bear due relations to or satisfy the wants of their enkindled souls. In vain do plodding, old-school fathers grumble at the wayward and preposterous ambition of their children—in vain do they attribute their perversity to laziness or folly, and wish 'the march of Mind,' would keep away from honest poor men's houses, and not spoil their sons. The simple truth is, that the Intellectual Culture of our age has outgrown its Physical and Social Progress, creating anarchy and confusion. Idle is all grumbling at or lamenting this advance—the shadow will not go back on the dial. What we have to do is not to draw back the van, but to bring up the rear. We must renovate and rëanimate our Iudustry, by bringing to bear upon its processes all the powers of Science, all the forces of Nature, all the vast economies of Combination. We must call on the college, the closet, the office, to send out their ablest and wisest to lead the advance of the grand army of Industrial Progress, as its engineers, staff, and officers of the line. We must replace the grim Knights of old War with a Chivalry of Industry, as honored and beloved as any Knightly Order, and infinitely more deserving of honor than the best. We must rëarouse and redirect that enthusiasm which for centuries precipitated myriads after myriads of Christendom's best and bravest to perish by sword or famine on the rocky wastes of Palestine, battling to the last to rescue the Redeemer's sepulchre from the defiling tread of the Infidel, and must bring its compact, resistless phalanxes to bear upon all the physical and tangible causes of Man's degradation and suffering. Guided by Science, impelled by a lofty devotion to Human Good, sustained by the sympathies and supplies of the whole civilized world, let us hope to see the vast armament of this new Chivalry advance to the draining of pestilent marshes by a single week's animated, arduous exertion—a triumph nobler than any

Cannæ or Waterloo—the reclamation of swamps, deserts, and sterile regions, until Sahara shall rejoice once more in verdure and fragrance, the Campagna become a garden, and stately forests belt the vast, bare plains which stretch away from either declivity of the Rocky Mountains. Of the physical improvement, whether as regards fertility or accessibility, whereof the Earth is susceptible, we have begun to entertain some glimmering notion; but of the facility with which Science, Experience, and Combined Effort shall enable us to effect this improvement, no adequate idea has yet been formed. The true idea, once formed and disseminated, will but briefly precede the consummation.

Enough, for the occasion, of the definitive and the critical. Let us bestow a few moments in closing on some broader, more animating aspects of Life in the Nineteenth Century.

Say what we will and justly may of the incurable depravity of Man, as evinced in the universality of Sin and Crime, this world is better and more hopeful than it has been. The robber and the murderer still skulk and prowl among us, insulting the lone majesty of Night with revealments of their hideous presence, but Murder in the face of Day and Heaven—the wholesale butchery of Nations, the robbery of Cities and Provinces—is no longer perpetrated without shame nor witnessed without indignant horror. The stifling to death of a few hundred Arabs in a cave, though shielded by the panoply of undoubted and relentless war, shocks the sensibilities of Christendom, and all apologies are instinctively rejected as adding sophistry to crime. The world regards admiringly the protracted defense of their homes and hearths by the bold mountaineers of Caucasus, wishing them a triumphant deliverance from the toils of their mighty oppressor, and every blow well struck at the minions of his power thrills with rapture the general heart. For Poland, the unfortunate, betrayed, crushed and bleeding, the tears of the nations flow in rivers, and the fervent prayers of sympathizing, sorrowing millions ascend unceasingly to God. And even Ireland, for seven centuries the prey of Domestic treason and Foreign rapine, prostrate and trampled beneath the heel of a double tyranny of Sword and Creed, at last lifts her eyes in hope and mute supplication, and, discarding the gory weapons of ruffianism and murder, trusts her cause wholly to Humanity and to God—even her sublime but less imposing appeal begins to be heeded and felt; it melts the hard crust of sectarian prejudice and hatred—it touches the souls of the generous and manly—and the glad shout of Earth's enraptured millions shall hail the swiftly hastening hour of her emancipation.

Nor am I discouraged by the fact that Kings and Courts still plot against Liberty and Justice, or even that Nations, blinded by rapacity or ambition, are led into the commission of gigantic crimes. I see also that these crimes, if not less atrocious than formerly, are less frequent, less unblushing, and require to be sugared o'er with sonorous, captivating phrases, indicating a devotion to Truth and Good. To steal provinces for the sake of stealing or of enjoying them would not pass uncensured now, as in the days of Xerxes, or Norman William, or Prussian Frederick. It must be styled tranquilizing a frontier, or putting an end to anarchy, or establishing justice, or extending the blessings of freedom, or something of the sort. Hypocrisy, that homage paid by Vice to Virtue, at least testifies the existence of that virtue without which the homage would be vain. In a former age, civilized men unceremoniously robbed savages of their possessions for God's sake and kept them for their own. Now it is deemed meet and decorous to incur the expense of making some few of the intended victims thoroughly insensible from strong drink, and thus procuring what can afterward be pronounced their signatures to a treaty of cession, surrendering lands which they had no more right to sell away from their brethren and their children than to sell the waters and the sky. And, with all this formality and seeming, the operation is often deemed imperfect unless sanctified by the presence and active participation of some Christian divine. These little attentions to the unities and proprieties, which the thoughtless would pass unheeded or with a sneer of contempt, are indeed cheering signs of Human Progress. They demonstrate the existence of an awakening though still drugged and drowsy National and Universal Conscience. They irradiate by contrast the raven darkness, unabashed ferocity and unbridled lust of Man's earlier career. The light they cast on the page of History heralds the dawn of a nobler and grander era, in which nations shall realize that for them no more than for individuals is there any possible escape from the inflexibility of God's Providence, which steadily puts aside all pretences, all shams, and looks intently into the impulse and essence of every action, awarding to each the exact and inexorable recompense of its merits. In the light of that era, Virtue will walk abroad unshielded by Force, unindebted to Opinion, winning all to obey her dictates if not from intrinsic love of her, then from love of happiness and themselves.

But this, though an effective defence against wrong-doing, can never be the true impulse to a life of active, positive goodness. That virtue which is based on a conviction of the advantage of virtue as a business investment will naturally waste too much time in calculating chances, to be of great value as a practical incitement to deeds. We need a loftier Ideal to nerve us for heroic lives. Only on forgetfulness of Self, or rather on a consciousness that we are all but motes in the beam whose sun is God, drops in the rivulet whose ocean is Humanity, can our souls be molded into conformity with the loftiest ideal of our race. To know and feel our nothingness without regretting it; to deem fame, riches, personal happiness, but shadows of which Human Good is the substance—to welcome Pain, Privation, Ignominy, so that the sphere of Human Knowledge, the empire of Virtue, be thereby extended—such is the soul's temper in which the Heroes of the Coming Age shall be cast. To realize profoundly that the individual is nothing, the universal everything—to feel nothing a calamity whereby the sum of human virtue or happiness is increased, this is the truest wisdom. When the stately monuments of mightiest conquerors shall have become shapeless and forgotten ruins, the humble graves of Earth's Howards and Frys shall still be freshened by the tears of fondly admiring millions, and the proudest epitaph shall be the simple entreaty,

'Write me as one who *loved* his fellow-men.'

Say not that I thus condemn and would annihilate Ambition. The love of approbation, of esteem, of true glory, is a noble incentive, and should be cherished to the end. But the ambition which points the way to fame over torn limbs and bleeding hearts—which joys in the Tartarean smoke of the battle-field and the desolating tramp of the war-horse—*that* ambition is worthy only of 'archangel ruined.' To make one conqueror's reputation, at least one hundred thousand bounding, joyous, sentient beings must be transformed into writhing and hideous fragments—must perish untimely by deaths of agony and horror, leaving half a million widows and orphans to bewail their loss in anguish and destitution. This is too mighty, too awful a price to be paid for the fame of any hero, from Nimrod to Wellington. True fame demands no such sacrifices of others; it requires us to be reckless of the outward well-being of but one. It exacts no hecatomb of victims for each triumphal pile; for the more who covet and seek it the easier and more abundant is the success of each and all. With souls of the celestial temper, each human life might be a triumph, which angels would lean from the skies delighted to witness and admire.

And, beyond doubt, the loftiest ambition possible to us finds its fruition in perfect, simple Manhood. A robber may be a great warrior; a pirate an admiral; a dunce a king; a slimy intriguer a President; but to be a thorough and true Man, that is an aspiration which repels all accident or seeming. And let us not fear that such are too common to be distinguished or famous. Could there appear among us a realization of the full idea of Manhood — no mere general, nor statesman, nor devotee, but a complete and genuine Man — he need not walk naked or in fantastic garb to gather all eyes upon him. The very office-seekers would forget for a moment their fawning, and prowling, their coaxing and slandering, to gather eagerly, though awed, around him to inquire from what planet he had descended. No merman nor centaur giraffe nor chimpanzee, mastodon nor megalosaurus, ever excited half the curiosity which would be awakened and requited by the presence among us of a whole and complete Man. And to form this character, inadequate as have been all past approaches to it by unaided human energy, the elements are visibly preparing. Men are becoming slowly but sensibly averse to whatever erects barriers between them and cuts them into fragments and particles of Manhood. The priest in his surplice, the *militaire* in his regimentals, the duke under his coronet, all begin to feel rather uneasy and shame-faced if confronted with a throng of irreverent citizens, hurrying to and fro, intent on their various errands. Among a corps, a bevy of his own order, the farce may still be played by each with decorous propriety, but apart from these it palls and becomes a heaviness. Day by day it is more and more clearly felt that the world is outgrowing the dolls and rattles of its childhood, and more and more disdains to be treated childishly. Direct, earnest speech, with useful

7*

deeds evincing lofty purpose—these are more and more insisted on, and whatever lacks them is quietly left to perish. An undeserved popularity, a sham celebrity, may still be got up by due incantations; but frailer, than the spider's gossamer, the first breath resolves them into their essential nothingness. Gas to gas, they mingle with the blue surrounding ether, and neither its serenity nor its purity is visibly affected by the infusion.

Yes, a brighter day dawns for us, sinning and suffering children of Adam. Wiser in its very follies, less cruel and wanton even in its crimes, our Race visibly progresses toward a nobler and happier realization of its capacities and powers. Compared century with century, this progress is not so palpable, since what is an age to individuals, is but a moment in the lifetime of the Race; but, viewed on a larger scale, the advance becomes cheeringly evident. Washington is a nobler exponent of humanity than Epaminondas or Scipio; La Fayette eclipses Phocion; and Burke has a larger nature, a more universal genius than Cicero. Wonderful as are the works of Homer, they bespeak the splendid barbarian, the thoroughly developed physical, animal man; but their range of imagination, of thought, is infinitely lower and narrower than Shakspeare's; the man they depict is infinitely poorer and more dwarfed than Goethe's, and I dare add even Byron's. Compare Achilles with Hamlet or Harold; the first is the more perfect of his kind, but of nature how infinitely grosser and less exalted! To him the stars are noteworthy but as battle-lanterns—they enable him to thrust the spear with deadlier aim to the heart of his enemy. To Harold, the bare presence of the stars, 'so wildly, spiritually bright,' would recall the nothingness of terrestrial aims and struggles—their searching glances would instantly rebuke and dethrone the fell appetite for slaughter, so that, throwing away the loathsome implements of human butchery, he would stand gazing intently into their serene deeps, regardless of the proximity, forgetful of the existence of a foe. Say, if you will that the former is more *natural*, I care not; in the universe of Mind there are scope and call for *more* than the natural—for the spiritual and celestial also. Never are we so truly human as when we most daringly transcend all the vulgar limitations of Humanity; and thus Hamlet, who, viewed with disparaging coldness and skepticism, is the most erratic and improbable creation of the brain, is instinctively recognized by all awakened souls as a veritable man and a brother. His unfamiliarity at first blush accused *our* deficiencies, not his—was caused by his combining more of the elements of our common nature than we had been accustomed to see embodied and developed in any one man. Had we but known ourselves, Hamlet had never seemed to us a stranger.

The ages of darkness—of unconscious wandering from the path of Right and Good—of that 'ignorance' which we are told 'God winked at' in its earlier and more excusable manifestations—are rapidly passing away. That generation is not yet all departed which witnessed the rise, progress, and termination of the struggle regarding the rightfulness and legitimacy of the African Slave-Trade. Commencing in the attacks of a few obscure fanatics on the usages, maxims, gains and respectability of the commercial aristocracy and sea-faring chivalry of nearly all Christendom, it has already become a struggle between nearly all that same Christendom converted, and a few abhorred, hunted, skulking pirates. Can any man rationally doubt that the discussion of Slavery itself, which had a similar beginning, is destined to run a like career, to a like termination? The fact that the latter is the more strongly entrenched in the interest, convenience, custom and seeming necessity of the superior caste, may somewhat protract the struggle; yet on the other hand the contest already past, the victory already gained in a kindred encounter, immeasurably diminish the difficulties and must abridge the duration of this. Men have learned and tested the applicability of moral laws to general and public as well as individual and private relations—to the acts of communities as well as of persons. Can any suppose that the application of this principle is to cease with the initial case which has established its efficacy and value? Far from it. We see it now operating upon rulers and nations, to restrain the most ambitious and blood-thirsty from war by a power far more dreaded than that of hostile bayonets. We see it operating at home in the Temperance agitation of our time, and especially that regarding the rightfulness of the traffic in Intoxicating Liquors. What is this but the Slave-Trade question over again?—varied in form, it is true, but differing nothing in substance. The essence of either controversy regards the right of any part or member of the Human Family to promote or countenance for private gain any practice or business whereby others are naturally degraded, impoverished, enslaved, or made wretched. Once determine that this right does not exist in any one case, and the principle instantly and naturally confronts other cases, and insists that these also shall be tested by its standard.

Let not the sensual hope, let the good never fear, that the vitality of this principle can be exhausted while moral evil or avoidable suffering shall linger on the face of the earth. The Reforms which have not yet begun to be prominent are vaster and nobler than any which have thus far been favored with the smiles, or even the frowns, of coteries and club-rooms. The world drowsily opens its eyes and yawns assent to the truth that the *direct* enslavement of Man is rebellion against Him who in His wisdom has endowed us with faculties and desires, with the development, use, and healthful satisfaction whereof the inevitable conditions of Slavery are incompatible. That perfect obedience which God requires can rarely be comprehended, and still more rarely rendered, by him who is born, lives, and dies the absolute chattel and convenience of another. And this truth condemns not the chattel relation only, but *all* relations in which Service degenerates into Servitude. Wherever one human being exists mainly for the convenience and advantage of another, or of others, there the elemental purpose, the essential economy of Providence is defied, and, for the moment, subverted. Wherever one requires of others more service than he willingly renders in turn, requiting it not with his own but the fruits of others' exertion, there is a principle asserted which tends to bankrupt the Race and defeat the highest end of its creation. Wherever one fancies himself exempted, by the inheritance or acquirement of wealth, from performing his fair proportion of the Labor demanded by human necessities, there is one whose example justifies the slaveholder on his couch, the absentee landlord rioting in luxury on the last potato of starving penury, the coward fleeing from the post of danger and of duty. In defrauding his kind of the service he owes them, he defrauds himself of the health, strength, and longevity, which were rightfully his portion until "vilely cast away." And the physical evils of luxury and sloth are but faint reflections of the moral. Every household constructed on the basis of a superior and an inferior caste—on the assumption that some of us were born to wait and serve, others *to be* served and waited on—that some must work to live, while others may justly live without working—the former being the less and the latter the more honorable class—*that* household, I say, is built on a foundation of un-Christian slavery and unmanly falsehood, whose tendencies are to eye-service, deceit, envy, hatred, sloth, pride, and all kindred vices. Not without a radical reform of the Household is any real approximation of the careers therein commenced to the Ideal of a True Life possible, save as a rare exception—a happy result of unobserved but potent influences, fortunately conspiring to overrule the more obvious and general laws governing the formation of character. If we are educated slaves or enslavers, we shall rarely and with difficulty outgrow our early lessons, and become true men and women.

As yet, the great Reform which shall abolish all Slavery, as it only *can* be effectually, really abolished, by leaving none coveting the position of a master, none possessing the soul of a slave, is in its infancy, silently and slowly but surely progressing to matured energy and vigor. Attractive Industry, the dream of the past age, the aspiration of the present, shall be the fruition and joy of the next. The re-union of Desire and Duty, divorced and warring since the Fall, restores Man at once to the unchanging, uncloying bliss of Eden. That this is a Moral renovation is indeed most true, but false is the deduction that it is wrought or endures regardless of Physical conditions. Idly do the lips of the widow murmur expressions of contentment and thankfulness when her children pine for bread and have no prospect of procuring it; vainly does the forlorn wretch essay to thank that Providence whose ways he can not fathom, but whose present results are to him famine, disease, and utter, hopeless destitution. Here and there the keen eye of Faith may pierce the deepest gloom of the Present, and rest exultingly on the compensating glories of the Future; but such are exceptions to the general law which renders present privation and anguish an Aaron's rod, swallowing up all thought, over-clouding all hope, of future bliss. We must know what happiness is, ere we can rightly appreciate the prospect of it; we must have exemption from pressing wants of the body, ere we can duly heed and be faithful to the loftiest promptings of the soul. The individual engrossed in a constant and arduous struggle for daily bread, makes slow and capricious progress on the path to Heaven. Those who can not obey the Divine precept, "Take no [anxious] thought for the morrow," can hardly hope to obey any precept relating to their own spiritual growth and elevation. Not till the pressing demands of our outward and bodily nature shall have been provided for, may we rationally look for a general conformity of our Actual State to the Ideal of sentient, intelligent being.

That the Physical conditions of a calmer and nobler existence for the great mass of mankind are slowly but surely preparing, I recognise with gladness; I will not doubt that the Moral elements are also commingling. In all the forms and shows of present and threatening Evil, I discern the shadows of approaching Good. The age now dawning shall reap in gladness the fields tearfully sown in defiance of tempests of contumely and reproach. It will have its Statesmen, who may continue to serve their Nations without stooping to flatter their worst and most dangerous passions; orators, whose trumpet-tones shall be employed to chasten and rebuke whatever is selfish in the thronging multitudes they address, rather than impel them to envy and hate their fellows; teachers of religion, meek, earnest followers of the carpenter's son of Bethlehem and Paul the tent-maker, who, living, or at all times ready to live, if need be, by the labor of their own hands, shall minister to God in houses unpartitioned to men, asking of a prospective field of labor, not what salary is to be paid, but what sin is to be cured, and setting forth the duties and reproving the delinquencies of Wealth, as few or none have dared to do since He who had not where to lay His head. Under such faithful ministrations, the truth must soon become apparent that Riches are desirable only to widen the scope and enlarge the opportunities of well-doing—that they impart no right to live prodigally, selfishly, or ostentatiously—still less to avoid the ways of Industry and benign Exertion. With wealth thus possessed and employed, vanish at once the privations and the envious discontent of the Poor—the dreams and the desire of Agrarian equality—since the most abject must then recognise the wisdom and beneficence of the dispensation which qualifies some to be the almoners and benefactors of the less gifted or provident millions, while the more fortunate would learn to feel, in extending the amplest encouragement and aid to the lowly, some faint reflection of the rapture of Creative goodness. Thus harmonized in feeling, exalted in purpose, convergent in effort, the re-united Human Family shall move on to greater and still greater triumphs over Physical obstruction, Elementary perversion, and Moral dissonance, until Evil and Anguish shall virtually be banished, our Earth be restored to its primal rank among the loyal provinces of God's empire, and Man, made 'a little lower than the angels,' shall realize in his Actual the noblest, the fairest Ideal of Life.

III.

THE FORMATION OF CHARACTER:

A LECTURE.

I STAND before you this evening to adduce some considerations connected with the right formation or malformation of the Human Character. It is not improbable that some of the views which to my mind are those of evident truth may to some among you wear the semblance of novelty—of extravagance—or, more strictly, of what the discreet and proper world has doomed to perdition under the vague but blighting designation of Ultraism. I say it *may* be so, because I am aware that each observing soul forms a world of its own, or at least establishes its own stand-point from which to look abroad on the universe; while the infinitely larger number who have forfeited by non-use their right of independent thought—who, never venturing a glance at Nature and Truth through their own, but always through others' eyes—whereby that which *was* Truth to the actual discerner becomes but its faint and imperfect shadow to them—will instinctively revolt at any view of the moral universe which professes to discover and hold up to the light that which *they* have never perceived, and thereby implies a rebuke to their blindness. I desire, therefore, to premise that, essentially, whatever of the philosophy I shall endeavor to set before you this evening shall seem original and peculiar is not mine by any right of discovery or authorship, but only by that cordial acceptance which the inquiring mind gives to all truth. I have shunned rather than sought novelty, so far as is consistent with the lesson I would inculcate; and if I shall be so fortunate as to present to any of you new ideas or illustrations—above all, if any of my views shall appear to any of you forcible or striking—you will do but justice in giving credit for its suggestion to those who have larger opportunities for contemplation and cultivation than I have—to the free-spoken, profound thinkers of our age; and foremost among them to RALPH WALDO EMERSON and the little band of earnest, clear-sighted spirits who are more commonly known by the contemptuous appellation of *Transcendentalists.* To these I acknowledge myself deeply indebted both for the perception and expression of moral truth generally; while my own aim has been to bring the diverging rays of that truth to bear focally on the Practical Education of Man.

I need not, surely, waste words in demonstrating to you the importance of a right Formation of the Human Character. Everywhere, in all ages, the world assents in words to the fact that the True Man is more than the rich man—that he who enters upon the stage of active life with all his faculties and capacities harmoniously and maturely developed, is more to be envied than the perverse heir of a principality. All men prize and reverence Knowledge, Wisdom, Virtue; they would readily add these to their possessions if the price were not too high. Nay, more—if that price could be told down on the counter to-day, and that were the end of it, most men would make the sacrifice, and buy. It is the endless effort necessary to preserve and sustain the purchase that discourages and disaffects. Every man, until thoroughly perverted, has his ideal of Truth and Goodness, on which he fixes his anxious gaze, toward which he paddles, or believes he is paddling, his frail bark over the Ocean of Life; but the soft breezes of Temptation, the strong but stealthy tide of Circumstance and Conformity, or the boisterous gale of Passion, is constantly bearing him farther and farther from his goal; he will not see that his safety lies in opposing his energies directly to the insidious foe; it costs less effort to yield; his vacant, wandering eye still discerns the beacon; his soul still feebly aspires to it; he idly trusts that to-morrow the adverse influence will be withdrawn, and he will then speed with ease to his haven. Vain, short-lived delusion! Every hour of non-resistance relaxes his energies while it increases the power of the adversary; at length the beacon, grown distant, flickers and disappears in the deepening haze, and the voyage whose outset was bland innocence and hope closes in darkness and despair.

Such is Life to unnumbered millions—such has it been through a hundred generations. And shall it so continue ever? Shall the earth weep tears of blood through centuries to come, over the perverseness, the infatuation, the wretchedness of her children? Let us conclude hopefully that such is not the order of Providence; let us search intently the nature and the history of our Race for the elements of a higher life.

All evils are mainly overcome by the eradication of their causes—rarely and partially by the administration of palliatives. The proneness to error, to self-abasement, to wrong-doing, which stands so prominently out on the page of the annalist as a characteristic of Man, argues an underlying necessity, so to speak—a steep proclivity in his nature toward the Forbidden. But let us not be deceived into confounding the superficial, the intermediate, the factitious, with the ultimate and the essential. Let us separate from this mass of tendencies and instincts which we rashly call Human Nature the super-imposed and the remediable, and we can better judge of the intrinsic and the eternal. I propose first, therefore—at the risk of being deemed puerile by the puerile—to point out to you some of the errors of our mistaken and thoughtless—nay, our vicious and destructive—Education, to which Man is subjected from his veriest infancy—which are entwined with the tenderest threads of his being, and so grow into and become a part of his nature—not a second nature, but his earliest perception of the relation which he holds to his fellow-creatures and the universe. It is by calling your attention, very briefly but frankly, to what we have all observed, with more or less interest, of the influences constantly at work to corrupt and pervert the dawning intellect, and insure the Malformation of the Human Character, that I shall best impress you with the nature and magnitude of the evil to be corrected, and determine the basis on which the Practical Education of the True Man, his harmonious development, and his growth to perfect moral and intellectual stature, must be established.

A gentle infant, fresh from the hand of its Creator, without guile, or envy, or stormier passion—without Fear, or Pride, or Discontent—exists in perfect harmony with Nature—with the breeze, the blossom, and the verdure laughing to the glad and glancing sunbeams. The most worldly and artificial are rendered truer and tenderer by its presence, in whose light the wrinkled brow of Age grows smoother, and shadows melt fleetingly from the marble face of Care. In that presence, it scarcely needs a Divine Teacher to assure us that 'Of such is the Kingdom of Heaven.' Yet a few years pass, and all how changed! On the averted though reckless countenance of Youth we too often see stamped indelibly the vices of mature depravity—of Covetousness, which needs but opportunity to become Robbery; of Sensuality, which has already well nigh effaced the Divine impress, and is hurrying its victim down to an early and shameful grave; of Cruelty, most hideous monster of all, which may at any moment be incited by passion to imbrue its hands in a brother's blood. Whence has come this rapid, this dreadful transformation? Alas! the germs of all this thorny wilderness of Evil are too often planted in tenderest Infancy itself, whose fertile soil nourishes into rapid luxuriance the richest plants or foulest weeds according as the seed is sown. Long before the thoughtless parent has deemed the child susceptible of a moral impression, the plague-spot has fastened upon the tender heart, whence years of patient culture and prayerful discipline may not avail to remove it.

The first lesson of Evil usually imprinted on the infant mind, is that of Sensuality, or more precisely, Gluttony. An excessive and diseased appetite is commonly created in earliest childhood, which is never fully conquered. Does its healthy instincts revolt against bandages which are stifling out its life, or an atmosphere which through stagnation and exhausting combustion or respiration has become noxious and insupportable, its cries are hushed with needless food. Whatever its ailing or source of disquietude, even though it be repletion and oppression, the universal elixir is more food. I need not speak of nourishment which is in itself, regardless of quantity, unsuitable and depraving—of sweetmeats, stimulants and spices. Against these a rational being needs no other caution than such as a moment's reflection must afford. Yet these are soon lugged in to spur the flagging appetite—to overcome the repulsion of Nature to a treatment which she feels to be fatally destructive. The sad result too commonly is that the child arrives at the knowledge of good and evil—if it be so fortunate or unfortunate as to survive the severe probation of infancy at all—completely depraved in all its physical instincts—a ready-made sensualist—a miniature glutton. To talk, after it has passed this point, of its *constitution* requiring this or that, or receiving benefit from one thing or the other, is to talk as blindly and absurdly as though we spoke of the constitution of an opium-eater in his last stages, or that of the victim of *delirium-tremens.* Would I could hope that the fearful infatuation on this subject in which the great majority are wilfully slumbering is breaking away, but facts will not allow it. The records of mortality in our own time and country undeniably show that, while the average duration of life is somewhat improving, the tenure of infant existence grows gradually frailer; and already one-half of the human race are consigned to the grave before attaining their fifth year—an increase of ten per cent. in half a century. I adduce this fact only to avail myself of its moral bearing; yet it has other relations which must ere long arrest the attention of the most heedless.

The second lesson of evil to which the child is subjected is *Fraud.* With all its perceptions fresh and wakeful, it early learns that human speech and action have two uses—the first, indeed, to express or convey ideas and emotions; but the second, hardly less common, to conceal them. Of what a perpetual comedy is not the little denizen of the cradle too often the quiet, but by no means unobservant spectator! The loud and angry altercation hushed into blandness on the appearance of a stranger; the vinegar aspect exchanged for one of 'wreathed smiles;' or perchance the slander just playing on the lip in his absence now turned to flattery and compliment in his presence! But not alone of these grosser forms of Fraud does the young observer, puzzled rather than amused, imbibe the spirit. The yawn of indifference chased by the smile of courtesy; the spruced appearance of robe or room; the hollow show of wealth and luxury with which Pride and Poverty, ill-assorted yet frequently inseparable pair, contrive to reconcile the semblance of their fortunes to the reality of their desires—these, and a thousand like incidents, are constantly teaching the infant mind that the world on which it is entering is not single but double — a world of things and a world of shows; and that the latter holds the higher place in the estimation and effort of the multitude.

The corrupting, fatal effect of this bitter fruit of the Tree of Knowledge can hardly be over-estimated. Half the energies and means, with far more of the true nobility of man, are wasted in striving to appear what he is not, but what he would wish to be believed. It is this which makes whatever is painful of the difference between the prince and the peasant, the rich man and his dependent. The latter sits uneasily in the presence of the former, because he is not satisfied with what he is, but would fain be something else. Let the frank, bold ranger of the forest come into that same presence, and, if at peace with himself, he feels no inferiority, dreads no sneer. Precisely because he does not wish to barter himself for something else, he is not afraid of being taken for less than he is worth.

Vain will be the effort, fruitless the toil, of the pastor, the pedagogue, the philosopher, to teach the Young the value and beauty of Truth so long as the lessons of the cradle and the fireside shall be in practical contradiction thereto. The pupil receives all monitions with a sedate attention, a demure propriety of manner, most edifying to behold. But in his heart he is comparing and classing every precept with those pithy maxims of moral science wherewith his infancy was refreshed, wherein he was daily instructed not to lie by those whose life was a perpetual falsehood, and to refrain from stealing by those who were constantly lying in wait to entrap the good opinions of their neighbors without possessing the qualities on which those good opinions should be based. The apt youth at once jumps to the conclusion that all these fine words are a part of the same system — a corner of the great mask of decorum and propriety behind which the world hides that portion of its selfishness and sensuality which could not be openly displayed without creating universal anarchy. Thus tutored, *he*, too, steps behind the mask, and becomes decorous, and has mouthfulls of moral saws at his tongue's end, and takes care not to blazon his vices uselessly, and not to expend any portion of his character when the gratification he seeks can be secured without, or at any rate without securing the full value of it. And thus he walks daintily through life, a fair-seeming, soft-spoken, reputable man, and in the world's facetious dictionary is classed 'respectable;' and if at last some great temptation impels him to some great villainy, the town rolls up its eyes in pretended astonishment that so respectable a man has turned out a forger, a libertine, a defaulter, though it has seen him educated for a knave, and at heart known him for one all along!

The third fatal vice of our system of Practical Education is the low estimate which we palpably put upon Labor. On this subject the world is not so specious and hypocritical as upon others, but wears its fault jauntily and with an air. In the Divine order, Labor is not merely a universal duty, but a universal necessity. 'Whoso will not work shall not eat' is the immutable law, and he who strives to evade it but vainly lacerates himself on the sharp thorns which everywhere hedge in the narrow path of Right. Take what you need at the bounteous table of Nature, says the decree, but pay its price. Fruitless the effort, preposterous the desire, to obtain by trick what can only come by equivalent. The fisherman is caught in his net—'the engineer hoist by his own petard.' The schemer reaches forth his eager hand to the fruit that looked so tempting on the bough, and grasps, not that which he coveted, but apples of Sodom—fair without, but within bitterness and ashes. What was coveted as luxury, unduly acquired, has become disease, satiety and death. All History, all Tragedy, all

Romance, is full of this; yet the blind world goes on scheming to circumvent God, and enjoy the pleasure without fulfilling the condition, as though all that the wise have observed and the good have written for its admonition were but a shallow fable, invented by the cunning of those who have, to secure themselves against the covetous assaults of those who have not. In fact, all vice, all transgression, roots itself in this fundamental error, that the laws of the Universe, which have vindicated themselves from eternity, may in this particular instance be evaded—that the good which is coveted may be separated from the condition which underlies it—that the magnet will for once have a positive pole and no negative—that there shall be summer without winter—day without night—sun without shade. To detach the sensual good from the moral good—the enjoyment from the use—the transient from the everlasting—has been the struggle of perverted Humanity through sixty centuries of wretchedness. Monstrous delusion! idle dreamings of a disordered intellect. The stone rolled with subtlest intent to the summit of the precipice rebounds instantly and vehemently to the bottom, overthrowing the contriver in its headlong career. If the primary requirement may be evaded, the penalty is swift, unrelenting, inevitable.

Now this first great lesson of Moral Truth, which all clear-sighted experience must teach, is one which is but blindly, imperfectly taught at all, but which is utterly set at naught in our popular inculcations with regard to Labor. What child of affluence or even of want is duly taught that if he would truly enjoy he must so live as to increase the means of enjoyment—if he would eat he must work? Love for love; truth for truth; service for service; this is the coin he must pay; for none other will be accepted. If he seek to procure these by force or subtlety, he obtains not what he desires, but only the counterfeit, which only his own correspondent corruption blinds him from perceiving to be as different from the thing sought as light from darkness. Let us not wait, then, for the world to teach this great truth through that rugged experience which is but another term for suffering. The child which is practically taught in the little world of Home that Labor is a burden and well nigh a disgrace — that Service is rightfully of constraint and not of affection — that the great end of Life is not nobly to Do, but skilfully to avoid Doing — that the service which requires humbler faculties and a ruder culture than some daintier avocation is therefore less honorable and meritorious — that the duties and obligations of the servant and the served are not throroughly mutual — that child has received already a moral perversity which not thousands of sonorous homilies — not years of scowling Pride, and gnawing Disappointment, and the drear vacuity of unloved existence, shall thoroughly efface from his being.

There remains one other monstrous error of our fireside Education which I can not refrain from exposing, though I am aware it is less common than those I have already reprehended, and in fact is but an off-shoot from them — a branch of that great Upas of false Formation of Character whereof I have endeavored to expose the gnarled and writhing roots to general scrutiny and abhorrence. I allude to the fatal practice of *paying for virtue*, or rewarding with adventitious indulgence acts of integrity and of duty. As in its nature and origin this is a compound of most of the errors I have enumerated, so it is in its consequences more pernicious than any of them. The child which, for performing a task nimbly and faithfully, or acquiring a lesson rapidly and thoroughly, is rewarded with some dainty confection or glittering toy, you have doubly corrupted; first, in making that a task which, being a duty, should also be a pleasure in itself; secondly, in pampering an appetite or a craving which, being factitious, can not fail to be evil. If that task were not properly his — if that lesson were not of itself worth acquiring — you should not have imposed it. If it were, you have blinded him to its true worth and meaning; you have taught him to look astray for the reward of well-doing; you have made that which was a simple and true action no longer such but a finesse — a dexterous feat — a sinister calculation. The child thus paid to do right will soon have learned not to do right without payment. It will not accept the harvest as the proper recompense of its toil and culture, but will clamor to be paid beside for sowing and nurturing it. Worse even than this is the delusion implanted that daintier food and gaudier toys are of more value than elevating knowledge and habits of healthful Industry — in fact, that they are of any value at all. But time would fail me to trace out all the evil consequences of that one woful folly by which you have polluted all the springs of action, clouded the moral vision, and corrupted the very soul of the victim of your fatally mistaken policy. Let us banish for ever the idea of a reward for well-doing extraneous from and unrelated to itself. There is nothing like it in Nature — in the vast universe. God never promised a reward thus detached from and alien to the obedience it would recompense; the Devil promises, but never pays. It is absurdity to desire, madness to expect anything like it.

I have thus glanced at some of the more prominent errors of Education and defects of Principle which enter into and determine the Malformation of the Human Character. Keeping steadily in view not merely the errors thus exposed, but the facts which their correction necessarily implies, so as to avoid useless repetitions, we approach the consideration of those principles and qualities which should enter into and govern the formation of a true character.

You have already anticipated the statement that first among these is Truth itself, or, more precisely, an entire Truthfulness, extending beyond the mere avoidance of verbal falsehood to the instinctive and rigid preservation of perfect integrity of being. It is not enough that the blush mantles the cheek at the thought of uttering a falsehood — the true man revolts equally at the idea of acting, dressing, appearing one. We must extirpate these nice, unmeaning distinctions of a heartless and unprincipled Opinion, the offspring of a lax Morality and a short-sighted Convenience, which teach us that we may swear by the gold upon the altar though not by the altar itself. The man who dresses, lives, entertains, in a style to which his means are properly inadequate, hoping thereby to be esteemed more affluent and thrifty than he is, is not merely enacting a daily lie, but one which comes home to his own door even sooner than the misdeeds of the hardier transgressor. Eternal justice for ever holds its balance true, and laughs at all puny attempts to evade its unerring decisions. Still the thief robs himself, the swindler defrauds himself, exactly as did his prototype four thousand years ago. The story of Haman and Mordecai is the epitome of universal History, could we read its page with the eye of spiritual discernment and with senses unclogged by the grossness of our groveling life. Yet the thief, the burglar has the wretched, demoniac satisfaction of imagining that he has not been the *only* victim of his own depravity — that if he has doomed himself to lasting misery he has at least inflicted some injury on another. But the hypocrite wears out his life in a constant effort to exchange his substance for shadows — to barter the stubborn wealth of his granary, his house, his heart, for its evanescent semblance in other men's eyeballs. Thus living in a world of shows and mockeries, he becomes a mockery to himself; to him there is no reality, no good, no knowledge; and God, Virtue, Confidence, Love, are but the bubbles with which men, themselves hardly more real, strive ever to delude and overreach each other. Thus deceived and mocked when he fancies himself deceiving, the hypocrite stands forth a perpetual alien in the earnest and kindly domain of Nature—the sorriest, saddest jest on the broad face of Creation.

I plead not for eccentricity, for roughness of manner—I am no stranger to the bland amenities and suavities of life. I acknowledge a fitness to time, and duty, and circumstance, in dress and in incidents of even lighter moment. I accept the common sense of mankind as the arbiter between what is real and natural and what is assumed and fantastic. The banker, the capitalist, the merchant, who should ape the dress of the carman, the hod-carrier, would be justly the ridicule of every healthy mind, and of none more than the carman himself. No man enjoys more keenly the stage-shown absurdities of the footman bedecked with his master's delegated authority, the valet personating the prince, than do footmen and valets. This is but the error condemned in another shape—the pendulum at the other extremity of its range. I would have no man do this or refrain from that in *contradiction* from the world, any more than in consistency with it. Nay, more: I admit and counsel acquiescence with the ordinary, the prescribed, the established, in all matters essentially indifferent or trifling. I loathe perverseness—it is at war with harmony and the supreme good. Convince me that the Quaker remains stubbornly covered in the presence of his equals, his seniors, from mere mulishness or whim, and I abandon him to your rebukes; I will second them with my own. But let me realize that that rude non-compliance stands to him for a vital fact—that it symbolizes to him a great principle, to wit, the stern uprising of a true manhood against servility and fawning adulation, and I will defend him to the last gasp—I will do him such reverence as befits a manly self-respect, for his stou fidelity to a conviction.

But in truth the vice of our time, and I apprehend of all times, with rare exceptions, is of opposite tendency, and it is to oppose this that our shields should be locked and our spears pointed. There is a simpering and dapper conformity, a blind deferring to other men's estimates, habits, tastes, which robs life of its freshness, its originality, its masculine strength. Where all are content to dress, to dine, to walk, and most to think, to feel, to act, as some dozen or score shall see fit to dictate, what wonder that invention is checked, that genius is caged, that existence becomes tame and vacant, or, if not torpid, still unmeaning as an idiot's tale? The waters of this dead sea of complaisance and barren formality need to be visited now and then by the rough gales of Heaven, even though they be shocked, and agitated, and driven helter-skelter thereby; better this than that they should become stagnant and putrid. Do not mistakenly imagine that you must go out of yourself—that you must become eccentric and extravagant to produce this effect. In the midst of universal ducking, and sidling, and compromise, you will seem sufficiently rigid and angular if you walk simply and naturally on.

The danger of this dead compliance—of living not your own genuine thought but other men's opinions, which even if true for them are not wholly so for you—is one of the most subtle and pervading of the many which track the ingenuous and timid through life. It is an evil which magnifies as our social relations become more artificial, and complex, and penetrating. It assails us even on the side of our virtues. Each of us is attached to some party in politics, some sect in religion, some coterie in morals, philanthropy or culture; and this is well, so long as that party, that coterie, shall represent to us the highest attainable good in that particular province which it contemplates. But the impulse which says, 'Do not proclaim that certain truth which you have discovered because other men have not discovered it, and your bold advocacy will be wielded to the prejudice of your sect or party, deserves only to be scouted and trampled under foot. What right has sect or party to intermeddle with your free thought, save to accept or reject it? What right to subject the line of your truth to the orbit of its policy—perchance its narrow policy and low though correct aims? O fear not to be wholly true and manful, and the devotees of policy and craft shall be driven into conformity with your lofty and earnest endeavor!

I have hesitated to place Temperance next to Truth as a primary element of a just character, in view of the low idea, the negative insignificance, to which the term has been degraded. Well may that Temperance which is satisfied with restricting its disciples and votaries to such quantities of an infatuating poison as shall not quite suffice to drown the reason and paralyze the frame—or even that better modification which counsels the entire abandonment of that one especial bane of life, leaving all others to work destruction at will, become the scoff of drunkards, the by-word of debauchees. But in that comprehensive and consistent signification, which implies the absolute subjection of the appetites to the government of the reason in all things—the satisfaction of each healthful and true desire with reference to the end of its creation and in obedience to the moral law of its existence—and, by consequence, the stern rejection of every proffered gratification, the repression of every appetite, which finds its consummation in itself, and shrinks from the thought of to-morrow—none can fail to recognize in Temperance a necessary moral as well as physical basis of the full and proper development of our being. I have already treated somewhat of this subject, though inversely; and I will not dwell on it here. That Man should be temperate, the vilest drunkard will agree; the great difficulty which meets us is that of awaking in him a whole and consistent idea of what Temperance is. When he shall no longer be schooled from the rostrum by lecturers themselves the slaves of tobacco-chewing and the like filthy vices, but in the language of consistency and love, I will hope that his restoration to manhood, its dignity, its healthfulness and true enjoyments, can not long be deferred.

Having established the basis of a true character in the elements of perfect Truth and Temperance in all things, we are ready to advance boldly toward the great central idea of Virtue. And here, as I deem the definitions of the Schools, and to some extent of the Pulpit also, imperfect and unsatisfactory, I shall not hesitate to expatiate fearlessly, and, accepting the best lights that are afforded, search vigorously for a true and solid foundation. You tell me Man should be virtuous, reverend Divine, and I ask you *why* he should be, not to dispute your self-evident proposition, but to aid me in determining what Virtue is. If you stop my inquiry with the crusty answer that he must be so because God commands it, you have neither satisfied nor profited me at all. I still need to know *why* He has commanded it—to know it not from arbitrary dogma but serene perception—or I shall be lost in a whirlpool of babbling sects, of unedifying jargon. I bow reverently to the axiom that God is to be obeyed, but I am still driven to inquire *which* God, or rather which of the thousand warring expositions of His will. Tell me, most self-sufficient Philosopher, tell me, pale Anchorite, absorbed in penitence and holy meditation, why am I to walk sternly in the jagged and dusty highway of Honor and Good, while a thousand flowery by-paths, more inviting to my wandering gaze, are opening on every side, and proffering ease and dalliance? Do not attempt to frighten me with the danger that if I diverge I shall not be able to return; for do I not see thousands in the path before me who *have* so diverged, and yet have made good their return? Do not attempt to frighten me with the chances of perdition; the gambler often knows that the chances are against him, yet, leave him but a hope of gain, and he plays eagerly, recklessly on. Once grant that there is a *chance*, though it be one in a thousand, to profit by wrong-doing, and you have confirmed millions in the way of error and ruin.

The true deduction of far-seeing wisdom imports that Virtue, in itself and for itself, is the most desirable thing, above all consequences, aside from all results, spurning all mercenary calculations of profit and loss. Whoso has performed an act of genuine love and service has no thought to look anxiously around and above him to discern if God and Man are taking heed of his sacrifice; for he already feels himself exalted and blessed by His deed. He has not climbed toilsomely a day's journey nearer to Heaven, but its radiance and bliss have come down to him; they have already shed a halo around his brow, a rapture in his breast. Well knows he from the depths of his own being that in the way of Truth and of Life there is no self-denial nor suffering; that Virtue is the one only thing too precious to be bought and sold. What is it to him that houses, lands, honors, power, are offered him in exchange for it? all this is not temptation, but absurdity. It is enough that he has already solved for himself that Divine problem, of universal and not particular application—'What shall it profit a man to gain the whole world and lose his own soul?'

I must be permitted to linger upon the homely enforcement of this Truth—to multiply and vary its illustrations—since its practical denial through grossness of perception is the one great error of perverse Humanity. Come not to me with your absurd repinings that you have lost by integrity some temporal advantage which your rival through greater suppleness has secured; if you had had any integrity worth preserving, you would rather thank God that *you* were not abandoned to temptation. Nay, more: were your eye single and your spiritual vision unobscured, you would have seen that a base success is the worst of discomfitures, dragging after it an interminable chain of miseries and mortifications. Swift and terrible is the retribution which follows him who has by violence or indirection succeeded to station, honors, affluence, which he has not deserved. The rustle of every leaf is to his ear the trump of the Archangel.

History has borne down to us the relation that the last and noblest Brutus, commending himself to death after the crowning disaster of Philippi, quoted this line from Euripides, 'O Virtue! I have followed thee through life, and I find thee at last but a shadow!' "I doubt not (says Emerson,) that the hero is slandered by this report. The great soul does not sell its nobleness. It does not ask to dine nicely, nor sleep warm. The essence of greatness is the perception that Virtue is enough. Poverty is its ornament. Plenty it does not need, and can very well abide its loss." I heartily accept this judgment, and would push it to its natural conclusions. I will not doubt that the last of the free Romans rendered up his spirit with a prayer for the country he had so truly served to the utmost, and a disdain akin to pity for her marble-hearted enslavers—that he scorned, even more than their parricidal ambition, that obtuseness which blinded them to the perception that in the fall of the Commonwealth they too fell irretrievably—that the enthroned, empurpled despot is but the first slave in his dominions, and that Fear and conscious Guilt are the most exacting and cruel of masters.

But this tradition would never have floated thus far adown the tide of time if it had not been founded in fact. Falsehood has never this vitality. Foul slander as it is to the spent and dying patriot, it is a pregnant truth as regarding the age which invented and perpetuated it. I read in that one line of practical Atheism the prophecy of a thousand years of dwarfing, darkening Humanity — of receding Civilization and deepening Night. By its lurid light, I see the haughty Mistress of the World sunken and still sinking in sloth, sensuality, corruption, and slavery; a military banditti selling her publicly in the market; the slaves of fools her capricious, exacting masters; a horse her Consul. I see the hordes of barbarians, so lately routed and panic-stricken, gathering again at the scent of her stiffening corpse; I see them pouring across the Rhine, the Alps, the Danube, which they so lately invoked to shield them from the terrible onslaught of her invincible legions. Barrier after barrier gives way before them; army after army melts like snow upon the sunny slopes of April; panic and despair precede them; desolation, blood, and ashes are behind; the steed in whose track grass springs never again drinks the water of the Rhone, the Po, the Tiber; and Rome, long tottering to her foundations, falls at length a gory wreck, an everlasting ruin. Her sons become the slaves of strangers, the scoff and football of barbarians. So perish they who in the fullness of lust, and pride, and sensuality, have vainly imagined Providence a delusion and Virtue an empty name!

I shall not err in commending a generous Self-Trust as an essential element of a manly and earnest Character; though chattering Conceit stand ready at the door, and strive to pass itself for that thing it would be but is not. They two are wide asunder as the poles. Conceit is founded in a low idea of the capacities of Human Nature — of brother, neighbor, countrymen. The coxcomb does not so much magnify his own abilities — for he has sounded their shallow depths and traced their narrow boundaries — as he depresses and distrusts those of others. Living ever in a home atmosphere of pretence and falsehood — of tinsel drapery, covering shabby raiment and ragged walls—he cheats himself into the belief that the possessions of others are alike hollow and meretricious—and that his assurance passes for knowledge, his insolence for authority, his impertinence for wit, so long as the world through complaisance or decorum refrains from laughing in his face! Miserable deception! that ostler who bowed to him in feigned deference has accurately weighed and measured him at a single glance; that chimney-sweep on whom he fancies he has made so profound an impression is already laughing at his folly. Let him betake himself to what market he will, he can not sell himself for one penny more than he is worth. But a genuine Self-Trust entrenches itself in the largest possibilities of Humanity. How shall it discourage you, faint heart and faithless, that Alexander conquered, that Columbus discovered, that Washington nobly withstood? That these have well done but proves that *you* too may do if you will, and to that end only do they exist for you. Excuse not your inglorious sloth by the assertion that the precise act of daring or endurance which was theirs can not be yours—that you have not the qualities, or it may be the opportunities, which have made their names immortal. You were not created to perform their acts but your own. If the deeds which they made theirs had remained unacted till now, they might have devolved on you; but the universe can not halt in its eternal career for needless iterations that you may gratify your petty and senseless ambition. But whatsoever act is truly yours, lies broad and palpable before you, if you will but turn from your mousing and heed it. For that act all the Ages have been silently, unerringly preparing; the wisdom of Omniscience, the power of Omnipotence, are pledged that your strength shall be equal to your day. Accept, then, with alacrity your position in the Eternal Order of things; and seek not to hide your sloth and sensuality beneath vain regrets that you are yourself and not another, and thus bury your talent in a napkin.

In truth, they who have put their heart into their work at the outset are rarely troubled with these qualms of incapacity. The traveler oftenest finds his road impassable as he sits by the tempting fireside, and listens shuddering to the howling of the storm. Let him but breast it with a smile of gay indifference, of conscious power, and the gale sweeps less fiercely, the darkness is no longer Egyptian. And thus, too, of our timid sensitiveness to Opinion. Ridicule, that weapon of fools, is harmless, save against themselves; it never yet pierced the solid armor of an upright and manly purpose. When Chivalry became a dead form, a cloak for rapacity and license, a senseless cumberer of the ground, Cervantes extinguished it by a romance; yet all the wits of Christendom could not have shaken it one iota so long as it remained a reality—a vital existence. Are you tempted to abandon your idea because a gaping multitude who can not realize, condemn, and make mouths at it? then it was never truly yours. You but borrowed it, in the silly hope that as it was novel and startling it might become popular. Vain imagining! if it had been worth anything to you, you would not have come by it so easily. Were it now truly your own, you would be ready to follow it over burning plowshares.

And yet we are deceived by our superficial philosophy in the presumption that Truth is rejected by the world. That it is not readily embraced and assimilated—that the good seed falls oftenest on rugged and thorny ground, or at least on that where the harvest is tardy, it needs no argument to show. Still is its utterance never without witness or efficacy; and the reverberation of its forgotten tones comes back to us from the opposite horizon to rebuke our hot impatience, our fragile faith. In our short-sighted leaping to conclusions, we misjudge and misinterpret. A wild, uncouth person suddenly appears among us, and begins haranguing in advocacy of Repentance, or Temperance, or Abolition, or some other revolt against established abuses. Forthwith there are commotion, and indignation, and violence; every voice and hand are raised against him; and we rashly decide that Public Opinion has condemned him. Not so: *he* has summoned Public Opinion to the judgment-seat, and condemned *it*. Incoherent and irrational his speech may mainly be, three parts error to one of truth; unsound and preposterous his theory; but not for this is the multitude incited to hiss or stone him. He might have babbled nonsense or raved in delirium till doomsday, and hardly have provoked a smile. But through all his folly there have gleamed rays of piercing truth; and this it is which has excited the uproar; not what the mob rejected, but what they unwillingly believed and dreaded. I would counsel you, then, give fearless utterance to your whole convictions; give free scope to your strongest energies, in the faith that whatever you shall do truly, simply, and uprightly, could be no better done by men nor angels, and will surely commend itself to the understandings of the highest, the consciences of the most perverted.

I approach with diffidence the consideration of Heroism, not as an element but as the complement and capital grace of the Human Character, in view of what has been so well said of it, as it were but yesterday, by Carlyle in a glorious volume; by Emerson in a transcendent essay. In the light of these, all truth that may be offered on the subject must seem but imitative, or at best the tame and needless elucidation of a transparent and living text. Of such as are familiar with these I can only expect pardon for my temerity in the event that it shall prove not wholly unsuccessful and useless.

By Heroism, then, I understand the overflowing of a generous and exalted nature into all acts of lofty daring and endeavor. In its purest condition it is Virtue militant; in any, it is Human Energy rising superior to inconvenience, obstacle, and the petty limitations which seem to hedge in our mortal condition; against the cobwebs by which Timidity and Sloth consent to be caged. Virtue calculates; weighs consequences; deliberates; while Heroism moves due on to the attainment of that good, the overthrow of that evil, which stands in the attitude of resistance before it. It does not stop to measure and balance its forces with those opposed to it, because it recognizes no terrestrial force higher than itself, and feels the soul superior to whatever of accident, circumstance or custom may oppose it. Virtue is calm, collected, forbearing; Heroism, impetuous, defying, advances eagerly to the combat with Fraud, with Wrong, with Oppression, instinctively recognizing in each its mortal foe. It is Michael and his angels battling the whole host of Darkness, and with not less but more of energy that they know intensely that the struggle can have but one result.

'Life,' says Emerson, 'is a festival only to the wise. Seen from the nook and chimney-side of Prudence, it wears a rugged and dangerous front. The violations of the laws of Nature by our predecessors and our cotemporaries are punished in us also.**** Insanity, war, plague, cholera, famine, indicate a certain ferocity in Nature, which, as it had its inlet by human crime, must have its outlet by human suffering.**** Our Culture, therefore, must not omit the arming of the man. Let him hear in season that he is born into the state of war, and that the Commonwealth and his own well-being require that he should not go dancing in the weeds of peace, but warned, self-collected, and, neither defying nor dreading the thunder, let him take both reputation and life in his hand, and, with perfect urbanity, dare the gibbet and the mob by the absolute truth of his speech and the rectitude of his behavior.

'Times of heroism (says this profound observer) are generally times of terror, but the day never shines in which this element may not work. The circumstances of man, we say, are historically somewhat better in this country, and at this hour, than perhaps ever before. More freedom exists for culture. It will not now run against an axe at the first step out of the beaten path of opinion. But whoso is heroic will always find crises to try his edge. Whatever outrages have happened to men may befall a man again, and very easily in a republic, if there appear any signs of a decay of religion. Human virtue demands her champions and martyrs, and the trial of Persecution always proceeds.

It is but the other day that the brave Lovejoy gave his breast to a mob for the rights of free speech and opinion, and died when it was better not to live!'

I think these true utterances of a serene spirit justly modify, in perfect accordance with what I have already urged when speaking of Virtue, the casual remark of the same writer, that 'every heroic act measures itself by its contempt of some external good.' Undoubtedly is this true in the sense in which it is intended—that, seen through the eyes of the prudent, the soul of the soulless, the action of the Hero is 'clean contrary to a sensual prosperity.' It is a riddle, a madness; at least a trap, an ambuscade. But from the consciousness of the Hero himself no idea is farther than that of relinquishment, or self-sacrifice. He has but accepted his place in Nature; had it been another's, he had not courted it to make a parade of his devotion or daring. A Washington never scores up the hours he has given, the perils braved, the sweet food and soft indulgence he has missed, in struggling for the salvation of his country. If he has been able to serve her triumphantly, it is well; if not, he has at least by action ripened and defined the capacities of his own being. Cæsar puts away the proffered crown with a sigh of regretful longing; Washington brushes it aside as the phantom of an abhorred, unnatural dream.

Human Virtue is generally tinged and not seldom utterly perverted by Human infirmity; yet I think we are inclining, with our easy assumption of immense superiority for our time and culture, to rate too meanly, to condemn too broadly, the ruder, harsher shapes in which the Heroism of earlier ages developed itself. In this we fall into the one great error of narrow and ungenial Criticism, in scanning the act of the individual on which we pass judgment, not from his point of departure but our own. We see the conqueror hurled on his path of carnage and conflagration, and our hearts revolt within us—we almost chide God for permitting so vast and wanton a ravage. But had we half the wisdom and insight our presumptuous judgment supposes, we should doubtless see in every state overturned the finale of myriads of rank and crying oppressions—in every City desolated, not one merely but ten thousand righteous retributions. Mourn not, then, sir philanthropist, over the devastating career of Alaric, the onward surge of the Saracen wave from Mecca to Vienna; nay, water not with your tears the grave even of hapless Poland; for, rely on it, if any true and healthful vitality had there existed, it would have vindicated itself in the hour of peril. Witness Greece, blackened, not subdued, by the innumerable hosts of Xerxes; witness Prussia withstanding the force of Europe under the lead of the Great Frederick. A nation is not surprised, is not circumvented into slavery; it can fall only beneath the weight of its own corruptions. It needs a Darius to make the fortunes of an Alexander. The inroad of a hostile force is to a stout-hearted people an electric shock, a ferment, a renovation. Cast your eye over the continent of Europe, and in that territory where Freedom and Culture are foremost, where the rank, accumulating abuses of many centuries have found their grave in this, you will recognize the soil which has latest echoed the tread of the invader. I trust the day has passed when the blood of civilized man required to be quickened and purged by this severe cathartic; but we need not therefore deny that War, too, had its uses in its day. Far hence be the infatuation which hailed the conqueror as a demigod; let us not err as widely by rashly pronouncing him a demon.

But happily to the Heroism of the Present and the Future is vouchsafed a higher pathway of duty—a holier endeavor. It is called no longer to thunder at the gates of capitals—to batter down the walls of citadels, in which venerable Abuse has entrenched itself. Though its mission is still as ever the abasement of pride, the redress of wrong, the vindication of unshielded right, the exaltation of the lowly, it moves no more to the field of conflict with lumbering catapult or echoing culverin. Its soul responds not now to the blast of the air-piercing trumpet; it starts not at the rude summons of the doubling drum. It troubles itself no more with ordnance, and towers, and armies, and Bastiles; for it knows that these dry bones of what were once dominion and power shall not protect their wielder an hour from the resistless might of offended Opinion. It sees the king sit to-day in proud security on his throne, surrounded by all of strength there is in walls and gates and weapons, and it smiles at his pomp and blazonry as it realizes that to-morrow he may be a friendless outcast and fugitive, fleeing from the stroke of a jest, a ballad, a newspaper. To-morrow the demagogue shall revel in his halls in utter blindness to the moral of yesterday; and the next day he too shall have vanished and been forgotten. But the ear of true Heroism is bent to catch the feeblest wail of suffering Humanity—its eye is fixed intently on the morning-star which heralds a brighter day for the enduring, the abject, the down-trodden millions of earth. It stretches forth an ungauntleted but sinewy and steady hand, and takes decided hold of this vast, ungainly framework of Society, and says to what end is this, and this? and does it remain here as a vital significance or only as a dead cumberer of the ground? It recoils not at the shriek of pain or the yell of indignation; for it knows by this that it has touched an ulcer; and, unhappily, it can hardly avoid touching one. It questions with firm speech all institutions, observances, customs, that it may determine by what mischance or illusion thriftless Pretence and Knavery shall seem to batten on a brave Prosperity, while Labor vainly begs employment, Skill lacks recompense, and Worth pines for bread. Its answer to that searching question of Divine arraignment, 'Where is thy brother Abel?' reverses that of the first murderer and all who are heirs of his spirit. It says to ostentatious Affluence and Splendor, 'Vaunt not to me of your icy charities, your gifts ill-sown because without heart; but rather ask pardon of God that as yet you have diverted so large a portion of his stewardship from the great end to which he designed it, and amend. You owe to the desolate, the crushed, the despairing, not the reluctant dollar, doled out with coarse and unjust upbraidings, but cordial sympathy, and the rekindling of hope in the benighted breast.' It says to timid and distrustful Power, 'Trouble not yourself with these labyrinthine passages of mazy policy, but lend your brawny arm to extend far and wide the blessings of Plenty, Culture, Improvement, and strengthen the fabric of your sway by laying broader and deeper its foundations in universal Happiness and Content.' It says to Genius, 'Immerse not yourself in these vain trifles of Convenience or Economy to which your best energies have so long been given. Why shall you waste your life in devising means for the better lighting or warming of the stately mansion, while you give not a thought to the utter darkness and inclemency in which the denizens of ten thousand adjacent hovels are groping and shivering?' Thus fearlessly the Heroism of the Nineteenth Century erects its judgment-seat in every breast, and weighs in its ready balances all custom, authority, assertion. From its serene exaltation above the low ambitions, the mousing schemes, the gross apprehensions of the sordid, it smiles benignly on the impotence of purblind hostility—the despot's bayonet, the bigot's scowl, the witling's sneer. This spirit shall yet renovate the world. Before the calm earnestness of its gaze shall Wrong, Slavery, and Ignorance vanish from the face of the Earth, and a pervading Intelligence, a clearer Insight, a higher Life, shall irradiate the future pages of the History of Man!

IV.

THE RELATIONS OF LEARNING TO LABOR:

A COMMENCEMENT ADDRESS.*

FROM the fierce turmoils and hot strifes of the passing day, I come at your bidding, to spend an hour with you in the interchange of more quiet thought, returning on the morrow to my wonted sphere and calling. I appear before you, not as a scholar among his equals, to descant on themes common and dear alike to all, but as one whose chief teacher has been the rugged world, and whose little all of knowledge has been gathered amid its rude jousts and stern encounters. You will not expect me, therefore, if you give me credit for sincerity and purpose in embracing this opportunity, to address you in the language nor unfold to you thoughts peculiar to the halls of learning. Were he some specimen of our fading Aboriginal Race whom you had thus summoned before you, you would hardly anticipate anything more than an outward deference to the genius of the place—a relinquishment, for the occasion, of the blanket, the tomahawk and the war-paint—not of whatever is intrinsic and essential. He could only hope to justify your daring choice by speaking to you his own words—by an utterance from the depths of his own being. And thus I, standing before you in some sort a humble representative of that large class sometimes termed the *self*-educated, by others (perhaps more properly) the *un*educated, shall speak to you from the

* Before the Literary Societies of Hamilton College, July 23d, 1844.

heart of that class—truths which may or may not have long since resounded through the halls of our Universities, agitating their venerable dust, but which in either case are certain ere long to make themselves heard and respected.

I have not hesitated to choose for my theme on this occasion—THE DISCIPLINE AND DUTIES OF THE SCHOLAR, vast and lofty though it be, and imperfect as have been my opportunities for its thorough appreciation and discussion. Few as are the fragments of hours that I have been able to seize for its contemplation, I am well aware that on its proper apprehension depends, in great degree, the Progress and the Well-being of the Human Race. You need not fear, my friends! that the advantages of a thorough Education, nor of a thoroughly educated Class, will be undervalued in our day, and especially by us weary marchers and combatants along the parched highways, beneath the fervid sun of active life, who have been able but to scoop, as it were, here and there a handfull from the grateful, invigorating waters of Knowledge, as they danced and bubbled across our too eager, headlong course. O, not from *our* panting ranks will ever arise the cry that solid and symmetric Learning is a boon to be rejected or lightly prized! The small coins of knowledge which we awkwardly handle and dispense are constantly reminding us of the priceless ingots of golden treasure which for us lie buried in the far recesses of halls like these, from which a grim Fate has forever debarred us. Limited as may have been our opportunities, it is not to us a sealed truth that the Present is only to be rightly read and interpreted in the full light reflected from the Past. We are not unaware that this uneasy, jostling throng of to-day is but a reproduction, with slight permutations, of the sweating, striving crowds of a thousand yesterdays, to be again and again represented, in the several throngs of countless to-morrows. We are well aware that faithful, graphic History is a diviner as well as a judge—that her magic mirror gives back the faces glowing around us as well as the forms in dust beneath us, and that he who rightly, intelligently, reads of Aristides and Cleon, of Brutus and Catiline, of smooth Augustus and deified Nero, may turn at once from the musty chronicle and see the living characters stalking eagerly around him. Must he not discern the Phocion of our Republic in that noble relic of our heroic elder time, the oft-baffled, defeated, decried, but dauntless, bravely struggling, unconquerable octogenarian of Quincy? Might he not be tempted at last to suspect that the difference between one age and another exists quite as often in its chroniclers as in its actors, and that the perishing hieroglyphics of Tlascala and Quito would reveal heroism as devoted and admirable as any of that more felicitously recorded by Homer or Polybius, had we but the skill to interpret them as thoroughly? In short, it is not alone the Educated who have learned that a knowledge of Man is the central truth, to which the study of men and their acts must be subsidiary; and that the mingled web of Divine beneficence and Human infirmity, termed History, is to be rightly scanned only in proportion as we apprehend its beginning and its destined conclusion.

There is, there must be, a preëminently Educated Class among us—I do not merely admit the notorious fact; I perceive the vital necessity. Whether the distance between that class and the many should or should not be as broad and palpable as at present, is not now the question. My theme implies its existence, and assumes that the greater number are relatively uneducated. However we might desire the universal diffusion and possession of the knowledge now confined to this class, we know it is, and long must be, impossible. Its attainment exacts a devotion of time and of means, to say nothing of tastes and habits, which can only be given by the comparatively few. My theme, then, involves the compound inquiry—What should be the *nature* of the education of the more cultivated class?—Under what *conditions* should Learning be acquired?—What *ends* should it contemplate?—What advantages secure to its possessors? I shall proceed to discuss it.

I would insist, then, as the primary requisition in the Discipline of the Scholar, on a THOROUGH AND HARMONIOUS DEVELOPMENT OF THE PHYSICAL MAN. I place this first, not as more important than Moral and Intellectual culture, but as the proper foundation of all culture unto perfection. You need not cite me to instances of intellectual giants who are physically dwarfs—of puny Genius and hypochondriac Wit—you may as well tell me that the fœtid, pestilent purlieus of a great City are favorable to health and longevity, because men have grown there to stature and vigor and died in hale old age. As well tell me that the bivouac and the battle-field are favorable to long life, because men have died peacefully at ninety, after a half century of camps and sieges. These are exceptions, which rather establish the rule than invalidate it. 'A sound mind in a sound body'—that is the order of Nature—you *may* find a sound mind elsewhere, but it will be most unfitly and inconveniently bestowed. The body can endure a divorce far better than the mind. In fact, we see bodies breathing, moving, acting all around us, which seem to perform their proper functions tolerably with the aid of very little mind—almost none—but a healthful, clear mind in a diseased, decrepit, decaying body is a far more pitiable spectacle. It is a diamond in the clutch of a lunatic—to be gazed at a moment in wonder, then hurled into the depths of the sea. It is a freight of the wealth of the Indies, embarked in a tottering wherry, which is certain to sink in the first tempest. When I look around me, and recall the many noble, and brilliant, and greatly useful, who have sunk after a meteor-like career into premature graves, under the assaults of diseases insensibly contracted during their years of study and mental acquisition—diseases from which any tolerable knowledge, any careful investigation, of the laws of Man's physical being must have preserved them — I am impelled to sound the alarm of danger alike to teachers and to students — to plead for the generation now in process of development and the generation to follow — and to warn the directors of Education of the fearful responsibility which rests upon them — a responsibility which it is but charity to presume very many of them do not even dimly comprehend. For, assuredly, they could not know that the hundreds of young men committed by anxious love to their charge were growing up in almost total ignorance even that they *had* physical constitutions to nurture and bring to vigorous maturity — in utter ignorance, quite commonly, of many of the inflexible laws on which their physical well-being depend — and not adopt some adequate measures to counteract and avert the danger. And yet, how little is systematically done, how little is even consistently, authoritatively *said*, in our seminaries of Learning, of the necessity and nature of a true Physical Education? Shall this deficiency continue?

True Education is Development. It does not create the statue from the marble — it only finds it therein and exposes it to the unimpeded, admiring gaze. But in what do our Educational processes tend to develop the physical man? From the high, uncomfortable bench on which the child sits for hours at the common school in abhorred constraint and suffering, watching in envy the flitting of every bird by the window, to the highest University, so called, we find scarcely a recognition that his mind is encased in a tenement of flesh and blood. He has teachers of Reading and of Grammar — Professors of Mathematics and of Ethics — of Languages and of Metaphysics — but the teachers of the laws of his own structure and relations to Nature — the Professors of Health, of Strength, of Longevity, I think are mainly yet to be appointed. Yet this ought not to be. The position of the young student is surrounded by peculiar perils. From the field, the forest, the bustling ways of home and neighborhood, he is transplanted at once to academic shades, whose genius demands quiet, meditation, seclusion. No longer is the climbing of rugged hills, or the levelling of stubborn woods, the preparation for the evening's study and the night's repose. He is instantly confronted by two formidable dangers—that of falling into habits of physical indolence and excessive study, inducing indigestion and its long train of enfeebling horrors; or his lithe frame revolts at the galling bondage, and he becomes a hater of books, a neglecter of studies, and gradually addicts himself to habits of turbulence and wild excess. Henceforward his career need not be indicated—its course and its end are inevitable.

I must press this point farther, for I feel that a reform with regard to it is most essential to the usefulness and honor of our seminaries. In too many instances has a Collegiate course, in view of all its consequences, proved a positive curse to a large proportion of the Class which sanguinely entered upon it as the unmistakable high road to eminent usefulness, recompense and fame. Alas! a deadly serpent lurked in those calm, bright bowers which seemed to their first eager glances so alluring. A few days of eager study jaded their spirits and unstrung their nerves; a languor and lassitude crept over them; they fell into the company of those who had traveled that road before them, who suggested—"All study is dry work—let us solace ourselves this evening with a bottle and a feast." Thus is laid the foundation of habits which have dragged too many a youth of rare promise down to an untimely and dishonored grave—which have quenched the fond, proud hopes of admiring relatives in a deluge of sin and shame.

Now it is the idlest folly to waste words in declaiming against these evils—we must trace them to their source and apply there an adequate preventive. We must begin by teaching our Young Men the nature of their own frames, and the shocking violence they do to that nature by overtaxing its powers, and then drugging it with narcotics and stimulants to reänimate them. We must demonstrate to them the fact that *any* use of stimulants is a certain and fearful evil—that the effect we term drunkenness is only a benevolent effort of Nature to expel the monster which has been treacherously admitted to her most sacred and vital recesses—and that the evil commences with the first particle of such substances which is thrust upon her, and the penalty is signal and certain although the second glass were never taken. All these truths and the kindred objections to narcotics, *may* easily enough be scientifically demonstrated—the mischief is that they *are* not. A man properly instructed, and as yet uncorrupted, would no more think of swallowing Alcohol than live coals or arsenic. And yet many have actually acquired the basest of habits—that of partaking of notoriously hurtful substances merely to produce a temporary and pernicious elevation of the spirits—within the precincts of our very Universities! Shame is it to human ignorance—shame especially to those whose duty it was to dispel that ignorance in the case of these victims, and yet neglected it! *They* can not be excused, but we may drop a tear of pity for the victim of their neglect, so distorted and misdeveloped that he knows how to construe Greek, yet does *not* know enough to reject and loathe Tobacco!

You have already anticipated my statement that, to a true and healthful development of the Man, I deem a constant participation in Manual Labor indispensable. Labor! blessed boon of God, to alleviate the horrors and purify the tendencies of our fallen state! when shall its benefits and its joys be brought home to each and to all? We may make it a curse and a burden by so regarding it, as we may any other blessing from Heaven, but the truth is irrepressible that only he who is familiar with Labor and loves it can either improve or enjoy life. The man whose only stimulant to exertion in any field is the hope of individual gain, can hardly have risen above the condition of a slave. We must learn to be true workers — our frames need it — our unperverted impulses demand it — our very souls, if unstifled, cry out for it. Most earnestly, then, do I record my protest against the all but universal prescription which divorces entirely profound Study from Manual Labor — which, in its attention to the intellectual and moral nature of the student, forgets that he has also a physical frame to be developed and invigorated. Of course, you will not understand me as assuming that the usual routine of student life forgets or disregards the necessity of physical exercise — I know better. I will not doubt that wherever thoughtful, conscientious and cultivated men have charge of the education of youth, there are, there must be, abundant inculcations of the necessity of exercise and the value of health; also of the danger of losing the latter through the neglect of the former. I will not doubt that abundant opportunities and facilities for exercise are everywhere afforded. Yet what is the result? Do the mass of our young men finish their studies with stronger constitutions, sturdier frames, more athletic limbs, than they brought away from their parental firesides? Not within the sphere of my observation — far otherwise. I have known many dyspepsias, consumptions, debilities, which traced their origin to seminaries: I do not remember any that were cured there; I have known the stout lad in the district school who graduated a feeble invalid from the university. My conviction is that the Physical department of Education has decidedly retrograded since the days of Greek freedom and glory. Our prevalent error is not one of method and detail — it is fundamental. We have lost the true basis ordained of God for the harmonious and healthful development of the whole human being, in separating the education of the Head from the education of the Hands. We have dared to disregard that Divine fiat, first of punishments and therefore first also of mercies — 'In the sweat of thy face shalt thou eat bread!' Shunning this appointed path, we have sought out inventions, which we term Exercise, Recreation, Relaxation. Heaven placidly but inexorably disallows them. I do not say that for the cramped, soul-dwarfed, undeveloped miner, delving for six days of each week in some stinted Egyptian labyrinth in the bowels of the earth, there may not be appropriate recreation in the free air and sunshine. Malign Circumstance has grudged him a full development—his class are significantly advertised for as '*Hands* wanted'—not men. But to the true and whole man each successive duty is the proper relief from the preceding, and in the regular alternation of labors—now those which tax mainly the Intellect, next those which appeal mainly to the Sinews—is the needed relaxation best attained. Thus only shall Life be rendered consistent and harmonious—thus shall each hour be dignified and rendered heroic. The division of the Race into two unequal, contrasted classes—the few Thinkers, the many Workers—has been and is the source of many and sore evils, including tbe loss of the fitting and manly independence of each. It is the source of infinite servility, falsehood and mean compliance. Not till we shall have emancipated the Many from the subjection of taking their thoughts at second-hand from the Few, may we hope to accomplish much for the upraising of the long trampled masses. Not till we have emancipated the Few from the equally degrading necessity of subsisting on the fruits of the physical toil of the Many, can we secure to the more cultivated and intellectual their proper and healthful ascendency over the less affluent in mental wealth. The plowman recognizes and appreciates Genuis, Talent, Learning; but he finds that these are too often directed to the acquisition of wealth and luxury by means which add little to the aggregate of human comforts, and rather subtract from his own especial share of them. The reprobate dreads the rebuke of the anointed reprover of sin; but says, 'He will hardly venture to arraign pointedly the transgressions of one who contributes liberally to the salary which barely supports his expensive family.' Thus the divorce of Learning from Manual Labor—the absolute dependence of the Educated on the Uneducated class for the means of supplying its physical wants—becomes the source of endless and fatal compromises of Principle and perversions of Intellectual power.

It avails nothing to point me to the failure, if it shall be so termed, of past attempts to rëunite Study with Physical exertion—the affluent mind with the ready and skillful hand. These failures only prove the inadequacy of the effort, not that the object is unworthy, nor even unattainable. They have been impelled too often by low ideas of their own scope and purpose—by a consideration of the necessity to the student not so much of Labor as of Bread. Commenced in this spirit, the number of workers will inevitably dwindle till only those labor who must subsist on the fruits of that labor; soon the class distinction of Gentlemen and Peasants rëappears; invidious comparisons, sneers and sarcasms beget hatreds and collisions; and one class or the other—probably both—make their exit; the institution explodes; and the superficial multitude unhesitatingly pronounce the idea of uniting Labor with Study proved impracticable and absurd!

The fatal error here was obviously that of putting the new wine into old bottles. The impulse to the enterprise was not a conviction of the necessity, healthfulness and dignity of Labor—not even the idea of Duty as commanding a participation in the toil needful to the sustenance and comfort of Man—but at bottom the pauper's necessity, the slave's dread of the lash. This may facilitate and insure the production of corn—never of true men. Not until Labor shall be joyfully and proudly accepted as a genial and beneficent destiny—as the needful exercise and complement of our else undeveloped or perverted faculties—may we rationally hope for any permanently satisfactory result.

And here you will permit me to hazard a criticism on so

much of our educational processes — no great portion of any college course, I will hope — as are undertaken for the sake, it is said, of 'disciplining the mind.' I ask a student-friend why he, who is aspiring to the Christian Ministry, should devote so much time to a science so little pertinent to his future calling as Mathematics, and he answers that the study of Mathematics is an admirable discipline for the mind! Need I say to you that I neither appreciate the force of the reason nor discern the benefits of the discipline? I do not say that this or any other science may not be eminently calculated to subserve the purpose contemplated — I simply demur to the necessity or fitness of pursuing mental discipline apart from healthful mental activity in the sphere of practical life. Does the youth contemplate the pursuit of Astronomy, Engineering, or any sphere of usefulness requiring the aid of the exact sciences — then let him devote his student years in part to Mathematics, and master them thoroughly. But if he contemplate pursuing either of the three leading professions, Theology, Law or Physic — I distrust the wisdom of such a devotion of his time. This life is too short to justify the acquisition of abstruse sciences on such grounds. The mind is best disciplined when it finds its pleasures in its duties — when all its laborious acquisitions are turned to direct and palpable account — when its every impulse is toward utility and beneficence. We give the child playthings because we know not or have not what we should give him — did we know all things, command all things, we should improve his every desire to subserve directly some useful end. His toys would be tools, or at least demonstrations of some truth adapted to his opening mind. He should be wiser for every walk — more skillful for each hour's diversion. In our ignorance or fond thoughtlessness, we waste half the golden opportunities of the most impressible period of life, and misimprove a portion of the remainder. It were well to remember that a benign Creator has enfolded the mental casket we contemplate, and that it needs not to be pressed and fashioned, but simply developed. The discipline it requires, if unstifled, unperverted, is induction into whatever is peculiar to that sphere of laudable endeavor to which it is specially devoted.

And here let me state fairly the objection of the Utilitarian school to the acquisition of the Dead Languages, which I find often commented on and controverted without being at all apprehended. We do not, we never did, deny the utility of these Languages to many—it would ill become us to do so—ill become any rational beings. We admit—nay, insist, that there are large classes to which a thorough knowledge of one or more of the Languages in which the noblest, most inspiring ideas of Antiquity lie inurned, is indispensable. The Christian theologian needs a mastery of Greek and Hebrew; the Physician, the Botanist, the thorough Lawyer, of Latin. But, beyond and above these, the world needs and is deeply indebted to the illustrious body of Scholars, Learned Men, who as Professors, (O most desecrated term!) Historians, Philosophers, Poets, Critics, are constantly irradiating and instructing the Present by the light of the Past. Noblest, least obtrusive of our teachers, we could not dispense with these—we are in no danger of honoring them too highly. But it is not given to every man—it is permitted to few—to be of these, and it is preposterous to subject the multitude of comparatively educated persons to their ordeal in the idle hope of producing any such result. You can not make Scholars of these—you have enough to do to render them passable attorneys and doctors, in the common way. And, if they are to be such and nothing more, you must allow me to believe that their College years might be better devoted than to the acquisition of Greek and Latin—oftener practically forgotten in two years than really learned in three. The simple and notorious fact that they usually *are* so forgotten—that they are to most educated men (so called) in the busy walks of life but a foggy reminiscence of dull days wasted and dry tasks slighted, is their sufficient condemnation.

The truth is that the fatal evil of *pecuniary dependence* is not always unfelt even by those who hold the responsible position of directors of the highest education of our youth. A President or Professor who should frankly tell the parents of a proffered student that their son might make an excellent blacksmith or carpenter, but would be neither eminent nor happy at the bar nor in the pulpit, would probably incur resentment and a withdrawal of patronage—and yet how often ought such truth to be frankly, kindly told! It would frequently save much waste of energies and means, much weariness and heart-ache. The true though rugged man who has nobly gathered a competence by following the plow, would feel offended if assured that his son was so fit for no other avocation as that of a farmer—though that were a genuine tribute of respect to the dignity of the vocation and the honest worth of the youth.

We are here confronted by the low idea which everywhere prevails of the true rank of useful manual toil—by none so cherished, as by those who themselves toil, except by the empty demagogue who windily babbles in bar-rooms of the rights and dignity of Labor, hoping to compass thereby the means of avoiding Labor. The farmer will not feel gratified, though he should, if assured that he can give his son no fitter, no better calling than his own; the hope of the family must be trained to the chicanery of Law or the futility of Medicine in order that he may duly honor his kindred, though he may be reluctant to enter, or at best have manifested no genius or taste for the calling thus thrust upon him. This is in the true spirit of the illiterate farmer who insisted on having a sermon in Greek, on the ground that he paid the clergyman for the best, and would have it. Thus our higher Education becomes a bed of Procrustes—

excellent for the few whom Nature has just adapted to it — but a very different affair for all beside. We shall learn yet to study the unfolding genius of the youth — to be guided by this rather than attempt to overrule it — and to leave to the directors of Education a larger discretion in the premises than they have usually hitherto enjoyed.

In the lamentable divorce of Learning from Labor — of the highest Intellectual culture from the greatest Industrial capacity and efficiency — do I detect the origin of that deplorable discord which prevails between the teachings of our Schoolmen and the edicts of Legislators, between the lessons of our Literature and the spirit of Communities and States, with regard to Political Economy. Vainly do our Colleges, the wide world over, indoctrinate nearly all the leading minds of the age with the distinctive principles of Adam Smith and his followers — their labor may be lighter than that of Sysiphus, but their fortune is inevitably like his. On a few minds, remarkable rather for speculative than for practical ability, they make a durable impression; but with the majority their plausible inculcations are overborne by the observation and experience of a few succeeding years. Those originally most captivated by the theory of '*Laissez faire*,' soon discover, on passing out into the actual world, that all Life is, all Legislation must be, in contradiction to its spirit. A man who should be left to grow up on this fundamental principle of the Free Trade philosophy, would, if by some miraculous chance he survived to maturity at all, be a most unmitigated savage, and a bad specimen even of that forlorn condition. A young Nation which should really and fully adopt the corresponding theory of National Economy, and, by dispensing with all Industrial and Commercial Legislation of its own, leave its Labor and Trade wholly at the mercy of Foreign regulation, would soon have little left wherewith to tempt the cupidity of Foreign policy. There never yet was, there never can be, a Government of a civilized, accessible, enlightened, wealthy Nation which acted consistently and thoroughly on the principle of Free Trade for a single generation — no, not for ten years. Superficial men may dilate on the unsafeness of following Theory, the discrepancies between Theory and Practice, and the like fig-leaves of seeming Wisdom wherewith Folly is wont to enrobe herself — but there is in truth no such discrepancy. A sound theory is always a safe one — it may fearlessly be reduced to practice and followed to the end. When a Statesman rises in your halls of Legislation and tells you that a certain theory is indeed sound and worthy of general acceptance, but it must be postponed in this particular instance, because of the depression of Trade, the distresses of the Laboring Class, or on any such ground, be sure that either he or his theory is hollow and untrustworthy. More probably, both of them are so. For, were the theory sound, the earliest moment would be the best moment to reduce it to practice, and whatever the embarrassments existing, they but furnish additional arguments for its instant adoption. Their existence argues a wrong somewhere, and demands that every known wrong be instantly redressed. To say that a theory is sound, and yet act in contradiction thereto, is to dethrone eternal Right and exalt a fleeting, unstable, unrighteous Expediency in its stead. Whatever is true in theory is desirable in practice, and desirable to-day.

But the elemental Free Trade assumption is *not* true. 'The best government is' *not* 'that which governs least,' or no government at all were clearly better still. 'Trade will' *not* 'regulate itself' so as to secure even 'the greatest good of the greatest number,' though I insist that it is not the good of the *greatest* number but of the *whole* number which communities and governments are bound unceasingly to seek and to secure. It is *not* true that the largest possible average or general reward of Industry is that which it would secure in the total absence of Governmental regulation. The grain-grower of the valley of the Wabash or Illinois, for example, can never receive the fullest reward of his toil, the largest return for his bounteous harvests, while the producer of his cloths, his wares, his glass, his cutlery, &c. remains on the other side of the Atlantic. The fact that they do remain there compels a larger export thither of his bulky Agricultural staples, at an enormous cost for transportation, and inevitably involves a corresponding and permanent depression of the prices of those staples. If England may obtain Wheat from the Black Sea and the Baltic at an average cost of one dollar a bushel, (as she can, very nearly,) then his must be largely sold in England at that price, though the cost of transporting it thither amounts to three-fourths of that sum. The residue, small as it is, must be the standard price of his wheat at the point of production. But change your policy so as to bring the producers of most of the fabrics which minister to his convenience and comfort from Sheffield and Birmingham to the banks of his own gentle rivers, or of their more impetuous tributaries, or divert a portion of the grain-growers already there into the various pursuits of Manufacture, and now you have insured a higher price for Grain and a larger reward to the industry of its producer. He will not merely receive more money for his yearly product than he could have done for a long, indefinite period if Manufactures had been left to grow up around him, by the slow, capricious efforts of unaided individual enterprise, exposed to the relentless hostility of their alarmed and skillful, wealthy and powerful Foreign rivals, but he will receive a far greater aggregrate of the various articles he desires in exchange for his own surplus productions. The reason why this is inevitable is that the number of actual producers, the amount of aggregate product, is immensely greater than formerly. Of a thousand workers there were originally three hundred in Illinois producing Grain, two hundred in Europe fabricating various products to be exchanged for the Grain, and the remaining five hundred employed as wagoners, boatmen, sailors, forwarders, merchants, etc., in interchanging the Provisions and the Manufactures between their respective producers, and living (as they must) out of the aggregate product. Now, with the workshops attracted to the westward of the Alleghenies, there are but one hundred required to effect those exchanges, releasing four hundred from various non-productive functions, and reinforcing by so many the body of actual producers of wealth. The consequence, most manifestly, is an increased production and accumulation of wealth, to be evinced not in store-houses filled to bursting with unneeded food and clothing, but in the improvement of wild or waste lands, the erection of buildings, and the multiplication of books, schools, implements, and everything which conduces to human comfort and well-being. There is no mystery, no magic, no juggle in the increase of National Wealth by an enlightened and judicious Protection of Home Industry — an increase of the wealth not of one nation merely, but of the People of all Nations. It operates by giving Idleness employment, and rendering Labor more effective. There is nothing narrow, partial, envious, exclusive, in the policy of Protection, rightly understood and rightly pursued. That we should systematically produce for ourselves and not purchase from other countries whatever articles may with substantially as little labor be produced here as elsewhere, is the dictate not only of a wise Patriotism but of a generous Philanthropy. It is the permanent, universal interest of the Toiling Millions of all climes that the exchanges of their productions be rendered as direct, simple, unexpensive, as possible; but a bloated and superflous Commerce, regarding simply its own profits and not the general good, may, in the absence of Protective Legislation, defeat this consummation, or at least postpone it for years. We may clearly be able — we *are* able — with our Home Market secured to us by such legislatlon, after vanquishing the difficulties presented by utter inexperience, to fabricate our own Hardware and Glass, our Pins and Penknives, much cheaper than we could purchase them from England — no matter though they were made somewhat lower there — and yet we should not be able in fifty years to naturalize and establish, under the batteries of destructive Foreign rivalry, so as to be beyond the reach of its capricious competition, the various arts and processes required for their production. A hundred farmers of Illinois, combining or resolving singly to purchase only Home Manufactures, might not raise the market price of their Agricultural staples one per cent. though the agreement of the Community, expressed through a Protective Tariff, to consume only or mainly Domestic fabrics, securing the Home Production of those fabrics and the consequent Home Consumption of the Agricultural staples, would inevitably raise the price of the latter by fifty to a hundred per cent. To repeat, then, the parrot phrase that 'Trade will regulate itself,' meaning that individual avarice and anarchical competition will work out the most beneficent general results, is a futility unworthy of this enlightened age. As well leave a necessary canal to dig itself, or be scraped out from time to time by the voluntary efforts of those who chance to live on its borders. The seeming personal interest of many of them will often be directly adverse to its construction at all, impelling them to impede rather than advance it. General good is only to be attained through general effort — systematic, harmonious and far-sighted. Left to the mercy of individual selfishness and caprice, it will rarely be compassed at all.

But I do not merely challenge the Economical soundness of the Free Trade system — my objection is deeper, broader, and more vital. I object that it fails to recognize and respect the more important use and purpose of Industrial effort. I object that it regards Labor only as a necessary means of supplying Man's sensual wants, and not at al as Divinely appointed for the discipline and development of our Race.

It regards the Corn and the Cloth as the only results of Industry; and takes no account of that nobler product, the Man.

It everywhere assumes as unquestionable that if our People, or those of any section, as a mass, a community, can realize a greater aggregate of wealth by devoting their energies wholly to some single function or department of Industry —the growing of Cotton, for example—then it would be clearly their interest and duty to do nothing but grow Cotton, and with this purchase everything else they need or desire, made ready for use abroad. But this I most strenuously deny. We might so have more goods for a season, but less good—more sensual gratification, but less intellectual expansion and force. A new art, a new calling, introduced among a people, is a new seminary for that people. It awakens inquiry, elicits ideas, suggests improvements even in old processes and inveterate habits. It has a decided value, though not precisely calculable in dollars and cents. The boorishness of manners, the vacuity or stupor of mind, of a youth trained in the dull routine of a single pursuit and ignorant of the processes of all others, contrasts strikingly with the rapidity of thought, freedom of manner, and fertility of resource, of his fellow who has been reared in observing contact with the multiform processes of a hundred surrounding avocations. It is thus that the city lad usually appears to advantage beside the rustic who has grown up in some secluded valley, even when the latter is the more favored by nature and more informed by the study of the schools. The vast domain of Industry is and must be the University of the great majority —it is of the highest public importance that none shall be restricted therein to a single acquirement, but that the education it affords shall be diversified and thorough.

But it is not merely true that the ultimate uses and full beneficence of the Divine appointment of Labor as the proper condition and essential element of human development and well-being can only be realized where that Labor is diversified and elevated, not monotonous and degraded—it is also true that, though the majority might possibly find a pecuniary and sensible advantage in a National Industry restricted to one or two pursuits, there would be numerous classes condemned to helplessness and dependence thereby. Let a whole community be purely Agriculturists, purely Iron-workers, or entirely devoted to any branch of Industry, and there must be a large proportion of its members who, from inadequacy of strength or of skill, from considerations of age or of sex, will be unsuited for efficiency in that especial field of effort—consequently, for the most part idle or but partially employed and meagerly rewarded. There will be seasons when, owing to unfavorable markets, the *whole* Industry of such a community will be suspended or unrecompensed, as well as classes which habitually earn little or nothing. Under such circumstances, the laborer becomes the thrall of the capitalist, just as the Egyptians did of Pharaoh during the seven years of famine; while those whose capacities are not suited to the demands of the branches of industry there mainly pursued, are habitually, inevitably dependent on others for the means of subsistence. A new branch of Industry naturalized in any country is a virtual Declaration of Independence for a portion of its before subject people. There can be no emancipation of the Laboring Mass from a virtual bondage without a liberal and thorough diversification of Industrial pursuits; and, though this is profitable in every way, it is too vastly important to be deferred to any mere pecuniary consideration. If it were true that it must cost us more, according to the narrowest dollar-and-cent reckoning, to manufacture for ourselves than to buy of others the products of manufacture, the interests of Labor and of Man would still imperatively require us to secure the supplying of our own wants, so far as Nature interposed no obstacle, by the skill and effort of our own People. Not individual Man only, but the Nation as an aggregate, demands that symmetric and thorough Development which is to be attained only through a many-sided Industry.

You will bear with one more illustration of the blindness which has befallen Learning through its divorce from Labor. I allude now to the discussions which have arisen in our day respecting the organic Reform of Society. We of the Movement are not surprised to hear from the lips of Ignorance and a purblind Selfishness the cavils which befit and bespeak their sources. We are not surprised nor vexed to hear from such that Industrial Association is but another device to get the goods of the thrifty and prudent within the grasp of the knavish and prodigal — that no house was ever large enough for two families — that no man will work unless impelled to it by appetite or avarice — or any of the sage and well-considered objections which we are required to meet as profound novelties or novel profundities, day after day. From the class wherein such objections properly originate, we receive and answer them with indomitable patience. Neither are we surprised that a well-meaning man, with a brain by nature and habit nicely adjusted to the reception and retention of one idea at a time, is afraid that if he accepts the thought of a Social condition based on brotherhood and love, he must eject his Religion, or his Family ties, or some other cherished possession, to make room for it. We see that the man wants expansion — he must have more room before he can render more hospitality — and we are but moved to more energetic and untiring effort in the great work of whose necessity he is so striking an evidence. But when the objections of the ostler and the nurse confront us from the rostrum and the pulpit — when they overwhelm us in the magisterial dictum of the Professor — when the annihilation that we can not realize in the Judge's argument overtakes us in the Judge's frown — what shall we think or say? The narrowness and obliquity of the depressed and benighted was saddening;

but when that which should be light but deepens darkness, whither shall we turn for a ray? Whither but to the great central truth of which we are the imperfect advocates?

We of the Movement maintain a position which need not be deemed ambiguous and ought not to be regarded with distrust or aversion by any generous, lofty mind—by any hopeful, loving heart. We maintain that Industry, now too often degraded and repugnant, may be everywhere elevated and rendered attractive, so that not the result only but the process shall be a source of daily joy. We contend that the anarchy between Labor and Capital which now glaringly prevails all around us may be replaced by a better system, wherein a just and settled proportion of product shall be accorded to each, and the present alienating, disorganizing, depraving, universal struggle to secure more wages for less work or more work for less wages, shall be banished forever, taking unfaithfulness on the one side and extortion on the other along with it. We maintain that, in this bounteous creation of our God, a man standing idle for want of employment, or even of suitable employment, when there is scarcely a square mile of the earth's surface which would not reward ten times the labor ever yet bestowed on it, is a grievous wrong and a bitter reproach to our whole Social Economy, wherein the cunning and the strong secure a certain portion of comfort and luxury to themselves by means which leave the simple and the feeble to famish. We contend that the Rights of Property in the earth, so wisely and necessarily guarantied to the fortunate possessors, were granted not that the many might be excluded from the common source of sustenance, but that they might be enabled more securely, peacefully, advantageously to derive their subsistence therefrom, and that the Right to Labor, and to receive the rewards of Labor, pertains to every individual where the right to the Soil, originally free and common to all, has been granted away to a part. We maintain that, as

12

no man, clearly, would have a moral right to acquire the ownership of *all* the earth and, forbidding any to cultivate or dwell on it, starve the Race to death, so no one can have the moral right to do this in part, by monopolizing the land and keeping it unproductive for the gratification of his pomp and avarice, while hundreds around him are suffering for the want of it. In fine, we hold that all individual rights are held subordinate to the demands of Universal Beneficence, and though Human Law may not prescribe the limits of such rights and provide against any overstepping them, yet the Divine Law condemns every act which finds its end in self-gratification by means which trench on the well-being of others. We maintain that the isolated family is not the most perfect form of the household — that immense economies, in both production and consumption, are attainable by Combined Effort, directed by combined experience and wisdom — that a true and full Education, such as is not possible under the isolated system, will be all but inevitable in the Combined Order, with its schools beneath the common roof for every department of Knowledge and Art, presided over by instructors chosen from the whole body because of their observed and tested capacity to teach, and not of their indisposition to work — but, above all, its extensive, infinitely diversified, carefully perfected processes of Industry in action all around the young learner. We maintain that only in such a relation, based on a profound sentiment of Human Brotherhood, can be wrought out the emancipation of the Laboring Class from practical servitude and the haunting dread of destitution — from Ignorance, Degradation and the apathy of departed Hope. We maintain that for Woman, from infancy a toy or a slave, so often condemned to mercenary and loathed marriages, or a useless and joyless loneliness, by an education and by Social usages which deny her the means of essential independence, there is no hope but in a true Social condition, and enlarged opportunities for Knowledge, liberal Culture and Industrial usefulness which the Phalanx alone can afford to all. We maintain that only in a Society which puts an end to the interminable vagrancy of Labor anxiously seeking employment, and often seeking long and hungrily in vain — which banishes Commerce and Wages, with their incessant temptations to selfishness, avarice and dishonesty — which secures Development and Opportunity to all, with Plenty and Comfort to every one who will use the means he possesses of acquiring them — wherein Love to God and Man will constitute the moral atmosphere, and Progress in all good the universal aspiration — can the benign purposes of Heaven be fulfilled and the Destiny of Man on earth accomplished.

If there be any who object that the Social Movement of our time is defective in method or in purpose, we simply invite them to embrace and pursue it by that better method, with that better purpose, which their criticism implies. If there be any who object that only publicans and sinners are engaged in it, we ask them to dignify it with their weight of character and hallow it with their sanctity. If they deem its advocates heretical in faith or deficient in piety, how much larger and more inviting is the field wherein they are called to exemplify the influences of a true faith and of a saintly life! Assuredly, there is no necessary heresy nor impiety in effort to supplant Divergence by Convergence of Interests — to replace envious Competition by generous Coöperation — to banish Strife and Want, and establish instead Concord and Plenty; and if any has been engrafted thereon by injudicious or inconsiderate partisans, it will be easy to demonstrate the fact by an effort based on better principles, and made in a more catholic spirit. We may be sure that every sincere, unselfish effort to do good is based on a Religion which can not be false, and a Faith which takes hold on Heaven.

Now it weighs little with us that those who never thought seriously, candidly, of this subject for two hours, perceive obstacles in our path which to them seem insurmountable —

for we have traversed the quagmires in which they now flounder and know that they are not impassable. It is no tidings to us that time, and effort, and sacrifice, will be requisite to secure what we contemplate, and that the grave will probably close over the present generation before half that we foresee and struggle for can be attained. Neither can failure in practical trials discourage us, for we anticipate successive and often mortifying failures. The inadequacy of means, the absence of that every-day wisdom learned only in the school of experience, the imperfection of men, all unite to assure us on this point. But we are sustained by an undoubting faith that whatever of possible good has been revealed to the understandings of men may be rendered practical by devoted and patient exertion. Through sacrifices, discouragements, reverses, and failures, the great work steadily advances step by step to its ultimate triumph. A hundred failures will not suffice to arrest it; a thousand lives are already pledged to its steadfast prosecution; and many thousands will be ready ere these are wholly spent. This wounded, bleeding body of Humanity shall yet be raised up and healed—the beneficence of God has decreed it; the silent transformations of the ages have prepared the way for it. For a time may the Priest and the Levite distrustfully pass by on the other side; but they shall yet recognize in this the work which they were appointed to aid and to compass, and shall exultingly share in the glory and the joy of its consummation!

I have thus far invited your attention to some of the defects, as they strike me, of our Educational methods and aims, as exemplified in the practical errors and deficiencies in which they result. I need not, surely, now reverse the picture and exhibit at length the amendments I would with diffidence suggest. That Education should be based on Labor and directed thoroughly, discriminately, to practical ends—this is the immovable and universal foundation. If a youth is destined to be a Professor, a Physician, a Lawyer, a Poet, a Clergyman, let his higher education at every step contemplate that fact; but let *all* his education, from infancy to maturity, regard the development and perfection of the Man. And, as one battle contributes more than ten reviews or sham engagements to form the soldier, so one acquirement which commends itself to the student's regard by a direct and palpable utility shall prove of more worth to him than a dozen which he is constrained to labor at as part of a prescribed routine, and (as he is told) to 'discipline his mind.' It is in life only that we learn how to live. The great ends of all study, of all acquirement, are ability and disposition to discharge more effectually our duties as men and as citizens. The benefits of a true education commence with the individual, but pass directly and inevitably to the community. He who is not a better brother, neighbor, friend, and citizen, because of his superior knowledge, may very well doubt whether his knowledge is really superior to the ignorance of the unlettered many around him. He whose education has not taught him to shun Vice and loathe Hypocrisy—has not taught him to prize lightly the pleasures of Sense, the possession of boundless Wealth, and the pomp of Public Station, has been taught to little purpose, and should be sent back to his hornbook.

Far be it from me to decry Ambition. There is a generous and lofty aspiration for the blessing of the present and the admiring regard of future generations, which has doubtless been the main-spring of many a self-denying act of devotion to human welfare—of many an illustrious and eminently useful career. Let this be held in due honor, that those who do not find in the consecration of their every faculty, every hour, to the good of their Race, the proper and ample reward of such consecration, may unite in the good work, though from a motive less exalted. I can comprehend an ardent desire for Public Station and even for Riches, springing from a consciousness of capacity to wield the power thence accruing to the signal benefit of mankind. It is this which excuses the thirst for office we often detect in men who by nature are clearly above receiving either consideration or renown from any post whatever. Yet I trust this will not much longer continue—that the increase and diffusion of Knowledge, insuring a more just and general discrimination of the real from the factitious, will gradually work a separation of real power, as well as of popular homage, from Station undignified by the Virtue and Ability which should be essential to its attainment. Our Country has enjoyed—shall I say, *has* enjoyed?—a remarkable example of the impotency of mere station, however lofty, to confer respect or substantial power—may we not hope that the salutary lesson will be widely and lastingly heeded?

Yet I confess that I find or fancy a perverted and groveling Ambition alarmingly prevalent among our Educated Young Men, and that the hope of awaking in some minds a nobler and loftier impulse has been instrumental in bringing me before you. It seems to me that, while our higher Culture is far more vague and indiscriminate than I could wish it, the purposes and aims of those who acquire that Culture are too generally special and personal to an extent equally faulty and even more pernicious. Nine-tenths of our Educated Youth pass through College to fit themselves for this or that profession—very rarely that they may be simply better men. If they intently explore and unseal the fountains of Knowledge, it is not that they, and all men and the parched earth, may be freely refreshed by the bubbling element, but that they may sell it by the penny's worth to the thirsty wayfarer. I am not satisfied with the aspect here presented. I do not object to the adequate reinforcement of the Professions from the ranks of the Educated; but I demur to the devotion of the Educated Class, of the entire facilities and means of a liberal Culture, to the filling of the Professions. It seems to me, if not a profanation, at least an impotent conclusion, when a young man who has spent some years in intimate and delighted communion with the Philosophers, Poets and Sages of all times, subsides into a mere dispenser of medicines or drawer of declarations. I would not undervalue the Professions as spheres of usefulness, though I am in small danger indeed of overvaluing them; but I insist that the Man and the Scholar shall not be swallowed up in the Lawyer or the Doctor. I insist that he shall not consider the Profession the object and end of his Education, but shall still employ the latter to qualify him for higher and more varied usefulness through all the scenes of life. What he has learned from Plato and from Newton, from the master-minds of our Race, let him, as opportunity shall offer, dispense freely and gladly to his less favored neighbors, till they too shall recognize and bless profound Learning as the guidance and the solace of mankind.

I have come naturally to the consideration of the position of the Educated Class in our existing Society, and the influence they therein exert. Will any contend that this is what it should and must be? Is our public opinion usually shaped and directed by that of the more elaborately Educated? I think no one will pretend it. There are points wherein, no settled or strenuous opposition being offered, the sentiment of the College-bred class is accordant with that of the uneducated; but let a vital question arise, on which the oracles of the grog-shops shall generally take ground against the oracles of the schools, and can we hesitate as to which will triumph? Were our Educated Class really the leaders of Opinion in this Country, could such atrocities as Lynch-Law and Repudiation ever be countenanced? There is manifestly unsoundness here—evil which needs to be probed and cured. The Educated Class is far less potential than it should be; the mischief may be the Country's, but the fault is primarily its own. Its sources I have throughout been endeavoring to detect and expose to your apprehension. It has been said by one of the most eminent scholars* of our time and country, "It is difficult for cultivated Pride to put its ear to the ground and listen to the teachings of a lowly Humanity." I see how this may be difficult for Pride of any sort, but I deny that the voice of Humanity, however lowly, ought to be less welcome or less intelligible to the truly cultivated than to the uncultivated ear — far otherwise. But there is a half-truth at the bottom of this sentiment, and it bears to us an admonition. There is too little cordial sympathy — too little familiar and friendly interchange of thought — between the better educated and the imperfectly instructed. There are too many barriers of form and usage between them. Each might learn much from the other — profit much by a nearer relation. Each may find admonition in the experiences of the other, if freely imparted. In the great convulsions now dimly apprehended but certainly at hand, the well-meaning and right-thinking of each class will find a union essential to both. That enlightened Conservatism, which asks what it *is* that we should conserve, and what there is of abuse or injustice that should be cut away in order that what is valuable and precious *may* be conserved — that genial Reform which recognizes Harmony and Love as the elements of all true Progress, and shrinks from any changes impelled by Hatred and compassed through Disorder — are learning to know each other as brethren and natural allies. On the altar of a common danger, a common interest, may their union be indissolubly consummated!

I have said that the practical and treasured acquirement of the Educated Class seems to me too special and individual, while their culture appears indiscriminate and general. Here in one of our rural townships is a limited number of persons — perhaps ten or twenty — who have enjoyed the benefits of a College education. Their literary acquirement of course

* Hon. Geo. Bancroft — Address of Massachusetts Democratic Convention.

far surpasses that of the great mass around them. But how are their neighbors and townsmen permitted to realize this? Is it not quite common that their only experience of it is based on the hard words in an attorney's prolix folios or an apothecary's account—words subsidiary to a still harder charge at the bottom of it? May we not hope that this shall be amended?—that the Educated Class shall yet be related to the less instructed many in a manner very different from this? Why should not this class create an atmosphere, not merely of exemplary morals and refined manners, but of palpable utility and blessing? Why should not the Clergyman, the Doctor, the Lawyer, of a country town be not merely the patrons and commenders of every generous idea, the teachers and dispensers of all that is novel in Science or noble in Philosophy—exemplars of Integrity, of Amenity, and of an all-pervading Humanity to those around them—but even in a more material sphere regarded and blessed as universal benefactors? Why should they not be universally—as I rejoice to say that some of them are—models of wisdom and thrift in Agriculture—their farms and gardens silent but most effective preachers of the benefits of forecast, calculation, thorough knowledge and faithful application? Nay, more: Why should not the Educated Class be everywhere teachers, through lectures, essays, conversations, as well as practically, of those great and important truths of Nature, which Chemistry and other sciences are just revealing to bless the Industrial world? Why should they not unobtrusively and freely teach the Farmer, the Mechanic, the Worker in any capacity, how best to summon the blind forces of the elements to his aid and how most effectually to render them subservient to his needs? All this is clearly within the power of the Educated Class, if truly educated; all this is clearly within the sphere of duty appointed them by Providence. Let them but *do* it, and they will stand, where they ought to stand, at the head of the community, the directors of Public

Opinion and the universally recognized benefactors of the Race.

I stand before an audience in good part of Educated men, and I plead for the essential independence of their class—not for their sakes only or mainly, but for the sake of Mankind. I see clearly, or I am strangely bewildered, a deep-rooted and wide-spreading evil which is palsying the influence and paralyzing the exertions of Intellectual and even Moral superiority all over our Country. The lawyer, so far at least as his livelihood is concerned, is too generally *but* a lawyer; he must live by law or he has no means of living at all. So with the Doctor; so alas! with the Pastor. He, too, often finds himself surrounded by a large, expensive family, few or none of whom have been systematically trained to earn their bread in the sweat of their brows, and who, even if approaching maturity in life, lean on him for a subsistence. This son must be sent to the academy, and that one to College; this daughter to an expensive boarding-school, and that must have a piano—and all to be defrayed from his salary, which, however liberal, is scarcely or barely adequate to meet the demands upon it. How shall this man—for man, after all, he is—with expenses, and cares, and debts pressing upon him—hope to be at all times faithful to the responsibilities of his high calling! He may speak ever so fluently and feelingly against sin in the abstract, for that can not give offence to the most fastidiously sensitive incumbent of the richly furnished hundred-dollar pews. But will he dare to rebuke openly, fearlessly, specially, the darling and decorous vices of his most opulent and liberal parishioners—to say to the honored dispenser of liquid poison, "*Your* trade is murder, and your wealth the price of perdition!"—To him who amasses wealth by stinting honest Labor of its reward and grinding the faces of the Poor, "Do not mock God by putting your reluctant dollar into the Missionary box—there is no such heathen in New Zealand as yourself!"—and so to every specious hypocrite around him, who patronizes the church to keep to windward of his conscience and freshen the varnish on his character, '*Thou* art the man!' I tell you, friends! he will not, for he can not afford to, be thoroughly faithful! One in a thousand may be, and hardly more. We do not half comprehend the profound significance of that statute of the old Church which inflexibly enjoins celibacy on her Clergy. The very existence of the Church, as a steadfast power above the multitude, giving law to the People and not receiving its law day by day from them, depends on its maintenance. And if we are ever to enjoy a Christian Ministry which shall systematically, promptly, fearlessly war upon every shape and disguise of evil—which shall fearlessly grapple with War and Slavery, and every loathsome device by which man seeks to glut his appetites at the expense of his brother's well-being, it will be secured to us through the instrumentality of the very Reform I advocate—a Reform which shall render the clergyman independent of his parishioners, and enable him to say manfully to all, "You may cease to pay, but I shall not cease to preach, so long as you have sins to reprove, and I have strength to reprove them! I live in good part by the labor of my hands, and can do so wholly whenever that shall become necessary to the fearless discharge of my duty."

A single illustration more, and I draw this long dissertation to a close. I shall speak now more directly to facts within my own knowledge, and which have made on me a deep and mournful impression. I speak to *your* experience, too, friends of the Phenix and Union Societies—to your future if not to your past experience—and I entreat you to heed me! Every year sends forth from our Colleges an army of brave youth, who have nearly or quite exhausted their little means in procuring what is termed an education, and must now find some remunerating employment to sustain them while they are more specially fitting themselves for and inducting themselves into a Profession. Some of them find and are perforce contented with some meager clerkship; but the great body of them turn their attention at once to Literature—to the instruction of their juniors in some school or family, or to the instruction of the world through the Press. Hundreds of them hurry at once to the cities and the journals, seeking employment as essayists or collectors of intelligence—bright visions of Fame in the foreground, and the gaunt wolf Famine hard at their heels. Alas for them! they do not see that the very circumstances under which they seek admission to the calling they have chosen almost forbid the idea of their succeeding in it. They do not approach the public with thoughts struggling for utterance, but with stomachs craving bread. They seek the Press, not that they may proclaim through it what it would cost their lives to repress, but that they may preserve their souls to their bodies, at some rate. Do you not see under what immense disadvantages one of this band enters upon his selected vocation, if he has the rare fortune to find or make a place in it? He is surrounded, elbowed on every side by anxious hundreds, eager to obtain employment on any terms; he must write not what he feels, but what another needs; must 'regret' or 'rejoice' to order, working for the day, and not venturing to utter a thought which the day does not readily approve. And can you fancy *that* is the foundation on which to build a lofty and durable renown—a brave and laudable success of any kind? I tell you, no, young friends!—the farthest from it possible. There is scarcely any position more perilous to generous impulses and lofty aims—scarcely any which more imminently threatens to sink the Man in the mere schemer and striver for subsistence and selfish gratification. I say, then, in deep earnestness, to every youth who hopes or desires to become useful to his Race or in any degree eminent through Literature, Seek first of all things a position of pecuniary independence; learn to live by the labor of your hands, the sweat of your face, as a necessary step toward the career you contemplate. If you can earn but three shillings a day by rugged yet moderate toil, learn to live contentedly on two shillings, and so preserve your mental faculties fresh and unworn to read, to observe, to think, thus preparing yourself for the ultimate path you have chosen. At length, when a mind crowded with discovered or elaborated truths *will* have utterance, begin to write sparingly and tersely for the nearest suitable periodical—no matter how humble and obscure—if the thought is in you, it will find its way to those who need it. Seek not compensation for this utterance until compensation shall seek you; then accept it if an object, and not involving too great sacrifices of independence and disregard of more immediate duties. In this way alone can something like the proper dignity of the Literary Character be restored and maintained. But while every man who either is or believes himself capable of enlightening others, appears only anxious to sell his faculty at the earliest moment and for the largest price, I can not hope that the Public will be induced to regard very profoundly either the lesson or the teacher.

Graduates, Students of Hamilton College! a parting word with you! Some of you have completed your studies and are now passing out into the actual world, to be followed in successive years by your brethren whom you now leave behind you. I will not doubt that you bid adieu to these scenes with lofty purposes of usefulness—with a proper appreciation of the advantages over the great mass of your countrymen which have been here afforded you, and of the obligations which these advantages draw after them. I am not so far removed from youth as to have forgotten all its sanguine visions and generous aspirations. I bid you cherish them each and all, for they are wiser than the cold lesson which disappointment and experienced treachery may afterward teach you. O be assured, above all things, that no generous and self-forgetting aspiration can ever be unwise or mistaken while the Universe obeys a scepter and Earth revolves beneath the eye of a benignant Father! I know not whether I may hope in this hurried communion to have implanted in one breast a clearer or nobler idea of the true purposes and aims of Life—I may not confidently trust that I have imparted to one mind a deeper disdain of those bubbles surnamed Luxury, Ease, Wealth, Power, Popularity, Honors, by which many an ardent and capacious soul has been deluded to its ruin. But you are by position Scholars, and by virtue of that position you must realize—at least, in your calmer and better moments, when that which is immortal is not stifled within you—that a true Life is the one thing desirable to Man on earth, for and in itself—that Virtue, being truly such, transcends all idea of reward, and becomes to the spiritual what gravitation is to the material world—a law which will not be evaded. He who truly, fully apprehends the one fact that GOD REIGNS, knows all that can be of morality—knows that no conceivable divergence from the line of strictest rectitude, of loftiest endeavor, can possibly be otherwise than calamitous in and of itself, wholly apart from all extraneous conditions and consequences. I shall not, then, exhort you to follow Purity and Righteousness, since the admonition would imply a possible ignorance on your part of the existence of the All-Wise—of the laws of your own being. But I may warn you, friends! of the mistake so commonly made by our educated youth of lingering long by the wayside of active life, under the pretence—very often alleged in good faith—of a want of opportunity. O, deceive not yourselves thus, young men! To the rightly constituted mind, to the truly developed Man, there always is, there always must be opportunity—opportunity to be and to learn, nobly to do and to endure—and what matter whether with pomp, and eclat, with sound of trumpets and shout of applauding thousands, or in silence and seclusion, beneath the calm, discerning gaze of Heaven? O realize that no station can be humble on which that gaze is approvingly bent—that no work can be ignoble which is performed uprightly and not impelled by sordid and selfish aims. It is a vital defect of our Society and our Culture, which you are bound to wrestle against and to overcome, that while an immensity of effort is ever needed, of true work remains undone, we are too generally dissatisfied with that which lies broad and plain before us, and waste our hours in seeking long and far for something loftier and nobler. We wander to the Poles and the Antipodes, vainly seeking for that which to the man at peace with himself is everywhere, to the unquiet nowhere. Vainly sighing for the opportunity of some other, which his genius and ready acceptance have made the basis of an illustrious and dazzling career, we neglect and sacrifice our own. We speak regretfully of the age of Chivalry, the age of Heroism or of perilous and doubtful struggle for Freedom, as if we did not recognize that Man's struggle with darkness and evil is ever in progress, and that to render any age one of heroism nothing is wanting but heroic souls. Waiting for the dead Past to be acted over again for our selfish gratification and aggrandizement, we suffer the precious and living Present to glide away from us undervalued and unimproved. Says a deep, fearless thinker* of our time, "To-Day is a king in disguise. To-Day always looks common and trivial, in the face of a uniform experience that all great and happy actions have been made up of these same blank To-Days. Let us unmask the king as he passes." Yes, my young friends, here is our high privilege and our imperative duty—to discern and honor the disguised angels whom God is ever sending to illumine and bless his earth. Not from

* Ralph Waldo Emerson—Lecture on 'the Times.'

among the children of monarchs, ushered into being with boom of cannon and shouts of reveling millions, but from amid the sons of obscurity and toil, cradled in peril and ignominy—from the bulrushes and the manger come forth the benefactors and saviors of Mankind. So when all the babble and glare of our age shall have passed into a fitting oblivion—when those who have enjoyed rare opportunities and swayed vast empires, and been borne through life on the shoulders of shouting multitudes, shall have been laid at last to rest in golden coffins, to molder forgotten, the stately marble their only monuments, it will be found that some humble youth, who neither inherited nor found but hewed out his opportunities, has uttered the thought which shall render the age memorable by extending the means of enlightenment and blessing to our Race. The great struggle for Human Progress and Elevation proceeds noiselessly, often unnoted, often checked and apparently baffled, amid the clamorous and debasing strifes impelled by greedy selfishness and low ambition. In that struggle, maintained by the wise and good of all parties, all creeds, all climes, I call you to bear the part of men. Heed the lofty summons, not the feeble messenger, and, with souls serene and constant, prepare to tread boldly in the path of highest duty. So shall Life be to you truly exalted and heroic; so shall Death be a transition neither sought nor dreaded; so shall your memory, though cherished at first but by a few humble, loving hearts, linger long and gratefully in human remembrance, a watchword to the truthful and an incitement to generous endeavor, freshened by the proud tears of admiring affection, and fragrant with the odors of Heaven!

V.

HUMAN LIFE:

A LECTURE.

To the piercing gaze of an unfettered spirit, unmindful of space, which should scan it from the central orb of our system, this fair globe must afford a spectacle of strange magnificence and beauty. Rolling on, ever on, in her appointed round, the earth must present new scenes of interest and grandeur with every hour of her revolving progress: now the swarming vales of China and Japan, the sultry plains of India, with its tiger-haunted jungles, relieved by the gaunt, bleak piles of the Himmalehs, piercing the very skies with their pinnacles of eternal rock and ice; then appear the more alluring and variegated glades of Southern and Middle Europe, and with them the scorched and glowing deserts of Africa, shining in silvery worthlessness and arid desolation. The broad green belt of the billowy Atlantic now unfolds itself, and then appears the deeper green of this immense, luxuriant forest, America, with the achievements of three centuries of advancing, struggling civilization, barely sufficing to dot irregularly its eastern border, and hardly equaling in extent those prairie openings in its center which Nature, or rather the Red Man's annual conflagration, has sufficed through many ages to hollow out by imperceptible gradations. From amid the all-embracing foliage, shine forth with steady radiance, with deep serenity, the mirror-like surfaces of the Great Lakes — the last surpassing in size, profundity, and beauty — the slender threads of the Father of Waters and his far-stretching tributaries are seen disparting vales whose exuberant fertility has known no parallel since Eden; while farther on, the tremendous chains of the Andes, the Rocky Mountains, heave up their scathed and rugged sides through the surrounding seas of verdure, as if in grim and haughty defiance to the utmost fury of the lightning and the hurricane, or in scornful exultation over the crouching world at their feet. Soon the broad, placid surface of the vast, unvexed Pacific presents itself, sprinkled with isles of deepest emerald where flowers perennial bloom. And still the earth rolls on, and every hour shall bring to view fresh marvels to awaken the soul to a consciousness of the Infinite, to deepen the fervor of piety, and exalt the glory of the Great Supreme.

Yet, beyond doubt, the central figure of this vast wonder-work of creation, around which all other entities and seemings cluster and revolve, is MAN. He is the presiding genius — the lord of the heritage. It is his presence which gives significance and interest to the landscape, which elevates fertility and beauty above barrenness and decay. Not in laughing meads nor rippling streamlets, not in broad blue lakes nor foaming cataracts — not even in these vast, eternal forests, with their cavernous depths, their waving, swelling expanse of surface, their changing garniture, so green, and now so golden — not in these — in any or all of them — does the soul of Nature find utterance. On no wild mountain-crag or lone savannah would the spirit-gaze dwell with clinging earnestness. But on the scenes of Man's earliest, sternest, most momentous conflicts with nature, with destiny, or with his own blinding, blasting evil passions — on the narrow defile where the Spartan handfull withstood the gathered might of a continent — the battle-field where a world was lost and won — on the widowed solitude wherein Rome broods disconsolate over the fading wreck of her grandeur and her power, or the wintry desolation wherein gray-haired Jerusalem crouches amid the ruins of her once impregnable towers and peerless temples—the ashes of her self-abasement trampled into her furrowed brow by the iron heel of sixty generations of tyrants. Through all circumstances, all events, this truth presents itself, that Man's being is the essential fact, his spirit the imparted vitality of the world.

Human Life! how inspiring, how boundless the theme! Sadly, wildly has the Poet sung of it—calmly, lucidly has the Historian traced its meanderings—earnestly, gravely have the Priest and the Sage exposed and reproved its errors from the birth of the Race. The Nurse's story depicts it—the Scholar's research illustrates—the Statesman's harangue illumines and exalts. From the cradle over which the young mother bends with a novel sensation of wondering delight, to the bier around which all are melted in the brotherhood of a common sorrow, this life of ours is a marvel and a poem.

Are we dwellers in the country? From that low-roofed cottage a youth is going forth, with lofty heart, to do and dare on the great battle-field of manly adventure. He has given ear to a father's counsel, he has knelt to receive a mother's blessing; he has smiled at the fears and regrets expressed by younger or tenderer hearts around him: for a sanguine spirit urges him on, and he sees already fortune and honors awaiting him in the distant city to which his eager footsteps tend. Not till the hour of parting has come and passed does he feel how heavy the chain *he* drags who goes forth for years from all he loves on earth—not till the stately, branching elms which overhang the dear spot have waved their last mute adieu to his backward glances—not till the stream which was the companion of his boyish pastimes has bent away from his rigid course and buried itself among the wooded hills, does he feel that he has shaken off the companionships and supports of his youth, and is utterly alone. Now nerve your quivering heart, young adventurer! Summon every thought of hope, and pride, and shame, and press sternly onward; for a feather's weight might almost suffice to dash all your high resolutions—to chase away the dreams of hope and ambition, and send you back, an early penitent, to that lowly home which never seemed half so dear before.

Are we dwellers by the sea-side? Here the sailor is bending the white canvas for a voyage—it may be around the world. Before he shall again drop anchor in the haven he deems his home, he may from his vessel's deck gaze on the peaks of the Andes, the sulphurous flames of Kirauea, or may thread with his bark the perilous windings of the forest-mantled Oregon—may survey the porcelain towers of Canton, or the naked site of Troy, whose very ruins have vanished, leaving no monument of their existence save in Homer's undying song.

Here, too, the emigrant is bidding adieu to the ungenial land of his birth and his love, and, with his household gods around him, is seeking on a distant shore a soil on which his hopes may expand and flourish. There is sadness, there is anguish in the parting hour: the tree most carefully transplanted must leave too many fibres in its native soil: and the life-long dweller in some secluded valley, who first finds himself confronted with a thousand leagues of raging brine, across which lies the way to his unknown future home, may well recoil and shudder at the prospect. But the hoarse order to embark is given and obeyed: the last adieux are looked from streaming eyes; the vessel swings slowly from her moorings; the young look out in wonder on the bleak waste of stormy waters, and turn inquiringly to those who are perchance as young in this hour's sensations as they. And so wears on the passage; and at length, amid new scenes, new toils, anxieties and troubles, the pilgrim finds that Care rests its eternal burden on Man wherever he is found—that Earth has no more an Eden. What recks it? The same blue heaven bends lovingly over all the children of men. New scenes, new hopes, new prospects, speedily dim the memory of keenest disappointments, of deepest regrets; and the heart, transplanted, sends out its tendrils in every direction, and learns to blossom and grow again. And thus do all of us, each in his appointed sphere and season, open new chapters in the great volume of Human Life.

But let us not contemplate only individual aspects. This Life of ours has grander proportions if we can but widen the sweep of our vision so as to reach its far horizon. Those daily acts, those common impulses, which, viewed individually, and with microscopic or with soulless gaze, seem insignificant or trifling, take on a different aspect if regarded in a more catholic spirit. Those myriad hammers which, impelled by brawny arms, are ringing out their rude melody day by day, and contributing to the comfort and sustenance of Man—those fleets of hardy fishers, now chasing the whale on the other side of the globe to give light to the city mansion and celerity to the wheels of the village factory—those armies of trappers, scattered through the glens of the Rocky Mountains, each in stealthy solitude pursuing his deadly trade, whence dames of London and belles of Pekin alike shall borrow warmth and comeliness—let us contemplate these in their several classes, unmindful of the leagues of wood, or plain, or water which chance to divide them. Readily enough do we perceive and acknowledge the grandeur of the great army which some chief or despot assembles and draws out to feed his vanity by display or his ambition by carnage; but the larger and nobler armies whose weapons are the mattock and spade, who overspread the hills and line the valleys, until beneath their rugged skill and persevering effort a highway of Commerce is opened where late the panther leaped, the deer disported—is not theirs the nobler spectacle—more worthy of the orator's apostrophe, the poet's song? Let us look boldly, broadly out on Nature's wide domain. Let us note the irregular yet persistent advance of the pioneers of civilization—the forest conquerors, before whose lusty strokes and sharp blades the century-crowned wood-monarchs, rank after rank, come crashing to the earth. From age to age have they kept apart the soil and sunshine, as they shall do no longer. Onward, still onward, pours the army of axe-men, and still before them bow their stubborn foes. But yesterday their advance was checked by the Ohio; to-day it has crossed the Missouri, the Kansas, and is fast on the heels of the flying buffalo. In the eye of a true discernment, what host of Xerxes or Cæsar, of Frederick or Napoleon, ever equaled this in majesty, in greatness of conquest, or in true glory?

The mastery of Man over Nature—this is an inspiring truth which we must not suffer from its familiarity to lose its force. By the might of his intellect, Man has not merely made the Elephant his drudge, the Lion his diversion, the Whale his magazine, but even the subtlest and most terrible of the elements is the submissive instrument of his will. He turns aside or garners up the lightning; the rivers toil in his workshop; the tides of ocean bear his burdens; the hurricane rages for his use and profit. Fire and water struggle for mastery that he may be whisked over hill and valley with the celerity of the sunbeam. The stillness of the forest midnight is broken by the snort of the Iron Horse, as he drags the long train from Lakes to Ocean with a slave's docility, a giant's strength. Up the long hill he labors, over the deep glen he skims, the tops of the tall trees swaying around and below his narrow path. His sharp, quick breathings bespeak his impetuous progress; a stream of fire reflects its course. On dashes the resistless, tireless steed, and the morrow's sun shall find him at rest in some far mart of Commerce, and the partakers of his wizzard journey scattered to their vocations of trade or pleasure, unthinking of their night's adventure. What has old Romance wherewith to match the every-day realities of the Nineteenth Century?

We are in no danger of estimating too highly the extraordinary character of the age in which our lot has been cast, and of the influences by which we are surrounded. The Present is the proper theme of Poetry, the fitting scene of Romance. Whoever shall even faintly realize the mighty events, the stirring impulses, the lofty character of our time, is in no danger of passing through life groveling and unobservant as the dull beast that crops the thistles by the wayside. The Past has its lessons, doubtless, and well is it for those who master and heed them; but, were it otherwise, the Present has themes enough of ennobling interest to employ all our faculties—to engross all our thoughts, save as they should contemplate the still grander, vaster Hereafter. Do they talk to us of Grecian or Roman heroism? They say well; but Genius died not with Greece; and Heroism has scarcely a recorded achievement which our own age could not parallel. What momentary deed of reckless valor can compare with the life-long self-devotion of the Missionary in some far cluster of Indian lodges, of Tartar huts, cut off from society, from sympathy, and from earthly hope? How easy, how common, to dare death with Alexander! how rare to live nobly as Washington, and feel no ambition but that of doing good! Take the efforts for the elevation of the African race in our day—ill-directed as some of them appear—and yet Antiquity might well be challenged to produce anything out of the sphere of Sacred History half so heroic and divine. Let us, then, waste little time in looking back to earlier ages for high examples and deeds that stir the blood. Let us not idly imagine that the Old World embosoms scenes and memorials dearer to the lover of Truth, of Freedom, and of Man, than those of our own clime. Let us repel alike the braggart's vain-glory and the self-disparagement of degeneracy, yet cherish the faith that nowhere are there purer skies, more inspiring recollections, or more magnificent landscapes than those in which our own green land rejoices. Where shall the patriot pulse beat high if not on Bunker Hill or Saratoga? Where has Nature displayed her grandeur if not in the great Valley of the Father of Waters? Are not the scenes of Man's noblest efforts, of God's rarest earthly handiwork, all around and among us? Have not *I* listened to the roar of Niagara and stood by the grave of Mount Vernon!

Let me not be accused of dwelling too long on the visible and the palpable—on external Nature when my theme regards internal Man. No reflecting mind can hesitate to admit that to a great extent the circumstances shape the man. None of us would have difficulty in pointing out among his circle one at least who would have been a Catholic at Rome, a Turk (if born such) at Constantinople, an idolater at Pekin—would it be as easy to instance one who would *not* be thus molded? As with the highest of all human affirmations—Faith in God—so with our lower deeds and developments. All know that the mountaineer is more hardy than the dweller in the vales beneath—the native of a rugged climate than he who is ripened beneath an equatorial sun. Have not the raw breezes from snow-clad hights been ever held an inspiration to the soul of Liberty? Is not the sailor oftenest born beside the heaving expanse which he chooses for his home? I would not explain all differences of character or capacity by the action of extraneous influences on the immortal spirit—the organs of the Phrenologist, the decree of the fatalist, the circumstances of the Owenite—and yet I shrink from the temerity of setting bounds to their sway. Though we speak of the inscrutable ways of the Deity, we accuse only our own imperfectness of vision. The eye of Faith, and not less that of Reason, recognize in all His ways regular successions of effect to cause, from the warming into life of an insect to the creation of a world. If, then, we read that the son and heir of a wise and good ruler proved a weak yet bloody tyrant, let us not rashly infer the procession of Evil from Good. We have yet to be assured that the good king was an equally good father — that pressing cares of state, or possibly some defect of character, did not incline him to neglect the great duty of training up his son, and imbuing him with the seeds of all moral good. So with the reprobate and outcast scion of an exemplary house — we *say*, indeed, that his opportunities of good were equal to those of his brethren, and his temptations to wrong no greater than theirs; but how do we *know?* It were well for the safety of our ready and confident assertion if we had first assured ourselves that no inherent vice of physical organization — no bodily defect preceding the susceptibility to a moral impression — no silent, unnoted, but yet potent agency, has produced the disparity we observe and lament, before we had so positively concluded that men may gather grapes of thorns, or figs of thistles.

Yet let us not hotly and heedlessly pursue this truth till we lose ourselves and it in the mazes of error, the opposite of that we would dissipate. There is very much of human attainment dependent on circumstances; let us not forget how much also — I will not say how vastly more — depends on essential Man. There is a deplorably immense multitude who live but to eat bounteously and daintily — with whom the sum of life is practically to compass the largest amount of rich viands and gaudy trappings with the smallest outlay of effort or perseverance to procure them — this mass will be at Rome Romans, at Moscow Russians, and nothing more. There will he some small varieties or shadings of individual character, calculated to gratify by their study the minute curiosity of an entomologist, and interesting to him only. But let one of these human ephemera be awakened, however casually or blindly, to the higher impulses, the nobler ends of our being, and he is instantly transferred to a different world—or rather, the world which surrounds him takes on a different aspect, and what before was bleak waste or dull expanse of wooded hight and low herbage, assumes a deep spiritual significance. To his unfolding, wondering soul, Nature is no more a Poet's rhapsody, a Chemist's generalization, but a living presence, a solemn yet cheering companionship. No matter whether he be, in social position, a peer or peasant, by birth Danish or Egyptian, one glance at the world within has placed him with those whose countrymen and brethren are all Mankind. He has no need now to change his daily pursuit or outward condition, for he has risen by inevitable force to an atmosphere of serenity, above the influence of merely external influences and petty limitations. He has not toilsomely but naturally attained a condition in which the soul no longer blindly pants for eminence or homage, but realizes intensely that nobly to Do for the sake of nobly Doing and its intrinsic results—rightly to Be for the sake of rightly Being—discarding 'the lust to shine or rule,' is the true end of life.

And here let me hazard the remark that our unquietness, our ant-hill bustle, is the severest criticism on our present intellectual condition and efforts. True greatness may be said to resemble the water in some perennial fountain, which rises ever and spontaneously, because in communication with some exhaustless reservoir more capacious and higher than itself; while the effort to be great is like the stream forced up by some engine or hydrant, which towers a moment unsteadily and then falls to water but the weeds by the way-side. And thus our young men of promise, who would seem to be touched by a live coal from off the altar of Genius—whom we are led fondly to regard as the light and the hope of our age—the heralds and the hasteners of that fairer future our hearts so throbbingly anticipate — seem for the most part to lack that element of natural quietude, of unconscious strength, which we are rightly accustomed to consider a prediction and an accompaniment of the highest Manhood. Here in some rude hamlet — in some boorish neighborhood — there starts into view a rare youth, whom the Divine spark would seem to have quickened — who bids fair to freshen by at least a chaplet the dusty pathway of human endeavor. But forthwith the genius must be bandaged into rigidity — some education society, or kindred contrivance for the promotion of dullness and mediocrity, must take hold of him and place him in its go-cart — there must be tomes of word-knowledge and the petrifactions of by-gone wisdom hurled through his cranium — he must be led away from all useful labor of the hands, and his already precocious intellect subjected to the hot-house culture of some seminary, no matter how unsuited to his mental or social condition; thus losing his independence, essential and pecuniary, and putting his whole life upon a single throw of the dice, and they so loaded that the chances are heavily against him. And this is called developing the man, and making the most of his natural gifts, though it would seem quite as likely to blast them altogether. With new scenes and an utter transformation of attitude and aims, come strange and dizzying excitement, extravagant hopes, inordinate ambition, along with novel temptings to dissipation on the one hand, as well as to excessive study on the other. I will not say that the result of this course may not in most instances be satisfactory; I only urge that you put at hazard the youth whom *Nature* has marked for noble ends, trusting to make of him the man of profound acquirement, who after all may be worth less than the material out of which he was constructed. May we not rather trust something to Nature? Would we willingly exchange to-day the Robert Burns she gave us for his counterpart educated in a University?

would we not prefer that the poor, rudely taught Ayrshire plowman had never seen Edinburgh and its cultivated circles at all?

And yet I have only taken hold of one corner of the forcing system. Its widest if not its worst evils are felt by those our *impromptu* collegian leaves behind him—in the conviction impressed upon the youth left in the hamlet that they can never be anything but ox-drivers, because they can not enjoy the advantages of what is termed a Classical Education. Hence the poison of disquiet and discontent—the irresolution to act worthily under a mistaken impression that adverse circumstances have forbidden that anything shall worthily be done. I confess I look with anxiety on what seems to me the perverted aspiration so universal among us. There is an incessant straining for outward and visible advantages—to be Legislators, Governors, Professional men, Teachers—there is too little appreciation of that greatness which is intrinsic and above the reach of accident. I am not insensible to the advantages of a systematic induction into all the arcana of Science—of a knowledge of Languages and a mastery of their vast treasures—the possession even of power and its honors. All these are well in their way, but they are not properly within the legitimate reach of all who feel that they have souls.

More intently than even these I would have our young men contemplate and be moulded upon such characters and lives as those of our FRANKLIN, the penniless, active Apprentice, the thriving, contented Mechanic, the peerless Philosopher, the idolized yet not flattered ambassador; our WASHINGTON, carrying the surveyor's chain through swamp and briar, forming with his own hatchet a rude raft for crossing the deep-shaded, savage-haunted Ohio; long and ably defending his country at the head of her armies; at length laying aside the care of a Nation's destinies, resisting the affectionate entreaties of millions that he would continue to bear sway over half a continent, in order that he may enjoy, for the brief remainder of an active, glorious life, the blessings of the domestic fireside, the untroubled sleep which comes only to the couch of private life. There is here a sweet unconsciousness of greatness that we realize and cling to at a glance. We recognise under every change of circumstance the strong and true Man, superior to any freak of Fortune. No culture could have made these men more or less than they appear alike to us and to all observers. Is not the lesson they teach us at once distinct and invigorating?

Let me not be misunderstood. I value and prize Learning, Knowledge, Culture, while esteeming Self-Culture and Self-Development the sum of them all. I would have no youth reject facilities for acquiring them which may fairly and justly present themselves, so that he may embrace them without sacrifice of his proper independence or neglect of his proper duties and responsibilities as a son, a brother, a citizen. What I object to is the too common notion that the higher Education of the Schools is *essential* to his development and his usefulness in life, thus making the Circumstances everything, the Man nothing. If I have not incorrectly observed, the effect of this prevalent impression is often to pervert and misplace the individual whom it specially contemplates, while it is morally certain to work injury to the great mass of his brethren by original condition. A youth in humble life evinces talent, genius, or the love of knowledge and facility of acquiring it, which are quite commonly confounded with either or both. Forthwith he must be taken hold of, and transplanted, and stimulated to acquirement, in an atmosphere and under influences wholly different from those which have thus far nourished and quickened him. Now I do not say that this novel, stimulating process will necessarily mildew or distort him—I do not say that he is inevitably thrust by it into a strange orbit for which he is unbalanced and unfitted — I do not say that he will be educated into flightiness or dunce-hood, though such cases may be — have been. What I would most earnestly insist on is this, that the continual repetition of this process confirms our aspiring youth in the mistaken impression that they can be nothing without a collegiate education and a profession, while it depresses and stunts the undistinguished many by a still keener humiliation. *They* had not hoped nor aspired to give light to others — they had presumed only to sun themselves in the rays of intellect which had burst on their own unnoted sphere. In the young aspirant to whom their village, their class, had given birth, they recognized with gladness and pride an evidence of the essential brotherhood of Man — a link between the lowliest and the most exalted. He has shed a redeeming halo of glory and beauty, of hope and joy, over the triteness and drudgery of their daily paths. But, in the first moment of their fond exultation, the unfolding genius expands its new-found wings and soars beyond their sphere, leaving them to gaze with sinking heart on its ascending, receding flight, troubled and depressed where they should have been assured and strengthened. As a farmer, an artisan in their midst, he would have been their glory and blessing — their 'guide, philosopher and friend' — for there is nothing in the contact of true genius which discourages nor disconcerts; but he hies away to some distant city or seminary; and now he is no longer of them, but has visibly enrolled himself in a different class, whose members they may admire, look up to, and even reverence, but can not clasp in the bands of a true and genial sympathy. There are too many folds of papyrus between his heart and theirs. What I would urge, then, is this, that the deep want of our time is not a greater number of scholars, professional men, pastors, educators, (though possibly there may be some improvement here in the quality;) the need of new, strong, penetrating and healthy men is felt rather in the less noticeable walks of life. We need to bring the sunlight of Genius to bear on the common walks—to dignify the sphere as well as facilitate the operations of the Useful Arts; to hallow and exalt the pathway of honest, unpretending Industry. It is here that the next decided movement is needed and will be made in the way of Human Progress—not a pushing forward of the vanguard, but a bringing up of the main body. The deep want of the time is that the vast resources and capacities of Mind, the far-stretching powers of Genius and of Science, be brought to bear practically and intimately on Agriculture, the Mechanic Arts, and all the now rude and simple processes of Day-Labor, and not merely that these processes may be perfected and accelerated, but that the benefits of the improvement may accrue in at least equal measure to those whose accustomed means of livelihood—scanty at best—are interfered with and overturned by the change. Not merely that these be measurably enriched, but that they be informed and elevated by the vast industrial transformations now in progress or in embryo, is the obvious requirement. Here opens a field for truly heroic exertion and achievement, far wider and nobler than that of any Political heroism of ancient or modern time, because its results must be deeper, more pervading, more enduring. I would insist, then, that our youth of promise shall not be divorced from the physical toil, the material interests of our and their natal condition, while qualifying themselves for the highest spheres of usefulness and endeavor. I would not have them, like Geography in our atlases, contemplate that hemisphere in which the greatest advances have already been effected, to the exclusion of that wherein the greatest triumphs yet remain to be achieved. I would not have them bedeck themselves in the spoils of by-gone victories, and forget that the adversaries, Ignorance and Obstacle, yet remain formidable and imminent.

But, above all, I would have no youth feel that he is debarred the opportunities of a useful and honorable, if he please, a lofty and heroic career, because the means of obtaining a Classical Education are denied him. I will not point him to the many who have inscribed their names high on the rolls of enviable fame without such Education, for the logic therein implied might as well be used to reconcile him to the loss of an eye or an arm. I will not argue to him that circumstances are indifferent or unimportant; I have freely admitted the contrary. But I would urge to such a one that the *essential* circumstance is the awakening of the soul to a consciousness of its own powers and responsibilities, and that this is determined in the very fact of his seeking, with eye single and heart pure, a larger development, a more thorough culture. This point attained, let him doubt nothing, fear nothing, save his own steadiness of purpose and loftiness of aim. Be not discouraged, then, awakened youth in some lowly cottage, some boorish valley, by the magnitude of others' attainments, the richness of others' facilities for acquiring and investigating, as contrasted with the seeming poverty of your own; but remember and be reverently thankful that the same high stars which, shining so brightly upon the palace, the university, the senate-house, have kindled the souls of philosophers, sages, statesmen in times past, now look down as kindly, inspiringly on you; and in the fact that they have touched an answering chord within you is an earnest that their companionship shall nevermore be sullen nor fruitless. From this hour shall all Nature be your teacher, your ministrant; her infinite grandeur no longer a barren pageant; her weird and solemn voices no more unmeaning sounds. Though they should come to you no more at second-hand from the lips of her Pindar, her Shakspere, they can never more be hushed nor unheeded; they have passed from the realm of darkness, of doubt, of speculation, and become to you the deepest and grandest realities of Human Life!

But Life is not all aspiration. Clouds and shadows overspread even its morning promise; they oftener settle densely and darkly down upon its evening horizon. Let us briefly regard them.

We must begin with that vast, deplorable fact of Sin, which early intrudes itself upon us in any attempt to measure the extent of external influences on the human character: How shall we regard it? It stands before us in all its towering altitude, throwing its gloomy shadows across the whole landscape of Human Life. We must look it fairly in the face, for no survey of our subject can be even superficially correct that affects to disregard it. Sin, without which this world would even now be an Eden, *with* which it is so nearly a Pandemonium—the haggard wrecks of its ravage are all around and among us: they stare upon us from the drunkard's hovel, the felon's dreary cell; they creak in the midnight wind from the murderer's gibbet; they meet us in the most extraordinary events; they hover and flit along our daily paths. The child opens its eyes on a world made foul and wretched by Sin alone, looks but fitfully around on the general desolation, and hastens to plunge in the polluted and polluting current, and dash its waves still higher up the banks which it threatens to overwhelm. Is there a stern fatality in this? Does Innate Depravity, taken in its most positive, emphatic acceptation, sufficiently account for it? I do not perceive that it does. Man's depravity never induces him in material concerns to act so blindly—to give much for nothing—to journey days through mire and thorn for that which is found abundantly at home, and can not be found by thus pursuing it. How shall we account, then, for this universal madness—this horrible infatuation? In pursuing this inquiry, I shall endeavor to state philosophic truth only, and to pursue it by philosophic methods. The *essential* depravity which leads man to trample wilfully on the laws of his Creator—to pursue his own ends indifferently through good and evil, uncaring who suffers so that his gratification is secured—I leave to be exposed and reproved by the Sacred Teacher, while I endeavor in all humility to consider transgression simply as error, and to trace out the nature and source of the immense mistake so generally fallen into by the hapless children of Adam.

The individual Man awakes on earth to moral consciousness, surrounded by warring influences—nay, endued, informed, possessed, by warring impulses. On the one side are arrayed his Passions, such as we now find them, demanding gratification at all cost—Luxury, Power, Ease, and all sensual delights. On the other side, stern as in the primal garden, gleams the Law, saying plainly to all, "Refrain! Obey!" Perhaps it does not become Omnipotence to reason with His creatures minutely and continually on the justice and propriety of His requirements—it is enough that those requirements are distinctly made known. Adam is not told that the interdicted fruit is unpalatable or intrinsically poisonous; it *should* be enough for him to know that it is forbidden. But here, where Divine Law stops, Human Education should begin. What is our knowledge but the collected experience of the Race? and what truth in this so important, so prominent, as that everywhere, in all cases, without the possibility of exception, Virtue secures Happiness and Vice produces Misery?

I insist that this be made the subject of scientific and palpable demonstration. I insist that this is the scope and the fullness of all true teaching, without which all beside is a hollow mockery of knowledge. I insist that the Education which excludes Moral and even Religious culture—using the term Religious in its legitimate relation to the *sentiment* of devotion, and with no regard to creeds or formulas—is at best superficial and defective—it may be, pernicious and destructive. I will not now say how much or how little of Education should be left to the school and its ministrations; but I *do* say, that to talk of a man being educated when he has not yet learned profoundly that any wrong action, however outwardly successful or unrebuked, is a deplorable *mistake* on the part of the wilful doer—a ruinous subtraction from the sum of his own happiness, considered simply in itself and its irresistible consequences—is to use words in utter contempt of their true meaning. Nay, more: our Education should not merely imprint on the mind the general truth already stated, but the full and particular *reasons* for it in all cases—should show why and how the miser, the swindler, the drunkard, the hypocrite, the libertine, all stand in their own light—all make war upon themselves, while they imagine they are draining others' measure of enjoyment to fill to overflowing their own. This truth thoroughly mastered, the road to all desirable knowledge, to all true happiness, lies open and easy before the learner. Shall it not be the triumph of our age to unfold and apply a truth so simple yet so mighty? The child but once suffers by clutching the glowing fire-brand; it knows thenceforth that the warmth so genial in its appointed sphere becomes anguish and destruction if grasped thus recklessly. Is it not time that civilized, cultivated Man were at least as truly wise as the infant?

Let none imagine that I am proposing to cure a cancer of the heart by some external ablution: I have not affirmed that the most lucid teaching, the most careful moral culture, will imbue man necessarily with a *right spirit*. But I do contend that, if all the natural and unavoidable consequences of Crime and Wrong-doing were clearly and fully set before our Youth from infancy, and the events transpiring, the influences surrounding them, were made to illustrate and enforce the lessons so imparted, there would be impediments to *actual* transgression which it would be outright madness to overleap. What thief would steal if he saw the officers of justice ready to seize him in the act, with the door of the State's Prison just opening to receive him? Though fallen as Lucifer, he plainly could not do it. What we need, then, in our Practical Education, is to bring home the consequences of transgression as clearly and directly to every man's understanding as in this instance; to show our youth that they can not possibly step aside from the path of duty without bringing upon themselves suffering and degradation. I would have them taught beyond cavil that any attempt to clutch enjoyment by Sin is as insane as undertaking to warm the hands by grasping a red-hot bar of iron. This teaching does not take the place of truly Religious discipline and culture—it is not intended to do so. A man may be too wise to do wrong, and yet be at heart far from right. I urge only that the community should secure itself by teaching the benighted the suicidal mischiefs of wrong-doing, even though the lesson be given without benevolence and received without essential amendment.

Alas for us! we are a dwarfed, distorted Race! We are but the fragments and pigmies of what we might and should be! Here and there we see a Judge, a General, a Ruler—perchance a Poet, an Orator, a Pastor—how seldom a whole and complete Man! Our excellence, what there is of it, runs in veins, in seams, in zig-zags—seldom is it found diffused and equable. Could a mental daguerreotype be held up before us—one on which the fullnesses and deficiencies of the character should vividly appear—what deformities and defects should we not be surprised to discern! far beyond any ability of paint and patches, of whalebone and padding, to disguise or conceal. What indiscreet Philanthropists! what godless Patriots! what uncharitable Devotees! Must we abandon in despair the hope of a truer Manhood? Must Human Virtue be ever a tiny rivulet meandering through a boundless bog of prejudice, selfishness, and passion? Let us hope otherwise.

And yet I derive less encouragement than many are enabled to do from that brilliant aurora in their eyes — in mine it has some suspicious likeness to a meteor, a will-o'-wisp — which they grandly propound as the "Progress of the Human Race." High-sounding words these, and most flattering is their sonorous iteration to our insatiable vanity and conceit. If they were intended only to assert that Human Nature has a *capacity* for vast improvement — that it *ought* to be wiser and better with each successive generation — or even that the small portion of our race which has enjoyed the greatest advantages of position, climate, traditional wisdom, and of Divine enlightenment, *have* improved, *are* improving — I accept it most heartily. But this is by no means all that the flowery orators of our time, the Philosophers of the latest French School and their admiring followers among us, assert and dilate on. They affirm (if I do not greatly misapprehend them) the existence of a principle of Progress in Man — a constant improvement founded in the very laws of his being, — and one of their latest essays declares that in those eras when the Race has appeared visibly, palpably to recede into deeper darkness — as in the centuries which witnessed the decline and subversion of the Roman power — that even then the light was not diminished, but obscured, as when a new load of fuel is thrown upon the roaring fire, diminishing for a season the brightness of the blaze, but increasing the intensity of the heat within. Not so have *I* learned history — not so regarded the monuments or the story of Human Advancement. Whether early Egyptian civilization and culture were in any sense the fruit of growth and progression, and not rather the result of some carefully treasured and guarded traditions of the primal state of Man, may I think be well doubted — I think has been successfully disputed by philosophic and critical observers. The means of positive solution to that deep enigma are doubtless buried for ever with the Priesthood of that mysterious realm. Greek elevation and refinement sprang so directly from a few mighty master-spirits—say Homer, Pythagoras, Plato—that, even under the inspiring influences of clime and scenery, of sea and skies, which will ever make the dwellers by the Ægean and the Adriatic a people eminent for genius and daring, without these we can scarcely imagine the Greece of Miltiades and Leonidas, of Epaminondas and Pericles, to have had an existence. From the humble cot of the peaceful and unregarded student of Nature and votary of Truth, from the tremulous and famine-enfeebled chant of the blind old beggar of Scio, went forth the power which hurled back into the Hellespont the legions of Xerxes and changed the destiny of a world. Roman culture, what there was of it worth recalling and commending, was so directly an imitation of the Greek, that it deserves no special consideration. And so far is continued Progress, higher and higher Attainment, from being, in my view, a law of Human Nature, that I believe the Civilization of Antiquity had attained and passed its zenith before the influence of Christianity began to be intensely felt; and that, but for that influence, so high a point of culture would never, within the range of natural causes, have been reached again. Only through some new infusion of the Divine, could the smouldering embers of Manhood have been kindled to a more genial warmth, a brighter radiance, than had already been manifested.

No! vain is the conceit, mischievous the illusion, that the Human Race progresses by some law of its being, and that the far Future, merely because it *is* future, shall be better and loftier than the Past. Let the dreamer of this flattering vision survey the vain-gloriously styled Celestial Empire, trace back its mouldy chronicles through thirty centuries of utter stagnation—stand upon the ruins (if he can find them) of mighty Babylon, above the fallen and imbedded pillars of her temples, theaters, and palaces, which no longer afford a shelter even for the wolf and hyena, and look abroad on the scattered hordes of miserable and famished robbers of the desert who roam here unconscious that a great city ever existed—explore, if you would rather, the crumbling monuments, the still towering pyramids and delicate sculptures of Palenque and Uxmal, inquire their origin and history of the degraded savages who dwell around them after three centuries of *Christian* teaching, and then judge of the fallacy which affirms Progress to be a law of our Nature, and its unebbing tides the land-marks of Time. No! friends of Man! only through ardent and patient effort, by heroic endurance and high-souled endeavor, aided, impelled by the good Providence of God, and led by those whom *it* leads and vouchsafes us, does the capacity of our Race for improvement and elevation evolve itself. Imperative is the obligation which rests upon us to stand not idly by, expecting the foaming current of human ignorance, error and wrong to exhaust itself, but to embark earnestly in the great work of resisting and overcoming it, assured that only through systematic exertion will it ever be diminished in volume or in force.

But Life has not rugged and repulsive aspects only—even perverted and degraded as it is, it smiles upon us through kindly and sympathizing eyes. Viewed in a genial spirit, it presents themes of elevating, chastening contemplation. Not in the rough and stormy collisions of the market-place, the forum, the senate, the battle-field, are its true nobility, its essential beauty manifested; but in the uncalculating hospitality of some rude squatter on a Texan prairie—in the heart-gushing charity of some Arab or African woman, who in the desert eagerly proffers the scanty morsel of food which stands between her and famine, to nourish the drooping stranger of whose nation she never heard till yesterday—in the clustering around some lowly New-England fireside of the long scattered members of a family which passed its childhood thereby, freely disbursing the hoarded coin they ill can spare, that they may gather from distant Ohio, Iowa, and Mississippi, once more beneath the dear old rafters, so blackened with smoke and age, to receive for the last time the tottering father's grave, affectionate counsel, the pious mother's fervent, tearful blessing. And still the great world rolls on, with empty noise and frivolous iterations, and the impatient soul exclaims, "How fruitless, how tiresome are these succeeding To-Days!—what use to bear with them longer, expecting the good which never comes?" Be not so hasty, choleric friends! Perchance at this very moment, in the brain of some nameless, noteless dreamer, some awkward, bashful boy, whom the world would not condescend even to laugh at, the Idea is silently maturing which shall transform and vivify the whole career of man. Whether it shall assume a Physical or Moral bearing—shall teach us to ride the thunderbolt or revel in the outermost ether—shall bridge the Atlantic, or only bridle its fiercest waves, and cause them to impel the calm, majestic vessel directly athwart their raving breakers—shall detect the hidden metals in the beds a hundred feet below the surface, where they have lain unimagined since creation, or draw from the unfathomed deep the treasures it has amassed through forty centuries, who may tell? Better, doubtless, than any, than all of these, could it secure to every child the blessings of Intellectual and Moral Culture—to every man and woman the means and opportunity of employing the faculties God has given in such manner as best to promote the welfare of all His creatures, while securing beyond contingency a competent support to each.

Of all Reforms not strictly spiritual, that which shall yet secure opportunity and a just and fair reward to every one who is willing to contribute his best exertions in any sphere of industry and usefulness to the aggregate of human efforts for the satisfaction of human wants—which shall secure to every man and woman the Right to Labor, and to enjoy reasonably the fruits of such Labor — appears to me the greatest, the most essential, and one which no generous and enlightened mind can afford to despair of attaining.

— The vital principle which must be the basis of a true life is forgetfulness of self in aspiration for general good. The act, of which selfish gratification or advantage is the impulse, can not be holy nor heroic — it can scarcely be other than ignoble and wrong. A life of selfish aims and exertions! how sordid and despicable! — how groveling its morality — how lean its virtue! — how icy and stolid its innocence! And yet this is the acme of much of the teaching and more of the example of the world. That evil inevitably leads to degradation and misery, this is a truth which should receive every practicable demonstration — which should be early and deeply imprinted on every heart. But the avoidance of evil is a lesson for infancy in moral culture — goodness for the sake of goodness, for the love of goodness, that is the highest inculcation. Not to do right for the sake of happiness, in the usual low sense of the term, but for the sake of Right, is the true precept. The whole life, even of the humblest, should be a spontaneous aspiration. Then Goodness is no more a holiday cloak, a Sunday feat, but a breath, an atmosphere. No longer is the week divided into six days for overreaching our neighbor and one for expiating it to God; but the life becomes integral and consistent, and the daily toil an unmeditated psalm.

The bane of guiltless life among us is excessive, perpetual Care. The eagerness to acquire, the dread to lose — the apprehension of loss of caste, poverty, want, famine — these furrow our brows prematurely with their scathing plowshares. The evils that we really endure are less formidable in amount, perhaps in intensity, than those we suffer from fear alone Not merely is it too true, that

'Getting and spending we lay waste our years;'

but the depressing dread that we shall be cut off from any opportunity to acquire and possess—this wears upon and crushes us. There is more bitterness than levity in the jest that "We have no National amusements but Banking and the Credit system." How many a child is early set to hoarding pence in a box which takes readily but returns none; while its simple, narrow-minded parents imagine that they have given it a noble start on the journey of life! To win money and keep it—this is the great achievement constantly held up before the eyes of our infant Alexanders and Cæsars. 'Whittington and his Cat' are more the objects of Childhood's admiring contemplation than an army of saints and martyrs. How shall such children afterward be taught to believe and realize that Life has higher aims than those of the counter and the market? that a competence is to be valued as enabling to live truly and nobly, and as affording the means of diffusing benefits and blessings, while Self-Culture, the training, development and elevation of the Man, are the true ends of life! It is idle to expect, save rarely, a result contradictory to early and deep impressions. Nay, it is idle to expect that the child which grows up surrounded and impressed by many and painful evidences of the privations and degradations, mental as well as physical, to which the pecuniarily destitute are everywhere subjected, will *not* learn to prize and struggle for Wealth as a chief good. It stands before him the practical barrier between Liberty and Slavery, Power and Insignificance, self-respect and abjectness. It is not merely a means of enjoying and dispensing physical comforts—it is the key to the treasuries of Thought and Knowledge—it is the power of retirement and self-communion. We may teach Man to limit his desires to the last degree, yet the question recurs to him—"Without Property, how shall I have means of satisfying the lowest necessities of physical existence? I may learn to live long on a dollar; but I can not learn to *com-*

mand that dollar, unless some one will employ me, and how shall I be sure of that? If I could live on grass and water, there are those depending on me who can not; what will secure comfort to *them?*" Alas, for this necessity of constant, anxious, earth-embracing care for the supply of temporal wants! Shall we never be able to obey the Divine injunction to 'take no thought for the morrow?'

And here is the root of that demand for a Social Reform which, springing up simultaneously in so many earnest hearts, is beginning at length to make itself heard and felt. The thoughtless Million may scoff, as their prototypes in all ages have scoffed, at ideas which look beyond the sensual wants of the individual and the hour; but the observing understand that these do not even comprehend the evil which is resisted—the change which is desired. It is not merely that the widow and the orphan lack food under our present Social Order—it is not merely the contemplation of the yawning abysses of degradation, misery and crime, into which millions after millions are constantly driven by our Society's harsh denial to them of any honest means of earning their needful bread—though this and its train of consequences are enough to drown a nation in tears of blood—but the cry for a truer Social basis has yet a deeper source than this. It is the Soul's indignant protest against its own perpetual involvement in a system of heartlessness and war—of chaffering and struggling for daily bread, when its healthful existence demands an atmosphere of serenity and love. It willingly proffers physical powers to obtain physical ends—the hands to plant and to build, to fashion and produce; but the surrender of itself to a perpetual round of ignoble anxieties and petty yet exacting collisions, is felt to be too much. The desolate and crushed heart that lives but on one cherished though saddening memory, is willing, nay, eager, to give faithful daily labor for the plainest daily bread; it is the constant, haunting dread that even that hard exchange will not long be attainable—the exposure to rude rebuffs and wounding suspicions in obeying the frequently recurring necessity to seek anew the privilege of giving much toil for little recompense—it is *this* which gnaws and kills. It is the conviction that Society—that of Christendom at least—ought to be a condition not of war but of peace—not of jarring rivalry but of generous emulation in good deeds—not calculated to develop and aggravate, but to chasten and correct whatever in man is selfish and unsympathizing—it is this which underlies and impels the great Social movement, not now prominent to the careless eye, but which is destined to render our age memorable in the history of Man. Let those who think slightingly of this idea of a pervading Reform—a Reform which shall embosom almost every other—ponder the following words of a great man lately departed—the philanthropic yet cautious, high-souled and far-seeing Channing:—

"Our present civilization is characterised and tainted by a devouring greediness of wealth. The passion for gain is everywhere sapping pure, generous feeling, and raising up bitter foes against any reform which may threaten to turn aside the stream of wealth. I sometimes feel as if a great reform were necessary to break up our present mercenary civilization, in order that Christianity, now repelled by the universal worldliness, may come into nearer contact with the soul, and reconstruct Society after its own pure and disinterested principles."

Such thoughts as these are already familiar to many generous hearts, and the number is daily increasing. Let us not fear that they will long remain unacted.

Let none accuse me of the enthusiast's common error—the presumption that the world is to be transformed in a day. I know well how great the interval which ever divides the perception of a noble idea by a few earnest minds from its hearty acceptance, its practical realization, by the great mass of mankind. I know how any such idea must ever suffer from the errors or imperfections of its apostles, from the faithlessness of the selfish and undiscerning, from its perversion and corruption by many on whom it makes an impression. But, on the other hand, I will not close my eyes to the decided progress which Society has made during the last two centuries, nor to the *direction* of that progress. When I perceive that UNITY OF EFFORT, resting on community of interest, has checkered Christendom with roads, bridges, canals, railroads, and before unimagined facilities for the interchange of products and of thought; when I see Universal Education, so recently regarded as a benevolent chimera, now admitted in theory to be essential and attainable, though but distantly approached in practice; when I find the right of the destitute to a support at the public expense admitted and acted upon — blindly, imperfectly, if you please, but still at so serious a cost and with such a uniformity both in time and space as to forbid the idea that it rests on any other foundation than that of acknowledged and imperative duty; when I consider that so few generations have passed since the ignorant and the destitute were left to live in darkness and die by unheeded famine, no man questioning its rightfulness, and the learned, the affluent, the noble blasphemously pronouncing all this the order of Providence! — I will not doubt that all these meliorations of the hard lot of the unfortunate are but slight precursors of the vast Reform which is yet to embosom all other reforms — which is to secure Education and Bread even to the deepest poverty and darkest misfortune, by simply making the sinews, the exertions, of any intelligent child of Adam worth the cost of his instruction and subsistence — which shall replace all our miserable and too often pernicious public and private alms to the vigorous, by a system of undegrading and self-sustaining General Industry, in which a place shall be open to every one who needs or asks it.

Happy he who shall be enabled to show forth in his own what human life should be, unpolluted by evil passions, uncorroded by sordid cares, unchafed by the disappointment of selfish aspirations, ever shielded from the access of temptation and error by finding delight in duty, and a tranquil joy in the widest diffusion of blessings. Happy beyond the power of evil destiny shall he be whose life flows on in one calm, full current of active goodness — of unceasing benevolence to Man, of unbounded reliance on God. Looking back in the evening of his days through the dissolving mists of the past, he shall discern in every trial, Discipline; in every sorrow, the salutary chastening of a Divine beneficence. And when the bowed frame and feeble limbs shall admonish him of failing power to execute the dictates of a still loving heart, he shall need no farther witness of the benignity of that dispensation which Sin recoils from as Death, but, pillowed on that blessed Book, whose promises have lighted the dim pathway to millions, shall sleep to be awakened in Heaven.

VI.

THE ORGANIZATION OF LABOR:

A LECTURE.*

WE are in the depth of Winter. Around us lie strewed the lifeless, decaying wrecks of a world of verdure, growth, and beauty, which has perished forever. Before us stretches a bleak, rugged prospect of ice and snow, of keen north-western blasts and raw north-eastern storms, rattling the bare boughs of a hemisphere of orchard, grove, and forest. All seems stern, joyless, transfixed, congealed as by the frost of Death.

Not so, however. The searching eye, impelled by the loving, trusting heart, discerns on these naked boughs the modest shrinking buds which bespeak the coming Spring — and the precursors of the abundant foliage and gladness of the approaching Summer. The pall of the Present shields while it shrouds the roses of the Future. Nature, so torpid, and dead to the dull, material eye, is even now in her profound laboratories preparing for her coming season of visible, palpable glory. Her night of wintry darkness heralds a rosy, genial dawn.

Thus also in the Moral and in the Social world.

For generations the old Social Machinery has been wearing out — giving way — breaking down. The original division of our Race into a Free class of Warriors and

* In part. The concluding pages as here published are quite different from the Lecture as read, under another title.

Rulers and a Slave caste of Laborers and Cultivators is with difficulty and but partially maintained. With the change of circumstances and of aspirations, the trade of War has fallen into comparative disuse and disrepute, and the governing class seek distinction and advantage on other fields than those of battle. The chiefs advance to the conflict in mail and hemlet as of old, while the undistinguished multitude still fight and fall in relative nakedness; but the armor of the Nineteenth Century is a plethoric pocket-book; its strong fortress is a fire-proof vault, well filled with notes, mortgages, and title-deeds. Ancient Chivalry wasted ten years, with countless lives and treasure, in burning one Troy; its modern counterpart builds half a dozen Lowells and Manchesters in a like period, and at a cost and risk immeasurably less. The 'king of men' of to-day, to whom honors and public trusts are tendered as of right, after whom new cities are named, is a Factory Agent and Railroad Director; a Cotton-spinner overturns the long-cherished policy of Great Britain; a cotton-spinner's son is the most eminent civilian of that mighty realm. Not to ravage and trample down but to cherish, upbuild and direct is the wiser impulse of the powerful of our day with respect to the operations and the results of Productive Industry. Very naturally, the progress and the efficiency of Useful Labor shame all recorded precedent.

But here, on the threshold of our survey, a painful fact confronts and startles us. *Human Labor is efficient beyond example, but the Laboring Class is hardly benefited thereby.* Houses multiply with extreme rapidity, but the number of the houseless is not diminished. The prolific Earth yields larger and larger harvests as wilds are reclaimed and Science is applied to Agriculture, but millions pine and thousands starve for lack of food. Our roads and means of transit are visibly improved from season to season; but our road-makers are no better circumstanced than their grandfathers were. Each year sees the number and value of arable acres increase, while the proportion of those who possess any land in their own right steadily diminishes. Each year produces more and more fuel and cloth, yet witnesses more and more shivering and nakedness. While new inventions and processes are daily rendering material life more smooth and comfortable to the affluent, the number of the destitute, squalid and miserable is steadily on the increase. With an immensely extended and widening demand on every side for Labor, to clear lands, blast rocks, construct houses, factories, dams, and Railroads, to dig Canals, drains, &c., &c., there is a large and increasing host of unemployed laborers, standing idle and gaunt in the market-place, anxious to work that their little ones may not famish, and in danger of sinking into dissipation and crime through despair. 'Men and brethren, what shall we do?'

That wealth and penury advance hand in hand, that the stately, sumptuous mansion implies the lowly, desolate hovel, was long ago noted. The mansion may rise in London or Paris, while the hovel covers in Irish Skibbereen or the Scotch Highlands: the distance of location does not break and should not conceal the chain of cause and effect by which the palace and the hovel are united. We may rehearse the babble of the accredited Political Economists till our own brains are addled and our eyes benighted, and still the fact remains that so long as one man shall be authorized to draw an income of, say $100,000 per annum, from the cultivators of a township or County for the use of the naked earth they stand on, to be increased as Power shall dictate and Need perforce assent, so long must the reward of the Labor expended thereon be meager and its subsistence scanty and precarious; and so long as the maxim is accredited and acted on that the powerful and the shrewd have a clear moral right to use their natural advantages with a single view to their own gratification and aggrandizement, so long must the weak and lowly be crushed and trampled on.

Of the tendencies and goal of the existing Social system, with its legalization of Land Monopoly and cardinal maxim of 'Every man for himself,' Ireland affords at this day the most eminent and striking example. There the soil is by law the property of the few, while the population is dense and relies mainly on Agriculture for subsistence. Vast estates and petty holdings are its main characteristics—estates whose incomes are squandered in luxurious dissipation from Dublin to Venice—holdings which it would seem scarcely possible to draw a family's subsistence from if the landlord's tax on God's naked bounty were a thing unknown. Yet from these mere patches of soil, varying from a rood to an acre in area, rents of five and twenty dollars per acre are extorted. And still men wonder that Ireland is so scourged and famine-stricken!—wonder that her common people are so ignorant and wretched! Is it not the real marvel that they have so long endured and survived their wrongs and oppressions?

Nor ought we to regret that the evil, so long brooding, has reached its crisis before our eyes—that the clouds so long gathering, lowering, muttering, have been rent by the artillery of Heaven and are discharging their furies. Whoever has thoughtfully studied our prevailing maxims of Social Polity, and clearly apprehends their radical vices, must realize that the visitations of Famine in our day are no less obviously judgments than mercies. For, as says the keen-sighted though erratic Carlyle:

"Great is Bankruptcy: the bottomless gulf into which all Falsehoods, public and private, do sink, disappearing; whither, from the first origin of them, they were all doomed. For nature is true, and not a lie. No lie you can speak or act, but it will come, after longer or shorter circulation, like a Bill, drawn on Nature's reality, and be presented there for payment—with the answer, *No Effects.* Pity only that it often had so long a circulation: that the original forger were so seldom he who bore the final smart of it! Lies, and the burden of evil they bring, are passed on; shifted from back to back, and from rank to rank; and so land ultimately on the dumb lowest rank, who, with spade and mattock, with sore heart and empty wallet, daily come in *contact* with reality, and can pass the cheat no farther. * * *

"With a Fortunatus' Purse in its pocket, through what length of time might not almost any Falsehood last! Your Society, your Household, practical or spiritual Arrangement, is untrue, unjust, offensive to the eye of God and man. Nevertheless, its hearth is warm, its larder well replenished; the innumerable Swiss of Heaven, with a kind of natural loyalty, gather round it; will prove, by pamphleteering, musketeering, that it is a Truth; or, if not an unmixed (unearthly, impossible) Truth—then better; a wholesomely attempered one (as the wind is to the shorn lamb,) and works well. Changed outlook, however, when purse and larder grow empty! Was your arrangement so true, so accordant to Nature's ways, then how, in the name of wonder, has Nature, with her infinite bounty, come to leave it famishing there? To all men, to all women and children, it is now indubitable that your Arrangement was *false*. Honor to Bankruptcy! Under all Falsehoods it works, unweariedly mining. No Falsehood, did it rise Heaven high and cover the world, but Bankruptcy, one day, will sweep it down, and make us free of it."

—'Ah! we know!' says the thoughtless conservative, 'that there is a bad state of things *in Ireland;* but what has that to do with *us?* You don't mean to say that *we* are in any such condition?'

Why, sir, do you realize that the anti-reformer in Ireland is just as oblivious to the existence or the curability of evils *there* as you are as to those which cluster or lower *here?* Of course, he does not wish to deny that evils exist; he readily admits that, and contends it is divinely ordained that so it should be. He seeks not to deny that whole neighborhoods are famishing;—but what of it? Did not Christ say, 'The poor ye have *always* with you?' And who should seek to falsify the Savior's prediction? Starvation and wretchedness are by Heavenly appointment—sent to discipline portly, well-to-do Christians in the exercise of Charity. Thus the Poor famish, but that only proves the extent of Human perversity, the desperate viciousness and depravity of the lower class, or the fierceness of the Divine wrath against Sin; and Society stands acquitted of injustice or even improvidence. When some poor peasant, living with his pigs and children in a mud-hovel unfit for the habitation of brutes, driven to despair by the impossibility of subsisting his family, and paying some dollars' rent for a scanty half acre of soil, falls into habits of intemperance, and is ejected for non-payment of rent, *his* fault is exaggerated and his calamity deemed a righteous retribution; while his landlord, who idly enjoys and uselessly expends an income of $50,000 or more, racked from just such half-acres and hovels, walks the earth an honored, smiling, self-satisfied, Christian gentleman, the pride of the County and the idol of those he honors with his intimacy; and when at a ripe age he is gathered to his fathers, florid sermons are preached in commendation of his exemplary life and in glorification of the munificent charity with which he gave back to plundered Poverty a hundredth part of what he took from it. So wags, not Ireland merely, but the world.

Yes, my Conservative friend! not in Ireland only, nor in Europe, nor in the Old World, are there grievous Social wrongs to redress, but here and everywhere. Man deals hardly with his brother—the rich with the poor, the strong with the weak, the landed with the landless. The base of our Social Edifice is not Justice, but Power—the right of the strongest to use his strength, not to upraise but to depress his brother, if he can seemingly profit thereby. Let a conflagration or an earthquake add some thousands to the number of those who must hire houses, and what Christian landlord hesitates to increase his rents? although he well knows that neither his outlay nor the ability of the tenants is increased an atom. Let bread become scarce, and what

Christian merchant, what affluent farmer, hesitates to advance the price of Grain, though the wail of the famished is ringing in his ears? Do we not know that the morality, and even the humanity, of so doing has, after a fashion, been demonstrated, and forms one of the corner-stones of the temple of modern Political Economy? And, the premises being granted, the conclusion is irresistible. The objection applies not to the stone but to the temple. Grant that the earth has been wisely and justly allotted to, or permitted to become, the property of the few to the exclusion of the many, and that every person has a right to use his strength, his skill, or his wit, expressly and primarily for individual gain or advantage, all we see and feel follows of course. The wrong lies at the very foundation of our Social Order, or there is no wrong at all.

But I have premised generally that our Society is unjust: let me briefly indicate in what respects and particular.

When a young man, having devoted the better portion of his minority to the acquirement of some useful trade or handicraft, finds himself of age and an adept in his vocation, yet unable to obtain employment in his calling and unfitted to earn a livelihood out of it—denied even an acre of bare earth on which to earn it—there is an instance of Social defect or injustice.

When a poor laborer, delving in weariness from day to day, finds a promising family growing up around him whom he can not lodge decently, clothe comfortably nor educate thoroughly, but is compelled to dismiss his sons to the temptations and corruptions of the street, while he is off through the day earning their scanty subsistence—there is another whom Society treats unjustly.

When a poor youth, who has devoted every hour of his time, every farthing of his means, to the acquirement of what is called a Liberal Education, finds himself afloat on the great sea without a haven before him—no call for him in any professional capacity, no influential friends to make a position—no fitness, but rather decided unfitness, for usefulness in any mechanical vocation—and has the simple choice afforded him, to beg, starve, or turn his acquirements to some gainful but infamous use—there is another victim of Social injustice.

When a poor man, after drudging steadily at day-labor through the warmer season, finds himself at winter thrown out of employment, with a family that must be fed, a rent that must be paid, and yet no means afforded him of doing either—no reliable barrier against starvation but the Poor-House—there is another whom Society is wronging and tempting to wrong.

Still more, when a poor widow, her earthly reliance and solace lately snatched away by death, finds herself driven by necessity into some miserable garret, there to keep the breath of life in her shivering children from the earnings of her needle—at best hardly twenty-five cents a day, however long that day may be made—from which the food, clothing, rent and fuel of that desolate family are somehow to be extracted—there is not merely grievous suffering but flagrant wrong, at which angels might weep tears of indignant commiseration.

Worse still is the case of the young maiden doomed to poverty and deficient training in one of our great cities, thrown early on her own guidance and exertions, impelled to earn a livelihood by sewing, bookfolding, or any of the principal avocations of women which at best affords a bare subsistence—cursed with 'the fatal gift of Beauty,' and with the necessity of constantly exposing herself, in the pursuit of her humble calling, to contact with all that is corrupt and licentious, and at length thrown out of employment by the paralyzing touch of Winter, with black Necessity drifting her to swift Despair, while Infamy eagerly proffers a life of dazzling Luxury and Ease in exchange for, at best, one of Poverty and Toil. That the exchange is oftener spurned with horror than accepted is honorable to Human Nature; but it is not *always* spurned, as the streets and alleys of our great cities mournfully attest. Accursed be the necessity which thus tramples down Virtue! detested be the Social Injustice in which originated the necessity!

And yet I have heard of such a mockery of Heaven as a clergymen rising before a wealthy and fashionable congregation on a Thanksgiving-Day to express gratitude that, in this favored land, *every one who chooses may earn a comfortable subsistence!* What could the man have meant? Where were his eyes? He might as well have given thanks that no person ever dies here except by his own hand. I can testify from personal experience that there is *not* always work even for the skilful who diligently seek it; much less is there for the unskilled and the simple. That Industry, Energy, Skill and Probity will *eventually* lead to Competence and Respect, may be affirmed without dispute, but to what purpose? The vital question remains: How shall the landless and virtually homeless *evince* these valuable capacities and thereby secure immediate Employment and ultimate Competence? How shall they live while they are waiting the moving of the waters? 'It is the first step that costs!' It is OPPORTUNITY to exhibit the desirable qualities and command a just recompense that I plead for as the natural right of all men; and that this is not now secured is the condemnation of our existing Social Order.

We, then, who stand for a comprehensive and all-pervading Reform in the Social relations of mankind, impeach the present Order as defective and radically vicious in the following important particulars:

1. It does not provide for the Physical, Moral and Intellectual training of the Young, but leaves all to the accident of parental ability and wisdom to nurture and instruct. But in most instances the father, and in many the mother also, is forced by the stern necessity of laboring for bread where

Labor can be obtained, to leave the children to the training of the street—that is, to the training of the most corrupt and worthless portion of the community. The little ones can not be tolerated in the factory, the foundry, nor even the grain-field, until they are fitted for useful toil therein; and the inevitable consequence, as to the most destitute and endangered, is the formation of habits of idleness, profanity and vice, and the utter waste of some of the most precious years of life.

2. It does not secure Opportunity to Labor, nor to acquire Industrial skill and efficiency, to those who most need both. It is a clear general truth that, in the world as we find it, the man who has the means of living for a time without labor need never stand idle; nor need he whose Industrial acquirements enable him to earn in one month the recompense of several months' merely physical toil. But he who is to-day without property and employment has but his chance among many others of finding something to do; and if he is at the same time unskilled for any but the rudest labor, his chance is by far the slenderer. Let him be infirm, or crippled, or by any means reduced below the medium standard of Industrial capacity, and his chance of finding employment is still more meager and doubtful. Thus Society, in strict obedience to its fundamental law, 'Look out for No. 1,' has established a sliding scale of opportunity, whereby every one's chance of finding work is in inverse ratio to the necessity of his obtaining it; and he who could hardly earn a poor subsistence if constantly employed and fairly remunerated, is morally certain to be more frequently idle and more scantily paid than anybody else.

3. We impeach our existing Society that it dooms the most indigent class to pay for whatever of comforts and necessaries they may enjoy—Food, Fuel, Shelter, &c.—at a higher rate comparatively than is exacted of the more affluent classes. The man who must buy as he needs, both

in time and quantity, always pays more than he who buys as he chooses. On this point no argument is necessary; but I apprehend that the extent of the injustice thus inflicted is very rarely considered and appreciated.

4. For the Physical evils it inflicts and renders inevitable, Society has barely two palliatives—Private Alms-giving and the Poor-House. But neither of these is curative in its nature; indeed, each is plainly calculated to render the evils its combats chronic and enduring. No man, I apprehend, was ever cured of Pauperism by the Alms-House; on the contrary, few have submitted to its conscious degradation and retained the moral power to struggle for and regain their independence. Over the entrance to this Hospital of Civilzation might fitly be inscribed the warning which Dante places over the gate of the Infernal Regions:

'All hope abandon, ye who enter here:'

For the man who enters the Alms-House as a pauper confesses that he has been utterly defeated in the grand battle of life and has surrendered at discretion; and he will hardly have the spirit, with his sanguine expectations disappointed, his hopes blasted, his means dissipated and his energies broken, to rally and renew determinedly the combat. To all practical intents, he is henceforth merely a clog and a burden. It is a little better, and but a little, with him who is reduced to receive assistance from friends or others without expecting ever to repay it. He may struggle on, in a dying way, for years; but each recurrence of the necessity and the bounty debases his spirit, relaxes his energies, and floats him nearer and nearer the abyss of utter abasement and listless despair.

Now what is proposed by Social Reformers, regarded merely in its Physical and Economical aspects, is the correction of these mistakes and the removal of their evil consequences. We contend that in a civilized, Christian land, in time and quantity, always pays more than he who buys as he chooses. On this point no argument is necessary; but I apprehend that the extent of the injustice thus inflicted is very rarely considered and appreciated.

4. For the Physical evils it inflicts and renders inevitable, Society has barely two palliatives—Private Alms-giving and the Poor-House. But neither of these is curative in its nature; indeed, each is plainly calculated to render the evils its combats chronic and enduring. No man, I apprehend, was ever cured of Pauperism by the Alms-House; on the contrary, few have submitted to its conscious degradation and retained the moral power to struggle for and regain their independence. Over the entrance to this Hospital of Civilzation might fitly be inscribed the warning which Dante places over the gate of the Infernal Regions:

'All hope abandon, ye who enter here:'

For the man who enters the Alms-House as a pauper confesses that he has been utterly defeated in the grand battle of life and has surrendered at discretion; and he will hardly have the spirit, with his sanguine expectations disappointed, his hopes blasted, his means dissipated and his energies broken, to rally and renew determinedly the combat. To all practical intents, he is henceforth merely a clog and a burden. It is a little better, and but a little, with him who is reduced to receive assistance from friends or others without expecting ever to repay it. He may struggle on, in a dying way, for years; but each recurrence of the necessity and the bounty debases his spirit, relaxes his energies, and floats him nearer and nearer the abyss of utter abasement and listless despair.

Now what is proposed by Social Reformers, regarded merely in its Physical and Economical aspects, is the correction of these mistakes and the removal of their evil consequences. We contend that in a civilized, Christian land,

nal principle or germ of vitality matter collects, disposes itself, attracts, organizes, until the rude and insignificant acorn has become the shapely and towering oak, a thing of infinite uses and of stern endurance. The principle of Organization, of assimilation, once lost, this storm-defying monarch of the hills is helpless, doomed, perishing. A summer breeze prostrates its unwieldy carcass, which has become the unresisting prey of all the elements—of insects the most weak and contemptible. Shall we not profit, morally as well as physically, by his origin and growth, his decline and fall?

Man has organized despotism, carnage, desolation, all with the most palpable and stupendous results. A drilled and well-appointed regiment of one thousand is a full match for an ordinary rabble of ten times the number. Why may not Production be likewise organized? Even in the midst of profound peace, he who would find work as a stabber and fusileer need never look long for an employer at any season, while his more peaceful brother, who revolts at the trade of death, and would gladly be hired to subdue and beautify rather than ravage and desolate the earth, may vainly seek opportunity from door to door, from city to city, and from week to week. Can it be impossible to render work at all times accessible to him also?

Stand by one of our crowded wharves as a steamboat from some other city approaches, and you see before you a very fair daguerreotype of Industry in Civilization. Here are two hundred passengers seeking their various destinations, one-half of whom will probably incur the expense of a ride; here are carriages enough for five hundred eagerly awaiting them; of which, after infinite crowding, jostling, cheating, lying, swearing, four-fifths must go away empty from their thriftless quest; while the residue, after half an hour's service, must each on the average spend three or four hours in anxious pursuit of another customer. Of course, those who are served must pay thrice the worth of the service, while those who wait to serve are in general meagerly rewarded. The chaotic, anarchical condition of the pursuit compels an abstraction of four times the needful amount of labor and capital from the general aggregate for the performance of this function, which, after all, is far less effectively, accommodatingly performed than it might be by one-fourth as many coaches, horses, and coachmen, under a carefully organized system.

Hawthorne, in his delightful 'Mosses from an Old Manse,' gives a vision of a Universal Intelligence Office, whereto all manner of people throng from every quarter, each inquiring for 'his place' in the general distribution of duties and functions, and insisting that that place be pointed out and assigned to him. A reasonable request, methinks, and one which Society should long since have recognized and complied with. As the world goes, many doubtless make it in envy, pride, petulance, or spleen ; they would not now be satisfied with such a place as they are entitled to and fitted for if it were allotted them. They have hardly been educated into fitness for any position of essential freedom and usefulness ; they need fitting as well as placing, and *before* placing. But visit the National Metropolis when a new Congress is about to be organized, or any State Capital on like occasion, and note the swarms of place-hunters whom such an occasion draws together ; they, too, shall teach us. Many of them are doubtless seekers for lucrative idleness or undue recompense, some for the imaginary consequence of official station, however menial, and of contact with the eminent and powerful. Yet I think the eagerness wherewith every place, even to the most laborious and least profitable, is sought and struggled for proves a very general desire to be employed and useful if each could but find his place and be reasonably sure of preserving and profiting by it. If steady employment with 'ust recompense, where Labor was neither unwholesome, uncomfortable, nor morally degrading, were this day proffered for half a million persons, of various ages and capacities, the whole number would gladly step forward and the requisition be promptly filled up, with no material and permanent abstraction from the ranks of existing employments. And what immense additions might the labor of this Half Million make to the aggregate of human comforts and enjoyments, even within the short space of ten years!

Labor *must* be organized. Apart from all theories and projects, this is inevitable. Our gigantic and ever-increasing Alms-Houses, our cots and hovels filled with shivering, famishing inmates, who suffer because they can not find work; our immense stretches of unbroken forest and uncultivated soil; our millions of children and youth, growing up in ignorance and idleness to lives of vice, misery, and crime, all demand an Organization of Labor which shall secure a place for every man, a man for every place. The aggregate waste of labor and faculty for want of such organization in any year excels the cost of any war for five years—ruinous and detestable as all War is. It is palpable fatuity, a criminal waste of the Divine bounty, to let this go on interminably.

But, assuming that Labor is to be, must be so organized, as a matter of pure Yankee calculation on the part of the landholding, capitalist class, who will not insist on maintaining a large and steadily increasing proportion of the community in pauperized idleness when they might clearly be enabled and stimulated to support themselves by useful industry, it still remains to be shown that a more intimate Social relationship is to accompany or result from this Industrial Reform. Dives might perhaps give Lazarus a steady job of oakum-picking, or even gardening, in order to keep the crumbs about his table for his dogs exclusively, without at all recognizing the essential brotherhood between them or doing anything to vindicate it. Beside, it is said that *Human*

Nature stands opposed to any such social aggregation as these 'Fourierites' dream of. Let us consider this:

The lowest Savage state is that of the most complete isolation of Family efforts and interests. The savage makes or mends a road or bridge if he wants one, but troubles no other savage concerning it; instructs his children after his fashion or neglects it, but never concerns himself with the instruction of his neighbors'; grinds his own grain as best he can, but never thinks of uniting with his tribe to construct or sustain a grist-mill; sends or carries his message through hundreds of miles of trackless wilderness, but has no idea of a public mail. As Civilization advances, all this is changed; public schools, mills, and mails are but a part of the vital machinery whereby Society progresses from Barbarism to Refinement, from poverty and misery to wealth and comfort. Even this is by no means the limit already attained. A bare century ago, it would have seemed quite incredible that the Patroon of Rensselaerwyck and the Governor of New-York should travel through the State in the same car with their barber, oyster-dealer, and shoemaker; yet they do it now without imagining there is anything remarkable in the circumstance. So the same carriage whirls through Broadway the dandy, the banker, the brick-layer, the fine lady, the washerwoman, and the milliner: and no one is discommoded nor offended; for it is the omnibus, and everybody rides with everybody in *that*, without regarding differences of caste or culture. The Omnibus and the Railroad car are among our latest adoptions; but who insists that we must stop here? These, we have found, do not contravene Human Nature: can we be sure that the Unitary Household must do so? Let us at least understand what it is before any settle obstinately into any such position.

We have seen that all the selfishness and depravity inherent in Human Nature has not prevented the gradual substitution of carriage-roads, turnpikes, canals, steamboats and railroads for the footpaths and canoes of the savage, nor the substitution of grist-mills for family mortars, common schools and seminaries for private tutors and family instructors, the steamboat and the rail-car for the scow and the palanquin; the spacious and luxurious hotel for the wanderer's tent and the oriental serai. This great change does not necessarily involve a moral regeneration, but simply a more enlightened appreciation by each of his own interest as a seeker of happiness. Human depravity is undoubtedly a formidable impediment to the perfect realization of the advantages of Association in efforts, interests and enjoyments; but we see that it has not prevented progress up to this point, and may justly conclude that it can not absolutely arrest and fix us at the spot we this moment occupy.

Indeed, we *know* it can not, from the testimony of all things around us. On every side we are confronted by evidences of movement, progress, advance, and all in the Associative direction. Trades Unions, Protective Unions, Sons of Temperance, Odd-Fellowship, Mutual Insurance, Life Insurance, Building and Mutual Benefit Societies of all shapes and sizes, attest the existence of a principle, an instinct, a perception, which is everywhere impelling the members of civilized communities to form closer and more intimate relationships and alliances for mutual assistance and protection. Many of these may seem narrow, partial, one-sided; still more may disclaim affinity with that universal reform for which they are all such palpable preparations and beginnings: we must have patience with all this, not exacting of the man who sees one truth an immediate and necessary recognition of all truth thence logically flowing. Enough that *we* can see plainly in these movements, however limited in their several aims, the workings of a great principle which is destined in time to overshadow and absorb them all—the principle of Social Unity, to be actualized in Industrial Association.

The first if not most important movement to be made in advance of our present Social position is the ORGANIZATION OF LABOR. This is to be effected by degrees, by steps, by instalments. I propose here, in place of setting forth any formal theory or system of Labor Reform, simply to narrate what I saw and heard of the history and state of an experiment now in progress near Cincinnati, and which differs in no material respect from some dozen or score of others already commenced in various parts of the United States, not to speak of twenty times as many established by the Working Men of Paris and other portions of France.

The business of IRON-MOLDING, Casting, or whatever it may be called, is one of the most extensive and thrifty of the Manufactures of Cincinnati, and I believe the labor employed therein is quite as well rewarded as Labor generally. It is entirely paid by the piece, according to an established scale of prices, so that each workman, in whatever department of the business, is paid according to his individual skill and industry, not a rough average of what is supposed to be earned by himself and others, as is the case where work is paid for at so much per day, week or month. I know no reason why the Iron-Molders of Cincinnati should not have been as well satisfied with the old ways as anybody else.

Yet the system did not 'work well,' even for them. Beyond the general unsteadiness of demand for Labor and the ever-increasing pressure of competition, there was a pretty steadily recurring 'dull season,' commencing about the 1st of January, when the Winter's call for stoves, &c., had been supplied, and holding on for two or three months, or until the Spring business opened. In this hiatus, the prior savings of the Molder were generally consumed—sometimes less, but perhaps oftener more—so that, taking one with another, they did not lay up ten dollars per annum. By-and-by came a collision respecting wages and a 'strike,' wherein the Journeymen tried the experiment of running their heads against a stone wall for months. How they came out of it, no matter whether victors or vanquished, the intelligent reader will readily guess. I never heard of any evils so serious and complicated as those which eat out the heart of Labor being cured by doing nothing.

At length—but I believe after the strike had somehow terminated—some of the Journeymen Molders said to each other: 'Standing idle is not the true cure for our grievances: why not employ ourselves?' They finally concluded to try it, and, in the dead of the Winter of 1847–8, when a great many of their trade were out of employment, the business being unusually depressed, they formed an association under the General Manufacturing Law of Ohio (which is very similar to that of New York) and undertook to establish the Journeymen Molders' Union Foundry. There were about twenty of them who put their hands to the work, and the whole amount of capital they could scrape together was two thousand one hundred dollars, held in shares of twenty-five dollars each. With this they purchased an eligible piece of ground, directly on the bank of the Ohio, eight miles below Cincinnati, with which 'the Whitewater Canal' also affords the means of ready and cheap communication. With their capital, they bought some patterns, flasks, an engine and tools, paid for their ground and five hundred dollars on their first building, which was erected for them partly on long credit by a firm in Cincinnati, who knew that the property was a perfect security for so much of its cost, and decline taking credit for any benevolence in the matter. Their Iron, Coal, &c., to commence upon were entirely and necessarily bought on credit.

Having elected Directors, a Foreman and a Business Agent (the last to open a store in Cincinnati, buy stock, sell wares, &c.) the Journeymen's Union set to work, in August,

1848. Its accommodations were then meager; they have since been gradually enlarged by additions, until their Foundry is now the most commodious on the River. Their stock of Patterns, Flasks, &c., has grown to be one of the best; while their arrangements for unloading coal and iron, sending off stoves, coking coal, &c. &c. are almost perfect. They commenced with ten associates actually at work; the number has gradually grown to forty; and there is not a better set of workmen in any foundry in America. I profess to know a little as to the quality of castings, and there are no better than may be seen in the Foundry of 'Industry' and its store at Cincinnati. And there is obvious reason for this in the fact that every workman is a proprietor in the concern, and it is his interest to turn out not only his own work in the best order, but to take care that all the rest is of like quality. All is carefully examined before it is sent away, and any found imperfect is condemned, the loss falling on the causer of it. But there is seldom any deserving condemnation.

A strict account is kept with every member, who is credited for all he does according to the Cincinnati Scale of Prices, paid so much as he needs of his earnings in money, the balance being devoted to the extension of the concern and the payment of its debts, and new stock issued to him therefor. Whenever the debts shall have been paid off, and an adequate supply of implements, teams, stock, &c. bought or provided for, they expect to pay every man his earnings weekly in cash, as of course they may. I hope, however, they will prefer to buy more land, erect thereon a most substantial and commodious dwelling, surround it with a garden, shade-trees, &c. and resolve to live as well as work like brethren. There are few uses to which a member can put a hundred dollars which might not as well be subserved by seventy-five if the money of the whole were invested together.

The members were earning when I visited them an average of fifteen dollars per week and meant to keep doing so. Of course they work hard. Many of them live inside of four dollars per week, none go beyond eight. Their Business Agent is one of themselves, who worked with them in the Foundry for some months after it was started. He has often been obliged to report, 'I can pay you no money this week,' and never heard a murmur in reply. On one occasion he went down to say, 'There are my books; you see what I have received and where most of it has gone; here is one hundred dollars, which is all there is left.' The members consulted, calculated, and made answer; 'We can pay our board so as to get through another week with fifty dollars, and you had better take back the other fifty, for the business may need it before the week is through.' When I was there, there had been an Iron note to pay, ditto a Coal, and a boat-load of Coal to lay in for the Winter, sweeping off all the money, so that for more than three weeks no man had had a dollar. Yet no one had thought of complaining, for all knew that the delay was dictated, not by another's interest, but their own. They knew, too, that the assurance of their payment did not depend on the frugality or extravagance of some employer, who might swamp the proceeds of his business and their labor in an unlucky speculation, or a sumptuous dwelling, leaving them to whistle for their money. There were their year's earnings visibly around them in Stoves and Hollow Ware, for which they had abundant and eager demand in Cincinnati, but which a break in the canal had temporarily kept back; in iron and coal for the Winter's work; in the building over their heads and the implements in their hands. And while other Molders have had work 'off and on,' according to the state of the business, no member of the Journeymen's Union has stood idle a day for want of work since their Foundry was first started. Of course, as their capital increases, the danger of being compelled to suspend work at any future day grows less and less continually.

The ultimate capital of the Journeymen's Union Foundry (on the presumption that the Foundry is to stand by itself, leaving every member to provide his own home, &c.) is to be eighteen thousand dollars, of which seven thousand dollars has already been paid in, most of it in labor. The remainder is all subscribed by the several associates and is to be paid in labor as fast as possible. That done, every man may be paid in cash weekly for his work, and a dividend on his stock at the close of each business year. The workers have saved and invested from three hundred dollars to six hundred dollars each since their commencement in August of last year, though those who have joined since the start have of course earned less. Few or none had laid by so much in five to ten years' working for others as they have in one year working for themselves. The total value of their products up to the time of my visit is thirty thousand dollars, and they were then making at the rate of five thousand dollars' worth per month, which they do not mean to diminish. All the profits of the business, above the cost of doing the work at journeymen's wages, will be distributed among the stockholders in dividends. The officers of the Union are a Managing Agent, Foreman of the Foundry, and five Directors, chosen annually, but who can be changed meantime in case of necessity. A Reading Room and Library were to be started directly; a spacious Boarding House (though probably not owned by the Union) will go up this season. No liquor is sold within a long distance of the Union, and there is little or no demand for any. Those original members of the Union who were least favorable to Temperance have seen fit to sell out and go away.

—Now is it reasonable that the million or so of hireling laborers throughout our country who have work when it suits others' convenience to employ them, and must stand idle perforce when it does not, can read the above simple narration—which I have tried to render as lucid as possible—and not be moved to action thereby? Suppose they receive all they earn when employed—which of course they generally do not, or how could employers grow rich by merely buying their labor and selling it again?—should not the simple fact that these Associated Workers never lack employment when they desire it, and never ask any master's leave to refrain from working when they see fit, arrest public attention? Who is such a slave in soul that he would not rather be an equal member of a commonwealth than the subject of a despotism? Who would not like to taste the sweets of Liberty on work-days as well as holidays? Is there a creature so abject that he considers all this mere poetry and moonshine, which a little hard experience will dissipate? Suppose the Cincinnati Iron-Molders' Association should break down, either through some defect in its organization or some dishonesty or other misconduct on the part of one or more of its members—what would that prove? Would it any more prove the impracticability of Industrial Associations than the shipwreck and death of Columbus, had such a disaster occurred on his second or third voyage to America, would have disproved the existence of the New World?

Can it be that I have not yet succeeded in making clear the feasibility as well as the importance of the Reform here indicated? Is there anything occult, or dubious, or mysterious in the process? Doubtless, the application of the principle to other handicrafts would require modifications in the details, which experience and practical knowledge will suggest; but what of that? What is there to hinder the immediate organization on this basis of such callings as do not involve complicated processes and the aggregation of large capitals for their economical and effective prosecution? Why should Tailors, Shoemakers, Hatters, Cabinet-Makers,

&c. &c., continue to work for masters instead of combining to work for customers? To illustrate still farther the facility and the advantage of the change proposed, I will take the case of the Boot and Shoemakers.

There are probably Ten Thousand Men and at least Five Thousand Women engaged in the manufacture of Boots and Shoes within half a day's ride of our City Hall—possibly twice that number. A few of them receive quite fair wages, but the great majority are working for very poor pay, and even at that can get nothing to do for some weeks if not months in every year. Nearly all are obliged every few weeks to troop from shoe-store to shoe-store, begging for work, and ready to accept it on any terms which will enable them to keep what little soul men so circumstanced can afford to have in their bent and crouching bodies.

On one of our street-corners is the store of a shoe-dealing firm—we will call it Stirrup & Co.—which has sold One Million Dollars' worth of shoes during the past year, and netted a clear profit of One Hundred Thousand Dollars—fifty thousand to each partner. I do not believe all the actual makers of Shoes and Boots between Philadelphia, Poughkeepsie, New-Haven and Sandy Hook were together enabled to lay up One Hundred Thousand Dollars in 1849.

Now don't fancy that I am about to preach a Jacobinic crusade against Stirrup & Co. They made their money fairly, as the world goes, and nobody has any right to reproach them. If Labor had seen fit to do without their services, it was at perfect liberty to do so; but it didn't. The fact that the Shoe business saw fit to find a channel through such stores as theirs proves that no better was in existence.

But there *should* be better, and the Shoemakers have nobody but themselves to blame that there is not. They might have steady instead of unsteady work, and full pay instead of part pay, if they only would. Let me endeavor in a rough way to show how:

Suppose One Thousand Workers on Boots and Shoes, old and young, male and female, good and indifferent, some living in our City and some around in its vicinity, were to meet here on some appointed day, and resolved to become their own employers. To this end they agree to pay in twenty-five dollars each to form a common fund, making in all twenty-five thousand dollars. The sole condition of their union is that each one shall have constant employment and full pay for his work — that is, in the first place, the regular journeymen's wages.

They proceed at once to elect a first-rate cutter or foreman and overseer of work, and the very best business man they can get, no matter though they have to pay him two thousand dollars a year. This agent must be a man of known integrity as well as capacity, able to give ample bonds for the safety of the funds. This agent and foreman proceed to take the right sort of a store or stand for business, and advertise the public that the Journeymen Shoemakers' Union is prepared to supply the public with Boots and Shoes of all kinds at the shortest notice and at fair prices. They buy stock with cash at wholesale prices, distribute it to the members with directions to make up such work as they are severally best qualified for, and as shall seem to be required to perfect an assortment for the demands of the trade. On the Saturday following, let the store be opened for customers, and the public called to enter and buy for cash at cash prices.

Each workman should be paid once a week, if he chooses to send in his work so often, as those living out of the city probably would not. Friday should be the general day for receiving work from associates and paying them off, all the work being passed upon as received, and paid exactly according to its value, leaving each worker the option of making poor or good work — fine boots, coarse shoes, ladies' gaiters, or whatever he should prefer; though of course a demand for any kind of work would be intimated by the foreman to the workers and some of them induced to supply it. Customers would be measured here as elsewhere, and promptly supplied with the best or poorer articles, as they might prefer. Each worker might stamp his own work with his name or mark, and any one choosing to order his work done by a particular maker would be obeyed. To the best workmen would naturally be assigned the best and most profitable work. But every person belonging to the Union should be furnished with stock on demand at all times, and credited with his products, when sent in, according to their value.

Twenty-five dollars per man would be a short capital—fifty would be better, but not so easily raised. With twenty-five, a good agent would be able to keep the wheels moving. If temporarily short of money, he would always have stock or shoes to pledge for it, and could borrow on security till money came in from customers. Such a concern, well managed, might sell ten thousand dollars' worth of Boots and Shoes per week at retail, at a profit of ten per cent. on the cost of stock and journeymen's wages for working it up.

At the end of each year there should be a settlement, and all clear profits carried to the credit of the shareholders. The first twenty-five thousand dollars should be divided to them in stock, increasing the cash capital to fifty thousand dollars, which would be sufficient for an inflexibly cash business. But the balance should not be divided and frittered away. It ought to be expended in buying for all the associates, first, an eligible and desirable plat of cheap land—say two miles square—on the Erie, Long-Island or some other Railroad; next in laying it out to the best advantage into streets and small allotments, and then setting to each one his separate acre. The balance might then be sold (after making suitable reservations for churches, school-houses, groves, squares, &c.) to grocers, artisans, &c., for more than the whole need cost, so soon as it should be decided that the Shoemakers were to occupy their allotments, thus making a village of a waste. Perhaps they would now see fit to put up a grand Shoe-shop, calculated to accommodate them all—and perhaps they would not stop at this—but let us not ask them to go too far. Suffice it that they might at all times divide the profits of their business and spend them if they thought proper.

—Such is a hasty outline of a plan for the Emancipation of the Shoemakers of New-York and vicinity from dependence on any employer but the shoe-wearing public generally. It is doubtless imperfect, and susceptible of many improvements. Well, *make them*, then, and let the enterprise be got under headway at once. The Shoemakers have been rather low down among Mechanics for some years. Why should they not go up to the head in the great work of making Labor its own master? They can if they will, and much easier than almost any other trade. Let us hope that, before this year expires, they WILL.

VII.

TEACHERS AND TEACHING:

A LECTURE.

To do good is the proper business of life—to qualify for earnestness and efficiency in doing good, is the true end of Education. The sum of all true knowledge in the child is a consciousness that he lives not for himself, but for his Creator and his Race. Let him but comprehend and accept this destiny, and all formal lessons of morality, all decalogues and criminal codes, become to him matters of small account. He needs no admonition not to steal, to lie, to covet, nor to slay; no doctor of divinity nor professor of ethics to decide whether slave-holding and war be right or wrong; if he has but received into his inmost heart the primal, central truth, that the human family live for and through each other, and that, in the abasement or exaltation of any, each is abased or exalted. "All the law and the prophets" may still be useful as counsel, as wisdom, as guidance; but no longer as conducing to whatever is intrinsic and essential. The one commandment, welcomed and obeyed in the sunlight of its manifest reasonableness and necessity as an elemental law of the universe, supplants or dwarfs all others. Know but that this is no barren abstraction, no oriental exaggeration, but the simplest dictate of heaven and nature, beaming alike from the loftiest star and from the humblest blossom, and all beside that philosophic lore, and pious exhortation, or even sacred writ, can convey to you, is subsidiary and incidental. 'Love God with all thy heart and thy neighbor as thyself,' is the sun of the moral universe, in whose presence the brightest stars become dim and invisible.

Well were it if the education of the heart could precede and prepare for the education of the mind and the body, but this may not be. With the earliest development of sensation and of muscular energy, while the child is still apparently unsusceptible of any thorough and enduring moral culture, come swarming shoals of perverted and misleading passions—untamed appetite, imperious temper, ungovernable will. The consciousness of self, of individual wants, sufferings, enjoyments, is felt with the first dawn of intellect; the knowledge of our relations and duties to others is the slow acquirement of maturer years. And, as distortion or misdevelopment in one sphere very surely induces defects and perversions in others, it is hardly possible to overstate the disturbing, deranging, blighting influence which moral obliquity exerts upon the education of the physical and intellectual being. From a chaos of moral infirmities, intellectual deficiencies and physical perversions in the child, is to be deduced the thoroughly informed, enlightened, wise, energetic, sternly upright, self-denying, all-loving, effective, healthy man.

Into the midst of this chaos, the true teacher fearlessly casts himself, the Van Amburgh of every-day life. It is his mission to grapple with all the elements of moral and mental disorder, and bid them 'stand ruled.' As 'out of the nettle Danger we pluck the flower Safety,' his task is to pluck from the unweeded garden of wayward childhood the rich fruit of a true and genial manhood. The marvels of chemical transmutation are tame compared with those he is required and expected to perform. To render the froward gentle, the reckless considerate, to dignify the degraded and spiritualize the clod, such are among the arduous requirements of his sphere and calling. That he should often fail is inevitable; the wonder is that he should ever succeed.

No engineer, no mathematician, is required to make allowance for so many disturbing and conflicting forces as he, the moral Leverrier, who is required not merely to discover but seemingly to create the Franklins and Washingtons of the time. His theories, be they what they may, must often give way to unwelcome but stubborn facts. He may, for instance, have adopted the principle that human beings are not to be constrained to do right by violence, but won to the love and practice of all virtue by attraction, by instruction, by admonition, by gentleness, by fervent love. That this is the true theory, I trust few at this day will dispute. But the public teacher often finds himself confronted with apparently insuperable difficulties in attempting to conform to this theory implicitly. For his instructions, his discipline, form at best but a small portion of the motley superstructure which composes the child's education; the lessons of the fireside and the wayside have been potential before his; are more numerous and pervading now than his; will be vivid and powerful after he and his are forgotten. He tries the virtue of moral suasion upon one who from the cradle has known no other power than physical force; no other dread but that of bodily pain; no influence but that of the appetite or the rod. To a mind so trained, all appeals to the heart or the conscience are flummery; the disuse of the rod can only seem the dictate of weakness or cowardice; and where penalty stops anarchy begins. How can any general rule be arbitrarily laid down to cover such cases as this? Invest the teacher with the authority and the intimacy of a parent; let the child be constantly under his supervision and care, and he may hope by patient endurance to translate and commend the principles by which he is guided to the apprehension of the most hardened and stolid. But while his lessons of six hours per day are contradicted by those of the other eighteen, especially with the immense advantage of several years' start to the latter, what shall the teacher do? How adapt the new wine to the old bottle? and to the bottle-imp confined therein? The system of discipline which eschews the infliction of physical pain as the penalty of moral aberration is undoubtedly the true one wherever its subject can be steadily exposed to its undisturbed influences; but where violence rules the hours out of school, as it has ruled the years before school, what is the teacher to do? What can we say more than that he must do the best he can?

The great work incumbent on him in this connection, however, is that of dispelling from the pupil's mind a false notion of the nature of Law, and of implanting a true one in its stead. Law, to the apprehension of the ignorant and the vicious, is but the exhibition of a Will as capricious and as selfish as their own, differing thence only in that it is stronger and more imperious. To the confutation of this error the teacher should sedulously devote himself. He should have as few prohibitions as possible; far better let two real offences pass unreproved, unnoticed, than to punish one act which involves no real culpability. He should devote all the time necessary — no matter how much — to demonstrating, even to the humblest capacity, the most perverse nature, the reasonableness of, the necessity for, every requirement and prohibition. As the exponent and minister of Law, it is his first duty to cause every subject to realize that Law is no arbitrary despot, no blind, remorseless Fate, but the loving, genial friend and guardian of all, himself included, and that it smites but to heal. Next to, and consequent upon the love of God and man, the love of Law, as a divinely-appointed guide, monitor, and beacon-light, is to be inculcated and implanted with the most devoted assiduity.

But this can never be consummated if the pupil finds himself hedged about with innumerable arbitrary and unreasonable commands and injunctions: if a look aside from the lesson, a smile at some passing drollery or incongruity, a movement of the weary muscles, is to be watched for and reprehended as a crime. To render authority respected, and obedience general, it is essential that Law should confront Inclination on the fewest points possible. We may not, indeed, be able to render the reasonableness and necessity of every separate command perfectly obvious to the infantile apprehension, but we can do this by adequate effort and earnest assiduity with the great majority of our inhibitions, and so create and justify a strong presumption that those whereof the reason is not so fully understood are equally well grounded in a regard for the subject's enduring welfare. When a child has once realized profoundly that the laws he is required to obey are founded in a thorough knowledge of his own nature and its requirements, and are calculated to increase the sum of his personal good, and not rather to subtract from the measure of his enjoyments in order to expand or secure those of others, his future government will be a work of guidance merely, and can cost but very little trouble.

As with Government or discipline, so with the more immediate business of Education itself. The teacher's first point is to impress thoroughly on the pupil's mind the truth that whatever of irksomeness or weariness of the flesh may be experienced by either in the process of instruction is encountered primarily and mainly for the learner's own sake, and not for that of his relatives or his monitors. He must feel that he is not fulfilling a useless task but securing an indispensable treasure. To grudge the youthful hours abstracted from the acquirement of useful knowledge as the spilling of some priceless fluid on the thirsty and remorseless sands of Sahara, is the feeling with which every pupil should be sedulously imbued and animated.

Of course, no one fit to be a teacher is likely to fall into the error of deeming the rudimental culture of certain well-nigh mechanical functions of the intellect Education, although the poverty of language and a colloquial convenience may tempt to such an accommodated use of the term. In the larger, truer sense, Education implies the development, drawing out, of the whole nature, moral, physical, intellectual, social. The acquisition of the mechanical facility of reading, writing, computing, &c., the sharpening of the youthful intellect on the rough grindstone of Letters, is no more Education than is learning to mow or to swim. The direct inculcations of the class can but supply the pupil with a few rude implements of Education — the ax wherewith he may clear and the plow wherewith to break up the rugged patrimony which has fallen to him in its state of primal wilderness. These are most valuable — nay indispensable — but they must be taken for what they are, and for nothing more. The youth who fancies himself educated because he has fully mastered ever so many branches of mere school-learning, is laboring under a deplorable and perilous delusion. He may have learned all that the schools, the seminaries, and even our miscalled universities, necessarily teach, and still be a pitiably ignorant man, unable to earn a week's subsistence, to resist the promptings of a perverted appetite, or to shield himself from such common results of physical depravity as Dyspepsia, Hypochondria, and Nervous derangement. A master of Greek and Hebrew who knows not how to grow Potatoes, and can be tempted to drown his reason in the intoxicating bowl, is far more imperfectly educated than many an unlettered backwoodsman. The public teacher is indeed virtually limited in his stated inculcations to a narrow circle of Arts and Sciences, so called, but he should nevertheless endeavor so to teach as to secure in the end a thoroughly symmetrical culture. The education of the prince will differ somewhat from that of the plow-jogger, but either should be consistent with itself and thoroughly adapted to the nature of both as well as to the circumstances of each.

Nor is this all. Each should be so educated that if Fortune should call him to fill the place of the other he would do so naturally, heartily, effectively. Being educated as a Man, he should be able promptly to qualify himself for and adapt himself to whatever a man may properly be required to do. Herein is laid the only solid foundation for a life of manly independence, and a readiness to brave all the possible consequences of a frank truthfulness, and a generous, fearless devotion to the highest and enduring good.

Herein, too, is the condemnation of our ordinary training. It is too special, narrow, one-sided. The merchant, we will say, educates his son for a merchant, and tolerably well with a view to that particular calling. But we live in a world and an age of mutation. The ground perpetually rocks and heaves beneath our feet, throwing up new eminences and opening chasms where hights have lately been. The young man who enters on the stage of action at twenty a trader, banker, doctor, will very likely be found pursuing a very different vocation at forty, or at least unable to follow advantageously that in which he began life. Joe Dobbs, the Yankee stable-boy of 1830, becomes the Western horse-dealer of '36, and very likely the South American Cavalry Colonel of 1840, thence branching off into running steamboats on the Paraguay, or working gold mines in the Cordilleras, unless he happen to have a taste for Politics, and so undertake a job of Constitution-making or accept the post of Foreign Secretary of State. On the other hand, a Nabob's son who does not quite graduate at Yale, owing to some trifling irregularities, is perfectly successful in doing so at wine-parties, gaming-saloons, and ultimately at Sing-Sing. No man's destiny, hardly his vocation, can be predicted with anything like certainty ; and the only safe plan of Education is that which shall prepare him for usefulness and independence in every imaginable contingency.

Now, while the teacher can not be allowed to forget that it is his primary duty, so far as purely intellectual culture is concerned, to supply his pupils with the mere implements of Education — with the ax, the saw, the plane, wherewith they are to work out an Education each for himself — he must never fall mentally into the error of confounding these with the essential thing itself. It is not enough that the child be taught to realize that he is to master the arbitrary and capricious spelling of a page of crooked words, not as an ingenious puzzle, a mental exercise, nor even for any intrinsic worth thereof as a mental acquisition, but simply because of the practical uses of that acquisition, and the indispensableness of this knowledge to a clear and accurate understanding of the meaning of written language. The farther use of a correct Orthography in fixing and throwing light upon the meaning of words and sentences is of course to be explained to and impressed upon the learner's mind. Yet after all, the central truth that all instruction in letters is but means to an end — an end immensely transcending in importance all scholastic eminence in itself considered — can not be too profoundly realized by the teacher nor too sedulously impressed on the learner. He whose admiring contemplation rests on the prizes of successful scholarship — who thinks more of the honors awarded to the most proficient in any branch of study than of the remoter uses of his proficiency — is readily perceived to be laboring under a baneful delusion ; but not less so is he who prizes Intellectual Culture unless accompanied by Moral, and except as conducive to ends of practical utility. *That* teaching has been most effective, however simple in manner or deficient in quantity, which has qualified, enabled the pupil to find a salutary lesson in every passing event, a healthful companionship in his own thoughts, a meaning and a wondrous beauty in every changing phase of Nature. He who knows how to do, when to do, and stands ready with a hearty will to do, whatever it is or fairly may be incumbent on him to do, perilous though it be, and apart from the sense of duty repulsive, is truly educated, though he knows nothing of logarithms or Latin; while the graduate with highest honors at Oxford or Gottingen may be as essentially ignorant as many a Typee or Hottentot. Fitness and utility are the only tests of the value of an acquirement.

I have reminded you, but am not satisfied with the mere suggestion, that Education is essentially Development. The teacher must never forget that he has much to learn of his pupil before he can safely assume to instruct him. Few of us will not readily recall instances within his own experience where a youth, wearied and sorely perplexed with some puzzling problem in his Arithmetic, has been caught by his instructer *flagrante delicto*, having been tempted by his aching brain into the astounding depravity of sketching a house, a ship, a tree, or a face, on his slate. Black grew the brow of the master at the sight of this enormity, and his virtuous indignation was only assuaged by the infliction on the shrinking body of the conscience-smitten culprit of sundry thumps and bruises, whereby Justice was satiated and the evil example carefully guarded against. But at length it has crawled through the hair of Pedagoguism that this propensity for sketching need not absolutely be treated as one of the seven deadly sins—that it may even be tolerated, patronized, licked into shape, so as to take rank in the end as a decent, well-favored pedagogical acquirement. How many millions of palms have been blistered by the ferule, how many backs have been warmed by the rod, to beat this tendency to linear drawing *out* of the minds of pupils before the first attempt was made to beat it *in*, it would be idle to guess at. The practical use of the notorious facts in this instance is to suggest farther inquiries in the same broad field, that we may see whether there are not other tendencies of the youthful nature which we rush eagerly to punish and repress when, were we wiser, we should rather guide, encourage, and rightly develop them. I can not doubt that many millions of lithe, graceful rods have been rudely torn from their parent trees and worse than wasted on juvenile backs in vain attempts to repress the superabounding muscular energies of boyhood, where wiser teachers would have said to the several offenders, "If you feel too restless to sit still and study, be good enough not to disturb others by whispering, or tickling, or other mischief, but step out, take a brisk run of half a mile or so, climb a smooth tree, or hurl heavy stones until you shall feel like coming in and studying quietly." That such liberty would sometimes be abused, is a matter of course; but that very abuse would tend promptly to correct the original fault and ultimately the superimposed truancy also. The mysterious luxury of breaking laws will lose its zest when the lawgiver evinces his readiness to obviate any needless severity involved therein, and to accommodate or even relax them in the subject's favor so far as is compatible with that subject's ultimate well-being. To defer our own to others' good is the perfection of moral culture, and can not be expected to precede the long course of wise and careful training which is required to produce it. Meantime, while keeping it ever in view, it is just and necessary to secure obedience and growth by means of laws of inferior scope and more personal bearing. To do right because it *is* right, without asking what will be the effect of so doing on our individual well-being, is the consummation, not the beginning of moral culture. Pending that consummation, attained as yet by so few, even of the ripe in years and in experience, we must guide and profit by such springs of action as we find already implanted in the youthful breast.

But let the great fundamental truth that 'No man (rightfully) liveth to himself,' be ever the pole-star of all moral inculcation. The child taught to practise virtue mainly that he may reap the rewards of virtue and to shun transgression because of the perils and penalties of transgression, is viciously taught, and will hardly fail to exhibit the fruits of vicious training in his subsequent career. Such good savors too much of enlightened, wary and cunning evil. The taint of utter selfishness poisons all it touches. What merit can there be in serving God for the best of wages when we know that the devil pays only in counterfeit coin? The truly virtuous do good from an inherent love of good, because it is the spontaneous dictate of their moral nature, and because it is calculated to increase and diffuse happiness. If it were possible to blot the Creator from his Universe, the good man would be no more deflected from his unvarying moral course than by the death of an earthly father. Against the temptations and trials of frail mortality there can be no absolute safeguard, but if there be any all-pervading, all-enduring security for rectitude, it is found in the conviction that Virtue is intrinsically more desirable than Honors, Rewards or personal Happiness. The mists of overmastering temptation may obscure every orb in the moral firmament, but this is the sun which shines longest and brightest of all.

That a pure Heart is of vastly greater moment than a sharpened Understanding, is a truth too palpable to be dwelt on here, and that it is the business of the teacher, however limited his sphere or imperfect his opportunities, to develop rightly the moral affections no less than the intellectual faculties of his pupils, I presume no one has ever questioned. Yet I apprehend that the truth is but half understood by or half impressed upon the minds of a majority of teachers. I fear that too many fail to appreciate the evil consequences upon some scores of ingenuous, receptive minds, of any casual exhibition of meanness, or falsehood, or unworthy passion, on the part of him who is their common exemplar and ruler. How dare a man do a base act, or harbor a base thought, when acting under such a tremendous responsibility ? Yet I have known instructors, directly under the piercing eyes of their charges, evince an unworthy and partial deference for the children of their more wealthy and honored patrons, or a mean conformity to fashion or popular prejudice, which could not fail to exert the most pernicious influence upon every immature observer. It is idle to expect that *his* influence will do anything toward inculcating the love or practice of virtue who himself evinces that he regards wealthy or powerful mediocrity above poor and humble excellence. Of all the lessons the teacher gives, that of his daily walk and conversation is the most potent and enduring.

I apprehend that there is a radical defect in our popular inculcations with regard to Manners, Breeding, Courtesy, though I do not know that I shall succeed in making it manifest. That we owe a certain deference to our fellow-beings generally, and should ever stand ready to serve them, is of course understood. That a manifestation of respect is likewise due to rank, station, authority, social eminence, is also obvious. But when the teacher requires his pupils to render certain outward symbols of deference to every one they may meet; above all, when he teaches them to observe a prescribed formula in entering or leaving the presence of others, is there not a peril that conformity will degenerate into rank hypocrisy or sheer grimace ? Is there not a clear demand for a spontaneity and hearty directness in all our intercourse with others ? Do the prescribed courtesies mean and are they intended to be understood only as ‘ Sir, (or Madam,) I proffer you that deference which I owe and am ready to pay to all my brethren of the Human Family ?’ If they mean this, and be tendered in sincerity, very well. But I apprehend that they are often intended to express more than this —to indicate a peculiar consideration or regard, which is not and can not be so widely cherished. If this be so, it becomes the teacher to warn against it as a virtual falsehood, and directly leading to the meanest of vices. He who does not shrink from acting a lie will not hesitate, when strongly tempted, to utter one; and the teacher who begins by exacting for himself or requiring toward others any farther indications of deference than are prompted by the inmost heart has launched his pupils blindly on an inlet of shams and seemings, whence the tide sets strongly out to the broad ocean of insincerity, hypocrisy, and all dishonesty.

I return to consider more fully the great end of all true Education — that of qualifying and inspiring to do good. He whose life is consecrated to the enhancement of general well-being, the diminution of wrong and wretchedness, is well educated, or needs farther instruction only to increase his efficiency in well-doing, or to teach him how he may surely discriminate between the truly good and the speciously, seeming good. Paul's education was perfected, not at the feet of Gamaliel, but on his journey to Damascus. We have only to consider how many, or rather, how few — have dedicated their lives to the widest diffusion of good, and we shall realize how low is the state and standard of Education among us, and throughout the world. We shall find on one hand an institute for instruction in the art of throat-cutting and joint-fracturing, and on the other a college for the education of surgeons to heal the mangled bodies; and a little farther on a seminary which turns out divines for the cure of gangrened souls. So far, Education would seem to be balancing its results, and likely to leave the world nearly as well as it found it, if we could forget that one battery will in an hour cut out work enough to last many surgeons for weeks, and that the saving of perverted souls is hardly less difficult than the healing of maimed bodies. That the world should realize as the fruit of such training many Murats or Neys to one Howard is inevitable. Yet I can not suppress the conviction that all our instruction looking to special ends — to make of the student a lawyer, doctor, engineer, merchant, or some such—is so shaped and managed as often to narrow and dwarf the intellect it is intended to sharpen. Each of us is trained for and started upon some special path, and incited to pursue it with primary reference not to general good but to his own. Not many of the children, even of Piety or Philanthropy, are urged to inquire out and select that sphere wherein they may contribute most directly and essentially to the general weal, while thousands on thousands are practically taught to consider only what career will probably secure them the most abundant supply of goods and chattels. From this pervading taint of selfishness, not even the inculcations of the pulpit are absolutely exempt. Men are exhorted to become religious, not so much because they ought as because they must, if they would avoid the most fearful penalties and woes. Hence many a man is impelled to strain every nerve to secure the saving of his soul, leaving out of view entirely the preliminary matter of *having* any soul to save. Whenever the time shall come that all men really *have* souls, their salvation will not be so arduous a work and need not absorb so much effort and attention.

I would not if I could conceal from you my conviction that, before Education can become what it should and must be, we must reform the Social Life whence it proceeds, whitherto it tends. To the child daily sent out from some rickety hovel or miserable garret to wrestle with Poverty and Misery for such knowledge as the teacher can impart, what true idea or purpose of Education is possible? How can he be made to realize that his daily tasks concern the Soul, the World, and Immortality? He may have drilled into his ears day after day the great truth that 'the life is more than meat and the body more than raiment,' but so long as his own food and raiment are scanty and precarious, his mind will be engrossed by a round of petty and sordid cares. (I speak here of the general fact; there will be striking instances of the contrary — brilliant exceptions which do not disprove but establish the rule I have indicated.) But the child whose little all hitherto of life has been passed in penury and consequent suffering — who lives in the constant presence, on the very brink, of Want — how can he have a higher idea of Life than that it is a struggle for bread, or of Education than that it is a contrivance for getting bread more easily or more abundantly, or else a useless addition to his toils and cares? He whose energies have been, must be, taxed to keep starvation at bay, can hardly realize that Life has truer ends than the avoidance of pain and the satisfaction of hunger. The narrow, dingy, squalid tenement, calculated to repel any visiter but the cold and the rain, is hardly fitted to foster lofty ideas of Life, its Duties and its Aims. He who is constrained to ask each morning, 'Where shall I find food for the day?' is at best unlikely often to ask, 'By what good deed shall the day be signalized?' Well did the Divine Teacher enjoin His followers to 'take no thought for the morrow,' and difficult will be the work of imbuing the general mind with any lofty ideal of Life and its ends until this commandment can be obeyed in verity, and until such obedience can be made to comport with the dictates of a reasonable forecast and with that care for his own household, lacking which the believer is 'worse than an infidel.'

And herein is the true foundation for that protest against the divorce of Learning from Labor which the world has not yet begun to comprehend, or at least to treat with decent consideration. The advocates of Manual Labor as an essential ingredient of a true Education cherish no fanatical regard for Physical Toil as alone deserving the name and rewards of Labor. They quite well understand and freely concede that much true Work has been done, elsewhere than in the fields and the factories; they know and cheerfully admit that the sage in his closet, the astronomer in his observatory, the legislator in the capitol, may be among the noblest and most deserving of toilers for universal good. But it is not given to all men, nor to most, to advance the general well-being from such exalted positions. The ship Common Weal can not be navigated from the quarter-deck alone; she needs men at the ropes as well as the speaking-trumpet, the wheel and the lead. It being thus certain that the many must live by hard labor, only the few by mental exertion solely, it does seem the most obvious dictate of prudence and wisdom that all should be qualified for efficiency in that sphere which may become the lot of any, and in which energy and skill will at all events insure a subsistence, independent of the opinion of others. Here, for illustration, is a youth just qualifying himself to enter upon the stage of active life, who desires and expects to be a clergyman, a physician, or a lawyer, and must at all events earn his bread in some sphere of manly exertion. He can not glide from one profession to another like a harlequin on the stage; he must choose one and abide his fortune therein. But suppose he should find, after exhausting all his means in fitting himself for his chosen career, that he can not succeed therein without a compromise of principle, a base deference to prejudice or falsehood — suppose, if a clergyman, he can not preach all the truth that is made plain to his mind without incurring ecclesiastical censure and ignominy — or as a physician, he stumbles upon some discovery in advance of his age, which raises the hiss of scorn from his brethren, as did Jenner's discovery of the great antidote for Small Pox or Harvey's theory of the Circulation of the Blood — or suppose that, as a Lawyer, he find or fancy such an oppugnancy between the maxims and usages of the craft and the dictates of a stern integrity that he can only succeed in the practice by kicking Conscience overboard and giving the command to circumspect, respectable Knavery — what alternative has the man educated to live only by his profession but to take the broad road and keep it, at whatever internal sacrifice? A Prime Minister once, to the courtier who said to him 'I must live, you know,' replied, 'Pardon me, Sir, I do not perceive the necessity,' but rarely has any one so decided in his own case. Even if living be to him personally a matter of indifference, there are those dependent on his exertions whom he can not so stoically resign to the buffetings of adverse fortune. Hence a life of mean compliances and self-condemned hypocrisies becomes a sort of necessity to thousands—nay, often, the seeming dictate of paternal or conjugal duty. Thus the landmarks which should separate Vice from Virtue are broken down, defaced, obliterated, and the ends of life are lost sight of in a desperate, degrading struggle for the means of living.

The most effectual remedy for this which is attainable under our present Social Order is the blending of Manual Labor with Education, so that they should be inseparable by the wealth or personal distinction of the learner. Let it be settled, as a fundamental base of our higher Popular Education, that a stated portion of each day shall be devoted to the acquisition of skill in some department of Industry—to Manual Labor for the sake of the strength it imparts, the disorders it baffles, the comforts it creates, the independence it secures, and the professional man may then stand up before his flock, his patients, his clients, in an attitude of conscious self-reliance, and say to them, "Employ and requite me if you choose: the earth and the kindly elements will reward my efforts if you do not want them; and, so long as vegetation proceeds and sunshine follows the shower, I can exist as well without you as you can without me. I have learned to labor efficiently with my hands; and I am neither afraid nor ashamed to do so, and whenever I have no other employment I shall joyfully earn my bread thus." Surely, the opinions and inculcations of the professional man in this attitude would deserve and command a degree of respect which is not now accorded to them. He could never more be rendered the slave of others' vices or prejudices; he would be master of his own aims if not of his destiny. The humiliating, fettering consciousness that any reckless following of Conscience out of the track of Prescription or Tradition would almost entirely deprive him of bread, would vanish for ever. In its stead would come self-respect and serenity; and not *self*-respect only, but the respect of those made to realize that his livelihood did not depend on his conformity to the standard of their opinions or desires. My profound conviction that the independence, adequate influence and proper dignity of the better Educated or Professional Class imperatively demands a reform in our systems of instruction which shall render the educated man skillful as well as knowing, *handy* as well as long-headed, will not allow me to neglect any fair opportunity of proclaiming and insisting on the requisition of Manual Labor as an integral part of our better Education. Not for their own sakes merely, though greatly for those, do I insist that the Thinking Class shall become a Working Class in the rude, palpable sense. I demand a more brotherly relation between the man who lives by turning clods and him who strives to turn hearts. That spectacle of the Emperor of China standing forth under the vernal sun a guider of the plow, can you think that it has no worth, no meaning, but as a state ceremonial—a relic of bygone ages? I tell you Nay!—it is to-day, and will be while time and it endures, a most inspiring, beneficent Reality and no sham. That single act shall lighten the heavy burthen on millions of aching shoulders—shall make the poorest and most heart-weary delver in all China more hopeful and joyous, at all events less miserable, than he else would be. Who shall deem himself degraded or dishonored by a calling which the Sovereign Majesty takes pleasure and pride in following, if not constantly yet statedly, as if to say that he would cleave to it daily did not imperious duties and the welfare of Three Hundred Millions sternly forbid? Rely on it, there is no other day in all the year when the 'Brother of the Sun and Moon' does half so much toward the right governing of those Millions as on that day when he turns the sward beneath the gaze of exulting thousands. Herein does he prove himself truly a Ruler, and more — a Teacher, by indisputable example — of truths which, if once universally accepted and lived, would make Governing easy and outward, forcible Government a quite subordinate matter. For let men but profoundly realize the dignity and true meaning of Labor — let them feel that not the fruits of it alone are, but the work itself is desirable, essential to the well-being of every son and daughter of Adam, and it is not possible that standing Armies and Armories, Forts and Magazines, multitudinous Police and Tipstaves, would be requisite to keep men from plundering and throttling each other, mainly for sordid pelf. It is the divorce of Work from the visible reward and outcome of Work — of laudable exertion from the palpable need of exertion — which fills the world with knaves and dastards, almost beyond the power of Authority to repress.

When that day shall have come which must come, which sees the truth that lurks in our aphorisms transferred to our popular convictions — when men shall find the highest reward of doing good in being good — when the heir of Wealth shall rejoice in his good fortune, in being able, not to fare more daintily and live more uselessly than his poorer neighbors, but to relieve more distress and diffuse more blessing — when the public opinion, not of the poor only but of the rich, shall hold the consumer in idle and selfish luxury of a bounteous income a craven-hearted object of pity rather than of scorn — when he who in cheerful poverty and serene humility most worthily hews out from stubborn wood or more obstructive stone the sustenance of a numerous family, shall, unseeking, be sought out for public trusts and honors —

when, in short, honest Industry and modest Worth shall be sure of respect and competence, while scheming Knavery and bloated Pretence shall be equally sure of detection and defeat—the work of the true teacher will be easy, the progress of the pupil rapid, compared with what we now witness. The perpetual and gigantic obstacle which confronts the instructor now is the opposition of the incessant teachings of the street, the gathering, and alas! the family fireside, to his own. Does he speak reverently of Virtue and its superiority to Rank, Wealth, Power, or any outward success—he finds his pupils puzzled if not perverted by the palpable, notorious truth that, tested by superficial and vulgar standards, Virtue is *not* popularly esteemed and rewarded. The coterie or the club-room rings with the general laugh at any supposition that a man has done a heroic act—has sacrificed popularity or property from any other than a sordid impulse, and the child is taught, if not expressly yet virtually, by the very mother that bore him, to ingratiate himself with school-mates excelling him in station, affluence, talents, expectations—anything, in short, but essential goodness. To combat and overbear these insidious influences, to make the pupil see through the misleading mists of Opinion and test every appearance and event by eternal instead of transitory consequences, is the high duty of the true monitor and guide of the feeble, faltering steps of Youth.

At the basis of all Morality, all true Knowledge, all lofty Endeavor, lies the truth that God reigns. I doubt not that there have been many worthy and useful men whose consciousness of this truth was obscured—whose minds the subtle mazes of metaphysical disputation had clouded or the pride of scientific attainment had made giddy, so that, bewildered in the very vastness and magnificence of the Universe, they had lost sight of its Creator. I disclaim all impeachment of the morals or characters of unbelievers when I say that I find it utterly impossible to demonstrate the certain and unvarying superiority of Virtue to Vice, of Right to Wrong, if there be no Discerner and Ruler of all things. I know and have said that the truly good man will do right though the Heavens were all swept from his vision, and this earth alone were left, whirling aimless and unguided through the depths of infinite space. But the question is, How shall we first convince the young mind that Virtue is more desirable, more precious than Pleasure? How shall we demonstrate to the passion-fired, hot-blooded youth, that the act which would yield him present ecstacy and yet may be shielded by secrecy from infamy or penalty is to be shunned and avoided at all hazards because it is in its tendencies adverse to general purity and well-being. Such unvarying resistance to temptation is plainly beyond the power of skeptical morality. Not vainly is Joseph solicited if Atheism possess his understanding—never fruitlessly does Satan proffer 'all the kingdoms of *this* world' to one who has no belief in any other. Archimedes must have a place whereon to stand or he can not move the world; and I see not how Virtue can be implanted in the human soul so firmly as to defy the blandishments of seduction, the tempest-gusts of Passion, the dazzling lures of Ambition, if it be not rooted and grounded in that faith 'which entereth within the veil' and undoubtingly realizes that every action is noted by Omniscience and rewarded by Omnipotent Justice.

Mere recognition of God as an Architect is not sufficient: still less is belief in Him as a blind Power—like the Destiny of the Greek Drama or the Fatalism which challenges the Turk's submission. Worse still is the vulgar idea of him as an African Mumbo-Jumbo, to be placated by flattery or won over by servile compliances in place of practical and hearty obedience. Whoever truly knows Him as He is, knows that no act nor thought, whether good or evil, can possibly fail of its due recompense, and that all attempts to evade this by finesse or formula are at once preposterous and audacious. That His mercy to the erring and the penitent never faileth, is a glorious, cheering truth; but vainly shall any hope for Vice, penitent on its death-bed, the rewards of enduring Virtue. Were He but known as He is, we should have more lives of active beneficence and fewer death-beds of abject repentance when too late to be of any earthly use. No Louis XV. worn out with fifty years of debauchery and tyranny, would think of 'making the *amende honorable* to God' by mumbling a wafer and a prayer in his death-throes, but all would realize that 'Whatsoever a man soweth that shall he also reap,' and that the Virtue which holds its even way through life, realizing that God governs and judges here as well as elsewhere, is alone deserving of his favor or calculated to secure it, and that hardly to Heaven itself is it possible to efface utterly from the soul the stains of a career of guilt and shame, save through the purifying fires of a righteous and fearful retribution.

I draw to the close of my hour; yet how shall I close without attempting to impress on your minds the great truth that *Education can never be what it ought until a vast and pervading improvement has been wrought in the Social and Physical Condition of the destitute Millions of mankind.* In vain shall we provide capable teachers and comfortable school-rooms, and the most admirable school-books, apparatus, libraries, &c., for those children who come shivering and skulking in rags—who sit distorted by the gnawings of hunger or suffering from the effects of innutritious or unwholesome food—who must sleep huddled in cellars or garrets unfit even for dog-kennels, hard Necessity overruling all distinctions of age or sex and crowding Modesty through the unglazed window to keep company with exiled Decency outside. You may fill the hovels of the famishing with Bibles and Tracts, sufficient to replace the chairs and tables which famine and the landlord have sent to the pawnbroker, yet you can not render those who grow up under such influences religious nor moral; you may cram them with Popularized Science and convert them into infant prodigies of intellect and culture, and they will yet be deplorably uneducated, untrained, undeveloped. No stimulation of one or two faculties ever yet produced a true or useful human character, nor ever will. The education which does not begin worthily in the cradle can rarely result in eminent worth or honor. Idly shall you labor to teach the child whose earliest recollections are of torturing hunger or of cloying surfeit that Food is not an end of life but a means of sustaining it—vainly shall you moralize to him whose youth was rendered bitter and abject by Want that Wealth is but an added responsibility and not necessarily a sovereign good. The actualization of grosser vice may be shunned from instinct, or fear, or habit; but the soul's native purity and delicacy can not be preserved where a single garret is made to afford the sleeping accommodations of a numerous family, nor can monitorial precepts restore it while the influences which wrought its destruction are still present and potent. It will be idle to expect true, beneficent attainment in school from those who have not the means of decent and comfortable existence at home. You may sharpen their wits; you may awaken in them a dread of shame or pain and a resolution to avoid them. But to impress the solemn injunctions, 'Thou shalt not steal,' 'Thou shalt not covet,' on him who daily casts famine-sunken eyes on the fruit ripening and rotting in the rich man's orchards, and who feels that the fuel which would warm his benumbed limbs is moldering to dust in the adjacent wood, unused and unwanted, this is the impossible task; yet who shall be deemed educated whose heart festers with rebellion against these essential commandments?

Not until we shall have achieved the emancipation of the Poor from the slavery of physical and absolute destitution—not till we shall have rendered possible to all obedience to the Divine precept, 'Take no thought for the morrow,'— not till we shall have relieved all who will work from the terror of constrained idleness and consequent starvation, can I feel that a secure basis has been laid for Universal Education. There will still remain obstacles in abundance— obstacles originating in perverted appetites, impetuous passions, narrow-minded parentage, false pride, mental incapacity, and the like; but before all these I place the impediments arising from extreme indigence and the degradations and dangers which have thence their origin. Let this be removed, and we shall have better opportunity to appreciate and encounter the residue.

Universal Education! grand inspiring idea! And shall there come a time when the delver in the mine and the rice-swamp, the orphans of the prodigal and the felon, and even the very offspring of shame, shall be truly, systematically educated? Glorious consummation! morning twilight of the Millennium! Who will not joyfully labor and court sacrifices, and suffer reproach, if he may hasten, by even so much as a day, its blessed coming? Who will not take courage from a contemplation of what the last century has seen accomplished, if not in absolute results, yet in preparing the approaches, in removing impediments, in correcting and expanding the popular comprehension of the work to be done and the feasibility of doing it? Whatever of evil and of suffering the Future may have in store for us—though the earth be destined yet to be plowed by the sword and fertilized by human gore until rank growths of the deadliest weeds shall overshadow it, stifling into premature decay every plant most conducive to health or fragrance—the time shall surely come when universal and true Education shall dispel the dense night of ignorance and perverseness that now enshrouds the vast majority of the Human Race—shall banish evil and wretchedness almost wholly from earth

20

by removing or unmasking the multiform temptations to wrong-doing—shall put an end to Robbery, Hatred, Oppression, and War, by diffusing widely and thoroughly a living consciousness of the Brotherhood of Mankind, and the sure blessedness as well as righteousness of doing ever as we would have others do to us. 'Train up a child in the way he should go, and when he is old he will not depart from it,' such is the promise which enables us to see to the end of the dizzy whirl of wrong and misery in which our Race has so long sinned and suffered. On wise and systematic training, based on the widest knowledge, the truest morality, and tending ever to universal good as the only assurance of special or personal well-being, rests the great hope of the terrestrial renovation and elevation of man.

Not the warrior then, nor the statesman, nor yet the master-worker, as such, but the teacher, in our day leads the vanguard of Humanity. Whether in the seminary or by the wayside, by uttered word or printed page, our true king is not he who best directs the siege or sets his squadrons in the field, or heads the charge, but he who can and will instruct and enlighten his fellows, so that at least some few of the generation of whom he is shall be wiser, purer, nobler for his living among them, and prepared to carry forward the work of which he was a humble instrument to its far grander and loftier consummation. O far above the conqueror of kingdoms, the destroyer of hosts by the sword and the bayonet, is he whose tearless victories redden no river and whiten no plain, but who leads the understanding a willing captive and builds his empire not of the wretched and bleeding fragments of subjugated nations, but on the realms of intellect which he has discovered and planted and peopled with beneficent activity and enduring joy! The mathematician who in his humble study, undisturbed as yet by the footsteps of monarchs and their ministers, demonstrates the existence of a planet before unsuspected by astronomy, unobserved by the telescope; the author who from his dim garret sends forth the scroll which shall constrain thousands on thousands to laugh or weep at his will—who topples down a venerable fraud by an allegory, or crushes a dynasty by an epigram—he shall live and reign over a still expanding dominion when the paste-board kings whose steps are counted in court circulars and timed by stupid huzzas shall have long since moldered and been forgotten. To build out into chaos and drear vacuity—to render some corner of the primal darkness radiant with the presence of an Idea—to supplant ignorance by knowledge and sin by virtue—such is the mission of our age, worthy to enkindle the ambition of the loftiest, yet proffering opportunity and reward to the most lowly. To the work of universal enlightenment be our lives henceforth consecrated, until the black clouds of impending evil are irradiated and dispersed by the full effulgence of the divinely predicted day, when 'All shall know the LORD from the least unto the greatest,' and when wrong and woe shall vanish for ever from the presence of universal knowledge, purity, and bliss!

VIII.

LABOR'S POLITICAL ECONOMY:

AN ESSAY.*

THE Political Economy of Trade is very simple and easy. 'Buy where you can cheapest and sell where you can dearest,' is its fundamental maxim; the whole system radiates from this. 'Take care of yourself and let others do as they can,' is its natural and necessary counterpart. Nay, this Economy insists that the best you *can* do for your neighbor and for mankind is to do whatever your individual interest shall prompt. That I do not misunderstand and may not be plausibly accused of misstating the scope of the Free Trade doctrine, so far as it applies to the action of states and communities, I will show by the following extract from 'M'Culloch's Principles of Political Economy:'

"Admitting, however, that the total abolition of the prohibitive system might force a few thousand workmen to abandon their present occupations, it is material to observe that *equivalent* new ones would, in consequence, be open to receive them; and that the *total aggregate demand for their services would not be in any degree diminished.* Suppose that, under a system of free trade, we imported a part of the silks and linens we now manufacture at home; it is quite clear, inasmuch as neither the French nor Germans would send us their commodities gratis, that we should have to give them an equal amount of British commodities in exchange; so that such of our artificers as had been engaged in the silk and linen manufactures, and were thrown out

* Mainly embodied in an American Introduction to 'Atkinson's Political Economy.'

only temporary. That this is a mistake, a few moments' reflection will establish. It assumes that the consumption of a given article is not diminished by the transfer of its production from the consumers' neighborhood to a distant shore, and that wherever a community receives its supply of cloths or wares from abroad, it necessarily follows that some staple or staples of equal value will be taken of it by the supplying nation in return. To prove that the fact is not so, I cite the memorable instance of the Dacca weavers of India, as stated in Parliament by the distinguished Free Trader, Dr. Bowring:

"I hold, Sir, in my hand, the correspondence which has taken place between the Governor-General of India and the East India Company, on the subject of the Dacca hand-loom weavers. It is a melancholy story of misery so far as they are concerned, and as striking an evidence of the wonderful progress of manufacturing industry in this country. Some years ago the East India Company annually received of the produce of the looms of India to the amount of from six to eight millions of pieces of cotton goods. The demand gradually fell to somewhat more than one million, and has now nearly ceased altogether. In 1800, the United States took from India nearly eight hundred thousand pieces of cottons; in 1830 not four thousand. In 1800, one million of pieces were shipped to Portugal; in 1830, only twenty thousand. Terrible are the accounts of the wretchedness of the poor India weavers, reduced to absolute starvation. And what was the sole cause? The presence of the cheaper English manufacture—the production by the power-loom of the article which these unhappy Hindoos had been used for ages to make by their unimproved and hand-directed shuttles. Sir, it was impossible that they could go on weaving what no one would wear or buy. Numbers of them died of hunger: the remainder were, for the most part, transferred to other occupations, principally agricultural. Not to have changed their trade was inevitable starvation. And at this moment, Sir, that Dacca district is supplied with yarn and cotton cloth from the power-looms of England. The language of the Governor-General is:

"'European skill and machinery have superseded the produce of India. The court declare, that they are at last obliged to abandon the only remaining portion of the trade in cotton manufactures, in both Bengal and Madras, because, through the intervention of power-looms, the British goods have a decided advantage in quality and price. Cotton piece-goods, for so many ages the staple manufacture of India, seems thus forever lost. The Dacca muslins, celebrated over the whole world for their beauty and fineness, are also annihilated, from the same cause. And the present suffering, to numerous classes in India, is scarcely to be paralleled in the history of commerce."

Here you see are Mr. M'Culloch's conditions made ready to his hand. 1. The people of India were formerly supplied with cotton fabrics from the hand-looms of their own Dacca weavers. 2. They are now supplied with such fabrics much cheaper (that is, at lower money prices) from the power-looms of England. 3. India being a dependency of Great Britain, the goods of the latter enter the former substantially free of duty, and have completely supplanted and ruined the native manufacture. 4. But, though this has now existed some thirty years or more, the supplanted Hindoo spinners and weavers *do not* (at least, they certainly *did* not, and their case is not yet materially improved) find employment in new branches of industry created or expanded to provide the means of payment for the British fabrics imported in lieu of their own. 5. That in consequence, "Terrible are the accounts of the wretchedness of the poor Indian weavers, reduced to the verge of starvation." [Yes, and many of them beyond it.] And 6. That the evil was by no means confined to the weavers, but that the present suffering of "numerous classes," (those whom Free Traders say Protection would *tax* for the benefit of the weaver) "is scarcely to be paralleled in the history of Commerce."

Here is the Free Traders' theory confronted by a Free Trader's notorious and undeniable facts. Can anything farther be needed to demonstrate the fallacy of the former, so far as it assumes unrestricted competition to be favorable to the interest of Labor?

Political Economy is among the latest born of the Sciences. Mainly intent on the horrid game of War, with its power-looms, the British goods have a decided advantage in quality and price. Cotton piece-goods, for so many ages the staple manufacture of India, seems thus forever lost. The Dacca muslins, celebrated over the whole world for their beauty and fineness, are also annihilated, from the same cause. And the present suffering, to numerous classes in India, is scarcely to be paralleled in the history of commerce."

Here you see are Mr. M'Culloch's conditions made ready to his hand. 1. The people of India were formerly supplied with cotton fabrics from the hand-looms of their own Dacca weavers. 2. They are now supplied with such fabrics much cheaper (that is, at lower money prices) from the power-looms of England. 3. India being a dependency of Great Britain, the goods of the latter enter the former substantially free of duty, and have completely supplanted and ruined the native manufacture. 4. But, though this has now existed some thirty years or more, the supplanted Hindoo spinners and weavers *do not* (at least, they certainly *did* not, and their case is not yet materially improved) find employment in new branches of industry created or expanded to provide the means of payment for the British fabrics imported in lieu of their own. 5. That in consequence, "Terrible are the accounts of the wretchedness of the poor Indian weavers, reduced to the verge of starvation." [Yes, and many of them beyond it.] And 6. That the evil was by no means confined to the weavers, but that the present suffering of "numerous classes," (those whom Free Traders say Protection would *tax* for the benefit of the weaver) "is scarcely to be paralleled in the history of Commerce."

Here is the Free Traders' theory confronted by a Free Trader's notorious and undeniable facts. Can anything farther be needed to demonstrate the fallacy of the former, so far as it assumes unrestricted competition to be favorable to the interest of Labor?

Political Economy is among the latest born of the Sciences. Mainly intent on the horrid game of War, with its various reverses and only less ruinous successes, it is but yesterday that the rulers of the world discovered that they had any duty to perform toward Industry, other than to interrupt its processes by their insane contentions, to devastate its fields, and ultimately to consume its fruits. And, when the truth did penetrate their scarcely pervious skulls, it came distorted and perverted by the resistance it had met, by selfish and sinister influences, so that it had parted with all its vitality, and was blended with and hardly distinguishable from error. When it began to be dimly discerned that Government had a legitimate duty to perform toward Industry—that the latter might be cherished, improved, extended by the action of the former—legislators at once jumped to the conclusion that all possible legislation upon and interference with Industry must be beneficial. A Frederick the Great finds by experience that the introduction of new arts and industrial processes into his dominions increases the activity, thrift and prosperity of his People; forthwith he rushes (as Macaulay and the Free Trade economists represent him) into the prohibition of *everything* but coin from abroad, and the production of everything at home, without considering the diversities of soil and climate, or the practicability of here prosecuting to advantage the business so summarily established. The consequence is of course a mischievous diversion of Labor from useful and productive to profitless and unfruitful avocations. But this is not the worst. Some monarch finds himself unable to minister adequately to the extravagance of some new favorite or mistress; so he creates in her favor a Monopoly of the supply and sale of Salt, Coffee, or whatever else is not already monopolized, and styles it a "regulation of trade," to prevent ruinous fluctuations, competitions, and excesses! Thus private ends are subserved under the pretence of public good, and the comforts of the people abridged or withheld to pander to the vices and sustain the lavish prodigality of princes and paramours.

From a contemplation of these abuses, pierced and uncovered by the expanding intelligence of the Eighteenth Century, the Political Economy of the Schools was evolved. In its origin a protest against existing abuses, it shared the common lot of all reäctions, in passing impetuously to an extreme the opposite of the error it went forth to combat. From a scrutiny and criticism of the gross abuses of the power of Government over Industry, it was impelled to the conclusion that no such power properly existed or could be beneficially exercised. Thus the Science became, in the hands of the latest professors of the 'enlightened' school, a simple and sweeping negation — a demand for incessant and universal abolishing — a suicidal science, demonstrating that to do nothing is the acme of governmental wisdom, and King Log the profoundest and greatest of monarchs.

These conclusions would have staggered the founders of the school, and yet it is difficult to resist the evidence offered to show that they are legitimately deduced by their disciples from the premises those founders themselves have laid down.

There are reasons for hoping that the raäction against a sinister and false regulation of Industry has spent its force, and that the error which denies that any regulation can be beneficent equally with the fraud which has cloaked schemes of personal aggrandisement under the pretence of guiding Industry aright, will alike cease to exert a controlling influence over the affairs of Nations. Experience, the great corrector of delusive theories, has long since settled this point, that any attempt to grow Coffee in Greenland, or dig Coal from the White Mountains, must prove abortive; that same Experience, it seems most obvious, has by this time established that it *is* wise, it is well, for each nation to draw from its own soil every desirable and necessary product which that soil is as well calculated to produce as any other, and to fabricate within itself all articles of utility or comfort which it may ultimately produce as advantageously—that is, with as little labor—as they can be steadily produced elsewhere. To do this may require fostering legislation at first to shield the infant branches of Industry against the formidable competition of their adult and muscular rivals, which would otherwise strangle them in the cradle; it may require efficient and steady Protection in after years, to counteract the effects of differing standards of money values, and different rates of wages for Labor—nay, of the disturbing rivalries and ruinous excesses of mere foreign competition, which often leads to underselling at the door of a rival, (especially if that rival be shut out from retaliation by duties on the other side) when living prices are maintained at home. A protected branch of Industry—cloth-making, for instance—might thus overthrow an unprotected rival interest in another nation without selling its products at an average price lower than that of the latter. Having its own Home Market secured to it, and unlimited power given it to disturb and derange the markets necessarily relied on by its rival, it would inevitably cripple and destroy that rival, as the mailed and practiced swordsman cuts down in the field of combat the unarmed and defenseless adversary whom fate or fatuity has thrown within his reach.

Those who profess an inability to see how Protection can benefit the producer if it does not raise the average price of his product contradict not merely the dictates of a uniform experience but the clearest deductions of reason. The artisan who makes pianofortes, say at three hundred dollars each, having a capricious demand for some twenty or thirty per year, and liable at any time to be thrown out of business by the importation of a cargo of pianofortes—will he produce them cheaper or dearer, think you, if the foreign rivalry is cut off, and he is thence enabled to find a steady market for some twelve instruments per month? Admit that his natural tendency will be to cling to the old price, and thereby secure larger profits—this will be speedily corrected by a Home Competition, which will increase until the profits are reduced to the average profits of business. It will not be in the power of the Home as it is of the Foreign rival interests to depress his usual prices without depressing their own —to destroy his market yet preserve and even extend theirs—to crush him by means of cheaper labor than he can obtain. If vanquished now, it will be because his capacity is unequal to that of his rivals—not that circumstances inevitably predict and prepare his overthrow. No intelligent man can doubt that Newspapers, for example, are cheaper in this country than they would be if Foreign journals could rival and supplant them here as Foreign cloths may rival and supplant in our markets the corresponding products of our own Country. The rule will very generally hold good, that those articles of Home Production which can not be rivaled by Importation are and will be relatively cheaper than those of a different character.

And here it may be well to speak more directly of the discrepancy between Theory and Practice which is so often affirmed in connection with our general subject. There are many who think the theory of Free Trade the correct, or at any rate the more plausible one, but who yet maintain, because they know by experience, that it fails practically of securing the good it promises. Hence they rush to the conclusion that a policy may be faultless in theory yet pernicious in practice, than which no idea can be more erroneous and pernicious. A good theory never yet failed to vindicate itself in practical operation—never can fail to do so. A theory can only fail because it is defective, unsound—lacks some of the elements which should have entered into its composition. In other words, the practical working is bad only because the theory is no better.

Let us consider, for illustration, the fundamental maxim of Free Trade, 'Buy where you can buy cheapest.' This sounds well and looks plausible. But let us hold it up to the light: What *is* 'cheapest?' Is it the smallest sum in coin? No—very far from it; and here is where the theory gives way. We do not, as a nation, produce coin—do not practically pay in coin. We pay for products in products, and the real question first to be resolved is, Whence can we obtain the desired fabrics for the smaller aggregate of our products—from the Foreign or the Home manufacturer? Take Woolen Cloths, for instance: We require of them, say One Hundred Millions' worth per annum. Now the point to be considered is not where we could buy most cloths for One Hundred Millions in money, for that we have not to pay; but where our surplus product of Pork, Lumber, Dairy Produce, Sheep, Wool, &c. &c. will buy the required Cloth most advantageously. The nominal or Money price paid for it may be Eighty Millions or One Hundred and Twenty Millions, and yet the larger sum be easier paid than the smaller—that is, with a smaller amount of our Produce. The relative Money prices do not determine the real question of cheapness at all—they may serve, if implicitly relied on, to blind us to the merits of that question. In the absence of all regulation, the relative Money price will of course determine whether the cloths *shall* be imported or produced at home, but not whether they *should* be.

But this is not all. We may obtain a desired product to-day and fitfully cheaper abroad, and yet pay more for it in the average than if we produced it steadily at home. The question of cheapness is not determined by a single transaction but by many.*

And again: We can not buy to advantage abroad that which, being bought abroad, leaves whole classes of our people to famish at home. For instance; Suppose one

* Madison's Messages, 1811–15–16.

hundred millions of garments are made by the women of this country yearly at an average price of twenty-five cents each, and these could be bought abroad for two-thirds of that sum: Would it be wise so to buy them? Free Trade asserts that it would—that all the labor so thrown out of employment would be promptly absorbed in other and more productive occupations. But sad experience, common sense, humanity, say Not so. The truth is very different from this. The industry thus thrown out of its time-worn channels would find or wear others slowly and with great difficulty; meantime the hapless makers, no longer enabled to support themselves by labor, must be supported in idleness. By indirect if not by public charity they must somehow be subsisted; and our citizens will have bought their garments some twenty per cent. lower from abroad, but will be compelled to pay another price for them in charities and poor-rates. Such is the effect of 'Buying where we can buy cheapest' in a low, short-sighted, miserly, Free-Trade view of cheapness.

But why, it is asked, should not a Nation purchase of others as freely as individuals of the same nation are permitted to trade with each other? Fairly as this question would seem to be put, there is a fatal fallacy lurking beneath its use of the term 'nation.' A nation *should* always buy where it can (in the long run) 'buy cheapest,' or most advantageously; where that may be is a question for the nation, through its legal organism, to decide. The query mistakenly assumes that the immediate, apparent interest of each individual purchaser is always identical with the interest of the community, which common sense as well as experience refutes. The lawyer or clergyman in Illinois may obtain his coat of the desired quality cheaper (for less money) from Paris than it can be fabricated in Illinois, yet it by no means follows that it is the interest of Illinois to purchase her coats or cloths from Europe—quite the contrary is the fact. Nay, it would be easy to show that the real, permanent interest of the lawyer or clergyman himself—certainly of his class—is subserved by legislation which encourages and protects the home producer of those articles, not only because they improve in quality and are reduced in price under such a policy, but because the sources of his own prosperity and income are expanded or dried up as the Industry of his own region is employed, its capacities developed, and its sphere of production enlarged and diversified. Let us illustrate this truth more fully:

The state of Illinois, for example, is primarily grain-growing, producing a surplus of five millions of bushels of Wheat and Indian Corn annually, worth in New-York four millions of dollars, and requiring in return ten millions of yards of Cloths of various kinds and qualities, costing in New-York a like sum. In the absence of all legislation, she purchases and consumes mainly English cloths, which can be transmitted from Leeds to Chicago in a month, at a cost, including insurance and interest, of not more than five per cent. and there undersell any Illinois fabricator of cloths equal in quality and finish. Is it the real, permanent interest of Illinois (disregarding the apparent momentary interest of this or that class of persons in Illinois) to persist in Free Trade? or, on the other hand, to concur in such legislation as will insure the production of her cloths mainly at home? Here is opened the whole question between Free Trade and Protection.

The advocate of Free Trade insists that the solution of the problem lies plain on the surface. The British broadcloth is offered in abundance for three dollars per yard; the American is charged twenty per cent. higher, and can not be afforded for three dollars. The true course is obvious —'Buy where you can buy cheapest.' But the advocate of Protection answers that the real, intrinsic cheapness is not determined by the market price of the rival fabrics in coin — specie not being the chief staple of Illinois, nor produced there at all — but *where may the required Cloth be bought with the smallest amount of her Grain?* Is not this true? What avails it to Illinois that she may have Cloth from England twenty per cent. cheaper if she is, by purchasing her supply there, constrained to sell her Grain at half price or less? Let us see, then, what is the inevitable fact:

That we can not buy, perpetually, without paying — that in paying for a single article, we must regard, not how much the payment is *called*, but how much it *is*, (that is, the amount of Products absorbed in paying for, or of the Labor expended in producing it) — we assume to be obvious or sufficiently demonstrated. Let us now consider what will be the inevitable cost to Illinois — the *real* cost — of one million yards of broadcloth obtained from England as compared with the same cloth produced at home.

The average value of Wheat throughout the world is not far from one dollar per bushel, varying largely, of course, in different localities; in the heart of a grain-growing region, away from manufactures or navigation, it must fall greatly below that standard; in other districts, where consumption considerably exceeds production, rendering a resort to importation necessary, the price rises above the average standard. The price at a given point is determined by its proximity to a market for its surplus or a surplus for its market. Great Britain does not produce as much as will feed her own population; hence her average price must be governed by the rate at which she can supply her deficiency from abroad; Illinois produces in excess, and the price there must be governed by the rate at which she can dispose of her surplus, including the cost of its transportation to an adequate market. In other words, (all regulation being thrown aside) the price which England must pay must be the price at the most convenient foreign marts of adequate supply, adding the cost of transportation; while the grain of Illinois will be worth to her its price in the ultimate market of its surplus, less the cost of sending it there.

Now the great grain-growing plains of Poland and Southern Russia, with capacities of production never yet half explored, even — with Labor cheaper than it ever can or should be in this country — are producing Wheat in the interior at fifty cents a bushel or lower, so that it is ordinarily obtained at Dantzic on the Baltic for ninety cents per bushel and at Odessa on the Black Sea for eighty, very nearly. With a Free Trade in grain, Britain can be abundantly supplied from Europe alone at a cost not exceeding one dollar and ten cents per bushel; with a competition from America, the average price in her ports would more probably range from one dollar to one dollar and six cents. What, then, is the prospect for Illinois, buying her Cloths from Great Britain, and compelled to sell *somewhere* her Grain to pay for them?

That she could not sell elsewhere her surplus to such extent as would be necessary, is obvious. The ability of the Eastern States to purchase the produce of her fertile prairies depends on the activity and stability of their Manufactures — depends, in short, on the market for their manufactures in the Great West. The markets to which we can resort, in the absence of the English, are limited indeed. In point of fact, the rule will hold substantially good, though trivial exceptions are presented, that, IN ORDER TO PURCHASE AND PAY FOR THE MANUFACTURES OF GREAT BRITAIN, ILLINOIS MUST SELL TO THAT COUNTRY THE GREAT BULK OF HER SURPLUS OF AGRICULTURAL PRODUCTIONS.

The rates at which she must *sell* this surplus, we have already seen; the cost of transporting it is easily computed. Seventy-five cents per bushel is considerably below the average cost of transporting Wheat from the prairies of Illinois to England, but that may be assumed as a fair average for the next ten years, in view of the improvements being

England to America, and placing them side by side with the producers of Grain, she has effected an enormous SAVING OF LABOR—of that Labor, namely, which was before employed in trasporting Grain and Cloth from continent to continent. One hundred thousand grain-growers and cloth-makers produce just as much now as they did with four thousand miles of land and water between them, while they no longer require the services of another hundred thousand persons as boatmen, sailors, shippers, forwarders, &c., to interchange their respective products. These now become producers themselves. By thus diminishing vastly the number of non-producers and adding to that of producers, the aggregate of production is immensely increased, increasing in like measure the dividends of Capital and the rewards of Labor.

Such is the process by which wise Protection increases the prosperity of a country, quite apart from its effect in discouraging ruinous fluctuations and competition, whereby thousands of producers are frequently thrown out of employment and thence out of bread. It is this multiplying and diversifying of the departments of Home Industry, bringing the farmer, the artisan, the manufacturer into immediate contact with each other, and enabling them to interchange their products without the intervention of several non-producers, which is justly regarded as the great end of an enlightened and paternal policy. To guard against the changes, fluctuations, depressions, which an unbounded competition and rivalry are sure to induce, is also well worthy of effort; but the primary aim of Protection is to secure a *real* cheapness of production and supply, instead of the nominal, indefinite, deceptive cheapness which Free Trade obtains by looking to the money price only of the staples purchased.

—But why, it is asked, have we need of any legislation on the subject, if the Home Trade and Home Production

England to America, and placing them side by side with the producers of Grain, she has effected an enormous SAVING OF LABOR—of that Labor, namely, which was before employed in trasporting Grain and Cloth from continent to continent. One hundred thousand grain-growers and cloth-makers produce just as much now as they did with four thousand miles of land and water between them, while they no longer require the services of another hundred thousand persons as boatmen, sailors, shippers, forwarders, &c., to interchange their respective products. These now become producers themselves. By thus diminishing vastly the number of non-producers and adding to that of producers, the aggregate of production is immensely increased, increasing in like measure the dividends of Capital and the rewards of Labor.

Such is the process by which wise Protection increases the prosperity of a country, quite apart from its effect in discouraging ruinous fluctuations and competition, whereby thousands of producers are frequently thrown out of employment and thence out of bread. It is this multiplying and diversifying of the departments of Home Industry, bringing the farmer, the artisan, the manufacturer into immediate contact with each other, and enabling them to interchange their products without the intervention of several non-producers, which is justly regarded as the great end of an enlightened and paternal policy. To guard against the changes, fluctuations, depressions, which an unbounded competition and rivalry are sure to induce, is also well worthy of effort; but the primary aim of Protection is to secure a *real* cheapness of production and supply, instead of the nominal, indefinite, deceptive cheapness which Free Trade obtains by looking to the money price only of the staples purchased.

—But why, it is asked, have we need of any legislation on the subject, if the Home Trade and Home Production be so much more beneficial than Foreign? The answer to this question is made obvious by the foregoing illustrations. The *individual* farmer, lawyer, teacher, of Illinois might with Free Trade obtain the Foreign fabrics cheaper than the Domestic, escaping, or seeming to escape, the consequent reduction in the price of Domestic staples which we have seen to be the result of a resort to distant countries for the great bulk of desirable fabrics; but *the community* could not escape it. On the other hand, the individual might perceive clearly the true policy to be pursued by all; but how could he effect its adoption except through the action of the Government? The Farmer, producing a thousand bushels of Grain, might see clearly that the *general* encouragement of Home Manufactures would build up a Home Market for Grain at a more adequate price; but *his* buying Domestic fabrics instead of Foreign, while importation remained unrestricted, and the majority purchased abroad, would answer no purpose whatever. It would only condemn him to sell his products for a still smaller return than the meager one which Free Trade vouchsafed him.

On this point it seems obvious that the inculcations of our leading Political Economists must be revised—the solecisms which they imbody have grown too glaring and vital to be longer endured. The distinction between real and merely nominal or money cheapness in marts of supply must be acknowledged and respected, or the flagrant contrarieties of Fact and Theory will impel the practical world to distrust and ultimately to discard the theory and its authors.

But not less mistaken and short-sighted than the First Commandment of the Free Trade Decalogue—'Buy where you can cheapest'—is the kindred precept, '*Laissez faire*'—'Let us alone.' That those who are profiting, amassing wealth and rolling in luxury, from the proceeds of some craft or vocation gainful to them but perilous and fraught with evil to the common weal, should strive to lift this maxim from the mire of selfishness and heartless indifference to others' woes to the dignity of Statesmanship, is not remarkable; but that any one seriously claiming to think and labor for National or Social well-being should propound and defend it, this is as amazing as lamentable. Regarded in the light of Morality, it can not stand a moment: it is identical in spirit with the sullen insolence of Cain—'Am I my brother's keeper?' If it be, indeed, a sound maxim, and the self-interest of each individual—himself being the judge—be necessarily identical with the common interest, then it is difficult to determine why Governments should exist at all—why constraint should in any case be put on the action of any rational being. But it needs not that this doctrine of 'Laissez faire' should be traced to its ultimate results, to show that it is inconsistent with any true idea of the interests of Society or the duties of Government. The Genius of the Nineteenth Century—the expanding Benevolence and all-embracing Sympathy of our age—emphatically repudiate and condemn it. Everywhere is Man awaking to a truer and deeper regard for the welfare and worth of his brother. Everywhere is it beginning to be felt that a bare *opportunity* to live unmolested if he can find and appropriate the means of subsistence—as some savages are reported to cast their new-born children into the water, that they may save alive the sturdy who can swim, and leave the weak to perish—is not all that the community owes to its feebler and less fortunate members. It can not have needed the horrible deductions of Malthus, who, admiringly following out the doctrine of '*Laissez faire*' to its natural result, declares that the earth can not afford an adequate subsistence to all her human offspring, and that those who can not find food without the aid of the community should be left to starve!—to convince this generation of the radical unsoundness of the premises from which such revolting conclusions can be drawn. Our standard Political Economists may theorize in this direction as dogmatically as they will, modestly pronouncing their own views liberal and enlightened, and all others narrow and absurd; but though they appear to win the suffrage of the subtle Intellect, the great Heart of Humanity refuses to be thus guided—nay, insists on impelling the entire social machinery in an exactly opposite direction. The wide and wider diffusion of a public provision for General Education and for the support of the destitute Poor—inefficient as each may thus far have been; is of itself a striking instance of the triumph of a more benignant principle over that of '*Laissez faire.*' The inquiries, so vigorously and beneficently prosecuted in our day, into the Moral and Physical, Intellectual and Social condition of the depressed Laboring Classes, of Great Britain especially—of her Factory Operatives, Colliers, Miners, Silk-Weavers, &c. &c., and the beneficent results which have followed them, abundantly prove that, for Governments no less than Communities, any consistent following of the 'Let us alone' principle, is not merely a criminal dereliction from duty—it is henceforth utterly impossible. Governments must be impelled by a profound and wakeful regard for the commōn interests of the People over whom they exercise authority, or they will not be tolerated. It is not enough that they repress violence and outrage as speedily as they can; this affords no real security, even to those exposed to wrong-doing: they must search out the *causes* of evil, the influences which impel to its perpetration, and labor zealously to effect their removal. They might rëenact the bloody code of Draco, and cover the whole land with fruitful gibbets, yet, with a People destitute of Morality and Bread—nay, destitute of the former alone—they could not prevent the iteration of every crime which a depraved imagination might suggest. That theory of Government which affirms the power to punish, yet in effect denies the right to prevent evil, will be found as defective in its Economical inculcations as in its relations to the Moral and Intellectual wants of Mankind.

The great principle that the Laborer has a Right of Property in that which constitutes his only means of subsistence, is one which can not be too broadly affirmed nor too earnestly insisted on. 'A man's trade is his estate;' and with what justice shall one-fourth of the community be deprived of their means of subsistence in order that the larger number may fare a little more sumptuously or obtain what they buy a little more advantageously? The cavil at the abuse of this principle to obstruct the adoption of all labor-saving machinery, etc., does not touch the vitality of the principle itself. All Property, in a justly constituted state, is held subject to the right of Eminent Domain residing in the State itself;—when the public good requires that it should be taken for public uses, the individual right must give way. But suppose it were practicable to introduce to-morrow the products of foreign needle-work, for instance, at such prices as to supplant utterly garments made by our own country-women, and thereby deprive them entirely of this resource for a livelihood—would it be *morally right* to do this? Admit that the direct cost of the fabrics required would be considerably less, should we be justified in reducing a numerous and worthy class, already so meagerly rewarded, to absolute wretchedness and pauperism? It does not seem that an affirmative answer can deliberately proceed from any generous heart.

I am not forgetting that Free Trade *asserts* that the necessary consequence of such rejection of the Domestic in favor of a cheaper Foreign production would be to benefit our whole People, the displaced work-women included!—that these would, by inevitable consequence, be absorbed in other and more productive employments. I am only remembering that facts, bold as the Andes and numerous as forest-leaves, confront and refute this assumption. To say nothing of the many instances in our own country's experience, where the throwing out of employment of a whole class of our citizens, owing to the overwhelming influx of Foreign fabrics rivaling theirs, has been followed, not by an increased but a diminished demand and reward for labor in other avocations, I need but refer to the notorious instance already cited—that of the destruction of the Hand-Loom Manufactures of India through the introduction of the cheaper product of the English power-looms. Not only were the Hand-Loom Weavers themselves reduced to beggary and starvation by the change—no demand whatever for their labor arising to take the place of that which had been destroyed—but *other classes* were inevitably involved in their calamity, while none in India realized any perceptible benefit unless it were a very few 'merchant princes,' who fed and fattened on the misery and starvation of millions of their doomed countrymen.

And here, as everywhere, it is observable that no *individual* action could have arrested the mighty evil. If every person intelligent enough to perceive the consequences of encouraging the Foreign instead of the Domestic fabric had early and resolutely resolved never to use any but the latter, and had scrupulously persevered in the course so resolved on, what would it have effected? Nothing. It would have been but a drop in the bucket. But an independent Government of India, with intelligence to understand and virtue to discharge its duties to the People under its protecting care, would have promptly met the Foreign fabric with an import duty sufficient to prevent its general introduction, at the same time prompting, if needful, and lending every aid to the exertions of its own manufacturers to imitate the labor-saving machinery and processes by which the foreigner was enabled to undersell the home-producer of cotton fabrics on the very soil to which the cotton-plant was indigenous, and from which the fibre was gathered for the English market.

Such a Government would have perceived that, in the very nature of things, it could not be permanently advantageous to the great working mass of either People that the Cotton should be collected and transported from the plains of India about twice the diameter of the globe to England, there fabricated into cloths, and thence, at some two years' end, be found diffused again over those very plains of India, to clothe its original producers. Obviously, here is an enormous waste of time and labor to no end of general beneficence—a waste which would be avoided by planting and fostering to perfection the manufacture of the Cotton on the soil where it grew and among the People who produced and must consume it. This policy would be prosecuted in no spirit of envy or hostility to the English manufacture—very far from it—but in perfect conformity to the dictates of universal as well as national well-being. The cost of these two immense voyages, and the commercial complications which they involve, though falling unequally on the Agricultural and the Manufacturing community respectively, yet fall in some measure on the latter as well as the former; they inevitably diminish the intrinsic reward of Labor on either side and increase the mischances which affect the steadiness of demand for that Labor and intercept that reward. Protection, as we have seen in considering the argument of cheapness, must increase the actual reward of both classes of producers, by diminishing the number of non-producers and the amount of their subtraction, as such, from the aggregate produced. Yet this is the policy stigmatized by the self-styled liberal and enlightened Political Economists as narrow and partial!—as looking only to local and regardless of general good!

The Moral effects of Protection, as resulting in a more intimate relation and a more symmetrical proportion between the various departments of Industry, can not be too strongly insisted on. Capital, under the present system of Society, has a natural tendency to centralization; and the manufacture of all light and costly fabrics, especially if their cheap fabrication involves the employment of considerable capital, is subject to a similar law. With universal Free Trade, those countries which are now foremost in Manufactures, especially if they at the same time possess (as is the case) a preponderance in Capital also, will retain and extend that ascendancy for an indefinite period. They will seem to afford the finer fabrics cheaper than they can be elsewhere produced; they will at any rate crush with ease all daring attempts to rival them in the production. That this seeming cheapness will be wholly deceptive we have already seen, but that is not to our present purpose. The tendency of Free Trade is to confine Agriculture and Manufactures to different spheres; to make of one country or section a Cotton plantation; of another a Wheat field; of a third a vast Sugar estate; of a fourth an immense Manufactory, &c. &c. One inevitable effect of this is to render the Laborer more dependent on the Capitalist or Employer than he otherwise would be; to make the subsistence of whole classes depend on the caprices of Trade—the endurance of Foreign prosperity and the steadiness of Foreign tastes. The number of hirelings must be vastly greater under this policy than that which brings the Farmer, the Manufacturer, the Artisan, into immediate vicinage and daily contact with each other, and enables them to interchange their products in good part without invoking the agency of any third party, and generally without being taxed on whatever they consume to defray the expense of vast transportation and of the infinite complications of Trade. A Country or extensive District whose product is mainly exported can rarely or never boast a substantial, intelligent and virtuous Yeomanry: the condition of the Laborer is too precarious and dependent—his average reward too meager. It may have wealthy Capitalists and Merchants, but never a numerous Middle

Class, nor a flourishing, increasing proportion of small but independent proprietors. The fluctuations of supply and demand soon reduce all but the few to the dead level of indigence and a precarious dependence on wages for a subsistence, unless prevented by absolute and undisguised Slavery.

But not alone in its influences on the pecuniary condition and physical comforts of the mass is the state of things produced by Free Trade conducive to their Social degradation. The external influences by which they are visibly surrounded are likewise adverse to their Intellectual development and Moral culture. The Industry of a People is, to a far greater extent than has been imagined, an integral and important part of its Education. The child whose infancy is passed amidst the activity of a diversified Industry—who sees the various processes of Agriculture, Manufactures, Art, in progress all around him, will be drawn out to a clearer and larger maturity of intellect—a greater fullness of being—will be more certain to discover and adopt his own proper function in life—his sphere of highest possible usefulness—than one whose early years are passed in familiarity with the narrower range of exertion which any one branch of industry can afford. Foreign as this consideration may be to the usual range of Economic Science, it is too vitally important to be disregarded.

I can not assent to the vital proposition so generally assumed as self-evident by the Free-Trade Economists that the ability to give employment to Labor is always in proportion to the amount of Capital, and that the increase of Capital as compared with Population necessarily leads to an increase of Wages. I will not deny that such *ought to be* the result in a perfect state of Society; that it *is* the result is plainly contradicted by glaring facts. The French Revolution diminished greatly the aggregate of Property in France as compared with its Population, yet the average rewards of

Labor were enhanced thereby. The amount of Capital as compared to Population is less in America than in England, yet the rewards of Labor are here higher. On the contrary, there are many instances where the Wealth of a People has increased, yet the condition and rewards of its Laborers, with the demand for Labor, have receded. Political Economy has yet to take to itself a broader field than that of discovering the means whereby the aggregate Wealth of a nation may be increased; it must consider also how its Labor may be most fully and equally rewarded, and by what means the largest proportion of the aggregate increase of wealth and comforts may be secured to those who have produced them.

I am not unaware that at present the current of opinion on this subject sets, or seems to set, against me—that the dead fish all float that way. I realize that the great majority of Authors and Professors who treat of Political Economy are Free Traders—that their writings are admired and commended as liberal, beneficent and of immutable soundness, while ours of the contrary part are derided as narrow, partial, and impelled by a transient or selfish expediency. I perceive that the paramount tendency of our time is toward Adventure and Speculation—that the great mass of the educated and intellectual are making haste to be rich, and generally by buying and selling other men's labor or its fruits rather than by laboring assiduously themselves. Commerce and Importation amass fortunes, and enrich the great journals with lucrative advertising, and found professorships, and fashion the public sentiment of the comfortable class with regard to Labor, its position, and requirements. I see that the very progress hitherto made in the Useful Arts under the shelter of Protective Duties, the progress still making by virtue of the impulse thus given, may render the existence of decided and stringent Protection less vitally, obviously necessary than it was in the infancy of our Country and her

Industry. Yet I see, too, that we who stand for Protection read, study, and endeavor to understand both sides of the question — are familiar with our adversaries' arguments, have considered them, and think we see why and wherein they are mistaken and inconclusive, while they habitually treat our arguments with studied contempt or with a radical misconception which argues gross ignorance or inattention. I can not doubt that this country is now losing many millions per annum for want of a more efficient and systematic Protection of its Industry, though some articles are really, others partially protected by it, and that our Labor is receiving in the average at least one-eighth less than it would be under a thoroughly Protective Tariff, while hundreds of thousands stand idle and earn nothing whom that Tariff would amply employ and adequately reward. So believing, I can not but hope that time, and discussion, and contemplation, and the cooling down of party asperities, and the progress of events, will work a silent but thorough revolution in our National Councils and that the adequate and comprehensive Protection of Industry will again be regarded by legislators and people as among the most urgent, essential, and beneficent duties of the Federal Government.

IX.

ALCOHOLIC LIQUORS:

THEIR ESSENTIAL NATURE AND NECESSARY EFFECTS ON THE HUMAN CONSTITUTION.*

ALCOHOL is a peculiar combination of Hydrogen, Oxygen and Carbon. It is a compound unknown to Nature, but evolved by art from certain vegetable substances in a peculiar stage of dissolution. The first step toward producing Alcohol is the *death* of the Grain or Fruit destined to yield it. When the life of any organic substance is destroyed, that substance tends by a law of the universe to decay and dissolution. More accurately, with the cessation of organic life the laws of vitality, by which the peculiar assimilation of elements forming the Grape, the Apple, the berry of Wheat or Rye, was created and sustained, now lose their power over this matter, and the opposite laws of chemical affinity take effect upon it, causing its several constituents to enter into new combinations with each other and with other substances wherewith they are brought in contact by the action of air, water, and otherwise. Thus the Sugar, which, in the form of Starch or Gluten, forms one of the bases of certain Grains and Fruits, is dissolved in an early stage of the process of decay, and, combining with other substances, ferments, or effervesces, and enters upon the stage known as

* Prepared by request of the NATIONAL DIVISION OF THE SONS OF TEMPERANCE, and published under the direction of a Committee appointed at the Session of May, 1849.

that of *Vinous Fermentation.* In this stage Alcohol is produced, a fiery, volatile, nearly transparent liquid, which, imbibed by itself, is a most undoubted and deadly poison to mankind, as well as to nearly or quite every animal constitution. Had Alcohol been originally and uniformly produced and imbibed independently of other fluids, there can be no question that it would have been recognized and shunned as a bane deadly as any other vegetable poison.

But Alcohol does not naturally manifest itself independently of other substances. The water which forms so large a proportion of the Grape, the Apple, the Peach, the Potato, and which must be commingled with the Grains in order to produce the Vinous Fermentation, remains combined with the Alcohol after the fermentation has produced it. Some small portion also of the other constituents of the original organic substance are held in solution or chemical combination by their affinities with the Water or Alcohol, or both united. Indeed, it was not till the ninth century that Alcohol was separated and recognized as a distinct substance by an Arabian chemist. Fermentation has been very generally practised, more or less rudely, from a very early age, and Alcoholic beverages of course produced ; and Intoxication just as naturally followed ; how or why seems to have been scarcely considered. But the Arabian's discovery induced or blended with the art of Distillation. Thenceforward, Alcoholic Spirits, more or less pure, began to find a place in the bottles of the apothecary, and, in minute quantities, among the physician's prescriptions. It was not till the sixteenth century, however, that Distilled Liquors began to be commonly used as a beverage or stimulant by persons in health.

Distillation is a more potent process, superinduced on Fermentation, rendering its liquid product more fiery, acrid and stimulating. In other words, it is the art of reducing the proportion of Water, &c. and increasing that of Alcohol in a given quantity of the stimulating fluid. Of the earlier stimulants, Ale and Porter contain but one-twenty-fifth of Alcohol, and Palm Wine one-twentieth; Cider, Perry, Elder and some of the milder Grape Wines about one-tenth. [It can hardly be necessary here to remark that none of these contain Alcohol nor any principle of Intoxication until they have fermented or '*worked*,' as the cider-makers say, and that many if not most of the ancient Wines were drank unfermented. That these were known to the Hebrews by a different word from that used to designate Alcoholic or fermented Wines has been fully shown by recent critical investigations, and the seeming contradiction between those passages of Scripture which mention approvingly and those which severely condemn Wine, is thus shown to be no contradiction at all. In the one case, a mild, harmless, palatable beverage, 'which cheereth god and man;' in the other a raging 'mocker,' a heating, corrupting, infuriating poison, was indicated. Those who have any doubt on this subject may dissipate it by consulting 'Bacchus,' 'Anti-Bacchus,' E. C. Delavan's essays, and other elaborate treatises in exposition and defense of Total Abstinence.]

The difference between Fermented and Distilled Liquors is one purely of degree. Alcohol, the intoxicating and poisonous quality, is precisely the same in the two, but there is *more of it* in an equal quantity of the Distilled spirit. While the different kinds of Beer contain from one-twenty-fifth up to one-fourteenth of Alcohol, and the Fermented Grape Wines from one-tenth to one-fourth, the Distilled Liquors known as Brandy, Rum, Gin, &c. are generally a little more than half Alcohol. Sometimes they are reduced far below this standard by the introduction of Water to increase the seller's profits; but this is very unlikely to diminish their poisonous properties, because the diminution of 'strength,' improperly so called, must be disguised by the infusion of drugs, often as poisonous as Alcohol and sometimes more concentrated. Whisky, for example, generally commands from twenty to twenty-five cents per gallon at wholesale in this City, yet it is known that what passes for Whisky (and often for Gin, Brandy and Rum as well,) in the lowest haunts of dissipation among us, is so concocted and 'doctored' as to cost its manufacturers but *fourteen* cents per gallon. The vile and baleful ingredients employed to conceal the infusion of so much water as will reduce the cost per gallon to this standard are such as, if fully exposed, would utterly shock credibility.

They greatly mistake who in this country hope to live longer by drinking Wines or Malt Liquors than they would expect to if addicted instead to Distilled Spirits. True, there is less Alcohol in the same quantity of the Fermented beverages, but *the same quantity will not content them.* Deceive themselves as they may, it is the Alcoholic stimulus that their depraved appetites exact, aud, if indulged at all, they will be indulged to the constantly receding point of satisfaction. The single glass of Wine or Beer per day which sufficed at the beginning, will soon be enlarged or repeated. It was enough to start the blood into a gallop yesterday, but falls short to-day, and will not begin to do to-morrow. And, even were the fact otherwise, the Wines and Malt Liquors drank in this country are nearly all so adulterated that drinking them would be foolhardy even if those liquids, when pure, were naturally wholesome instead of being the poisons they are known to be. White Lead, Red Lead, (Litharge,) Copperas, Sugar of Lead, Rhatany, Logwood, Alum, Elder-Berries, Opium, Henbane, Quassia, Aloes, Tobacco, Nux Vomica, Oil of Vitriol, Coculus Indicus, Grains of Paradise. and even Arsenic, beside many comparatively harmless ingredients, are all in current use among the preparers of Wines, Malt and Distilled Liquors for consumption. Few of the Wines drank out of the wine-producing districts are even comparatively pure, while nine-tenths of the liquids imbibed by the drinkers of this country never smelt of a grape.

Even in the Wine-producing districts of France and Germany, there have been formidable and fatal epidemics, raging through a lifetime, caused solely by the adulteration of wines with lead. So with Cider in England and Rum in Jamaica, in the very regions where these beverages were respectively produced. 'Lead Colic' is a well known disease, whereof drinking drugged liquors is the source. The facts here stated do not rest upon anti-Alcoholic authority. In the standard Vintners' Guides, Brewers' Manuals, &c. you will find directions for correcting acidity, producing paleness, clearness, briskness, body, color, bead, &c. by the use of the notoriously poisonous substances above enumerated. Sometimes the reader is warned *against* liquors so drugged, or the practice of using such deadly poisons is condemned and less objectionable substitutes are suggested; but the manufacturers take the hint. British Custom-house returns show indisputably that the use of Nux Vomica, Coculus Indicus, &c. has rapidly increased of late in England, as it doubtless has also in this and other civilized countries. Nine-tenths of these poisons are consumed in the form of drugged liquors, and that alone. The British Channel Islands are not subject to the British Tariff of Duties, and are consequently places of deposit for wines destined for British consumption, which the dealers choose to have within easy reach, while they defer the payment of duties as long as practicable. The official returns show that for every pipe of wine imported into those islands some *ten* or *twelve* pipes are in due season exported thence to London. It is the same the world over, save that the farther the liquors are transported the greater is their probable adulteration. In Southern Europe, half the wines consumed may contain no other poison than the Alcohol; but in more Northern countries, it is not probable that one-fourth are thus uncorrupted; while in America not one bottle in ten is free from gross adulteration. Our home-made Whisky,

New Rum, &c. is a little better; our Porter, Ale and other Malt Liquors generally worse. Adulteration with regard to these is the law; purity the exception. Of Liquors ostensibly imported, observing, experienced drinkers habitually observe that they grow worse as you recede from the seaboard, so that the pretended French Brandy, Holland Gin or Jamaica Rum which is a tolerable imitation of the genuine in New-York or Boston, becomes one-fourth Whisky and drug at Albany to Syracuse, half ditto thence to Buffalo, three-fourths ditto to Chicago and Milwaukee, beyond which points it is difficult to detect the flavor of the genuine article at all. Now, while this fact does not necessarily imply the pernicious character of Alcohol, it *does* show that the use of Alcoholic Liquors is pernicious and perilous. If we waive altogether the proof that Alcohol is *essentially* a poison, the fact that it is habitually mingled in beverages, with ingredients whose poisonous qualities no man ever disputed, should induce us to let it carefully alone. Partridges are naturally wholesome and savory; but they sometimes eat obnoxious berries which render their flesh a poison. When it is known that some of them have done so in any locality, the eating of partridges in that locality is at once desisted from by all but the grossly ignorant or stupid; and if it shall ever become a habit with these birds to eat the poisonous berries freely and generally, so that their bodies shall be usually poisonous, who can doubt that their flesh will be generally rejected and uneaten? In nothing else do sensible, moral, intelligent men act so irrationally as when they persist in the habitual use of Alcoholic Liquors.

The first production of Alcoholic Liquids was doubtless accidental—caused by the spontaneous fermentation of Grape-juice, Milk, or Grain, under peculiar circumstances, finally evolving a fiery, transparent fluid. (When we term Alcohol an unnatural product, we simply place it in the same category with carrion, malformations, idiots, &c. which are not produced in the regular and healthy course of Nature, but evidence her defeat and disappointment.) Ten thousand times this phenomenon may have occurred unnoted, before some stern necessity of thirst, faintness, and destitution induced some one to imbibe cautiously of the product, in spite of the reluctance and revolt of the senses. The effect was immediate and palpable—elasticity, energy, courage, invigoration,—the first pair and the apple over again. The depression, prostration, and pain came afterward, and could be forgotten or referred to some other cause. If the first bold experimenter in Alcohol did not choose to repeat the dose, the second, the fifth, or the tenth was doubtless less wise. It crept gradually into use—first, as a medicine or wonderful elixir, capable of curing almost any disease; and very soon repaid the confidence reposed in it by creating many new disorders and aggravating those previously known. While it may have been medically employed in some cases with effect, it has unquestionably created a thousand pains where it ever removed one, and caused more deaths than all the medicines on earth have postponed or prevented.

Throw a fierce bloodhound into the cage of a young leopard or tiger, and, although neither ever before saw an animal of the other's species, each instantly, instinctively recognizes the presence of a deadly foe. Each summons every energy for the imminent and deadly encounter, places himself in his best attitude, rallies all his strength, quickens his circulation—'bristles up,' as we say. He is more strongly nerved, resolute, formidable now than he was a minute since, precisely *because* he feels himself confronted by an implacable enemy, before whom to quail is immediate death.

So with the use of Alcohol. A man swallows a glass of Alcoholic Spirits—his first. At once his whole vital economy recognizes the presence of an unnatural intruder—a deadly enemy. The stomach, disturbed in all its functions, says,

'You must not stop here—I can not digest you'—and throws it off upon the liver, which repels it as peremptorily, and thrusts it toward the heart, which with like emphasis repels it. It is thus hurried from one to another of the vital organs, and repulsed by them all; but the necessity for disposing of it is pressingly imperative, and it is expelled in one way or another—partly through the kidneys, partly through the lungs, and partly through the pores of the skin. Unless the outrage be repeated, a short time sees the enemy banished, but only through an extraordinary exertion, an unnatural activity of all the vital forces. The pulse bounds, the blood gallops, the heart quickens its movements, and even the endangered brain is goaded to unwonted exertion. Of all these exhausting efforts, the mind perceives only the impulse, the exhilaration. The happy neophyte almost walks on air—he feels richer, more generous, and of more consequence than hitherto—he has a great mind to give somebody a fortune. (The illusive exhalation produced by opium and some other poisons is known to be even more intellectual and ethereal than that produced by Alcoholic Liquors.) But all this elevation of spirits is not really *created* by the stimulus—it is simply so much vivacity and elation of spirits borrowed at ruinous usury, and of which payment is sure to be demanded to-morrow. To-morrow comes, and the demand with it; but the debauched consciousness fails to attribute the intolerable exhaustion and depression to its real cause. 'When the liquor was present, and potent,' it perversely reasons, 'all was better than usual; but, now that it is gone, I feel horribly.' 'Take more,' chimes in the depraved appetite, and the counsel is deferred to. More is taken, and momentary relief thereby secured, by means which shall necessitate a still more abject prostration on the morrow, which will require a still stronger potion to overcome it. And thus the blind victim goes on, cherishing the adder which daily stings him, and fancying he is revived and upheld by that which is constantly depressing and destroying him.

But it is said that very many drink moderately and guardedly through a long course of years, preserving to old age a sound constitution and vigorous intellect, which could not be the case if the natural effects of Alcoholic Drinks were such as has been depicted.

Now that some men live long in spite of moderate drinking no more proves that practice safe and healthful than the fact that some soldiers who fought through all Napoleon's wars are still alive proves fighting a vocation conducive to longevity. That some persist in drinking without drinking immoderately is true ; but the natural *tendency* of drinking at all is nevertheless from less to more, and from more to indisputable excess. There are many vices of which the natural, obvious penalty is not inflicted on every one who commits them, yet no man doubts the connection between the sin and the punishment. Some men steal so moderately and slily that they are never detected by man; yet no one doubts that stealing is a crime, and that every crime meets its proper punishment. That some men drink liquors yet do not die drunkards is true, as it also is that some habitual drunkards live to old age ; and yet it is none the less true that drinking leads to drunkenness, and drunkenness shortens life. The laws of the universe are vindicated alike by their usual consequences and the apparent exceptions. There may be men who began to drink one glass of liquor per day forty years ago, and whom one glass per day still suffices ; but if so they are exceptions to a law almost universally vindicated; and it is safe to assume of them that a less amount of self-denial than was requisite to keep their allowance down to one glass per day would have preserved them from drinking at all. And if any moderate drinker of forty years' standing will recall to mind the subsequent career of the fifteen or twenty associates in whose company he began to drink, he will, if well informed and candid, admit that seven-eighths of them are now dead, and that full three-fourths, whether now living or dead, have been seriously injured by drinking.

If what has been said of the nature and essential properties of Alcoholic Liquors be correct, there can be no such thing as a *temperate* or moderate use of them as beverages. No man in the enjoyment of health and vigor can need such beverages nor innocently imbibe them, whether in large or small quantities. The whole controversy properly hinges on this question—'Is Alcohol naturally a poison to the human constitution?' If the proper answer be Yes, then it can never be innocently and safely imbibed, except where it is medically prescribed as an antidote to some still more dangerous and deadly evil which it is calculated to dislodge. If Alcohol be naturally a poison to man, then there can be no more temperate and innocent use of it as a beverage than temperate forgery, adultery, or murder. Is Alcohol, then, essentially a poison? I have already expressed my own conviction, which is that of the advocates of Total Abstinence generally. I will proceed to quote a very few Medical authorities in support of that conviction. I can not quote one in a hundred, but I affirm that no candid, intelligent adversary will deny that the great mass of the scientific and able writers who have investigated and treated of the subject concur substantially in the views here presented.

Sir Astley Cooper who has no superior as a British Medical authority, observes:

> "I never suffer Ardent Spirits in my house, thinking them evil spirits; and if the poor could witness the white livers, the dropsies, the shattered nervous systems which I have seen, as the consequences of drinking, they would be aware that spirits and poisons are synonymous terms."

Dr. Wm. Beaumont, Surgeon in the U. S. Army, was stationed at Mackinac, Lake Huron, in 1822, when Alexis

St. Martin, a robust French Canadian eighteen years of age, was severely wounded in his side by the accidental discharge of a musket within a yard of him, whereby part of a rib and a large portion of his side were blown off, lacerating one of his lungs and perforating his stomach. His life was nevertheless saved, and the wound was healed but not closed; the stomach finally forming a sort of fold or overlap, which prevented any exudation of its contents through that orifice, but did not forbid the introduction nor withdrawal of nutritive substances by way of it; nor did such operation occasion any pain. The whole process of digestion was thence observed and experimented upon by Dr. Beaumont, just as plainly as you may observe the working of bees in a glass hive. The time required for the digestion of any substance eaten by St. Martin; the effects of various combinations of food or of different liquids with any one or more of them; the diseases of the stomach and their causes—all were watched and the results noted through a series of years. Dr. Beaumont's book is purely scientific; it has no theory to establish, no party nor school to subserve; it simply details his experiments and observations and draws the obvious deductions therefrom. St. Martin frequently drank Alcoholic Liquors, though not what is called intemperately, and this is Dr. Beaumont's statement of the consequences of such drinking observed by him:

"The mucous membrane of the stomach was covered with inflammatory and ulcerous patches; the secretions were vitiated, and the gastric juice diminished in quantity, and of an unnatural viscidity; yet he described himself as perfectly well and complained of nothing. Two days subsequent to this, the inner membrane of the stomach was unusually morbid, the inflammatory appearance more extensive, the spots more livid than usual; from the surface some of them exuded small drops of grumous blood; the ulcerous patches were larger and more numerous; the mucous covering thicker than usual, and the gastric secretions much more vitiated. The gastric fluids extracted were mixed with a large proportion of thick, ropy mucus, and a considerable muco-purulent discharge, slightly tinged with blood, resembling discharges from the bowels in some cases of dysentery. Yet, notwithstanding this diseased appearance of the stomach, no very essential aberration of its functions was manifested. St. Martin complained of no symptoms indicating any general derangement of the system, except an uneasy sensation and tenderness at the pit of the stomach, and some vertigo, with dimness and yellowness of vision, on stooping down and rising up again."

Dr. Beaumont farther remarks that

"The free use of Ardent Spirits, Wine, Beer, or any other intoxicating liquor, when continued for some days, has *invariably* produced these changes.....The use of Ardent Spirits *always* produces disease of the stomach if persevered in," &c. &c.

Is there on the face of the earth any tangible evidence in conflict with this testimony? I know of none.

Dr. Muzzy, an eminent American physiologist, says:

"That Alcohol is a poison to our organization is evident from observation.....What *is* poison? It is that substance, in whatever form it may be, which, when applied to a living surface, disconcerts life's healthy movements. * * * * Such a poison is Alcohol; such in all its forms, mix it as you may. It is never digested and converted into nourishment.

Dr. Dods, an eminent English physician, being called before a Committee of the House of Commons, testified as follows:

"Writers on Medical Jurisprudence rank Alcohol among narcotic-acrid poisons," of which "small quantities, if repeated, always prove more or less injurious," and that "the morbid appearances seen after death occasioned by Ardent Spirits exactly agree with those which result from poisoning caused by any other substance of the same class."

Dr. Dods, in the course of his testimony, farther says.

"The effects of Alcohol on the blood-vessels seems to be two-fold —increased excitement and contraction in the diameter of the vessels; this tends to produce enlargement in some parts of the blood-vessels, or effusion, should their coats give way at any part of their course

Diseased deposits are frequently formed where a branch is given off, or in some wider portion of the blood-vessels, which give rise to the most painful symptoms, such as are common in gout or rheumatism."

It would be as easy to multiply quotations of similar purport — far easier than to refrain. — But to keep within the necessary limit of a tract I am compelled to stop here. Let the candid and reasonable drinker say whether he can safely and innocently imbibe Alcholic beverages in any quantity.

'How is it,' asks a doubter, 'if Alcohol be so poisonous, that the best doctors often use it in their medical prescriptions?' — The question implies ignorance in the querist that other poisons, and indeed most poisons, are likewise used as medicines, including the most deadly. Mercury, Opium, Nightshade, Hemlock, Arsenic, and even Prussic Acid, are in daily use by the ablest physicians for the cure of human maladies, and, though often abused and misapplied, there can be no doubt that each and all of them may be and are prescribed by the experienced and skillful to remove pain and preserve life. But who thence argues that these articles may be harmlessly and beneficially swallowed by men in health as their own fancy or depraved appetite may prompt? The laws of Health and those of Disease are so different that the fact of a particular substance being useful in certain stages or forms of disease, would rather argue its unfitness to be profusely swallowed in health merely for the sake of a sensual gratification. But I do not press that argument. Suffice it that the fact of Alcohol's being sometimes useful as a medicine does not and can not prove that it is innocent as a beverage.

I have aimed to demonstrate the physical evils of Temperate Drinking (as it is improperly called, since no drinking of liquids essentially poisonous for the sake of a sensual gratification can be truly Temperate) by other considerations than those connected with Drunkenness. It is very true that he who drinks, however moderately, is in danger of dying a drunkard; but if there were no such thing as drunkenness it would still be most unwise and culpable to drink. Indeed, it has been forcibly argued that the physical evils of drinking would be greater if Drunkenness were unknown. Inebriety dethrones the reason, often making of a naturally inoffensive, good-natured man, a furious, raging fiend; but it does not originate the mischief—it rather serves to expel and finish it. It is the demoniac spirit tearing his victim because commanded to come out of him. Thousands die prematurely every year in consequence of drinking who never were thoroughly drunk in their lives. One man drinks three glasses and loses his reason; another drinks six, or even ten, and seems wholly unaffected. Men say of the latter, 'He has a strong head;' and cigar-puffing, wine-bibbing youngsters are apt to envy him; yet he is far more likely to die in consequence of drinking than his neighbor whom three glasses knock over. The former retains the poison in his system, and it silently preys upon him: in the latter, Nature, revolting at the deadly potion, makes a convulsive effort and throws it off. He is damaged by the liquor, but not by its ejectment, whatever he may fancy. Intoxication is a kindly though ungentle ministration whose object is relief and recovery. Drinking is not evil because it produces Intoxication, but Intoxication is ordained to limit the physical evils of Drinking. Let no free drinker, therefore, glory in his ability to drink much without Intoxication; for, in the natural course of events, he will need his coffin much sooner than if liquor easily overcame him.

If the propositions affirmed in this essay be true, how *can* any youth read them and yet become or continue a drinker of Alcoholic Liquors? Banish, if you can, all thought of God and His judgments—forget or deny your immortality—deride the idea of restricting or qualifying your own gratification for the sake of kindred, friends, country or race—regard yourself merely as an animal that has happened here to sport a brief summer, then utterly perish—and still is it not a palpable *mistake* to drink anything that intoxicates? Why *should* it intoxicate if it be not essentially a poison? Is there any other substance claimed to be innocent and wholesome in moderate quantities which drowns the reason if the amount taken be increased? Why seek enjoyment in such a perilous and dubious way—a path paved with the bones of millions after millions who have fallen in pursuing it—when innocent and healthful pleasures everywhere surround and invite you? Lived there ever a human being who regretted at death that he had through life refrained from the use of stimulating drinks? and how countless the millions who have with reason deplored such use as the primary, fatal mistake of their lives? Surely, from the radiant heavens above us, the dust once quickened beneath us, comes to the attentive ear a voice which impressively admonishes, BE WISE WHILE IT IS CALLED TO-DAY.

[NOTE.—The writer does not pretend to know anything on the subject of Temperance which others have not known and well said before him. He acknowledges his obligations for ideas herein presented to Sylvester Graham, Rev. B. Parsons, and several others, beside those he has expressly quoted in the foregoing pages.]

X.

THE SOCIAL ARCHITECTS—FOURIER.

A LECTURE.

By the term Society I indicate that indefinite circle of relations, usages, unwritten laws, duties, obligations, whereby every human being is surrounded from birth to burial, the hermit who flees from the face of his fellows and dwells beyond the reach of human control or influence alone excepted. Wherever two or more human beings exist, recognizing some relations or duties to each other, there is Society.

Yet the Social Structure has varied from age to age and from country to country. Its lowest form is probably that exhibited in our own day by the savages of Australia and some other isles of the Southern Ocean. Looking upon this from *our* point of view, we can readily see that it is exceedingly imperfect, and ill suited to promote the happiness of the People living under it. The wandering, foraging, hunting, fighting tribe which abandons its aged and decrepit members to perish by famine, frost or the wolf, doubtless conforms reluctantly to the dictates of a hard necessity. It commits its burdensome members to such Alms-Houses as it has. Our criticisms upon its conduct, which at first blush appeared so unfeeling, must, if just, go behind the simple *act* at which our humane feelings revolt. *That* was unavoidable, except by preceding arrangements and provisions—in other words, by a better Social structure. To secure this must all wise efforts for the prevention of such tragedies be directed.

Four distinct orders of Society, variously modified as they are unfolded, one from another, have existed and now exist on the earth—the Patriarchal, the Savage, the Barbarian, and the Civilized. Sacred History assures us that the Patriarchal is the oldest, and that while population was sparse and Man's desires few and simple, it assured a moderate degree of happiness to those who reposed in its shade. But a Patriarchal Society is not formed to resist the rude shocks of War nor to repress the effervescence of vehement passions. The few possess and rule; the many labor and obey. Soon, laborers are more abundant than employment; the patriarch's people are "servants born in his household"—in other words, Slaves; his sway is vigorous, his dispensations of food and raiment scanty; the aspiring, the turbulent, the criminal become fugitives or outcasts in large numbers; he is attacked and plundered by these or by the troops of some marauding conqueror, and the Patriarchal System is no more. The world outgrows it, as the son his father's rule—not always, it must be conceded, to his own advantage. But of the various orders of Society which the world has yet known, I need not farther speak. War, Conquest, the subjection of Race to Race, and a general aversion to Industry, are the proper characteristics of the Savage and Barbarian eras, but Civilization has never yet been able to rise above them. The fear of starvation is an inducement to labor only less degrading than the dread of the lash.

Civilization, as manifested in the most favored Christian countries, is unquestionably a great advance upon, as it is a wide departure from, any Social order which had preceded it. The brilliant sophisms of Rousseau and his school have never really convinced any considerable number that the well-being of mankind is to be sought in a return to the wigwam and bark canoe of the Indian. Doubtless, the city has many vices, many diseases, many forms and occasions of suffering, unknown to the simpler, hardier life of the savage. But it has its enjoyments also — pleasures of the Intellect and the Soul — which those who have once tasted them can never willingly relinquish. We may look back with a sigh to the simple joys of Childhood, yet we are rarely in earnest when we wish we were children again. If to the feeble glimmering of the stars has succeeded the indistinctness of the morning twilight, we must not waste time in idle lamentations, but look steadfastly upward and onward to the day.

The idea of a direct and systematic effort for the better ordering of the Social relations of Men, is almost as old as History. The 'Republic' of Plato is its most ancient expression now extant. In that remarkable essay of one of the profoundest minds of antiquity, the critic detects the most glaring incongruities. A rigorous maintenance of rank and caste on the one hand, with an abolition of all individual property and even of the ties of family on the other — here are conditions which could not possibly coëxist for any considerable time. But the 'Republic,' regarded in its proper light as a protest against existing evils and the suggestion of a comprehensive plan for Political and Social improvement, has great worth. It was the remonstrance of a great and pure soul against the usages founded in selfishness, injustice and perverseness, by which the lives of a great majority of the human family were made bitter. That it was not in all respects worthy of acceptance is the fault not of the author but of the age — an additional evidence of the existence and universality of the evils it exposes and combats. If each succeeding philosopher whom the world has reverenced as a teacher and a guide, had done but half so much as Plato to promote it, a great Social revolution would ere this have been accomplished.

But the world has been rarely blessed with a Plato. Inquirers have found suggestions of a Social reconstruction, more or less earnest and thorough, in the writings of St. Pierre, of Campanella, of Morelly, of Fenelon, of Rabelais, of De Foe; and many others might doubtless be added to the list.

The 'Utopia' of Sir Thomas More deserves a separate notice. As the production of an eminent as well as wise and good man, a Lord Chancellor of England two centuries, ago, and one who has made his mark legibly and brightly on the Jurisprudence, as well as the literature of his eventful age, 'Utopia' demands our earnest regard. Its simplicity and beauty of style, its manliness of thought and benevolence of spirit, have won it many admirers among those who would have been most shocked at the idea of any practical realization of its pictures of a better social system.

Utopia is depicted as a Republic, in which every exertion, every impulse tends to and promotes the public good. All Property is common, but every one labors a certain portion of each day for the general weal, the hours of toil being agreeably relieved by music and recreations. Innocent pleasure is the general aspiration, and to secure the widest possible enjoyment the object of the Political and Social Institutions. The laws are few and simple, and the penalties of offences are mild, that of death being never inflicted. The author says, what would hardly be expected from a judge, save one in whom manhood was too strong to be overpowered by any circumstance of position or official duty, 'that as crimes spring oftener from the injustice and wrong 'of Society than from the inherent depravity of the individual, it is clearly our duty and our true policy to prevent 'offences and reform offenders rather than hope to deter by 'the severity of punishments.' It is remarkable and would seem not a little inconsistent that the author, while he eschews individual property, yet tolerates Personal Slavery.

The last writer who need be noticed in this class of theoretical reconstructors of Society is Harrington, author of 'Oceana,' who lived in the time of Cromwell. He, too, depicts to us an imaginary Commonwealth, in which he recasts Society for the sake of constituting a perfect Government. Power, he assumes, always follows the Land, and so, in order to a proper distribution of power he ordains an equal distribution of Property, though recognizing the distinction of castes or orders in Society.

I may not linger over details. Let me remark, however, that these speculators on the reconstruction of Society, from Plato to Harrington, were not weak men; they were not fanatics; they were not outlaws. They were among the wisest and best men whose names have come down to us. They were generally men held in high honor and entrusted with power; who, according to the vulgar estimate, had everything to lose and nothing to gain by such changes as they proposed. No conceivable motive for their inculcations can be adduced, if we reject the hypothesis of a profound conviction that the welfare of mankind imperatively demanded some radical change.

I can not at all concur with those who in our day have professed to find in these productions of lofty and generous minds only the sportive sallies of lively and ardent imaginations—mere castles in the air, intended but to amuse a passing hour. Their authors—I speak of those upon whose works I have mainly dwelt—were not novelists. They were not writers for bread nor for popular applause. They were grave statesmen, eminent sages, profound philosophers. Silence would to any one of them have been more grateful, more joyous, more fruitful, than inditing romances to dazzle coteries and win admiration from the empty and the idle. I conclude, therefore, that each of them had a meaning and a purpose, and that this purpose is clearly indicated by the works themselves. Doubtless, the exposure and demolition of some immediate practical errors of policy or of habit—some deforming accretion which long years of ignorance or vicious passion, of state-craft or priestcraft, had built up, drop by drop, on the face of Society — was aimed at, as in the wilder fancies of the satirists and fabulists of their times. Doubtless, if any one of them had been called upon to establish at once, with such men and means as he saw around him, such a Social condition as he had portrayed, he would have wisely shrunk from the task. But I can not doubt that each of these radiant minds was penetrated by the conviction that the Social structure wherein they and all men lived and struggled, and sinned and suffered, was in itself radically vicious and wrong — that it inevitably tended to create the evils which all good men deplored and resisted, and that a Social Order was possible in which these evils, if not utterly abolished, should be greatly modified and restrained, while happiness and purity should be immensely increased and far more impartially distributed. To incite men to seek for and obtain that better condition was the motive by which they were impelled and directed.

The practical attempts to realize a better Social structure are almost as old as the theoretical inculcations of its possibility — perhaps older. To speak of no other — the Essenes of the time of our Savior afford a well-known example. They were a community of mild and simple ascetics, holding all property in common, discarding Marriage and living in pure celibacy, refraining from War, and Oaths, and Slavery, and bloodshedding on whatever pretense. They were in short very much like the Shakers, so called, of our day, with fewer prejudices and a deeper intellectual life. Their existence was terminated by the stupendous calamities which overwhelmed the Jewish People and scattered their remnant over the face of the earth.

Perhaps the most satisfactory experiment of the power of a true and heartfelt Religion to render practicable and enduring a more genial and trustful Society is that of the Hernhutters or Moravians of Germany. Their example has fully demonstrated the feasibility of combining that universal Philanthropy which spurns the thought of individual and exclusive possessions with the natural sentiment of peculiar love for family and kindred, so as to preserve and cherish both. They, not rejecting but exalting the basis of the family union, have demonstrated that true Marriage is loftier and purer than Celibacy, and that to live truly and wholly to God it needs not that we contravene or contemn any part of the nature wherewith He has endowed us.

I am not personally acquainted with the Moravians, and know not what changes may have been wrought in their relations to each other by time, and personal ambition, and the contagion of evil example. It may be that an intimate knowledge of them might somewhat modify the admiration which a general acquaintance with their history and their character is calculated to excite. But, after making every allowance, it seems to me that the Moravians are to Christendom a rebuke and an example, an incitement and a condemnation. If men may live, have lived, a life of perfect equality and brotherhood, why should any man be content to live otherwise?

With the Shakers, so nick-named, I have some personal acquaintance, and I am not ashamed to own that I have been instructed and cheered by them. They have never been fairly appreciated by the world. Their utter condemnation of Marriage and of Individual Property, their grotesque ceremonials of Divine worship, and their incessant declamation against all departures from celibacy as impure and sinful, have repelled and disgusted nearly all who are not of their own body. But might not a more expansive philosophy, a more liberal culture, discover in these very excesses a moral worthy of the gravest attention? Are our relations as men and women so universally pure and exalted that we may rightly despise those who, unable to separate the palpable evil from the latent good, reject both together? Is exclusive property so beneficent a feature of our Social Order, as practically exemplified around us, that we may fairly stigmatize those who, not needing its incitements to thrift or industry, see fit to decline them? The peculiarities of Shaker worship I readily abandon to the ridicule of the caviler, only wishing that theirs were the only absurdities committed in attempting to honor our Father in Heaven, and that no Religious errors more popular and more enduring than theirs were worse than simply ridiculous.

When all that may be said against these simple-minded ascetics has been freely admitted, there is yet left enough in their character and history to challenge our admiration. They present the sublime and hope-inspiring spectacle of a Community founded and built up on the conquest of the most inexorable appetites. Lust, Avarice, Ambition, Revenge—these are not merely discountenanced by the Social economy of the Shakers, but this economy is based on their entire crucifixion. Nor can I see how any man can rationally conclude, as some have nevertheless asserted, that all this show of subduing the appetites is a hypocrisy and a delusion. I can conceive no earthly motive for practicing so much outward self-denial, at so great inconvenience, and with no hope of honor, or popularity, but a certainty of the reverse, if not based on obedience to an inward conviction. The uncharitable theory supposes a refinement of absurdity and self-annoyance which never yet possessed for any period the brain of any one sane man, much less of a whole community for ages. Let us, then, profit by the lessons which these enthusiasts read us, while discarding their pardonable errors. Let us remember tha' they have solved for us the problem of the possibility, the p acticability, of a Social condition from which the twin curses, Pauperism and Servitude, shall be utterly banished. They have shown how pleasant may be the labors, how abundant the comforts, of a communit) wherein no man aspires to be lord over his brethren, no man grasps for himself, but each is animated by a spirit of devotion to the common good. When I have stood among the quiet homes of this unaspiring, unpoetical people, and marked how they have steadily, surely advanced from abject poverty to amplest competence—when I have observed how their patient but never excessive toil has transformed rugged barrenness into smiling fertility and beauty, how could I refrain from thinking lightly of that blind dogmatism which asserts the impossibility of inducing men to labor except for their own selfish gratification, and affirms the necessity of the stimulus of personal acquisition to save mankind from sinking back into the darkness and the destitution of barbarism?

—I have not time to speak fully of the first of the Social Architects of our own day who attracted the attention of the learned world—of Claude Henri, Count St. Simon, a descendant of Charlemagne—in youth a soldier of our own Revolution, in later years an impassioned seeker of all knowledge possible to man, and an ardent explorer of every field of human experience; falling at length into extreme poverty, and dying substantially of want; yet insisting, through all, not merely on the practicability but the certainty and imminence of a great Social renovation, to be wrought out through the operation of Christian Love. This man, without securing our entire respect, challenges our admiration. Impulsive and sanguine in temperament, he was calculated rather to inspire others than to direct wisely the movement which he originated. Blindly confident that Love would solve all difficulties, redress all inequalities, reform all abuses in the condition of mankind, he does not seem to have considered means at all requisite, but trusted to the simple enunciation of the sentiment. Adversity, destitution, misery, could not shake the convictions of a better day past in better days to come; and the last words he uttered to the few friends who stood around his desolate death-bed of famine joyously proclaimed 'THE FUTURE IS OURS!'

His few surviving disciples, catching new inspiration from a faith so quenchless and sublime, eagerly rushed to the work of propagation, and soon a large number of the best spirits of Europe did reverence to the genius and devotion of St. Simon. But the fatal defect of a want of system, of definite plan, of seeking to base Society on a sentiment merely, was soon evident. The little band who gathered to form the first community or family of St. Simonians soon found their ardor cooled and their sentiment of brotherhood abated. Differences arose which they had no appointed means of adjusting or preventing; many were repelled, while the few who remained are reported to have fallen at length into gross sensuality. Their dissolution was inevitable, and, if I mistake not, was hastened by the Government, which, regarding St. Simonism as a new and specious form of Jacobinic attack on all Public Order, broke up their establishment on a charge of immorality.

The counterpart of St. Simon's is exhibited in the system of Robert Owen, a man in whom it is hard to say whether personal virtues or speculative errors have predominance. Mr. Owen relies as blindly on Reason as did St. Simon on Love. We do not need Law; we need no Religion; we need no hope of personal advantage, to induce us to do whatever is just and beneficent, says Mr. Owen in substance, as I understand him; all that is required is that we shall conduct ourselves *rationally*. All, indeed; but this is very much. If men were but truly reasonable, they would not butcher each other, whether for the honor which neither party possesses, nor the territory which neither needs; they would not grasp, nor covet, nor degrade themselves by all manner of unseemly vices. But how comes it that so few *are* rational?—that so few have been so in the course of a hundred generations?

To say that the fault is in Society scarcely helps the matter toward a solution: for this Society is made up of these very men and women whose irrationality is our puzzle, and is such as they have chosen to make it. The problem is how Society and its members have gone so far wrong altogether. Its solution Mr. Owen finds in the existence of formal Religion, Priests and priestcraft, superstition and blind obedience to the irrational behests of an unknown superior being—these, according to Mr. O. are the causes of the vice and misery wherewith the world abounds. These convictions, no doubt earnestly entertained, have cut him off from the sympathies of the believing, and greatly impaired if not destroyed his efficiency as an apostle of Social Reform. His followers are now mainly confined to the anti-Christian, and the general scope of his exertions is now directed quite as much against Religion as against Social Evils. I regret this, not only because it tends to prejudice, and has already prejudiced, thousands against all plans for Social melioration, but because Mr. Owen's earlier efforts at practical reform, which resulted in the substitution of Temperance, Cleanliness, Thrift, Comfort, Intelligence, for the Drunkenness, Filth, Idleness, Misery and Ignorance which had previously prevailed in the manufacturing district of New Lanark, where his attention was first drawn to the subject, proves that much good might have been anticipated from his undivided attention to the wants and woes of his fellow-men and the best means of removing them.*

The last of the Social Architects to whom I shall invite your attention is CHARLES FOURIER; and if I ask more of your time for a development of the nature and details of his system, it is because I consider his plans far less imperfect in themselves than any other, and more likely to lead to beneficent results.

* For many of the foregoing facts I am indebted to the writings of PARKE GODWIN.

Fourier, born at Besançon, in France, in 1772, was trained to Commercial pursuits in the shop of his father, a woolen draper, where at five years of age he was punished for telling the truth to a customer, whereby a purchase was prevented. From this time his infantine mind pondered anxiously on the means of obviating frauds in Commercial dealings, and of establishing uniform Truth and Justice in the business relations of mankind. At twenty-one years of age he engaged in Commerce for himself on a capital of $16,000, his portion of the family property, which was swept away before the close of that year in the siege and capture of Lyons during the convulsions which attended the French Revolution. His life was barely saved by escape and flight, but he was again arrested at Besançon, and, to avoid execution, compelled to enter the army, whence, after two years' service, he was discharged on account of ill health. He afterward engaged as a clerk in Marseilles, where he was employed to throw into the river an immense quantity of rice, which had been monopolized in a season of public scarcity in the hope of realizing an enormous profit, but which, having been held too high and kept too long, became worthless and unsalable. Other incidents conspired to stimulate his early resolution to discover the means of preventing the calamities resulting to mankind from the frauds, extortions, falsehoods and adulterations of Commerce. Pursuing this inquiry, he saw the field widen before him, disclosing and embracing the broad domain of Industry and the whole Social condition of our race. He became convinced that nothing short of a Universal Science could solve the difficulties and obscurities in which this vast subject was involved. This Science, of which the outline was, as he believed, discovered by him in 1799, was first set before the public in 1808, in his earliest work, the 'Theory of the Four Movements,' or of Universal Attraction and Repulsion. (This was four years previous to the appearance of Owen's 'New Views of Society.') The volume which was published was but one of eight of which the whole work was to have consisted, and was rather a prospectus of what was to follow, than a complete work. Those who know anything of the common or probable fate of such works will not need to be told that the other seven were never published—at least not in their author's lifetime. I have heard that a copy of the published volume was submitted to Napoleon, then in the zenith of his power and glory. The relentless warrior, then involved in his Spanish War and about to plunge into another desperate struggle with Austria, bestowed but little thought upon it. 'The earth must first be plowed by the sword,' said he, 'before it will be fitted to produce such harvests as this man thinks of.' It *was* plowed with the sword—how thoroughly, let Wagram, and Borodino, and Leipsic, and Waterloo, bear witness. In the event, Napoleon was hurled to his island rock, having found no time to look farther into the undistinguished citizen's far-reaching speculations on Divine Benignity and Human Destiny.

The name of Fourier's first work will have indicated that, though he may be condemned as visionary, he can not rationally be considered narrow or superficial. Though his primary object was the prevention of Fraud and whatever induces men to act in opposition to the general or highest good, his researches took the widest scope, and he undoubtingly believed that their result was the discovery of the laws of Universal Unity or those Divinely ordained Harmonies by a knowledge and observance of which all discord, all evil, shall ultimately be banished from the earth. Attraction and Repulsion being the laws by which the planets are held in their orbits, oceans in their beds, and the multiform races of animals nurtured in infancy and impelled to do whatever is proper and needful to them, Fourier held that these same laws, rightly understood and duly applied to the Organization and mechanism of Society, will there produce equally benign results. Some of the more important of Fourier's deductions from a profound and critical investigation of Nature I have very freely rendered as follows:

1. *The Attractions of all beings are proportioned to their Destinies.* Thus every animal is fitted by nature and inclination for the element he is to inhabit and the life he is destined to lead. So man is precisely fitted for that Social Harmony for which he was created, but which he has not hitherto discovered and realized.

2. *The Harmonies of the Universe are distributed in Series*, stretching from the highest to the lowest order of beings. Whatever law exists for one exists for every other, though necessarily modified in its applications. To understand thoroughly the laws which govern one is to understand the laws which govern all.

3. *The Human Race exists not as many but as one.* The ignorance, vice, misery, which seem to afflict but a part, do truly mar the happiness of all. Hence no reform can be perfect which is not universal, and no happiness unalloyed until all evil is vanquished. The good should labor and strive for nothing less than the emancipation and elevation of the Race.

4. *All needful Labor may be rendered Attractive.* By this he means not merely that all Labor may, by proper inducements, be procured without constraint or degrading servitude, but that, under proper arrangements, men will love Labor for itself, will prize it as an intrinsic good, and as contributing to health, vigor, enjoyment, and true dignity. To this law Fourier admits in practice some exceptions, consisting of labors now requisite which are intrinsically repulsive and disgusting, for which he prescribes increased rewards and the highest Social honors. All other Labor, he insists, may and will be performed as freely and willingly as

hunting, fishing, and other sportive functions are in our existing Society.

5. *The Right to Labor, and to the fair reward of Labor, inheres in all men*, and can not be withheld from any without grievous wrong and injury. The man who has no resource but in the strength of his sinews, the skill of his fingers, has a positive claim on the possessors of Land and of Property for opportunity to earn and receive a subsistence.

On these principles, here most imperfectly stated, is based Fourier's system of Society.

Let me endeavor to set before you some rude idea of a community constituted according to his suggestions. But, in order that you may understand the change he proposes, let us first briefly consider the society he would supersede.

A New-England rural township (answering to the French commune, and, in some respects, to the English parish) is, we will say, a tract some six miles square, inhabited, in the average, by about two thousand persons, divided into four hundred families. Of these families one-half obtain their subsistence by farming, a fourth by the various mechanical or manufacturing arts, half a dozen by merchandise, three or four by religious teaching, two or three by law, as many by physic ; a few are so wealthy as to be above the necessity of labor ; some are paupers, supported by the town ; while perhaps a dozen live as they may by hiring out to labor when they must, and picking up whatever they can, at all times. Such are the avocations by which the township is subsisted. It would be a liberal estimate to say that three hundred good days' work are performed daily on the average in all branches of *productive* labor among these two thousand people, while perhaps as much more labor is performed by women, children, and servants in the less profitable but still essential duties of the household. Out of the products of this labor, often rudely applied and unskillfully directed, the whole community must obtain such a livelihood as it has.

Fourier's system would make of these four hundred families one community or association, inhabiting one vast, capacious edifice, (instead of four hundred scattered dwellings of all grades from comfortable to miserable,) with half a dozen spaciously and perfectly constructed granaries, instead of three hundred ill-adapted, leaky barns, the safe harbors of countless destructive vermin. These buildings he would locate conveniently to the choicest lands of the Association, and near its water-power, if such were among its possessions. Instead of some twenty thousand acres of land, (the area of the township,) the Association would require less than half so much, but of this the arable portion would be brought to and kept in the highest state of fertility and cultivation. The property would be represented by stock, as in a railroad or bank ; each member, whether resident or not, holding shares and receiving dividends according to the amount of his investment. The whole of the produce is to be sold or valued annually, a proportionate dividend paid to the capital, and the residue apportioned to all the members, according to the amount and efficiency of the labor and skill of each. Meantime, education is zealously prosecuted in the Association, the fittest persons being chosen for teachers in the various departments, who are to initiate all the children, not merely into the rudiments of learning, as now taught in schools, but into the principles of Mechanics, the knowledge of Chemistry, Geology, Botany, but, above all, into the love and practice of Industry. From earliest infancy they are to be familiarized with the various processes of Agriculture, Manufactures, and the Arts ; they are to see Labor, however rude or repulsive, the main source of honor and distinction, as well as wealth ; and they are to be thus taught to seek the knowledge and skill which shall fit them for eminence in the domain of Industry, and to arrest the earliest opportunity of winning her cherished rewards. Such is a very meager outline of the means by which Labor is to be rendered attractive.

Among the material advantages reckoned by Fourier, as inevitably resulting from Association, as contrasted with the present modes of life and industry, are these:

1. A saving of at least nine-tenths of the fuel now required, of the land set apart to produce, and the labor needed to prepare it.

2. A saving of nineteen-twentieths of the fences now required, covering and defacing the land, and requiring endless repairs, materials, and attention.

3. A saving of the time now consumed in the endless exchanges of products between the various classes of producers, and in petty trade.

4. A saving of the labor now misapplied and wasted, by reason of the want of skill or science in the workman, or rendered relatively inefficient by the want of the best labor-saving machinery. The small farmer can not afford to purchase, for his few acres, all the costly implements of the most skillful modern husbandry.

5. A saving of three-fourths of the labor now required for the preparation of food, and in the various departments of the household. It is evident that these would require far less labor in one house than in five hundred, and that the food of two thousand persons may be prepared in three or four spacious apartments, amply supplied with every convenience, with infinitely less labor than in four hundred petty kitchens with scarcely any conveniences at all. Whether the members shall partake of their food at common tables, in small groups, or in families, is to depend on the free choice of each, the actual cost being ascertained and charged to each in every case.

6. A saving of the entire services of those now employed in the unproductive functions of retail trade, and of most of those now living by Law, Physic, &c., &c. One good Physician would be enough, one Lawyer, it is hoped, too much, for an Association, while fewer but better teachers

than are now required, would impart a far wider range of instruction to the young.

These are but a part of the economies insisted on by Fourier, who is sanguine in the faith that the annual product of the community would be four-fold what it now is, while an immense saving, on the other hand, of property now destroyed by waste, and ignorance, and subdivision, and want of skill, is also predicted.

The general results which he affirms are these:

1. *All needful labor skilfully and cheerfully performed.* In so large a community there would be found capacity for every duty and a duty for every capacity, so that each individual would find that employment best suited to his abilities, and which, by a general though not inflexible rule, would be to him most attractive. In the exceptional instances of duties to be performed which no one would undertake of choice, their recompense is to be raised until some one is induced to undertake them.

2. *Every individual, infants, idiots and disabled persons excepted, will be secured the means of earning an ample subsistence and of acquiring property ahead.* The vast economies and vastly increased production of the community are to redound to the benefit, not mainly of capital, but of labor. Each man, woman, and child is guarantied the fullest opportunity to labor and earn, in the vocation of his or her choice, as nearly as may be, and with assurance of the just and fair reward of his or her exertions. To women and children, gardening, horticulture, the care of fruits, and the prosecution of a great variety of manufactures, in addition to the cares of the household, proffer industrial careers as ample, varied and independent as those of men. With each individual an account is kept, in which he is charged the fair cost of his subsistence, the rent of his apartments, and whatever he draws from the common stores, while he is

credited for his labor or the fruits of that labor, whether used by the Association or sold, at its fair market price.

3. *The most thorough Education is guarantied to every individual.* The schools, though ample, well-taught, and never intermitted, are not, according to Fourier, the main sources of Knowledge to the child; but the fields, the edifices, work-shops, manufactories, and all industrial processes are to be rendered his books and his monitors. From earliest infancy, a thirst for information is to be studiously excited. The child is to be trained to seek honor in usefulness, pleasure in duty, and to plead for instruction in letters and in arts, as the means of enjoyment, of efficiency and of personal distinction.—To become familiar with some new truth, some new process, some application of science to the promotion of human well-being, is his daily step-stone on the path to manhood and its honors. The Library of the Association, open to all, will afford the amplest stores of knowledge to old and young, while stated meetings of those engaged in each branch of industry will be held to receive and to impart the results of experience, of observation, and of study, until the knowledge and skill of each shall be combined in the understanding and practice of all.

Such are some rude, imperfect outlines of Fourier's system. Of the means by which he proposes to secure to each his just dividend of the aggregate product—to each family the domestic privacy and sanctity of its own apartments—to each individual or family the freedom of living more or less sumptuously according to ability or inclination, I have not room to speak in this lecture. Unlike every other notable Social architect, from Plato to Owen, Fourier is wholly averse to communism or the denial of individual property as utterly subversive of justice, not merely, but of individual freedom. Basing his system on a rigorous analysis of the Divine economy as evinced in Nature, he holds that diversity, not uniformity, is the fundamental law to which all human regulation must conform. Many are indifferent to present gratification but eager for permanent acquisition; others are careless of the future, so that the present be but joyous. Some choose to devote a large proportion of their income to dress; others to food; others delight in spacious and richly furnished apartments. Some grudge every moment abstracted from their work; others regret rather those hours wherein they *must* work. Fourier, insisting that work may be rendered as attractive as play now is, leaves to each individual the perfect control of his hours and their uses, the Association taking care only that his earnings shall equal the cost of his subsistence — in default of which, if not caused by sickness or other calamity, his stock is sold to make up the deficiency, until it has entirely disappeared, when his rights of residence and membership are at an end.

In short, while St. Simon bases his Social fabric on universal Love, and Owen on calm, enlightened Reason, Fourier builds on absolute and carefully administered Justice — a justice which secures to each his own, whether of Development, of Opportunity, or of Recompense. Give every one the work for which he is best fitted, give him knowledge and skill, and guaranty him the full reward of his exertions; but disturb not the foundations of Property, nor transfer to any one, save in charity, the earnings of another. This keen sense of justice is the basis of his hostility to Commerce, other than the wholesale interchange of the products of different climes and communities. Traders, as such, have no place in his Social economy. The extent and minuteness of his arrangements to obviate the possibility of injustice, and to reconcile perfect order and harmony with the largest individual freedom, can only be apprehended by those who are familiar with his works.

Yet I could not, with any confidence of a favorable result, invite the mass of readers to study Fourier's system in his own writings. Replete as they are with profound observation and the most searching analytical criticism, they will not impress happily the casual or careless student. The author is too positive in his self-assurance—too dogmatic—too contemptuous in his regard for whatever opposes his views. He has no adequate patience with our difficulty in seeing through his spectacles on the first trial. A lonely, obscure, thoughtful, studious man, treated with obloquy, or more commonly a disdainful silence, by the world's flattered teachers and arbiters, as though he were an idiot or a madman, we may not wonder but must regret that he returned scorn for scorn, and that many of his later works are marred by fierce denunciations of the duplicity, barrenness, and sophistry of the leaders of public opinion.

The world without and that within such a man must present a strange and striking contrast. Around him poverty, neglect, derision—a settled hostility or a more humiliating indifference; within, the consciousness of mighty discoveries—of truths competent now and certain ultimately to transform and electrify mankind. Around him obstruction and want—perhaps hunger and cold; within, the deep conviction that he had discovered the means ordained of God for banishing want from the earth, by quadrupling production, diminishing wasteful consumption, renovating and beautifying the earth, until at last even the Polar Ices should be dissolved, and a joyous, exhilarating spring-time envelop our planet. The reclamation of deserts, of pestilential marshes, of wildernesses and snow-capped mountains, until all earth shall praise Heaven by comforting and blessing mankind—all these, and many more dizzying, are among the ultimate consequences of Social Reörganization anticipated by Fourier.

This sanguine spirit waited eight years after his first work appeared for a disciple—perhaps for his first attentive reader. Six years later, he published his second work, which was met, like the former, by absolute silence and indifference on the part of the press, and so remained unknown to the public. It was not till ten years afterward, on the dispersion of the St. Simonian fraternity in 1832, that he obtained any general hearing. Then a considerable number were attracted by his theory, a journal was started, and, in spite of his earnest remonstrances, an estate was purchased near Paris, and an attempt made at practical Association. It failed at the outset for want of means; though if this had been surmounted, the want of Knowledge and of fit men would doubtless have been found as serious an obstacle to success. The unthinking many were repelled by the failure, of which they neither knew nor cared to know the reasons; the judicious few stood unmoved. Their journal was kept up and its circulation extended; and, abandoning the idea of practical experiment until knowledge shall have been adequately diffused and the confidence of men of wealth and influence obtained, they are still laboring in the cause with spirit and success. In France, they number thousands, including many eminent in station, in intellect, and in worth; in England, they have made some progress; in Germany more, though there are they checked by the prevalence of Communism; in this country, the doctrines of Fourier have gained adherents in every State, and in some sections in almost every neighborhood, and are still making steady progress. Meantime, Fourier himself has gone down to the grave in obscurity, but in undoubting conviction of having pointed the way to a loftier and happier career for Humanity on Earth. He died in 1837.

I have thus hurriedly traced the outlines of Fourier's life and Social System—the Industrial and Economical rather than the Intellectual and Spiritual features of the latter. I doubt not that I have exposed him to objections which a better knowledge of his works would remove; but, on the other hand, I have passed over many of his speculations on subjects having no necessary connection with Social Reform that would be likely to provoke opposition. He was a bold adventurer in unknown seas, and whether he brought back more pearls or bubbles I need not here discuss. I stop not for criticism nor panegyric even on his Social theory, though it seems to me to invite the one and deserve the other. What time I may trespass farther on your attention shall rather be devoted to the Living and the Practical—to a consideration of our own duties, our hopes, and our responsibilities in connection with Social Reform.

—The famous pamphlet of the Abbe Sieyes on the Third Estate or Commons of France, which gave so powerful an initial impulse to the Great Revolution, assumed to propose and answer three questions—'What *is* the Third Estate? *Nothing*. What *might* it be? *Everything*. What should it be? *Something*.' In a kindred spirit I am accustomed to regard the various efforts in our day for effecting a radical Social Reform. * * * *

What, then, may we reasonably hope from these efforts?

If this question contemplate only immediate results, I shall be constrained to answer, Very little. True, I know many noble men and women engaged in these enterprises, and who bring to the work a spirit worthy of our reverent admiration. These can not fail, though the enterprises with which they are connected may. If all of this stamp were united in one undertaking, with means at all adequate to its prosecution, I should indulge ardent hopes. But I can not put aside the impress which sixty centuries of grasping and suffering, of avarice and want, have made on the Human Character. I can not forget that these who are now embarking it would seem so bravely, so heroically, in the various efforts to realize a higher and less sordid Social condition, have lived from infancy amid scenes and under influences whereof Self was the master-spirit, and the ever-cherished even if unuttered maxim, 'Look out for Number One.' Some have doubtless risen, above these influences; others mistakenly *think* they have. But the great majority, even of those who are ready to embark in undertakings to reform Society, have not yet reformed themselves. The motive which impels them, even in this, is at bottom selfish — the hope of ease, of abundance, of consequence, or of fame. As this selfish expectation is disappointed, and disappointed it must be, since no great and true Reform was ever effected except through privations and sacrifices — their zeal will grow cold, their enthusiasm vanish, their faith die out. Their undertakings will fail, and they abandon the cause in the full conviction that the idea is chimerical and can never be realized.

And, besides, we must consider that the individuals easiest induced to embark in any novel enterprise like this, are usually those who have not been strikingly successful in their undertakings hitherto, and who may fairly be presumed less fitted than many others to deserve and command success generally. The fortunate, the skilful, the thrifty, are usually content to remain as they are. They *feel* no necessity, and are slow to perceive any, for a radical change in Society. These are seldom tempted to embark in novel enterprises, while the luckless, the portionless, the unskilled in the crafts of trade and the ways of 'getting on,' are sure to be well represented. I do not note this distinction to cast reproach on any. Every observer is aware that the faculty of making headway in the world is something quite distinct from moral qualities, good or bad. But it is fair, it is essential, that this distinction should be borne in mind.

I am not surprised, therefore, to hear of the failure of most of the rash, ill-considered, ill-provided attempts in our day to furnish practical models of a better Social condition. I should have been greatly disapppointed if they had all succeeded. Of those which remain to buffet the gales of adverse or sport in the breezes of prosperous fortune, a part will doubtless share the fate of those already broken up; while some, I think, are destined to survive and ultimately flourish. But this is conjecture only; while the fact that men *have* lived, *do* live, in a more intimate and trustful Society than the mass of us believe possible, is abundantly established. Apart from the familiar examples of the Moravians, the Shakers, there are in this country communities which have existed twenty thirty, and forty years, holding all things in common, and finding thrift, economy, abundance, happiness, freedom, in their chosen condition. Of these are the settlement known as Rapp's or Economy, in Beaver Co., Pennsylvania, that at Zoar, Ohio, and one or two others. They do not appear to have been held together by any special sympathy or fervor of Religious feeling, nor by any disposition to act as models for the guidance and imitation of mankind. They have no theory to commend, no anxiety to make proselytes. In each case, the Social appears to have been preferred to the Individual economy from a mixture of choice and necessity, and in each it has fully answered the expectations of its choosers. Abundance and thrift have amply rewarded the moderate labor of the associates, and no reason has been given us to doubt their entire satisfaction.

I think, then, we may consider this fact already established, that a more intimate and trustful Social relation is practicable than that which prevails among the mass of mankind —that men may labor and possess in common without jealousy, envy or strife—at any rate, without an increase thereby of these cankers of existence. The vulgar cavil that no house is large enough for two families, is as thoroughly refuted by one demonstration as it would be by a million repetitions of it. Association in life and industry is not a chimera—it is not a bubble—it is not a mere possibility, but palpably and certainly practicable.

But what then? Are we to abandon our old-fashioned and not altogether comfortless dwellings, our settled ways and maxims, because a different Social economy has been found practicable? Certainly not. There are many thousands of us whose condition could hardly be improved by such a change, and whose sense of security and comfort would surely not be. There is many a humble home of which the happiness of the inmates would not be enhanced by a transfer to the stateliest palace, even though a few crowns and scepters were to be thrown in to sweeten the bargain. We need not disparage the old in order to commend the new. There is no probability that the mass of the well-placed and comfort-girded thousands will desert their happy homes to accept any which Association may proffer them, nor that they would be gainers by it if they did. Let all who are satisfied and useful where they are remain so; they are very unlikely to receive benefit or do good by rushing into untried and to them most unnatural relations. Unspeakable is the worth of Habit—of the fact that matters have been so ordered, or have so ordered themselves, for a time whereof the memory of Man runneth not to the contrary. Custom not only serves to reconcile us to privations and sufferings, but it has even impelled mean men to do heroic deeds, hardly conscious that such was their nature. For the great mass of human beings, it is eminently desirable that they should jog on as nearly as possible in the paths worn smooth and plain by their ancestors' footsteps, profiting much by the secondary instinct which the usage of successive generations has called into being, until something better shall be plainly demonstrated. Well is it for them and for their race if 'the wisdom of our ancestors' be not invoked by this immense class to support and justify their adherence to the folly which has encrusted and obscured that wisdom, so that they may be found admiring less the block of amber than the fly therein imbedded.

But on the other hand there is a small number—very small, it may be, but I think it increases—to whom the old ways, the old purposes of life, have become impossible of pursuit—who must breathe more freely or be stifled—who can not live longer to merely personal ends—who will readily dig ditches, if that be the most useful employment which solicits them, but who must do even this heroically, not sordidly, or not at all. They are ready to welcome drudgery, privation, obscurity, but not willing that the covering and cherishing of their own bodies shall be the purpose of their life-long struggle. To this small class the idea of a Social Reform commends itself with irresistible force; they can not banish it from their minds; they can not even affect indifference to it. Need I urge that these should be aided from the abundant wealth of the contented class to give their several plans a fair trial? There is no possible shape of evil, no suggestion of depravity, which has not been bodied forth in acts; why should sanguine hopes of universal good alone be coldly set aside as fantastic and chimerical?

And then, again, that immense multitude whose lives are but a weary round of incessant and meagerly requited drudgery—who herd in hovels, exposed to the visitation of every annoyance and discomfort—with whom the contemplation of the miseries incident to their filthy, noisome, unventilated workshops is forbidden by the overmastering horror of the apprehended time when even this employment shall vanish, taking their subsistence along with it—shall not the thought of *their* world-wide sufferings impel us to do something? The universal spectacle of Wealth and Poverty increasing side by side—of side-boards of glittering plate accumulating here, while the thin diet *there* grows more meager and scanty—all this is calculated to compel reflection, at least. The labor of this generation produces nearly twice as much as did a like amount a century ago; yet that immense proportion of the laborers who must subsist on the Wages of rude manual toil live no better as a class—in the average even worse, than of old. In the great City of my residence, a metropolis of wealth, of commerce, civilization, art and enterprise, not less than forty thousand human beings at this moment vainly seek employment—have sought it for days and weeks without success, and at length almost without hope. Shall this be accepted as the final, God-ordained condition of Humanity on earth? I can not, will not believe it. No: through effort and vicissitude, through aspiration and stern resolve, through the flashes of electric Genius and the slow approaches of prosaic Calculation,—if need be, through reproach and obloquy—the humane and the Christian must patiently toil on, until at length, with bent frames and beaded brows, they shall have attained the summit of the Mount of Vision, and may thence perceive with exulting gladness the glories of the second Eden.

IN MEMORY

OF THE

MARTYRS TO HUMAN LIBERTY,

WHO FELL

DURING THE SIEGE, MAY AND JUNE, 1849.

AS

DEFENDERS OF ROME,

AGAINST

THE MACHINATIONS OF DESPOTISM, THE WILES OF AMBITIOUS HYPOCRISY,

AND

THE INFERNAL PERFIDY OF MONARCHICAL VILLAINS WHO HAVE STOLEN POWER IN FRANCE,

BY MEANS OF

HOLLOW PROFESSIONS OF THAT REPUBLICANISM THEY MORTALLY HATE, AND SWEARING FIDELITY TO THAT CONSTITUTION WHICH THEY HASTENED MOST GLARINGLY TO VIOLATE;

Thus Richly deserving,

The loathing detestation of the honest and just.

NOT SO THEY

WHO FELL ON THE RAMPARTS OF ROME,

sternly Struggling

AGAINST OVERWHELMING NUMBERS, AGAINST AMPLE MUNITIONS, AGAINST FATE:

THEIR HIGHEST HOPE THAT IN THEM, LIVING OR DEAD, THE SACRED CAUSE SHOULD NOT BE DISHONORED.

Their proudest wish

THAT FREEDOM'S CHAMPIONS THROUGHOUT THE WORLD MIGHT RECOGNIZE THEM AS BRETHREN,

Nobly Dying

THAT SURVIVING MILLIONS MAY DULY ABHOR TYRANNY AND LOVE LIBERTY:

Closing their eyes serenely,

IN THE GENEROUS FAITH THAT RIGHTS FOR ALL, DOMINION FOR NONE, WILL SOON REVIVIFY THE EARTH BAPTIZED IN THEIR BLOOD.

Stay, heedless Wanderer!

DEFILE NOT WITH LISTLESS STEP THE ASHES OF HEROES!

BUT

ON THE RELICS OF THESE MARTYRS SWEAR A DEEPER AND STERNER HATE TO EVERY FORM OF OPPRESSION.

Here learn to Feel

A DEARER LOVE FOR ALL WHO STRIVE FOR LIBERTY.

Here breathe a Prayer

FOR THE SPEEDY TRIUMPH OF RIGHT OVER MIGHT, LIGHT OVER NIGHT;

AND FOR ROME'S FALLEN DEFENDERS,

THAT THE GOD OF THE OPPRESSED AND AFFLICTED MAY HAVE THEM IN HIS HOLY KEEPING.

"They never fail who die
In a great cause; the block may soak their gore;
Their heads may sodden in the sun; their limbs
Be strung to city gates and castle walls—
But still their spirit walks abroad."

BYRON—*Marino Faliero,* Act II., Scene 2.

XI.

BRIEF REFORM ESSAYS.

DEATH BY HUMAN LAW.

DEATH is the universal doom. The time, the mode of individual decease are to human vision inscrutable; the event is inevitable. We do not know whether it is better for us to die early or later—by sudden violence or slow decay. Many who die at twenty are doubtless more fortunate in life and death than others who lived to eighty. Many who perished by flood or fire, by famine or frost, by rack or poison, by ax or halter, are more to be envied than the mass of those who lounged through a long life of pomp and ease, and breathed their last on beds of down amid the tears of idolizing thousands. Who can say that a man should be pitied or congratulated that he is doomed to die to-morrow?

Society must live though individuals should die. All speculation on the *right* of the community to take human life is preposterous. Self-preservation is the primal law; and if the death of any individual is necessary to the safety of the commonwealth, he must die. I doubt whether there is one theoretical denier of the right of society to take life who—if he saw a man forcing his way into the window of his family's sleeping apartment, and knew that the ruffian would, in order to rob securely, murder the mother and babes there lying in unconscious slumber—would hesitate to catch up a rifle and shoot the burglar dead on the spot. This would imply no malice toward the victim of his own evil designs — no desire to harm him — no wrath, even — but a simple choice that of two evils the greater should be averted by interposing the lesser.

Thus we hear that in the California of 1849 men were frequently hung by a summary process for simple theft — I do not say wantonly, nor cruelly. There were no courts, no sheriffs, no prosecutors, grand juries, police, nor prisons. The legal forms of indictment, arraignment, trial, sentence, and punishment, were clearly unattainable. Yet theft must somehow be repressed, though at the cost of guilty or even innocent lives. To allow it impunity and triumph would be to arrest the arm of Labor, palsy Production, Transportation, Commerce, and doom the entire community to ruin and starvation. Yes, though it were certain that a dozen innocent men would be put to death under the Lynch-law which precedes and partially subserves the end of the regular Administration of Justice, we must still say, Welcome this dire alternative — welcome anything rather than Anarchy, chaos, and the unchecked domination of devils!

In such a state of things, it is idle to talk of the duty of Society toward its erring, sinful members — for Society's first duty is to exist. That it can not do if the lazy villain may break at pleasure into the frail shanty of the delving miner and carry off the fruits of his patient, exhausting toil. The moment it is established that this is a safe operation, the vicious and unprincipled will hasten to ravage and rob, while the honest and industrious must inevitably cease to dig. They will hasten to collect their valuables in some strong position, to strengthen it with fortifications and defend it by arms. They can do nothing as yet with the rascal but to make him keep his distance, or, if he *will* persist in robbing, to deprive him of the ability in the only way yet practicable, by depriving him of life.

The condition of the Children of Israel at the time the Law was given through Moses was not unlike that of California in 1849. Fugitives and wanderers in a rugged wilderness, surrounded by hostile tribes, and soon to engage in a protracted, exterminating warfare for the land destined to be their home for many centuries—a land certain to be frequently overrun by invading hosts and to be harassed by robber hordes from the adjacent desert—it would have been idle for a people so situated to talk of perpetual imprisonment or anything of the kind. They could treat offenders no otherwise than with severity. Punishment must be prompt or it could not be inflicted, for no prisons existed, nor could any be constructed which could be reasonably expected to hold prisoners through a lifetime. A wise Law-giver could not overlook these facts. He could give no other laws than such as his people's condition and circumstances required, leaving to later times and a Diviner guide the announcement of the Law of the Universe—of Eternity.

The infliction of Death on flagrant offenders is not, under such circumstances, necessarily nor naturally an act of vengeance any more than the farmer's destruction of the weeds, briars, and thistles which infest his fields and meadows is. Man must live—Society must exist—the Right must maintain its ascendency—Cultivation and Food-producing must have scope, though robbers should die, the wrong should suffer, and weeds be exterminated in consequence. Whatever degree of severity and amount of destruction may at any time be necessary to maintain this rightful supremacy of good over evil stands justified by the constitution of the universe. It is not cruel but merciful; not wrathful and vindictive but benignant and humane.

The moral guilt or innocence of the causer of evil is not material to the issue. Suppose an insane man were now wandering and skulking among the nountains and ravines of interior California, so possessed by the spirit of destruction, of slaughter, that he missed no opportunity to kill a human being whom he could surprise when defenseless and alone. He could not be taken, and, if taken, could not be kept secure. He has killed several already, and every week adds to the number of his victims. Now the miners would say, 'True, we know this man is insane and morally irre-'sponsible—that there is no essential guilt in his homicidal 'frenzy; but we know also that many of us must die by 'his hands if he does not by ours. We know that life is 'unsafe and rendered hideous by terror, so long as we re-'main exposed to his destroying fury. Therefore, the first 'man among us who gets within rifle-range of him will 'shoot him down as if he were a wolf'—which he would do, and be perfectly justified in doing—not in revenge for past but in deprecation of future killing.

So with regard to War. If a farmer were to shoot a boy whom he caught robbing his orchard or fleeing from such robbery, the whole country would cry Shame, and the law would not hold the slayer guiltless. But if that youth were an avowed burglar, robbing the farmer's dwelling at midnight and threatening death to all who resisted, shooting him would be deemed justified, not by the robber's guilt but the farmer's peril. The principle is the same with regard to nations as individuals. A nation which should declare war and proceed to invade another's territory, burn its towns and slaughter its resisting people, because of past depredations on the property or outrages on the persons of some of the citizens of the former within the territory of the latter, would surely be guilty of a wanton and inexcusable resort to bloodshed. True, if these depredations and outrages were defiantly proclaimed and gloried in by the offending nation, they might afford some pretext for hostilities—or rather, the *spirit* evinced in their perpetration might be esteemed dangerous to the National and individual security, and so demanding resistance with a view to repression. To embark in wholesale slaughter simply because those outrages had been committed would be wanton and inexcusable crime.

But a nation is invaded and its very existence threatened by some powerful neighbor — as that of Greece was by Xerxes, that of France by the Saracens, that of Russia by Napoleon. It is the plain duty of its people to resist with all their might, and roll back the tide of invasion across their frontiers. It is better for Humanity that thousands should die than that millions should be made slaves, and their children after them. But there is necessarily and properly no vengeful feeling on their part — no wish to harm an individual of the invading host — nothing but submission to the stern, sad necessity of sacrificing the invaders or themselves to the preservation of the most sacred Rights of Man. Since the path to security and perpetuated Freedom lies through the center of that invading, advancing host, the patriot pursues and clears that path, though in so doing he should cleave an invader's heart on the point of his bayonet. Yet he may very probably regard the individuals composing the invading army with pity rather than wrath — may consider that they are, nevertheless, men and brethren, whom deceit and constraint and a perverted love of country have thus armed and impelled on their errand of devastation and enslavement. He must resist and even slay them so long as no other way lies open to him of defeating the baleful purpose whereof they are instruments; but, the moment that peril is averted, by their capture or discomfiture, that moment his acquiescence in this sad necessity of doing them physical harm is at end. To kill one of them now would be a crime — a wanton and guilty effusion of human blood. He is henceforth their friend, their host, their good Samaritan, and in due time dismisses them on their homeward road, heartily wishing them a pleasant journey thither and a long and happy sojourn in the land of their fathers.

—And now to killing malefactors by sentence of law. Is it ever justifiable? I answer Yes, *provided* Society can in no other way be secured against a repetition of the culprit's offence. In committing a murder, for instance, he has proved himself capable of committing more murders—perhaps many. The possibility of a thousand murders is developed in his one act of felonious homicide. Call his moral state depravity, insanity, or whatever you please, he is manifestly a ferocious, dangerous animal, who can not safely be permitted to go at large. Society must be secured against the reasonable probability of his killing others, and, where that can only be effected by taking his life, his life must be taken.

—But suppose him to be in New-England, New-York or Pennsylvania—arrested, secured and convicted—Society's rebel, outcast and prisoner of war—taken with arms in his hands. Here are prison-cells wherefrom escape is impossible; and if there be any fear of his assaulting his keeper or others, that may be most effectively prevented. Is it expedient or salutary to crush the life out of this helpless, abject, pitiable wretch?

I for one think it decidedly *is not*—that it is a sorrowful mistake and barbarity to do any such thing. In saying this, I do not assume to decide whether Hanging or Imprisonment for Life is the severer penalty. I should wish to understand clearly the moral state of the prisoner before I attempted to guess; and, even then, I know too little of the scenes of untried being which lie next beyond the confines of this mortal existence to say whether it were better for any penitent or hardened culprit to be hung next month or left in prison to die a natural death. What is best for that culprit I leave to God, who knows when is the fit time for him to die. My concern is with Society—the moral it teaches, the conduct it tacitly enjoins. And I feel that the choking to death of this culprit works harm, in these respects, namely:

1. *It teaches and sanctions Revenge.* There is a natural inclination in man to return injury for injury, evil for evil. It is the exciting cause of many murders as well as less flagrant crimes. It stands in no need of stimulation—its prompt repression at all times is one of the chief trials even of good men. But A. B. has committed a murder, is convicted of and finally hung for it. Bill, Dick and Jim, three apprentices of ordinary understanding and attainments, beg away or run away to witness the hanging. Ask either of them, 'What is this man hung for?' and the prompt, correct answer will be, 'Because he killed C. D.'—not 'To prevent his killing others,' nor yet 'To prevent others from killing.' Well: the three enjoy the spectacle and turn away satisfied. On their way home, a scuffle is commenced in fun, but gradually changes to a fight, wherein one finds himself down with two holding and beating him. Though sorely exasperated and severely suffering, he can not throw them off, but he can reach with one hand the knife in his vest pocket. Do you fancy he will be more or less likely to use it because of that moral spectacle which Society has just proffered for his delectation and improvement? You may say Less, if you can, but I say More! many times more! You may preach to him that Revenge is right for Society but wrong for him till your head is gray, and he perhaps may listen to you—but not till after he has opened his knife and made a lunge with it.

2. *It tends to weaken and destroy the natural horror of bloodshed.* Man has a natural horror of taking the life of his fellow man. His instincts revolt at it—his conscience condemns it—his frame shudders at the thought of it. But let him see first one and then another strung up between heaven and earth and choked to death, with due formalities of Law and solemnities of Religion—the slayer not ac-

counted an evil-doer but an executor of the State's just decree, a pillar of the Social edifice—and his horror of bloodshed *per se* sensibly and rapidly oozes away, and he comes to look at killing men as quite the thing provided there be adequate reason for it. But what reason? and whose? The law slays the slayer; but in his sight the corrupter or calumniator of his wife or sister, the traducer of his character, the fraudulent bankrupt who has involved and ruined his friend, is every whit as great a villain as the man-slayer, and deserving of as severe a punishment. Yet the Law makes no provision for such punishment—hardly for any punishment at all—and what shall he do? He can not consent that the guilty go 'unwhipt of justice,' so he takes his rifle and deals out full measure of it. He is but doing as Society has taught him by example. War, dueling, bloody affrays, &c., find their nourishment and support in the Gallows.

3. *It facilitates and often insures the escape of the guilty from any punishment by human law.*—Jurors (whether for or against Capital Punishment) dread to convict where the crime is Death. Human judgment is fallible; human testimony may mislead. Witnesses often lie—sometimes conspire to lie plausibly and effectively. Circumstances often strongly point to a conclusion which is after all a false one. The real murderers sometimes conspire to fasten suspicion on some innocent person, and so arrange the circumstances that he can hardly escape their toils. Sometimes they appear in court as witnesses against him, and swear the crime directly upon him. A single legal work contains a list of one hundred cases in which men were hung for crimes which they were afterward proved entirely innocent of. And for every such case there have doubtless been many wherein juries, unwilling to take life where there was a *possibility* of innocence, have given the prisoner the benefit of a very faint doubt and acquitted him. Had the penalty been Im-

prisonment, they would have convicted, notwithstanding the bare possibility of his innocence, since any future developments in his favor, through the retraction of witnesses, the clearing up of circumstances, or the confession of the actual culprit, would at once lead to his liberation and to an earnest effort by the community to repay him for his unmerited ignominy and suffering. But choke the prisoner to death, and any development in his favor is thenceforth too late. Next year may prove him innocent beyond cavil or doubt; but of what avail is that to the victim over whose grave the young grass is growing? And thus, through the inexorable character of the Death-Penalty, hundreds of the innocent suffer an undeserved and ignominious death, while tens of thousands of the guilty escape any punishment by human law.

4. *It excites a pernicious sympathy for the convict.*—We ought ever to be merciful toward the sinful and guilty, remembering our own misdeeds and imperfections. We ought to regard with a benignant compassion those whom Crime has doomed to suffer. But the criminal is not a hero, nor a martyr, and should not be made to resemble one. A crowd of ten to fifty thousand persons, witnessing the infliction of the law's just penalty on an offender, and half of them sobbing and crying from sympathy for his fate, is not a wholesome spectacle—far otherwise. The impression it makes is not that of the majesty and Divine benignity of Law—the sovereignty and beneficence of Justice. Thousands are hoping, praying, entreating that a pardon may yet come—some will accuse the Executive of cruelty and hardness of heart in withholding it. While this furnace of sighs is at red heat, this tempest of sobs in full career, the culprit is swung off—a few faint; many shudder; more feel an acute shock of pain; while the great mass adjourn to take a general drink, some of them swearing that *this* hanging was a great shame—that the man did not really deserve

it. Do you fancy the greater number have imbibed and will profit by the intended lesson?

—But I do not care to pile argument on argument, consideration on consideration, in opposition to the expediency, in this day and section, of putting men to death in cold blood by human law. It seems to me a most pernicious and brutalizing practice. Indeed, the recent enactments of our own, with most if not all of the Free States, whereby Executions are henceforth to take place in private, or in the presence of a few select witnesses only, seem clearly to admit the fact. They certainly imply that Executions are of no use as examples—that they rather tend to make criminals than to reform those already depraved. When I see any business or vocation sneaking and skulking in dark lanes and little by-streets which elude observation, I conclude that those who follow such business feel at least doubtful of its utility and beneficence. They may *argue* that it is 'a necessary evil,' but they can hardly put faith in their own logic. When I see the bright array of many-colored liquor-bottles, which formerly filled flauntingly the post of honor in every tip-top hotel, now hustled away into some side-room, and finally down into a dark basement, out of the sight and knowledge of all but those who especially seek them, I say exultingly, 'Good for so much! one more 'hoist, and they will be—where they should be—out of sight 'and reach altogether:'—so, when I see the Gallows, once the denizen of some swelling eminence, the cynosure of ten thousand eyes, 'the observed of all observers,' skulking and hiding itself from public view in jail-yards, shutting itself up in prisons, I say, 'You have taken the right road! Go 'ahead! One more drive, and your detested, rickety frame 'is out of the sight of civilized man for ever!'

LAND REFORM.

The Rights of Man—his natural, unchanging, inalienable Rights *as* Man—have fitly become, in our day, the theme of general and earnest discussion. We find little of this in the world's early ages and their enduring monuments—in Homer, or Plato, or Cicero—in Magna Charta, or the Constitutions, so called, of ancient Republics, or more modern Limited Monarchies. Only since Paine met The Crisis of our Revolutionary struggle with those brief, terse, vigorous essays which brought the whole philosophy of Government into the strong, clear sunlight of Common Sense—only since Jefferson condensed the truths so enunciated into the Declaration of our Independence—have the Rights of Man been prominently considered and discussed. And, when Jefferson and the Continental Congress proclaimed, in tones to which the world, however unwilling, has been compelled to listen, that 'all men are created equal,' and that among the 'inalienable rights' with which their Creator has endowed them are those of 'Life, Liberty, and the pursuit of Happiness,' they uttered truths of whose fullest import even they were not clearly conscious, and whose ultimate influences on Human well-being and destiny no man can even yet conceive.

Let us consider their bearings on the newly agitated Land Question—on the Right of Man to the Soil. The Earth's surface undoubtedly contains good arable land enough to give to every family in existence a farm of ample dimensions, even though all the unhealthful or inhospitable portions of the globe were left utterly uninhabited. But of the One Thousand Millions of human beings who are supposed to be in existence, what proportion practically enjoy the Right to any Soil except that with which their lifeless bodies are finally covered? What proportion are at liberty to obey God's command, 'Six days shalt thou labor,' save in the contingency that some one else knows that he can buy that labor and sell its product on such terms that he may realize a pecuniary profit on the speculation?

Now these deductions can hardly seem far-fetched: Man, having a conceded right to live, has a necessary right also to a reasonable share of those means of subsistence which God has provided for and made virtually necessary to the whole human family: Having a right to Liberty, he must have consequently the right to go *somewhere* on earth and do what is essential to his continued existence, not by the purchased permission of some other man, but by virtue of his manhood: Having the right to pursue his own happiness by any means not inconsistent with the welfare and happiness of others, he has the right to do so *somewhere*, and to be protected and justified in so doing. In short, the terrestrial Man, possessing the well-known properties of matter as well as of spirit, can only in truth enjoy the rights of 'Life, Liberty, and the pursuit of Happiness,' by being guarantied some *place* in which to enjoy them. He who has no clear, inherent right to live *somewhere*, has no right to live at all.

But look at the question from the side of Labor: God expressly commands men to labor six days of every seven, and has made obedience to this command a vital condition of healthful and comfortable existence. (Alas that one man should obey and another enjoy the reward of his obedience!) Here, in a State or County, are fifty thousand persons able and willing to labor, with an abundance of arable land to employ them all constantly and reward them generously: But the land mainly belongs to a few dozens or hundreds of this population, (or, still worse, of absentees,) who virtually say to the twenty or thirty thousand would-be laborers who own no land, 'You can only be allowed to work here 'on condition that you will allow us [in the shape of rents, 'price of land, or depressed wages] one-half to three-fourths 'of the entire product of your toil.' Is not here a heavy tax levied by man upon obedience to the laws of Nature and of God? Who does not see that Labor is discouraged and Idleness immensely increased by this exaction, and the power vested in the few to impose it?

Yet the most appalling feature of our present system of Landholding is the manifest tendency of its evils to become more and more aggravated and intolerable—nay, the inevitable necessity that they *should* become so, if the system itself be endured. If the population of the British Isles were this day no more dense than that of Indiana or Russia, the average recompense of its labor would doubtless be increased, the condition of its laboring people greatly improved. The gradual increase of population therein from three or four millions to thirty or forty, has, in connection with the monopoly of the Soil by a class who are not its cultivators, gradually carried up the market value and the yearly rental of arable land to prices which enable the land-owning few to riot in unparalleled luxury, and doom the landless many to toil evermore for the barest necessaries of life, while hundreds of thousands vainly beg from door to door an opportunity to earn the blackest bread by the most repulsive and meagerly recompensed drudgery. Like causes will produce like effects here and elsewhere. It is not the fact that the landlords are few that is so baneful; if they were ten times as many, the evil would hardly be mitigated. So long as the millions, whom God has doomed in the sweat of their faces to eat bread, shall be constrained to solicit of others the privilege of so doing, and to propitiate the land-owning class by such a share of their products as Cupidity may exact and Necessity must concede, the increase of population will be paralleled by the depression of labor and the laborer. Other influences may come in to modify or counteract this—new inventions which vastly increase the efficiency of labor; improved processes, more scientific culture, &c., may do something to mitigate the ills of poverty; but the master evil, a monopoly of land by those who do not use it, tends ever to sink the landless multitude into a state of more abject dependence, while it restricts the demand for and the price of their sole commodity and resource.

Suppose the usage and the law were so changed that no man were permitted, in this boasted land of equal rights, to hold as his own more than half a square mile of arable soil (which is enough for fifty men to cultivate) so long as a single person needing land in the community should remain destitute of any, what a mighty and beneficent transformation would be effected in the reward of labor and the condition of the laboring class! Then, instead of a constant increase in the proportion of landless seekers for something to do, resulting in a constant jostling and underbidding among laborers wanting employment, we should see a continual division and subdivision of large estates, with a steady increase in the number and proportion of small proprietors, each his own employer and his own laborer, whereby the mass of landless seekers for work as hirelings or tenants would be rapidly diminished. It is not proposed to disturb any individual in the full enjoyment of his possessions, but to make the operation of the proposed reform wholly prospective, so that, while each proprietor or landlord, at the enactment of the Limitation, should retain his estates until death, all future aggregation shall be sternly forbidden, and the principle applied to each existing estate on the decease of its present owner. Even the right to transmit property to heirs or devisees would not be interfered with, except so far as to say, 'Man of Millions! bequeath your wealth as 'you choose; but that part of it which consists of the Soil 'can only be inherited and held by any one to the extent of 'the limit prescribed by law. If you see fit to devise more 'than this to any one person, he may select from your be-'quest, and any he may previously own, so much as the law 'allows him to retain, and sell the rest: or, if he does not do 'this within a year, the State will do it for him, holding the 'proceeds of the portion sold subject to his order.'

That this will seem arbitrary and impracticable to many is a matter of course, and the hardship of not allowing a man to *do as he likes with his own* will doubtless be dilated on in tones of moving eloquence. But the principle here involved has already been asserted in our Usury Laws and many others which tend to fetter or check the spirit of personal acquisition when it is found encroaching úpon the domain of public good. A man may *not* 'do as he likes with his own' money, nor even with his own house—he is forbidden to burn the latter, though built with his own hands, and entirely unconnected with any other. Many if not most States already limit the area of land which may be acquired and held by a Bank or Moneyed Corporation; probably none allow Aliens freely to acquire and enjoy it. Coëval with the great Hebrew Lawgiver and very thoroughly enforced by him, reäppearing in the noblest periods of Roman republicanism, but gradually sapped and overthrown by an ever-grasping Aristocracy, the principle of Land Limitation has received the approval of some of the most gifted and philanthropic of ancient or modern times. Its triumphant establishment, wherever Popular Education and Universal Suffrage shall have preceded it, is well nigh inevitable.

A ready objection of those who have scarcely thought on the subject imports that any attempt to remedy by law the inequalities of fortune in the matter of Land involves the principle of an arbitrary distribution of Property equally to everybody. But this is an egregious error. What Nature indicates and Justice requires is *Equal Opportunities* to all. To maintain that he who has idly frolicked through the summer has an equal right to food and clothing in the winter with his frugal neighbor, who by patient toil has produced five hundred bushels of grain and some hundreds of pounds of flax and wool, is to contravene the Apostle's precept, 'He that will not work shall not eat.' But Land Limitation contemplates a gentle and gradual restoration of that equal right to the Soil which was ordained by the Creator in the constitution of the globe. Instead of giving to the idle the products of other men's labor, it is intended to countervail that dispensation of human policy whereby millions labor ceaselessly for scanty and bitter bread while thousands revel sumptuously on the lion's share of the products of the toil so meagerly recompensed. Not to transfer the toiler's earnings to the idler, but to *prevent* such transfer, is the object of Land Reform.

But if it be possible to resist the force of the considerations which dictate the enactment of laws looking to a more equal apportionment of the Soil now private property, how *can* it be to oppose with even plausibility the application of the Land Reform principles to our vast and bounteous National Domain? Here we have a public patrimony equal to the habitable portion of Europe, and calculated to support in generous abundance a population of Two Hundred Millions of People. Under our present system, (the best the world has known since the overthrow of the Hebrew Commonwealth,) this Domain is becoming private property at the rate of some Three to Five Millions of Acres per annum. Making a reasonable allowance for the steadily increasing demand, arising from the enlargement of our population and the swelling tide of immigration, we may safely calculate that in fifty years our Public Lands will have been diminished by at least Three Hundred Millions of their very choicest portion, namely, that bordering or approaching the navigable waters of the Mississippi, the Columbia, and their tributaries. The remainder must be far inferior in soil and natural advantages generally. What then will be the condition and prospects of the landless millions among our people, pressed upon by European competition and European immigration on the one side, and deprived in great measure of the present safety-valve of Western migration on the other?—But look forward another half-century, and judge what will then be the state of 'the disinherited classes,' should no change be made meantime in our land-laws. Look to Saxony, to Belgium, to Ireland, for a parallel.

National Reform is the broad and sure basis whereon all other Reforms may be safely erected. A single law of Congress, proffering to each landless citizen a patch of the Public Domain—small but sufficient, when faithfully cultivated, for the sustenance of his family, and forbidding farther sales of the Public Lands except in limited quantities to actual settlers, with a suitable proviso against future aggregation, would promote immensely the independence, enlightenment, morality, industry, and comfort of our entire laboring population evermore. It would improve the condition of the laboring class in our cities, not by drawing away all to the new lands of the West, but by so enlarging the stream of emigration thither as to diminish the pressure of competition in the Labor market throughout the country, and enable the hireling to make terms with his employer as to the duration of his daily toil and the amount of his recompense. It would render settlements more compact and continuous, insuring a more rapid establishment of Roads, of Schools, of Divine worship, &c. It would enlarge immensely the demand for the products of our manufactories and workshops, and thus aid the laborers remaining in the Old States by increasing the demand for their labor as well as diminishing the competition to supply it. It would hardly be possible to exaggerate the ultimate benefits of the proposed Reform, and the day of its triumph should be hailed by the poor and lowly as the birthday of *their* independence, as the Fourth of July is celebrated as that of the Nation.

THE RIGHT TO LABOR.*

"In the beginning God created the heaven and the earth."

The earth, the air, the waters, the sunshine, with their natural products, were divinely intended and appointed for the use and sustenance of Man (Gen. i. 26, 28)—not for a part only, but for the whole Human Family.

Civilized Society, as it exists in our day, has divested the larger portion of mankind of the unimpeded, unpurchased enjoyment of their natural rights. That larger portion may be perishing with cold, yet have no legally recognized right to a stick of decaying fuel in the most unfrequented morass, or may be famishing, yet have no legal right to pluck and eat the bitterest acorn in the depths of the remotest wilderness. The defeasance or confiscation of Man's natural right to use any portion of the Earth's surface not actually in use by another, is an important fact, to be kept in view in every consideration of the duty of the affluent and comfortable to the poor and unfortunate.

It is not essential in this place to determine that the divestment of the larger number of any recognized right to the Soil and its Products, save by the purchased permission of others, was or was not politic and necessary. All who reflect must certainly admit that many of the grants of land by hundreds of square miles to this or that favorite of the power which assumed to make them were made thoughtlessly or recklessly, and would not have been so large or so unaccompanied with stipulations in behalf of the future occupants and cultivators, if a reasonable foresight and a decent regard for the general good had been cherished and evinced

* From a discussion on Socialism, with H. J. Raymond.

by the granting power. Suffice it here, however, that the granting of the Soil—of the State of New York, for example—by the supreme authority representing the whole to a minor portion of the whole is a "fixed fact." By a Law of Nature, every person born in the State of New York had (unless forfeited by crime) a perfect right to *be* here, and to his equal share of the Soil, the woods, the waters, and all the natural products thereof. By the law of Society, all but the possessors of title-deeds exist here only by the purchased permission of the land-owning class, and were intruders and trespassers on the soil of their nativity without that permission. By law, the landless have no inherent right to stand on a single square foot of the State of New-York except in the highways.

The only solid ground on which this surrender of the original property of the whole to a minor portion can be justified is that of PUBLIC GOOD—the good, not of a part, but of the whole. The people of a past generation, through their rulers, claimed and exercised the right of divesting, not themselves merely, but the majority of all future generations, of their original and inherent right to possess and cultivate any unimproved portion of the soil of our State for their own sustenance and benefit. To render this assumption of power valid to the fearful extent to which it was exercised, it is essential that it be demonstrated that the good of the whole was promoted by such exercise.

Is this rationally demonstrable now? Can the widow, whose children pine and shiver in some bleak, miserable garret, on the fifteen or twenty cents, which is all she can earn by unremitted toil, be made to realize that she and her babes are benefited by or in consequence of the granting to a part an exclusive right to use the earth and enjoy its fruits? Can the poor man who day after day paces the streets of a city in search of any employment at any price, (as thousands are now doing here,) be made to realize it on his part? Are there not thousands on thousands—natives of our State who never wilfully violated her laws — who are to-day far worse off than they would have been if Nature's rule of allowing no man to appropriate to himself any more of the earth than he can cultivate and improve had been recognized and respected by Society? These questions admit of but one answer. And one inevitable consequence of the prevailing system is that, as Population increases and Arts are perfected, the income of the wealthy owner of land increases while the recompense of the hired or leasehold cultivator is steadily diminishing. The labor of Great Britain is twice as effective now as it was a century ago, but the laborer is worse paid, fed, and lodged than he then was, while the incomes of the landlord class have been enormously increased. The same fundamental causes exist here, and tend to the same results. They have been modified, thus far, by the existence, within or near our State, of large tracts of unimproved land, which the owners were anxious to improve or dispose of on almost any terms. These are growing scarcer and more remote; they form no part of the system we are considering, but something which exists in opposition to it, which modifies it, but is absolutely sure to be ultimately absorbed and conquered by it. The notorious fact that they do serve to mitigate the exactions to which the landless mass, even in our long and densely settled towns and cities, are subject, serves to show that the condition of the great mass must inevitably be far worse than at present when the natural consummation of land selling is reached, and all the soil of the Union has become the property of a minor part of the People of the Union.

The past can not be recalled. What has been rightfully (however mistakenly) done by the authorized agents of the State or Nation, can only be retracted upon urgent public necessity, and upon due satisfaction to all whose private rights are thereby invaded. But those who have been divested of an important a vital natural right, are also entitled to compensation. THE RIGHT TO LABOR, secured to them in the creation of the earth, taken away in the granting of the Soil to a minor portion of them, must be restored. Labor, essential to all, is the inexorable condition of the honest, independent subsistence of the Poor. It must be fully guarantied to all, so that each may know that he can never starve nor be forced to beg while able and willing to work. Our public provision for Pauperism is but a halting and wretched substitute for this. Society exercises no paternal guardianship over the poor man until he has surrendered to despair. He may spend a whole year and his little all in vainly seeking employment, and all this time Society does nothing, cares nothing for him; but when his last dollar is exhausted, and his capacities very probably prostrated by the intoxicating draughts to which he is driven to escape the horrors of reflection, *then* he becomes a subject of public charity, and is often maintained in idleness for the rest of his days at a cost of thousands, when a few dollars' worth of foresight and timely aid might have preserved him from this fate, and in a position of independent usefulness for his whole after-life.

But the Right to Labor — that is, to constant Employment with a just and full Recompense — can not be guarantied to all without a radical change in our Social Economy. I, for one, am very willing, nay, most anxious, to do my full share toward securing to every man, woman, and child, full employment and a just recompense for all time to come. I feel sure this can be accomplished. But I can not, as the world goes, give employment at any time to all who ask it of me, nor the hundredth part of them. "Work, work! give us something to do! — anything that will secure us honest bread," is at this moment the prayer of not less than Thirty Thousand human beings within sound of our City-hall bell. They would gladly be producers of wealth, yet remain from week to week mere consumers of bread which somebody has to earn. Here is an enormous waste and loss. We must devise a remedy. It is the duty, and not less the palpable interest, of the wealthy, the thrifty, the tax-paying, to do so. The ultimate and thorough remedy, I believe is found in ASSOCIATION.

HOMESTEAD EXEMPTION.

THE general policy of exempting certain necessaries of life from seizure and confiscation for debt no longer stands in need of vindication. The Roman barbarism of selling the debtor to satisfy the demand of his creditor and the more absurd and recent enormity of shutting him up in jail, to be an expense to the creditor and no benefit to himself nor anybody else, are now generally exploded. Instead of depriving the debtor of all chance to earn a livelihood, or to support his family, it is the wiser effort of our time to encourage him to work and earn by reserving of his property certain household articles of prime necessity and his implements of labor from the clutch of the sheriff. And I feel very sure that these exemptions, though sometimes abused, have in the main operated justly and beneficently. A man hitherto in easy circumstances is often rendered bankrupt by misplaced confidence, by endorsing for friends, by a commercial revulsion, or by a mistaken estimate of his own resources, by a fire, a flood, or some other calamity. Of course, as soon as it is known that he is unable to pay, everybody insists on being paid, and his remaining property is sacrificed for less than half its worth, just when he most needs that it should command its full value. The law, as it has been, steps in not to protect and comfort but to harass and skin him, until he finds himself not merely destitute of property, but of the ability to earn any. His implements of labor, the shelter of his family, their bedding, clothes and cooking-ware, are dragged away and sold for a song; and he has the pleasant prospect before him of seeing anything that he may henceforth be able to earn carried off and sacrificed in like manner, without paying his debts or contributing sensibly toward that consummation. Law costs eat up pretty much all that such small matters will fetch, and he is, if left out of prison, hardly better off than if in it. Discouraged, despairing, avoided by his sunshine friends, he is, in the expressive language of the street, *ruined.* He sinks in stupid lethargy under the crushing load weighing upon him, and becomes feeble, heartless, inefficient—very often a dependent on the grudged charity of kindred, an idler, a pauper, a drunkard.

Public sentiment, enlightened by observation and reflection, has outgrown this policy and subjected it to many important modifications. Imprisonment for debt is nearly extinct; liberal exemptions of implements of labor and household furniture have been enacted in most States; and now the question is fairly presented—'Shall a shelter for wife 'and children, a piece of ground wherefrom to grow their 'food, be added to the present list of exempted articles?' To this question I most emphatically answer, 'Yes! Let the 'bankrupt's wife and children have a shelter in spite of his 'misfortunes. Let him still have an assured opportunity to 'labor on and produce from the soil now that his other 'resources are cut off. In our diseased and unstable social 'condition, the banker of to-day may be the bankrupt of to-'morrow. Let us all in prosperity remember the teachings 'of adversity and be merciful.'

—Now I know all that may be said, and have said a part of it against the selfishness, the dishonesty, the gross culpability, of a large proportion of the debtor class. I know that no man has a moral *right* to give entertainments, to buy fine clothes and jewelry, to inhabit a costly house and live sumptuously, while he is or pretends to be unable to pay his honest debts. Such a man is a swindler, no matter though 'Hon.' is prefixed to his name or 'D. D.' appended to it. I will go as heartily and as far as any man for punishing him *as* a swindler, but not for turning his family into the street on a simple allegation of debt. Indeed, it is one of my reasons for urging the further prosecution of the Exemption policy that I wish to see loose, idle livers deprived of the facilities they now enjoy for running into debt. Credit, credit everywhere—credit to men of doubtful character or principles—credit for articles that never should be bought except by those who have the money to pay for them and more behind it—credit absorbing half the movable capital of the country in channels where it is least useful—such credit is among the sorest evils of our time. Credit should be given to the upright, the frugal and the industrious only—to farmers for farms, implements or stock; to mechanics or artisans for machinery or material; to forwarders and exchangers to enable them to purchase produce with cash and market it advantageously for all parties. But credit for silks, pianos and Brussels carpets—for wines, liquors and perfumes—this is about as common and as extensive as the right sort, and it is bad policy to encourage such by legislation. I did hope that a mortal blow had been struck at such credit by the National Bankrupt Law; but faction and folly destroyed that law just when its evils had been all encountered and its blessings were about to be experienced. I shall rejoice if the same end is reached, to a more limited extent, by Homestead Exemption.

The soundness of the principle of Homestead Exemption is not generally questioned by the adversaries of the policy. They have a safer mode of warfare than that. No bill can be drawn so as to hit their several tastes—if the amount exempted is high enough for one it is too high for another; and if you reduce it to the pattern of the latter, the former will vote against it as a mockery and worse than nothing. If a

House passes a bill notwithstanding, the Senate will amend, or postpone, or fail to act upon it, and the measure fails. Yet already Wisconsin, Georgia, Texas, New-York, and I believe some other States, have Homestead Exemption laws, and nobody even suggests their repeal. Those States would as soon think of going back to the cast-off atrocity of stripping a man of all he has and shutting him up in jail without trial on a mere allegation or suspicion of debt. A secure though humble home to every family is one of the generous aspirations of our age, and it will yet be established as one of the cardinal principles of a Republican polity. It will prove a potent element of a true and genial Conservatism. The timorous people who used to declaim against the unsafety of a Government swayed by all manner of vagrants and loafers were not so very wrong as to the evil, though grievously mistaken as to the remedy, which is to be found in supplying these vagrants with Homes and not in depriving them of Votes. A Republic in which every man shall feel that he has interests to protect, rights to defend, must be the strongest government on earth, and such will ours be when every inhabitant shall have his own secure Home. Now Homestead Exemption will not directly provide any one with a freehold who is without it, but it will secure one to each man or woman who has it, and thus strongly impel every man to acquire one. The young man will naturally say, 'If I work 'for and pay the price of a dwelling and piece of land while 'I am single and can save, I may be very sure that no mis-'fortune in after-life can deprive me of a home so long as I 'choose to retain it.' That the end of this will be frugality in youth and independence in after-life to thousands, who otherwise would stumble on to maturity heedless and improvident, I can not doubt. And, in spite of distrust, timidity, indolence and avarice, the good work will go on, until the enjoyment of Inviolable Homes shall be commensurate with the existence of Republican Freedom.

LIVING AND MEANS.

One of the most mischievous phrases in which a rotten Morality, a radically false and vicious Public Sentiment disguise themselves, is that which characterizes certain individuals as destitute of financial capacity. A 'kind, amiable, 'generous, good sort of man,' (so runs the varnish,) 'but 'utterly unqualified for the management of his own finances' —'a mere child in everything relating to money,' &c. &c.— meaning that with an income of five hundred dollars a year he persisted in spending one thousand; or with an income of two to three thousand dollars, he regularly spent five to eight thousand, according to his ability to run in debt or the credulity of others in trusting him.

The victims of this immorality—debtor as well as creditor—are entitled to more faithful dealing at the hands of those not directly affected by the misdemeanors of the former. It is the duty of the community to rebuke and repress these pernicious glosses, making the truth heard and felt that inordinate expenditure is knavery and crime. No man has a moral right thus to lavish on his own appetites money which he has not earned and does not really need. If Public Opinion were sound on this subject—if a man living beyond his means when his means were commensurate with his real needs, were subjected to the reprehension he deserves—the evil would be instantly checked and ultimately eradicated.

The world is full of people who can't imagine why they don't prosper like their neighbors, when the real obstacle is not in banks nor tariffs, in bad public policy nor hard times, but in their own extravagance and heedless ostentation. The young mechanic or clerk marries and takes a house, which he proceeds to furnish twice as expensively as he can afford, and then his wife, instead of taking hold to help him earn a livelihood by doing her own work, must have a hired servant to help her spend his limited earnings. Ten years afterward you will find him struggling on under a double load of debts and children, wondering why the luck was always against him, while his friends regret his unhappy destitution of financial ability. Had they from the first been frank and honest, he need not have been so unlucky.

Through every grade of society this vice of inordinate expenditure insinuates itself. The single man 'hired out' in the country at ten to fifteen dollars per month, who contrives to dissolve his year's earnings in frolics and fine clothes; the clerk who has three to five hundred dollars a year and melts down twenty to fifty of it into liquor and cigars, are paralleled by the young merchant who fills a spacious house with costly furniture, gives dinners and drives a fast horse on the strength of the profits he expects to realize when his goods are all sold and his notes all paid. Let a man have a genius for spending, and whether his income be a dollar a day or a dollar a minute it is equally certain to prove inadequate. If dining, wining and party-giving won't help him through with it, building, gaming and speculating will be sure to. The bottomless pocket will never fill, no matter how bounteous the stream pouring into it. The man who (being single) does not save money on six dollars per week will not be apt to on sixty; and he who does not lay up something in his first year of independent exertion will be pretty likely to wear a poor man's hair into his grave.

No man who has the natural use of his faculties and his muscles has any right to tax others with the cost of his support, as this class of non-financial gentlemen habitually do. It is their common mistake to fancy that if a debt is only paid at last the obligations of the debtor is fulfilled, but the fact is not so. A man who sells his property for another's promise to pay next week, or next month, and is compelled to wear out a pair of boots in running after his due, which he finally gets after a year or two, is never really paid. Very often, he has lost half the face of his demand by not having the money when he needed it, beside the cost and vexation of running after it. There is just one way to pay an obligation in full, and that is to pay it when due. He who keeps up a running fight with bills and loans through life is continually living on other men's means, is a serious burden and a detriment to those who deal with him, although his estate should finally pay every dollar of his legal obligations.

Inordinate expenditure is the cause of a great share of the crime and consequent misery which devastate the world. The clerk who spends more than he earns is fast qualifying himself for a gambler and a thief; the trader or mechanic who overruns his income is very certain to become in time a trickster and a cheat. Wherever you see a man spending faster than he earns, there look out for villainy to be developed, though it be the farthest thing possible from his present thought.

When the world shall have become wiser and its standard of morality more lofty, it will perceive and affirm that profuse expenditure, even by one who can pecuniarily afford it, is pernicious and unjustifiable—that a man, however wealthy, has no right to lavish on his own appetites, his tastes or his ostentation, that which might have raised hundreds from destitution and despair to comfort and usefulness. But that is an improvement in public sentiment which must be waited for, while the other is more ready and obvious.

The meanness, the dishonesty, the iniquity, of squandering thousands unearned, and keeping others out of money that is justly theirs, have rarely been urged and enforced as they should be. They need but to be considered and understood to be universally loathed and detested.

'PITY HIS FAMILY.'

A MAN falls into embarrassments, which ultimately overwhelm him in bankruptcy or drive him into roguery and crime. He was yesterday respected, influential and supposed to be affluent, and his family were treated and treated themselves accordingly; but to-day he is disgraced and steered clear of—without resources or prospects—very likely in prison and exposed to ignominious punishment.—'Vile wretch!' say the million; 'it is good enough for him, but we must pity his poor family.'

—Certainly, we must pity them—pity all who suffer—still more all who sin and suffer. They need pity, and there is no danger that we shall pity them too much.—But the impression conveyed of the innocence of the fallen man's family and their unmerited exposure to want and ignominy, is often very far from the truth.

In fact, half the men who are loathed as dragging down their families to shame and destitution are really themselves dragged down by those families—driven to bankruptcy, shame and crime by the thoughtless and basely selfish extravagance of wife and children. Let a man be in the way of receiving considerable money, and having property in his hands, and his family can rarely be made to comprehend and realize that there is any limit to his ability to give and spend. Fine dresses and ornaments for wife and daughters; spending money and broadcloth for hopeful sons—costly parties every now and then, and richer furniture and more of it at all times—these are a few of the blind drains on 'the governor's' means which are perpetually in action. 'O, what's a hundred dollars to a man doing such a business?' is the indignant question in case of any demur or remonstrance on his part. Not one of them could bear to disgrace him by earning a dollar; they could n't go out shabbily dressed, for fear his credit would suffer. They can't see how a man who can get discounts in Bank need ever be short of money or stingy in using it. All his talk of difficulties or hard times they regard as customary fables, intended to scrimp their drafts on his purse or enhance their sense of his generosity. When it is so easy to fill up a check, why will he be hoggish? Let him give fifty dollars to any philanthropic object, or invest five hundred, however safely, in any attempt to meliorate the sufferings of the Poor, and they now see clearly that he has hoards of gold, and can just as well give them all dresses and jewels as not.—Thus the man of means or of business is too often regarded by his family as a sponge to be squeezed, a goose to be plucked, an orange to be sucked, a spring to be drank from when thirsty without at all diminishing its flow. The stuff is there in profusion—the only trouble is to make him give it up.

In vain he remonstrates—implores—puts down his foot. He can not be eternally contending with those he loves best—he wants quiet at home in order to mature his plans and perfect his operations. If he resists importunity, the pumps are set going, and what man can stand the April showers of feminine sorrow? He gives way at last and throws down the money demanded, hoping that some great news by the next steamship, some turn of luck in his business, will make it up to him. Perhaps it does, and he floats on; perhaps it do n't, and this last feather has broken the elephant's back. The end, however near or distant, is morally certain. Treated always as a mine to be opened at will, he finally grows desperate and rushes into reckless speculation or blasting crime, and is overwhelmed with ruin. 'Selfish villain!' say the ignorant crowd; 'how *could* he run such a career? How we pity his family!'—No doubt of it! But if you knew more, perhaps you would pity *him*.

FLOGGING IN THE NAVY.

The primary division of the human species on shore resolves the individuals into Men and Women; on shipboard into Officers and Men, though the latter term very unfitly expresses the light in which Seamen are regarded by Officers. The crew are practically Hands; sometimes Legs also; at others Backs; but as to any clear conception that they are truly Men, it is neither expressed nor implied in our theory or practice of Naval discipline. In the contemplation of that discipline, the crew are beasts, dogs, devils—anything but men.

A seaman enlists into the Navy, allured by the notion of serving his country and helping to maintain and extend the glory of the Stars and Stripes. He has the faults of his class and condition—is reckless, headstrong, easily provoked to quarrel, and has an appetite for grog and other sensual depravities. Yet he means to behave himself and to do his duty, and for a time no complaint is made. But, as a part of his rations, an allowance of Alcoholic Liquor is daily dealt out to him—not enough to make him drunk, but quite enough to maintain and increase the appetite for Alcohol if he has already acquired it, and to create it if he has hitherto escaped or overcome it. Not to drink it would be to subject himself to ridicule and dislike among his messmates, so he takes it down. By-and-by the ship reaches port, and he with others has a few hours' liberty to go on shore. With appetites for liquor thus formed or increased on shipboard, the jolly mess betake themselves in hot haste to the grog-shop first, and then to other dens of debauchery, and when their leave has expired, some are too confused and brutified clearly to know or seriously to care where they are or what they are doing.

If all hurry on board at the last moment, some of them are pretty certain to be grossly intoxicated, which is of course a punishable offence. These are to be hauled up as soon as the ship's convenience will permit, their backs stripped and lashed with a heavy, cutting, torturing whip known as the cat-o'-nine-tails, plied with all the strength of an athletic sub-officer. One dozen lashes is the usual allowance for such an offence as drunkenness; and each lash makes at least a black-and-blue stripe across the offender's back of the width of your finger—often takes off the skin and causes the blood to fly freely, leaving the back as raw as a beef-steak. More serious offences are punished with more lashes—striking an Officer with death. But lashing, threshing, gashing, is the great reliance for 'discipline' on board our Republican Navy, and many officers resort to it on the most trifling pretexts. 'Looking insolently at an officer,' is one of the more serious offences, while there are cases officially reported by the commanders themselves where men have been thus gashed for not cooking an officer's dinner to his liking, for spilling water on the deck, not stowing a hammock away neatly, &c. &c. Six thousand lashes, such as I have described, have been dealt out during one cruise to the crew of a single vessel—that is, so many were reported to the Navy Department by the commander, while it is notorious that nothing like all are reported, and officers have boasted that they never would report all, nor any more than they chose. That men have been flogged by the dozen for no better reason than such as the drunkenness of their superior supplied, is notorious. The appetite for cruel spectacles grows by what it feeds on, and an officer accustomed to order and oversee the flogging of half a dozen men just before morning prayers might as well be expected to do without his bitters as without the added stimulus of writhing flesh and spirting blood. If there are no real offences, his gloomy fancy, his flagging spirits, will invent or imagine some, for the sake of the fillip they crave so insatiably.

What must be the effect of this on the seamen, whether personally flogged or spared?

They have no hope of promotion — no chance of ever rising to the quarter-deck — no prospect of an honorable niche in history nor of laying their bones beneath a marble monument. If they are lucky enough to spend their last days in a hospital and be buried at all, they do well. Every year sees a new squad of greenhorns, — mere boys, and not favorable specimens at that — sent aboard the ship, not to learn and serve, but to govern and direct. These sons and nephews of Congressmen or local dignitaries of some sort are often provided with commissions in the Navy because their past careers of idleness and dissipation have unfitted them for usefulness on shore, and rendered them a burden if not a terror to their respective families. (Of course, there are many of a different order, but there are many of this stamp as well.) They step on shipboard immature except in depravity, knowing not even the alphabet of their novel profession, but thoroughly comprehending that they are officers and thus gentlemen, while sailors are the dust beneath their feet. Let 'an old salt' who fought with Bainbridge, Porter or Perry, venture to look queer at one of the new mid's hourly exhibitions of ignorance in nautical matters, and wo to that unlucky soul! The scars won in capturing the Guerriere or Macedonian shall be as feathers in the way of that dignitary's vengeance. And thus the brutalizing of men and officers by lash and gash goes on from day to day. The officers have been educated to deem it necessary; it magnifies their importance and draws the line sharply and broadly between the flogged and the flogging classes. The seamen are dumb — nobody hears nor heeds them. The People are ignorant and indifferent; Congress is prëoccupied and hostile. 'The Navy,' in its contemplation, means the officers, and possibly the vessels; the men are of no account there. Commodores, Captains, Lieutenants and Midshipmen have fathers, brothers and cousins in either House, Jack has none. So Reform is shirked or scouted, and Lash and Gash go on. There is no hope of a change but through enlightening and arousing the mass of the People.

What is essentially needed may be summed up in a very short sentence—*Make the Navy Republican.* Open a gangway from the forecastle to the quarter-deck. At the end of every year make it the sworn duty of the commanders and lieutenants to report to the Navy Department the names of the ablest and best seamen in the ship for promotion, and if the crew consist of more than a hundred men, let one such be reported for every hundred or major fraction of a hundred. Let the crew in like manner assemble by themselves, and each giving his word of honor to render a true judgment, let each man cast a ballot for the seaman who in his opinion has best served and displayed most nautical ability during the past year. Let these votes be duly authenticated and transmitted unopened to the Department, and if the judgment of the officers and men be found to accord in any case, let a commission issue forthwith. If not, let future commissions be given in equal numbers to those recommended by the officers and seamen respectively, the Department exercising a discretion as to which among the recommendations from the various vessels seem most emphatic and reliable. But make the rule absolute and inflexible that *no one shall henceforth receive a commission in the Navy until he shall have earned it by manifest ability and faithful service as a sailor therein.*

Let this system have two years' fair trial, and it would matter little, except for the principle of the thing, whether Congress directed the Abolition of Flogging or not. It would be dead, beyond the power of resurrection. Officers promoted from the forecastle would have a tenderness for

Jack's infirmities, which those manufactured as at present can never feel. Seamen, with the eyes of both officers and messmates steadily watching to see who ought to be reported for commissions, would have a very different and far more effectual stimulus to well-doing than Lash and Gash can ever afford. And the Navy, thus proffering an honorable career with ultimate distinction and a liberal support through life to every well-behaving seaman, would be crowded with the noblest spirits that sail the ocean, instead of being left to those who have banished the hope of rising in the world and to whom the scourge is no longer a conscious degradation. Make the Navy Republican, and the spirit will be aroused which carried the arms of Revolutionary France in triumph to Rome, Cairo, Vienna, Berlin and Moscow by simply opening the road of promotion to good conduct, without regard to birth or breeding. Make the Navy Republican, and it will be the most efficient and formidable of its size that the world has ever seen. In thus doing justice to the fundamental principles of our Political Fabric, we shall palpably hasten the advent of universal freedom and happiness, wherein Lash and Gash shall be banished for ever from the world.

THE UNION OF WORKERS.*

THE ancient Egyptians had a custom of seating at their feasts the robed skeleton of some departed friend, whose stern silence contrasted strikingly with the mirth and hilarity of his living companions. I believe scholars are not agreed as to the purpose and meaning of this strange custom—whether the rigid, silent guests were intended to say to the festal throng—"Enjoy and revel while you may, for Time

* An Address to the Printers of New York, delivered before the N. Y. Typographical Society, at their Celebration of Franklin's Birth-Day, Jan. 17th, 1850.

'flies, Man perishes; in a few years all is dust, is nothing—'therefore, make haste to quaff the wine while it sparkles, to 'seize pleasure while the capacity of enjoyment remains to 'you"—or rather to impress the opposite sentiment—"Life 'is short; Life is earnest; stupendous consequences hang 'suspended on your use or abuse of the speck of time allot-'ted you; therefore, be temperate in your indulgence, mode-'rate in your festive mirth, and, seeing in what I am what 'you soon must be, consider and beware!"—I shall not of course pretend to decide this grave question, though I shall assume for the occasion that the latter is the true rendering; and, in accordance with the elemental idea, I venture to assume among you to-night the functions of the Egyptians' silent monitor, and while others stir you with lofty eloquence or charm you with dulcet flatteries—with pictures of the grand achievements of our Art in the past and its brilliant prospects for the future, I shall speak to you frankly of our deficiencies, our failings, and the urgent demands upon us for new and more arduous exertions in yet unrecognized fields of duty.

It is now some four centuries since the discovery or invention of our Art, fully three since our continent began to be the home of civilized men, and more than two since the Pilgrim fugitives first landed on Plymouth Rock. Since that landing, and even within the last century, what amazing strides have been made in the diffusion of Knowledge and the perfection of the implements and processes of Industry—in the efficiency of Human Labor and the facilitation of intercourse between country and country, clime and clime! The steam-engine, the spinning-jenny, the power-loom; the canal, steam-ship, power-press, railroad and lightning telegraph—these, in their present perfection and efficiency, are a few of the trophies of human genius and labor within even the last century.

But while Labor has hus doubled and quadrupled its own

efficacy in the production of whatever is needful to the physical sustenance, intellectual improvement and social enjoyment of Man, I do not find that there has been a corresponding melioration in the condition of the Laborer. That there has been some improvement I do not deny; but has it been at all commensurate with the general progress of our race in whatever pertains to physical convenience or comfort? I think not; and I could not help pondering this matter even while our orator's silvery tones were delighting our ears with poetical descriptions of the wonders which Science and Invention have achieved and are achieving. I could not help considering that, while Labor builds far more sumptuous mansions in our day than of old, furnishing them far more gorgeously and luxuriously, the laborer who builds those mansions lives oftenest in a squalid lodging, than which the builders of palaces in the fifteenth century can hardly have dwelt in more wretched; and that while the demands for labor, the uses of labor, the efficiency of labor, are multiplied and extended on every side by the rush of invention and the growth of luxury around us, yet in this middle of the Nineteenth Century (call it the last year of the first half or the first year of the last half as you please) Labor is a drug in the market—that the temperate, efficient, upright Worker often finds the comfortable maintenance and proper education of his children beyond his ability—and that, in this thriving Commercial Emporium of the New World, this trophy and pride of Christian Civilization—there are at this day not less than Forty Thousand human beings anxious to earn the bread of honest industry but vainly seeking, and painfully, despairingly awaiting opportunity for so doing. This last is the feature of our condition which seems to me most important and commanding, and it is to this, on occasions like the present, and in listening to such orations as that which has just delighted us, that my thoughts are irresistibly turned.

What can be the reason of this? Why is it that these Forty Thousand strong-handed, willing Workers stand here thus fixed, enchained, in loathed, despairing idleness? Why are they compelled to wear out our pavements in hurrying hither and thither in anxious, heart-sick quest of something to do?—with downcast looks and trembling voice beseeching some fellow man to give them leave to labor for their bread? I trust no one here gives any heed to the mumbling of self-styled Political Economists about 'Over-Production' and the kindred phrases with which counsel is darkened. 'Over-Production'—of what? Where? Can there be over-production of Food, when so many, even in our midst, are suffering the pangs of famine? 'Over-Production' of Clothing and Fabrics, while our streets swarm with men, women and children who are not half-clad, and who shiver through the night beneath the clothing they have worn by day? 'Over-Production' of Dwellings, when not half the families of our city have adequate and comfortable habitations, not to speak of that large class whose lodgings are utterly incompatible with decency and morality? No, friends! there is *no* 'Over-Production,' save of articles pernicious and poisonous, like Alcoholic Liquors, Lewd Books, implements of Gaming, &c. Of whatever conduces to human sustenance, comfort or true education, there is not and never has been too much produced, although, owing to imperfect and vicious arrangements for Distribution, there may often be a glut in the warehouses of Trade, while thousands greatly need and would gladly purchase if they could. What the world eminently requires is some wise adjustment, some remodeling of the Social machinery, diminishing its friction, whereby *every person willing to work shall assuredly have work to do, and the just reward of that work in the articles most essential to his sustenance and comfort.* It may be that there is indeed a surplus of that particular product which some man's labor could most skillfully or rapidly produce,—Pianos, Watches, or Gauzes, for example—and therefore it may be advisable to intermit for a season the production of these—yet the skill, the faculty, the muscular energy not required in that particular department of production might nevertheless be made available, even though in a subordinate degree, in the fabrication of some kindred product for which there *is* a demand among the general mass of consumers. I maintain, then, that in our day no man should be compelled to stand idle or wander vainly in search of employment, even though that particular calling for which he is best fitted has now no place for him, but that the palpable self-interest of the community should prescribe the creation of some Social Providence expressly to take care that no man, woman or child shall ever stand uselessly idle when willing and anxious to work. Even the most injudicious application of the labor now wasted through lack of opportunity could not fail to increase the National Wealth to the extent of millions on millions per annum, while its effect on the condition of the Laboring Class, in preserving them from temptation, dissipation and crime, would be incalculably beneficent.

—Now what I stand here to complain of is the indifference and inattention of the Laboring Mass, and especially of those entitled to a leading position in it, like the Printers, to the discussion of a truth so grand and so fruitful as the Right to Labor. It is more discussed, more pondered, to-day, by Merchants, Capitalists, Scholars, and men who are called Aristocrats, than by the mass of those who earn their living by the sweat of the face. It is now eighteen years since I came to this city a journeyman printer, during which years I have been intimately connected with our craft in one capacity or another, and yet I have never heard of a meeting of Printers to consider and discuss the Rights generally of Labor, the causes of its depression, the means of its advancement. During these eighteen years there have been hard times and good times, so called; seasons of activity and seasons of depression—in the course of which the country has been 'saved,' I forget how often—our city has doubled in population and more than doubled in wealth—and yet the Laboring Class *as* a Class is just where it was when I came here, or, if anything, in a worse condition, as the increased valuation of Property has caused advance in Rents and in some other necessaries of life. Individuals have risen *out* of the Laboring Class, becoming buyers of Labor and sellers of its Products, and grown rich thereby; but the condition of the Laboring Class, as such, has not improved, and I think is less favorable than it was twenty years ago. Why should it not investigate, determine and develop the causes of this? Why not consider the practicability of securing Work and Homes to all willing to work for them? Can we imagine that improvement is to come without effort or even inquiry? Is it the order of Nature or of Providence that it should? Do blessings come to other classes without foresight or calculation? I have heard complaints that Machinery and Invention do not work *for* the Laboring Class, but rather against them. Concede the assumption, and is not the inquiry a fair one, What has the Laboring Class ever done to *make* Machinery work in its favor? When has it planned, or sought, or calculated, to render Machinery its ally and aid rather than its enemy and oppressor?

I am here to-night to tell you that you, and our Trade, and the Laboring Class of our City have been glaringly, unfaithful in this respect to yourselves, your posterity, and your Race, and that the Workers of Paris, for example, are in advance of their brethren here in knowledge of and devotion to the interests and rights of Labor. And I am here not to find fault merely, but to exhort you to awake from your apathy and heed the summons of Duty.

I stand here, friends, to urge that a new leaf be now

turned over—that the Laboring Class, instead of idly and blindly waiting for better circumstances and better times, shall begin at once to consider and discuss the means of controlling circumstances and commanding times, by study, calculation, foresight, union. We have heard to-night of a Union of Printers and a Printers' Library, for which latter one generous donation has been proffered. I have little faith in giving as a remedy for the woes of mankind, and not much in any effort for the elevation or improvement of any one section of Producers of Wealth in our City. What I would suggest would be the Union and Organization of *all* Workers for their mutual improvement and benefit, leading to the erection of a spacious edifice at some central point in our City to form a LABORERS' EXCHANGE, just as Commerce now has its Exchange, very properly. Let the new Exchange be erected and owned as a joint-stock property, paying a fair dividend to those whose money erected it; let it contain the best spacious Hall for General Meetings to be found in our City, with smaller Lecture-Rooms for the meetings of particular sections or callings—all to be leased or rented at fair prices to all who may choose to hire them, when not needed for the primary purpose of discussing and advancing the interests of Labor. Let us have here books opened, wherein any one wanting work may inscribe his name, residence, capacities, and terms, while any one wishing to hire may do likewise, as well as meet personally those seeking employment. These are but hints toward a few of the uses which such a Labor Exchange might subserve, while its Reading-Room and Library, easily formed and replenished, should be open freely and gladly to all. Such an edifice, rightly planned and constructed, might become, and I confidently hope would become, a most important instrumentality in the great work of advancing the Laboring Class in comfort, intelligence, and independence. I trust we need not long await its erection.

THE TRADE REFORM.

ALL great changes proceed slowly, and if any seem to be sudden, it is because the real change had long been going on unnoticed, and that which is mistaken for it is only the disclosure or discovery. You will only hear from the vulgar and shallow that repeated attempts at renovation have failed or broken down, until at last the ignorant and credulous are astounded by the admission that what they have so often been told had exploded has actually triumphed! Even now they will not comprehend that what they have been taught to consider failures was but the necessary foundation of what they must now admit is success—that the latter is but the complement and fruition of the former. They admit the particular fact, but shut their eyes to the general principle, and the very next reform that is commenced finds them as blind and shallow as ever.

There is to be, there must be, a great reform in the mode and means of effecting exchanges of products between producers and consumers generally. The average cost of such exchanges is absurdly higher than it need be and will be. There are certain marked exceptions to this general statement—one of them in the case of cotton. The manufacturer, whether in Old or New England, in France or Pittsburg, regularly buys his stock of cotton for seldom more and often less than the grower's price with the usual charges for brokerage and transportation. The same is the case with a few other great staples which are mainly bought and sold in large quantities, and which suffer little injury from time or change of climate. But with regard to the great majority of vendibles the fact is gloomily otherwise. There are very many articles which cost large classes of consumers three to six times what the producers receive for them ; while on more than half the goods sold in the world there is an advance of twenty-five to fifty per cent. above what they need cost the consumer. This advance is a tax on productive labor which can not long abide the neighborhood of common schools, cheap newspapers, and electric telegraphs. It must come down.

Do you ask *why* the rate of mercantile profit is too high? Count the number of stores in any county, and you have a ready answer. There are five to ten times as many persons employed in and subsisting by trade as there need or should be. As the taxes of a nation must be in proportion to the number and salaries of those quartered on its treasury, so the profits of trade must be graduated by the number they are required to support. If twenty mercantile establishments are kept up where three would be abundant, the average advance on the cost of the goods must be three or four times what it should be. Of course, we do not forget the use of competition in counteracting selfish rapacity, but there are ways of attaining the good here contemplated far more cheaply than by employing twenty men to do the work which three could do better.

We shall have an end of this. The diversification of industrial pursuits will do much to promote it. As a general rule, the profit charged on any article to the consumer is proportioned to the distance from the point of production. A fabric which the manufacturer will gladly sell to the people of his own county for five per cent. on its cost, and think he is doing well, will sell a thousand miles away at twenty per cent., and across a continent at fifty or even a hundred. When the nations of the earth shall have become wise enough to purchase freely of each other such raw materials as the nature of their soil or climate forbids them respectively to produce, each fabricating and commingling for itself, the aggregate tax levied on labor by traffic will be immensely diminished. But that is a work of time.

The more immediate instrumentalities through which a reduction of this tax is to be effected are, as briefly as may be stated, the substitution of Cash payment for Credit as the common law of mercantile transactions, and an immense and systematic extension of Advertising. And though on these heads I have little to offer that is novel, I would earnestly commend them to public attention.

Credit, I need hardly affirm, is an excellent, an indispensable thing, but grossly abused, as excellent things are apt to be. It ought to be based on substantial security. We give credit to a bank-note which we know to be based upon and secured by a deposit of state stocks in the public coffers of our state; we give credit to the man who proffers a pledge of undoubted property for the punctual payment of his debt; we give credit to the man we thoroughly know as a man of integrity and pecuniary ability. So far all is legitimate, though it should still appear that the person giving credit is thoroughly able so to do. Credit should be given because the creditor is able and willing to intrust some share of his means to the less fortunate debtor, and not merely because the former is a seller and the latter a buyer. Selling and giving credit are two entirely distinct operations, and one should never suppose nor involve the other.

But the existing system of mercantile credit is as loose and vicious as it could be and not lead directly to general ruin. Our importers buy in Europe on credit; our manufacturers are too often constrained to sell through commission-houses on credit—not because they desire or are really able to give it, but because such is the course of trade, and they must conform to it or not sell at all, except at a ruinous sacrifice. The jobber, of course, jobs on credit, and when his payments crowd him he is forced to credit not less, but more; for his stock in store will not pay his notes, but when turned into retailers' paper, though not absolutely known to be good, it can, well indorsed, be ground into cash. It is no mystery, therefore, that a failing house has lots of bad paper among its assets, it is as natural as life. It has been making sales to keep the mill going, and could not stop to be nice. Thus green country youth, not worth a thousand dollars in the world, but backed up by such letters as most people will write or sign without much consideration or conscience, can come here and get in debt for five thousand dollars' worth of goods, when they have no legitimate claim to credit for one-fourth the amount. These they go back to retail, nine-tenths on credit, to Tom, Dick, and Harry, at glorious prices, but with dubious prospects of payment. The notes fall due all around; payment is demanded; a part of the retailer's customers have paid in work on his new store, or in provisions, furniture, or fuel, for his family, a few pay punctually, their goods costing them twenty to forty per cent. more than they need if there were no such thing as mercantile credit; others pay at the end of an execution, and of course pay nearer a hundred per cent. more than the cash value; many have started for "the west," or have no tangible property, and never pay. Finally, but not when due, the retailer pays twenty to fifty per cent. of his debt, compromises with his creditors, and is ready to begin again. The jobber pays the importer and the commission-house if he can. The upshot is, that the goods are not half paid for—but those who paid at all have paid far too much. The whole transaction has been an encouragement to knavery, improvidence, and over-trading; for, if there were no system of mercantile credit, not half those now engaged in trade could pretend to be in it at all. They could not buy a decent stock of goods if obliged to pay for them; and a system of cash sales would speedily reduce profits so that a petty business would not be worth doing. The mere simplification of business consequent on the disuse of credit in trade, would save half the time and talent now absorbed in mercantile pursuits. The selling of one hundred thousand dollars' worth of goods in a county, by two or three establishments, entirely for ready pay, need not engross the time of ten persons in all; while selling the same goods through ten or fifteen concerns, with the usual paraphernalia of daybook, ledger, note-book, &c., winding up with the interposition of lawyers, sheriff, county court, &c., will keep at least fifty employed the year round.

I have remarked that extensive advertising is one of the means by which the reform in trade is to be accomplished. The two classes, buyers and sellers, have a common interest in finding each other: that is to say, it is the interest of him who can supply a certain want cheapest, to have every buyer aware of the fact; and it is the interest of the buyers no less. An expenditure of fifty dollars may be too much, one of five thousand may be too little, for that purpose. If, for example, somebody has discovered—as I see stated in a southern paper—a substance, or chemical compound, which will dispense with the labor now required in washing clothes, or the half of it, at a very small cost, the owners of his patent may spend fifty thousand dollars a-year in advertising it, and then not spend enough. There are inventions within my knowledge worth hundreds of thousands, if the patentees knew how, and had the enterprise, to bring them home to the knowledge of all interested; these failing, they will never realize twenty thousand. Whoever can supply this city cheapest with almost any article in general use, or can cheaply furnish an article which will meet a general want hitherto more expensively met, can not advertise too much if he knows how to advertise at all. And yet many a dealer in our city pays a thousand dollars more for an eligibly located store than he need pay in a less frequented street, and does not pay a hundred dollars a-year for advertising! He willingly pays a thousand dollars merely to let some ten thousand people know that he has certain articles to sell, but grudges five hundred dollars as the cost of extending the same knowledge to millions!

This can not, in the nature of things, long endure. It is simply a blind following of old rules and habits, after they have become utterly inapplicable. The time was when the circulation of the most popular journal was counted by hundreds, and an advertisement in its columns was about equivalent in publicity to a handbill on a blacksmith's shop. It is different now, and there are men in trade who understand the difference and profit by it. Many pay thousands a-year for advertising, and the number is yearly increasing. There will be hundreds where there are now tens within five years.

Fools can be fools in this as in anything else. He who keeps a corner grocery, and does not look for customers beyond the four blocks around him, need not advertise—it would only be throwing away his money. So of many others. But he who has a cargo of fresh tropical fruits to-day, which he must speedily sell or see spoil on his hands, can not too quickly make known the fact to every purchaser within five hundred miles: so of many others. Whenever the difference in cost or quality is worth looking after, then it is an immense economy of cost and labor to let the fact be known at once and as widely as possible. Extensive advertising of itself is morally certain to work a revolution in trade, by driving thousands of the easy-going out of it, and concentrating business in the hands of the few who know how to obtain and keep it. Unite with this the substitution of cash for credit, and one-fifth of those now engaged in trade will amply suffice to do the whole—and will soon have it to do. The revolution is already begun.

WHAT FREE TRADE IS DOING.

"You ought to go to England," said a mercantile friend lately from Europe the other day, "to see how triumphant is the success of the Free Trade Policy there."

'Indeed! is it?—I had not heard that the British Poor-Rates had fallen off materially. Is the Labor of England better paid and subsisted than it was ten years ago? If it is, the fact is new to me.'

My friend could not say that Labor was higher or Paupers fewer in Great Britain under what is called Free Trade than they had been previously. Indeed, the condition of Labor and the extension or diminution of Pauperism did not seem to have specially engaged his attention abroad. But he had seen Commerce active, Business prosperous, London swelling on every side, Liverpool extending its borders, Manchester and Leeds increasing their looms and mills, and capitalists plethoric and satisfied. They told him that England was flourishing under her present policy, and he joyfully believed it. Had he gone into the workshops and dwellings of the Laboring Poor—of the spinners, weavers, tailors, shoemakers, hatters, stevedores, &c.—and inquired as to the condition and wages of the millions who just manage to exist there, he would have learned that those millions were never more scantily paid, more meagerly fed, nor more utterly wretched and hopeless than they are in this year of grace 1850. If the blessings of Free Trade have been realized around the London Docks and the Welsh iron-mines, in the mills of the Cobdens and the banks of the Barings, they have never yet traveled down to the shops of the toiling and the cottages of the humble.

But this is not the whole truth that demands consideration.

I bear no ill will to England. She is in part the land of my ancestry. She has produced many great and noble men, to whom the world is deeply indebted. Among the predominant characteristics of her People are many which challenge admiration — patient courage, fortitude under adversity, laborious energy, and love of home and kindred. I as warmly desire the well-being of her people as of any other except our own, and yet — say rather, because of this — I desire and hope for the downfall of that Commercial and Manufacturing supremacy which she now enjoys. I believe such an ascendency by any one nation over others, is based on and compels the depression of Labor and the degradation of Man. So long as the whole world shall be laid under contribution to gild the palaces and expand the cities of Great Britain — so long as the Cotton, Wheat, Wool, Meat, and other staples of all nations are collected in the London and Liverpool docks to be fabricated and consumed by British skill and industry, and their product re-distributed over the whole face of the earth, just so long must Labor everywhere be depressed and plundered. The wrong is in the system, and can not be averted by any modification of it. The British manufacturer may well say to his workers, 'I 'must have your services for a shilling or so per day; for 'how else can I pay the cost of bringing hither the Cotton 'of Alabama, the Pork of Ohio and the Wheat of Illinois, 'and make my fabrics so cheap that they may undersell 'and drive out the rival American fabrics from the market 'of their own country?' Then the American manufacturer turns round upon *his* workers, and says, "I can't sell my 'goods except at a loss, for the British fabrics are cheaper; 'I must have labor cheaper or shut up my works: say 'which it shall be?" — and they, clinging to their homes and an assured though meager subsistence, say, "Cut us 'down ten per cent if you must; we will try to live under 'the reduction." So down go the wages, and Yankee cloth is cheapened; but British capital gives the screw another wrench, and gets its labor still cheaper and consequently its cloth also; and there is a chance for our operatives to try another stage on the road to famine, and so on. The natural, inevitable tendency of this struggle of British Manufacturers to permeate and monopolize the markets of the world is to aggrandize Speculation and useless Traffic with the sweat and blood of helpless, undefended Toil. Labor is everywhere driven by it to bid against itself—is driven to engage in a cannibal warfare whereof the only issue is ruin. If there be for it a season of seeming prosperity here or there, the reäction is certain and terrible. Half the recompense which Labor fairly earns is swallowed up in the cost of taking its product from one country to undersell and ruin on their own soil the workers of another. And, bad as the job is, it is never thoroughly done. The moment the labor of one country or class has been thus undermined and crushed, it becomes a potent instrument for undermining and crushing the labor of others—perhaps of those who wrought its overthrow. The lower the Capital and Commerce of any country can depress its Labor, the greater is their chance of securing bountiful gains—the more thorough is their command of the markets of the world. *They* can hold up when a business don't pay, or seek out some other investment; but Labor must delve on, even at ruinous rates; with it to stand idle is to famish. And even its victories are defeats; for, as the Spitalfields silk-weaver told Mr. Mayhew, "We've driven the French out of the market in umbrellas and parasols; but *the people are starving while they're driving of 'em out.*"

Earnestly believing, therefore, that the gigantic fabric of modern Commercial and Industrial Feudalism whereof Great Britain is the center and soul is at deadly war with the vital interests of mankind, I do *not* rejoice in what men of business call the prosperity of England, for I believe it is based on the robbery of Labor at home and results in its depression and derangement abroad. I do not rejoice that Manchester builds new factories and London excavates new docks, for I see in these new instruments for the colonial subjugation and industrial depression of the rest of the world. Profoundly convinced that it is best for the Toiling Millions of all nations, Great Britain included, that each country should learn to spin and weave, to roll and hammer for itself, I regret any evidence afforded us that the retrograde policy anywhere gains ground. I would not regret that British Manufactures are expanding, British Commerce flourishing, British Revenue redundant, did I not feel that these are but links in the chain which holds Portugal in virtual vassalage, renders Brazil in effect a British colony, and leaves our own vast, fertile and energetic country in her blindness to grind corn like Samson in the house of the Philistines. She ought to be out of debt, independent in her circumstances, with her labor fully employed and justly rewarded; yet tens of thousands of her people to-day vainly beg employment in her streets and villages, while, in the midst of peace and bounteous harvests, she is silently incurring a Foreign Debt of many millions per annum in the shape of Government and State Stocks, Railroad Bonds (for Iron that our workers would gladly make, and suffer for want of opportunity to make,) and other Stocks, Bonds and Commercial balances generally. Why *should* we run in debt for the fruits of other nations' labor, while a superabundance of our own labor is left unemployed and famishing?—No, I do not rejoice in what is regarded as British prosperity; for I believe it is the upholding and apparent triumph of a system whose downfall is necessary to the emancipation and elevation of Labor throughout the world.

SLAVERY AT HOME:

ANSWER TO AN INVITATION TO ATTEND AN ANTI-SLAVERY MEETING.

NEW-YORK, June 3, 1845.

Dear Sir:—I received, weeks since, your letter inviting me to be present at a general convention of opponents of Human Slavery, irrespective of past differences and party organizations. I have delayed to the last moment my answer, hoping I might this season indulge a long-cherished desire and purpose by visiting your section and city, in which case I should certainly have attended your Convention. Being now reluctantly compelled to forego or indefinitely postpone that visit, I have no recourse but to acknowledge your courtesy in a letter.

In saying that I should have attended your Convention had I been able to visit Cincinnati this month, I would by no means be understood as implying that I should have chosen to share in its deliberations; still less that I should have been likely to unite in the course of action to which those deliberations will probably tend. Whether there 'can true reconcilement grow' between those opponents of Slavery whom the late Presidential Election arrayed against each other in desperate conflict, I do not venture to predict. Most surely, that large portion of them with whom *I* acted and still act, have been confirmed in our previous convictions of duty by the result of that election, and by the momentous consequences which it has drawn after it, not merely with regard to this question of Slavery, but to all questions, I have by that result been warned against pledging myself to any special and isolated Reform in such manner as to interfere with and fetter my freedom and ability to act decisively and effectively upon more general and immediately practical considerations of National interest and of Human well-being. You and yours, I understand, have been confirmed in an opposite conviction. Time must decide on which side is the right.

But, while I can not hope that I should have been able to unite with you upon any definitive course of action to be henceforth pursued by *all* opponents of Slavery, irrespective of past or present differences, I should have gladly met you, conferred with you, compared opinions, and agreed to act together so far as joint action is not forbidden by conflicting opinions. Animated by this spirit, I shall venture to set before you, and ask the Convention to consider, some views which I deem essential as bearing on the present condition and ultimate success of the Anti-Slavery movement.

What is Slavery? You will probably answer, "The 'legal subjection of one human being to the will and power 'of another." But this definition appears to me inaccurate on both sides—too broad, and at the same time too narrow. It is too broad, in that it includes the subjection founded in other necessities not less stringent than those imposed by statute. We must seek some truer definition.

I understand by Slavery, that condition in which one human being exists mainly as a convenience for other human beings—in which the time, the exertions, the faculties of a part of the Human Family are made to subserve, not their own development, physical, intellectual, and moral, but the comfort, advantage, or caprices of others. In short, wherever service is rendered from one human being to another, on a footing of one-sided and not of mutual obligation—where the relation between the servant and the served is one not of affection and reciprocal good offices, but of authority, social ascendency and power over subsistence on the one hand, and of necessity, servility, and degradation on the other—there, in my view, is Slavery.

You will readily understand, therefore, that, if I regard

your enterprise with less absorbing interest than you do, it is not that I deem Slavery a less but a greater evil. If I am less troubled concerning the Slavery prevalent in Charleston or New-Orleans, it is because I see so much Slavery in New-York, which appears to claim my first efforts. I rejoice in believing that there is less of it in your several communities and neighborhoods; but that it does exist there I am compelled to believe. In esteeming it my duty to preach Reform first to my own neighbors and kindred, I would by no means attempt to censure those whose consciences prescribe a different course. Still less would I undertake to say that the Slavery of the South is not more hideous in kind and degree than that which prevails at the North. The fact that it *is* more flagrant and palpable renders opposition to it comparatively easy and its speedy downfall certain. But how can I devote myself to a crusade against distant servitude, when I discern its essence pervading my immediate community and neighborhood? nay, when I have not yet succeeded in banishing it even from my own humble household? Wherever may lie the sphere of duty of others, is not mine obviously *here?*

Let me state what I conceive to be the essential characteristics of Human Slavery:

1. Wherever certain human beings devote their time and thoughts mainly to obeying and serving other human beings, and this not because they choose to do so but because they *must*, there (I think) is Slavery.

2. Wherever human beings exist in such relations that a part, because of the position they occupy and the functions they perform, are generally considered an inferior class to those who perform other functions, or none, there (I think) is Slavery.

3. Wherever the ownership of the Soil is so engrossed by a small part of the community that the far larger number are compelled to pay whatever the few may see fit to exact for

the privilege of occupying and cultivating the earth, there is something very like Slavery.

4. Wherever Opportunity to Labor is obtained with difficulty, and is so deficient that the Employing class may virtually prescribe their own terms and pay the Laborer only such share as they choose of the product, there is a very strong tendency to Slavery.

5. Wherever it is deemed more reputable to live without Labor than by Labor, so that a gentleman would be rather ashamed of his descent from a blacksmith than from an idler or mere pleasure-seeker, there is a community not very far from Slavery. And,

6. Wherever one human being deems it honorable and right to have other human beings mainly devoted to his or her convenience or comfort, and thus to live, diverting the labor of these persons from all productive or general usefulness to his or her own special uses, while he or she is rendering or has rendered no corresponding service to the cause of human well-being, there exists the spirit which originated and still sustains Human Slavery.

I might multiply these illustrations indefinitely, but I dare not so trespass on your patience. Rather allow me to apply the principles here evolved in illustration of what I deem the duties and policy of Abolitionists in reference to their cause. And here I would advise:

1. *Oppose Slavery in* ALL *its forms.* Be at least as careful not to *be* a slaveholder as not to *vote* for one. Be as tenacious that your own wives, children, hired men and women, tenants, &c., enjoy the blessings of rational Liberty, as that the slaves of South Carolina do.

2. *Be at least as ardent in opposing the* NEAR *as the* DISTANT *forms of Oppression.*—It was by beginning at home that Charity was enabled to perform such long journeys, even before the construction of railroads. And it does seem clear to my mind that if the advocates of Emancipa-

tion would unite in well-directed, persistent efforts to improve the condition of the Colored Race in their own States and neighhorhoods respectively, they could hardly fail to advance their cause more rapidly and surely than by any other course. Suppose, for example, they were to resolve in each State to devote their political energies in the first place to a removal of the shameful, atrocious civil disabilities and degradations under which the African Race now generally labor, and to this end were to vote systematically for such candidates, whom their votes could probably elect, (if such there were,) as were known to favor the removal of those disabilities: Would not their success be sure and speedy? But,

3. *Look well to the Moral and Social condition of the Blacks in the Free States.* Here is the refuge of the conscientious slaveholder. He declines emancipating, because he can not perceive that emancipation has thus far conduced to the benefit of the liberated. If the mass of the Blacks are to remain ignorant, destitute, unprincipled, degraded (as he is told the Free Blacks are) he thinks it better that his should remain Slaves.

I know that the degradation of the Blacks is exaggerated. I know that so much of it as exists is mainly owing to their past and present wrongs. But I feel also that the process of overcoming this debasement must be slow and dubious, while its causes continue to exist. I entreat, therefore, that those who have the ear of these children of Africa and of their philanthropic friends, shall consider the propriety of providing for them cities of refuge, townships—communities, I would say—wherein they may dwell apart from the mass of our people, in a social atmosphere of their own, not poisoned by the universal conviction of their inferiority, at least until they shall have had a chance to show whether they are or are not necessarily idle, thriftless, vicious and content with degradation. I most earnestly believe the popular assumptions on these points erroneous; I ask that the Blacks have a fair chance to prove them so. A single township in each Free State mainly peopled by them, with churches, schools, seminaries for scientific and classical education, and all Social influences untainted by the sense of African humiliation, would do more (if successful, as I doubt not it would be) to pave the way for Universal Freedom, than reams of angry vituperation against slaveholders. These are in good part men of integrity and conscience; they see the wrong almost as clearly as you do; it is the *right* which they should see and can not; will you enable them to see it?

Yours respectfully, HORACE GREELEY.

TOBACCO.

LETTER TO MESSRS. O. S. & L. N. FOWLER.

Gentlemen:—You ask me for a statement of what I know and think respecting tobacco. I have had a good deal of experience on this subject; in fact, I once smoked nearly an inch of cigar myself. It served me right, and I have never since had an inclination to outrage human nature and insult decency in any such way. I was then some six years old, and naturally aspiring to the accomplishments of manhood and gentility; but the lesson I then received will suffice for my whole life, though it should be spun out to the length of Methuselah's. I have since endured my share of the fumigations and kindred abominations of tobacco, but I have inflicted none.

I wish some budding Elia, not a slave to narcotic sensualism, would favor us with an essay on "The Natural Affinities of Tobacco with Blackguardism." The materials for it are abundant, and you have but to open your eyes (or nostrils) in any city promenade, (glorious Boston excepted,) in any village bar-room, to find yourself confronted by them. Is Broadway sunny yet airy, with the atmosphere genial and inviting, so that fair maidens (and eke observing bachelors) throng the two-shilling sidewalk, glad to enjoy and not unwilling to be admired? Hither (as Satan into Paradise, but not half so gentlemanly) hie the host of tobacco-smoking loafers, to puff their detested fumes into the faces and eyes of abhorring purity and loveliness, to spatter the walk, and often soil the costly and delicate dresses of the promenaders with their vile expectorations. And, even should the smokers forbear to besmear the outraged but patiently-enduring flag-stones with their foul saliva, the chewers will not be far behind (as the Revelator saw 'Death on the pale horse, and Hell following after,') industriously polluting the fair face of earth, as their precursors have poisoned the sweet breath of heaven. How long, oh! how long, must all this be suffered?

I have intimated that the tobacco-consumer is—not indeed necessarily and inevitably, but naturally and usually—a blackguard; that chewing or smoking obviously tends to blackguardism. Can any man doubt it? Let him ride with uncorrupted senses in the stage or omnibus, which the chewer insists on defiling with the liquid product of his incessant labors, seeming unconscious of its utter offensiveness; and which even the smoker, especially if partly or wholly drunk, will also insist on transforming into a miniature Tophet by his exhalations, defying alike the express rule of the coach and the sufferer's urgent remonstrances, if he can only say, "Why, there's no *lady* here." ['No *ladies*' is *his* expression, but the plea is execrable enough, though expressed grammatically.] Go into a public gathering, where a speaker of delicate lungs, and an invincible repulsion to tobacco, is trying to discuss some important topic so that a thousand men can hear and understand him, yet whereinto ten or twenty smokers have introduced themselves, a long-nine projecting horizontally from beneath the nose of each, a fire at one end and a fool at the other, and mark how the puff, puffing gradually transforms the atmosphere (none too pure at best) into that of some foul and pestilential cavern, choking the utterance of the speaker, and distracting (by annoyance) the attention of the hearers, until the argument is arrested or its effect utterly destroyed. If he who will selfishly, recklessly, impudently, inflict so much discomfort and annoyance on many, in order that he may enjoy in a particular place an indulgence which could as well be enjoyed where no one else would be affected by it, be not a blackguard, who *can* be? What could indicate bad breeding and a bad heart, if such conduct does not? "Brethren!" said Parson Strong, of Hartford, preaching a Connecticut election sermon, in high party times, some fifty years ago, "it has been charged that I have said every Democrat is a horse-thief: I never did. What I *did* say was only that every horse-thief is a Democrat, and *that* I can prove." So I do not say that every smoker or chewer is necessarily a blackguard, however steep the proclivity that way; but show me a genuine blackguard—one of the b'hoys, and no mistake—who is not a lover of tobacco in some shape, and I will agree to find you two white blackbirds.

HORACE GREELEY.

COMING TO THE CITY.

CITIES are the result of certain social necessities of civilized or semi-civilized Man,—necessities of Trade, of Manufacture, Interchange of Ideas, and of Government: they rest upon and are supported by the Country. Their support is of course mainly voluntary; its amount is controlled by the ability and desires of the rural population. Thus, while almost any farming County might give employment and ample subsistence to five or even ten times its present population, there is scarcely a city in the world whose population is not already quite as large as it has business to employ and income to sustain, while the greater number are constantly crowded with surplus laborers, vainly seeking employment and underbidding each other in the eager strife for it, until thousands can hardly sustain life on the scanty reward of their exertions, and other thousands are forced to live on public or private charity. Many perish every year, not perhaps of absolute starvation, but of diseases induced by hunger, want and exposure, while a larger number are driven by destitution into evil courses, and close their brief careers of guilty mockery of enjoyment by deaths of shame and horror. Such are some of the dire consequences of the continual over-population of our cities, caused by the insane desire very generally felt to escape the ruder toils and tamer routine of country life. Until some marked change shall have been wrought in the general condition of our rural Industry, so as to render it less repulsive than it now is, our cities must continue over-crowded and full of misery. The naked truth that, as a general rule, no one lives by *bona fide* physical labor who can obtain a living without, and very few live by farming or the like who can live by what are esteemed the lighter and more genteel avocations mainly pursued in cities and villages, explains much of the misery so prevalent all around us. Doubtless, the Monopoly of Land is one of the ultimate causes of this deplorable state of things; thousands annually quitting the country for cities who would cling to the homes of their infancy if they were not the property of others, and would cultivate soil like their fathers if they had any soil to cultivate. Having none, they are tempted to seek in some city the employment and independence which seem denied them where they were born.

This choice is almost always an unwise one. In the Country, the young man heartily willing to do anything honest and useful for a livelihood, need seldom wait long for employment that will at least insure him a subsistence. In the Cities, the case is sadly different. A capable, willing, trustworthy man may earnestly seek employment here for months without finding any. And the reason is very clear: There are more seeking work in the cities than work can be found for; and, though the business of most cities annually increases, through the growth of the Country trading with them, yet the pressure for employment in cities constantly outruns the demand for labor, and if New-York were to increase its trade and consequently its population by ten or twenty per cent. a year for the next century, there would at all times be thousands waiting here for chances to do something, and many starved out or impelled to evil courses for want of honest business. The gigantic sea of Foreign Immigration incessantly rolling in upon us, bringing thousands each month to our City (some of them most ingenious, expert and capable) who must have work promptly or go to the Poor-House, and who are inured to lower wages and poorer living than Americans will submit to, will keep the general Labor market glutted and the average recompense of hired labor low for a term of which I can not foresee the end.

—'But do you contend that no American youth should *ever* migrate from the country to one of our Cities?' No, Sir, I do not. What I *do* maintain is this—Whoever leaves the country to come hither should feel sure that he has faculties, capacities, powers, for which the Country affords him no scope, and that the City is his proper sphere of usefulness. He should next be sure that he has ability to procure a livelihood while he shall be laboring to attain that sphere which he regards as his ultimate destination. No youth should migrate to a City without a thorough mastery of some good mechanical trade or handicraft such as is prosecuted in cities, although he may not intend to follow it except in case of dire necessity. Teaching, Clerking, Law, &c. are so very precarious, except to men of established reputation and business, that it is next to madness for a youth to come here relying upon them. With a good trade, a hearty willingness to work, strict temperance and habits of economy, it will be hard to starve out a man who has once found employment; not so with one who is trained only for a Teacher or Clerk, or who 'is willing to do anything'—which means that he knows how to do nothing. With these, our City always has been, always will be crowded—it pays for burying the greater part of them.

The young man fit to come to a City does not begin by importuning some relative or friend to find or make a place for him. Having first qualified himself, so far as he may, for usefulness here, he comes understanding that he must begin at the foot of the class and work his way up. Having found a place to stop, he makes himself acquainted with those places where work in his line may be found, sees the advertisements of 'Wants' in the leading journals at an early hour each morning, notes those which hold out some prospect for him, and accepts the first place offered him which he can take honorably and fill acceptably. He who commences in this way is quite likely to get on.

But for him whose chief object is to live comfortably, or even to acquire wealth by honest industry, the City is not the place. The mass of men and women work far steadier and harder here for a bare subsistence than they do away from the Cities. To say nothing of the ruder manual toil by which no man can support a family in comfort, the average earnings of good mechanics here will not exceed eight dollars per week the year round, or four hundred dollars per annum. This will seem considerable to mechanics who can hire a good house and garden for thirty to sixty dollars, with often a strip of pasture or meadow attached; but let such consider that here almost any kind of a house costs from three to five hundred dollars per annum, and the meanest dog-hole into which a family can be crowded—perhaps up two flights of stairs—will cost one hundred dollars, with like charges for Fuel, Milk, Vegetables, &c. and they will understand the whole subject much better. A good mechanic can support his family better by five days' labor per week in the country than by six in this or almost any great city.

'But men do get rich in the city,'—Yes, they do. One in a thousand of those who come here in quest of fortune achieve it, and they are generally men who would do the same anywhere. Scrutinize closely the lives of those who have made fortunes in cities, and you will find that they were early risers, hard workers, sharp dealers, and close calculators—a sort very difficult to starve. Having thus obtained a good start early in life, the rest was easy; for he must be a natural-born fool or worse who can not with money and credit accumulate property anywhere. The problem we are considering is, How men are to do who have *not* money, or at best have very little.

I am not forgetting that there are some rare but showy instances of men who have made fortunes by some dashing speculation or run of luck in trade—but these are too few to disturb the general calculation. Whoever wishes to try his luck at gambling is not obliged to come to the City for that purpose, or at least need not remove hither. Three days will usually suffice for his purpose.—And, for every large fortune rapidly acquired in Trade or Stocks, fully forty small fortunes (and some large ones) have been lost in the same way. The mushroom millionaire dazzles all eyes by his horses and equipage, his palace, and his plate—he is thought of, talked of—while those who have lost everything by the same turn of the wheel crawl away to die in some out-of-the-way corner, silent and forgotten.

—A single class remains to be spoken of—that of men past their youth, who, often with families dependent on them, seek employment in cities because they have not been successful elsewhere, and, without any special faculty, plunge into some emporium of Commerce to earn in some novel vocation the livelihood among strangers which they can not amid their friends at the pursuits to which they are accustomed. Such men are downright suicides—if they have families, they are worse than that; and whoever aids them in their mad folly is an accessory to their crime. No man should ever change his vocation after thirty unless he has hitherto been a pirate, gambler, pickpocket, or something of the sort, and even then he has but a sorry prospect before him; but for a poor unlucky man to bring a family of children to a City and hope there to support them in some novel pursuit, is the wildest, most desperate infatuation. There is no chance of success—no rational hope that he can struggle on except in the most abject dependence and beggary.

Such are some of the reasons which impel me uniformly to reply unfavorably or not at all to those seeking encouragement in their plans of removing to the City. To bring more here is to increase the prevalence of want and misery among our present redundant population. I might say much more on this theme, but can it be needed?

STRIKES AND THEIR REMEDY.

THE recent Strikes for Wages in different parts of the country, but especially those of the Iron-Puddlers of Pittsburgh, suggest grave and yet hopeful thoughts. In reading the proceedings of the Strikers, an observer's attention will be arrested by their emphatic though unconscious condemnation of our entire Social framework as defective and unjust. Probably half of these men never harbored the idea of a Social reconstruction—never even heard of it. Ask them one by one if such an idea could be made to work, and they would shake their heads and say, 'It is all well in theory, but it will never do in practice.' But when they come to differ with their employers, they at once assume the defectiveness of our present Social polity, and argue from it as a point by nobody disputed: "We *ought* to be paid so much, [thus runs their logic] because we *need* and they can *afford* it." '*Ought*,' do you say, friends? Don't you realize that the whole world around is based upon *must* instead of *ought?* Which one of you, though earning fifteen dollars per week, ever paid five cents more than the market price for a bushel of potatoes, or a basket of eggs, or a quarter of mutton, because the seller *ought* to be fairly paid for his labor, and couldn't really *afford* to sell at the market rate? Nay, which of you well-paid puddlers ever gave a poor widow a dollar a piece for making your shirts when you could get them made as well for half a dollar, even though at the dollar you would be getting three days' work for one? Step forward from the ranks, you gentlemen that have conducted *your own* buying and hiring through life on the principle of '*ought*,' and let me make my obeisance to each of you! I shall do it right heartily, and with no fear of being rendered neck-weary by the operation.

Yet that '*ought*' is a glorious word when applied to the relations of Business and of Labor—we must not let it be forgotten. There is in it the seeds of a revolution more gigantic and pervasive than any Vergniaud or Kossuth ever devised. Heaven speed the day when, not only in Iron but in all branches of Industry, the reward of Labor shall be regulated not by 'must,' but by 'ought.'

* * * * * * * * *

The most melancholy feature of these strikes is the apparent indisposition on either side to discover any law whereby these collisions may be terminated for the present and precluded in future. It seems so natural for the workmen to say, "You tell us that you can pay but three-fourths of our former wages because of the low price of Iron now suppose we accept your terms, *will you agree that our wages shall advance whenever and so fast as the price of Iron shall improve?*"—'Yes,' would be the natural and proper answer of the masters, '*if you will agree that they shall be reduced whenever and so fast as Iron shall decline still further.*' This being accepted, the entire relation of Capital to Labor in this particular department is reädjusted on the basis of Proportion or Common Interest instead of that of arbitrary Wages, evolving contrariety of interests. Now the puddler gets so much, although the Iron should not sell for enough to pay him, and cares very little whether the business is prosperous or depressed, save as its suspension may turn him out of work. But with the establishment of Proportion as a law of the trade, every worker's interests would be on the side of prosperity, and his wages every week depend on the price which Iron should bear at the end of it.

But from neither party to this controversy do I hear one fruitful or reconciling word. From the journeymen's side, we have all manner of Jacobinic clamor against the oppressions of capital, wealth, monopoly, &c., but no practical suggestion for their removal. No one says, 'Let us hire Iron-works [of which there are abundance shut up] and go to making Iron as our own masters.' Even in Wheeling, where there has been a great meeting of Iron-workers to sympathise with and encourage the Pittsburgh puddlers, no voice uttered the creative words, 'Stop depending on masters, and go to making Iron for yourselves!' How is it that a course so obvious, so decisive, and now rescued from the fatal taint of novelty by a signal success, should remain unadopted and even unconsidered?

NOTE.—Since the above was written and published, the organization of the various branches of Iron-making and manufacture on the basis of Proportion or Association has been earnestly considered by the workers of Pittsburgh, and several attempts at practical Association are now in progress or in contemplation by them.

GLIMPSES OF A BETTER LIFE.

I KNOW that the speculations of those who dream of a better framework of Society are distasteful to the greater number of readers, but shall we, therefore, hold our peace? Shall we follow the advice of our adversaries, and choose only those opportunities to speak when they who condemn unheard will surely not be among the number of our auditors? Shall we politely smother the light under a bushel, lest its piercing rays inflame the eyes of a long benighted and wilfully slumbering world? So policy dictates, and the World imperatively commands. The dull, voluptuous World! it demands flattery for its amazing charities, not rebuke for its indifference to the wants and woes of the Poor! Beauty in her boudoir will be complimented on her generous bestowment of pence on some famishing invalid, and not confronted with the stern, reproachful ghosts of the hours due to Humanity she has wasted in Sloth or Selfishness; of the coin lavished on dress or decoration, which might have raised a sister from despair to love of life. Wealth rocks indolently in its easy-chair, contemplating its ample hoards, and broadly fertile domains, and laboriously digesting its dainty viands, and petulantly asks if it is *never* to have a moment's peace from the importunities of want, and the cant of deputy beggars. And even Religion oft discards the example of the Divine Teacher who hesitated not to say, "How hardly shall they that have riches enter into the 'kingdom of God!" and no longer ventures to test the sincerity of her neophytes by the sharp criterion, "Sell *all* thou 'hast, and give to the poor; then come and follow me." Wisely and truly does she warn the Poor against envy, hatred, and agrarian convulsion—rightly and forcibly does she teach them that no change in society can be beneficent unless based on Justice, Concord, and Love—that from strife and malevolence can come nothing but aggravated squalor and misery—that Content and Competence may be found quite as readily, and far more effectually, by most of us, by limiting and regulating our wants, than by increasing our possessions—that a heart at peace with the Father and with its allotment is more to be prized than all the wealth of Peru—but does her duty stop here? How speaks she to the successful devotee of gold who is constantly adding to his broad domains estate after estate, as though he would monopolize the Earth's wide surface and leave his brethren of the Race no dry spot whereon to stand but by his gracious permission?—who would deem it an exorbitant exaction if he were asked to contribute a tithe of his annual gains to improving the condition of his unfortunate-fellow-men?—How seldom do her oblique and vague denunciations of avarice and worldliness disturb the enjoyment of their well-placed, richly furnished pews, though directly under the eye and voice of the preacher?

Well, thus be it, so long as it must. Let the champions of Society as it is eulogize its structure and its blessings, only let us few Dissenters realize and proclaim the approach of a better. Ay, even on this earth, it is ordained that a better condition shall be realized for Man,—the toiling, striving, suffering, famishing! Not until the dark valley is passed shall our Race be doomed ever to wait ere they see the kingdom of God! The radiant vision of the Prophet, the living dream of the Poet, do not transcend the reality which the Father has decreed for his earthly children. It needs but that the principles of Divine Order shadowed forth (perchance dimly to gross apprehensions) in the life and words of Jesus be embodied in the daily acts and efforts of His professed disciples, and Earth shall once more be enrobed in the vesture of Eden. The old Record of the proffer that even five righteous persons should suffice to save a guilty and doomed city, is written for our admonition and profit. It needs only that goodness *be* goodness, openly and veritably, to commend it to all consciences and all hearts. Were there but one community whereof the love of God, as evinced in entire devotion to the welfare of Mankind, were the ruling impulse, the whole world would speedily be illumined by its light, and transformed by its example. But the life, even of the noblest, is devoted to partial ends; its aims are narrow and partisan; its efforts discordant and fragmentary. The manifestations of whatever Philanthropy there is in our wide world jostle each other; Religion regards with doubt, if not with aversion, the efforts for Human advancement which are not made through the Church, and the Church is in turn distrusted, or deemed inadequate, by the philanthropist. Thus suspicion, division, discord, convulse and darken the world.

Yes, Division, Alienation, Isolation, are the bane of our Race. We have lost the knowledge that the blessing of each is bound up in the blessing of all. Fallen Cain blindly imagines that he slays but his brother, his rival, his triumphant competitor: he feels not that he is slaying himself—that henceforth a sky of fire shall be above him, and an earth of blood beneath—that all Nature's voices shall speak to him the wrath of God, and that his curse shall be to live. When shall the At-One-ment through Christ become a living reality to the common heart, and the scales of Selfishness and Discord fall from our eyes as of old did those of Prejudice and Hate from the eyes of Saul of Tarsus?

A Social condition founded on and penetrated by the vital truths of Christianity—this is the Problem of our Age—a Society which shall be the embodiment and palpable expression of the great Law of Love, in which servant and master shall be obsolete distinctions, Labor no more a drudgery nor a degradation, and Usefulness, whether exalted or lowly, the sure and only path to Honor. It shall yet be achieved, through struggles, through errors, through failures, if the imperfections of those who dimly and unworthily apprehend, and strive to give expression to the great truth, shall render these inevitable. The wintry sullenness, the frozen apathy of the mass may delay the dawn, but the bright Day shall come at last. Christ never intended that of His disciples a few should enjoy every costly luxury which Imagination could suggest, while millions famished and shivered, wanting the veriest necessaries of life. How should he recognise as a follower him who walls up thousands of fertile acres as a hunting-ground, and leaves hungry thousands all around to pine in hunger for the food which that fair domain would abundantly render, and which they have now no place to produce, no opportunity to procure? To my mind, the most formal and hard-natured Pharisee of olden time, the most sensual, soul-denying Sadducee of our own day, would be recognised as a disciple by the "good Master" far sooner than this pillar of "Church and State," who complacently deems Christ under obligations to him for his efforts and contributions to spread what he calls the Gospel.

Man has fallen and is divided; he must be raised and re-united. Darkened in understanding, and made gross by sensuality, he needs to be taught his first duty to his brother. "Thou shalt love thy neighbor as thyself!"—how read you this, upholder of War, and Slavery, and of that Social Order which leaves millions to grow up in Ignorance, Want, and Temptation; which provides prisons for the guilty, and poor-houses for the helplessly starving, but makes no provision that the still innocent and nobly striving shall have Opportunity to earn needful Bread? His children look up to him with hollow, anxious eyes; he rushes into the street, determined to find employment, however repugnant, and however meager its reward, but in vain! He returns at night only more weary and more wretched, to a home more desolate and despairing than ever. Vain is the strength in his sinews, while strength remains there; he is one of the landless millions, and has no resource but the *chance* that some one will appreciate and require his services, and when that fails — what then? The prison of the pauper may be opened to his entreaties, and it may be shut sternly in his face; the fact that he has energies and health remaining is often regarded as evidence, *prima facie*, that he needs no alms; as if muscles must command food, with or without opportunity to use and profit by them. The prison of the felon is his only certain resource.

Tell me not that this is Christian Society, in which the widow sits toiling from dawn till midnight, consuming her slender remnant of health and vision, to earn of her sister in the church the smallest modicum of food and shelter with which her tender babes can exist, and shivering with dread that, — by the delay of payment, or the failure to obtain further work, — food and shelter may fail to outlast the week. Tell me not that these Cities, in which thousands are annually driven, by keenest want, to shame and destruction, do truly worship that Maker with whose costly temples they are so thickly studded — the benighted savages who abandon the decrepit and incurable to famine and the wolf in the lonely wilderness, are better Christians than these. They at least have the plea of a seeming Necessity to palliate their conduct; we create the necessity we witness, by placing Virtue on a rugged, flinty eminence, and presenting a flowery declivity to Crime. Not till at least the Christian who possesses wealth shall hold it as the trustee of the Creator for the benefit of his children — till it be recognised as a practical axiom that "the Earth is the Lord's, and the fullness thereof," — given not to aggrandize the few, but to bless and strengthen all — never till it be established as a maxim of Political Economy that Pauperism is, in most cases, far easier prevented than supported, and that those who possess nothing have a Right to labor and to live, a Right to education and healthful development, which those who possess all are bound to recognise and give effect to — not till it is felt and admitted that Society commits a great crime when one of its members is left to famish, or falls into sin, through defect of education or of Social providence in any way — may we hope to withstand triumphantly the host of moral and physical evils which now overwhelm the Race.

In view of these evils and their causes, how shall we have patience with the cavil that it is not reform of Social Arrangements that is needed, but of the individual heart? Ay, truly does the individual need reform to induce him to enter heartily and effectively upon the great work for which that is a preparation. "This ought ye to have done, and not have left the other undone." But when he *is* regenerated, what then? Shall he go on adding estate after estate to his possessions? Shall his daily life, his business, his dealings with those around him, remain unaffected? Shall servants swarm around him, living for his convenience, and ministering to his luxury or his pride? Shall the poor dread ejectment from his tenements, when misfortune or miscalculation shall have rendered them unable to meet his legal demands? Shall his garrets and cellars be tenanted by those whose every hour must be held subordinate to his wishes, and of whose education, moral culture, and happiness he takes no more account than of those of the beasts in his stable? Away with this Pharisaic pretence! Christianity demands a life renewed in all its aims and relations, in which there are no more servitors of pomp and sloth, to be treated superciliously and paid grudgingly, but a true and essential Brotherhood, linking the noblest and most fortunate with the most dependent and benighted of mankind.

To constitute a Society which shall conform, in both its outward structure and its inward life, to this Divine ideal is the great duty of our time — a duty which will yet be consummated. Despite the sway of selfishness, seemingly so universal, nobler and truer thoughts are everywhere breaking in on the human mind. The Statesman in debate, the Poet in his visions, the Novelist in his exposures of the workings of guilt and the daily tragedy of life, begin to lay bare the roots of Social Evil, often unwarily or with imperfect apprehension, but yet so that the world begins to startle in its lethargy and dream uneasily of a better day. That day shall surely come — nay, it is now not afar. The Chivalry of Industry is already replacing that of War. It is not Napoleon nor Wellington, but some Fulton or Arkwright, who shall stand forth in the future as the hero of the Nineteenth Century. The frightful excess of Social anarchy, misery, and destitution, in the midst of the most abundant wealth and prodigality the world has ever known, is driving millions to inquiry and study with regard to their causes and their cure. Knowledge and light with respect to the whole subject are borne on the wings of the wind to every nation, to every neighborhood, and even the most stolid or wilfully adverse can not long refuse to listen and to learn. And yet farther: Practical attempts are in progress to test and exhibit the possibility, the feasibility, of a life of true Brotherhood — a life harmoniously adjusted to blend and secure the rights and the happiness of each in those of all — a life devoted to noble and exalted purposes — a life ultimately freed from selfish anxiety, from want and from abounding temptation — a life of which the atmosphere shall be Innocence, and the labor Worship. Little enough of these vast aims will be realized immediately — they may be pursued for years under adverse circumstances, discouragements and difficulties — but is it not something to have conceived and adopted them? Let us not doubt that the ultimate realization shall transcend the initial hope, and that through their triumph a way shall be opened for the Social emancipation of our Race.

THE AIMS OF LIFE.

Q. What is the chief end of Man?
A. Man's chief end is to glorify God, and enjoy him for ever.

Westminster Catechism.

It must be deemed unfortunate that, in a summary of religious doctrine from which so many human beings have received their first distinct notions of God's government and man's duties, the primary and most important truth should have been set forth so vaguely and obscurely. How many of the young learners of that catechism have any clear perception of what is meant by either question or answer?

But dissipate all obscurity in the statement of the problem and in its solution, and the matter is still seriously objection. able. The existence of each individual is made to have two purposes or aims—first, God's glory; next, his own enjoyment. He is called into being to gratify two selfish ends—one the Creator's, the other his own. This must be wrong. God has not created us to the end that He may be glorified, nor with any such purpose, but in obedience to the dictates of His infinite beneficence. He has given us being in order to increase the infinity of good which pervades the universe. He has endowed us with reason and consciousness, not commanding us to glorify Him, not bidding us to enjoy Him, but exhorting us to omit no opportunity of doing good, of diffusing true Knowledge, Wisdom, Happiness, Blessing. In short, God has not created us to subserve any selfish end of His own, nor will He hold us guiltless if we pursue only such ends of our own.

Am I wrong in assuming that our ethical and clerical teachers are generally deficient in their inculcations on this head? that their point of view is insufficiently elevated, and their requisitions too scanty? Is not the vulgar notion that to refrain from doing ill to our neighbor is virtue, somewhat countenanced by the usual tenor of moral exhortation? Does not the commandment-keeping squanderer on his own luxurious appetites of the average earnings of ten human beings, pass in society as an innocent and often as an exemplary man?

It seems evident that a radical reform in the popular apprehension of religious teaching, if not in the teaching itself, is here needed. Since the earthly pilgrimage of the Divine 'Man of Sorrows,' we have had few preachers who said frankly and pointedly, 'How hardly shall they that have riches enter into the Kingdom of God!'—'Sell all that thou hast and give to the poor; *then* come and follow me,' and so forth. Do we realize that these were not the exaggerations of petulance or asceticism, but the simple, natural conditions of spiritual health, illumination, and progress? What He required was but the disencumbering of the soul of clogs which impeded and bore it heavily earthward. What Christ said of wealth, its influences and proper uses, had no mere local or transitory significance. It is as true in New-England as it was in Palestine,—as true in 1846 as it was in the year one.

In truth, wealth, employed only or mainly to subserve personal ends, is in its nature incompatible with a true life, or with the purpose of such a life. The man of substance, who regards his riches as means of luxury, of elegance, of power, (other than the power to relieve and bless,) or of continuing such advantages to his descendants, is inevitably, palpably beclouded as to the very purpose for which life was given him. His aims are selfish and groveling, his understanding darkened, his faltering, grudging, feeble efforts at goodness, are tainted by the sin of Ananias and Sapphira. His fealty to Mammon will ever clash with his duty to God.

The true disciple of Christ regards himself but as the steward of whatever worldly goods Providence has placed in his hands. From these he is to satisfy the necessities of those dependent upon him; all beyond belongs to his Master, and is to be dispensed according to His plain directions. Not that he is compelled to divest himself to-day of the means of relieving wants to-morrow; that would be acting the part of a prodigal and thoughtless steward; but he is to dispense or reserve whatever has been confided to him with single reference to the highest good of all. All that he has, being the rightful property of his Creator, is to be dispensed according to the model ever before him in the dispensation of rain and sunshine. He whose sympathies or beneficent efforts are circumscribed by any boundary of family, sect, neighborhood, or nation, is most imperfect in his obedience to the Father of lights. He who is content to enjoy the fruits of others' toil, rendering mankind little or no positive service in return, can be but a very distant follower of the Divine Redeemer.

On no point is error more common or more vital than on this. A life devoted mainly to what is deemed innocent though selfish enjoyment is not usually regarded as inconsistent with a Christian profession. The wealthy disciple may devote half his time to a round of visits, dinners, tours, and entertainments, without fear of reprehension from the sacred desk, and with little danger of reproach from his own drugged conscience. Yet it would be difficult to say wherein such a life excelled that of the less depraved heathen of our own or ancient times. He that lives mainly to himself and his kindred can not truly be said to live to God, no matter whether he pray with his face to Jerusalem, Mecca, Rome, or the sky. There is no savor of real godlikeness in a life so devoted.

The assumed innocence of a life of pomp and luxury will never bear a searching examination. It is not possible that such a life may be lived innocently, no matter how liberally it may be garnished with tithes and prayers. The man of substance who lives in luxury, can not fail to render the lives of other human beings merely auxiliary to his own enjoyment. Where some are only served, others must needs be merely servants; where some one is to be habitually gratified, others must degenerate into the mere instruments of gratification — the machine whereby a certain quantum of supposed enjoyment is produced. Wherever one man deems the services of other human beings essential to his comfortable subsistence, and repays those services otherwise than by service in turn — wherever a family is divided into two or more classes, holding respectively superior and inferior positions, so that their reciprocal obligations differ wholly in kind and degree — so that one class, and but one, lives in constant dread of incurring the displeasure of the other, or rather, of incurring the consequences of that displeasure — there is a relation which Christ never recognized, and which all His teachings tend to condemn and overthrow.

I do not know that I am more strongly moved by any ordinary spectacle than by that of the assembling for worship of a fashionable and wealthy congregation in one of our great cities. As the rich and the great roll up in their carriages to engross the superbly adorned pews, the poorer and humbler shuffle in on foot, and take the less desirable seats, leaving the worst of all to the crushed children of Africa, whose understanding, it would seem, is deemed so acute that they need not hear more than half the service in order to comprehend it thoroughly. The same equivocal compliment is paid to the decrepit, the deaf, the superannuated, if they happen to be hopelessly poor. But the great man's coachman is not even supposed to hear at all. Were he at liberty, he would not venture to present himself at the door of the family pew — such a stretch of presumption would cost him a lecture on manners to superiors, and very likely his means of subsistence. *His* business in that solemn hour is not to worship God, but to take care of horses. While he assiduously fulfills this function in the shadow of the church outside, and the gilded prayer-books are in requisition within, half a dozen other human implements are busy at home preparing the sumptuous meal. For these, 'Sunday shines no holyday;' it hardly witnesses a relaxation of their labors They may have some vague idea that the obligations, duties, and hopes of religion are divinely intended for all, but the whole atmosphere, the daily necessities of their life condemn such a notion. It may be their masters' duty to obey God; it is theirs to obey their masters; and in this service conscience is well nigh superfluous, and would often be an embarrassment and obstruction. Thus they wear out their lives in mere brutishness and serfdom, with no more mental exercise nor development than the domesticated animals which are their fellow servants and daily companions. How many families contribute annually to send the gospel to the heathen, without once reflecting that their practice and example make a great many more heathen than their money will ever convert!

To insure the speedy diffusion and triumph of Christianity throughout the world, it needs but to be carried fully and fairly into practice by a part of its present adherents, so as to be plainly observed and understood. Were a single county thoroughly Christianized in all its institutions, laws, polity, usages, the world could not resist its noiseless appeal for universal conformity to its order, justice, harmony, and happiness. It is because Christians are content to differ so little from the pagan world, except perhaps in theology, that gross darkness still overspreads nine-tenths of the habitable globe.

The time is at hand when the significance which once dwelt in the disciples' washing each other's feet, (and not those of each other only,) in the office of deacons, in the

Lord's Supper, and so forth, shall again be apprehended and realized. Christianity has been preached, expounded, and moralized upon, long enough ; it is yet (by the mass of its professors) to be really *lived.* In the new age now dawning upon humanity, the Christian slave-trader and the Christian living in idleness and luxury will stand on the same platform. The professor who lives sumptuously on the unrequited toil of his slaves, and he who consumes largely without himself laboring to add anything to the store of human comforts, will be regarded as neighbors ; while he who requires service but renders none, will be deemed a most unfaithful subject of the great law of Love. In short, living to self, or to any ends which do not embrace love to God and the highest good of mankind, will be deemed the one great departure from rectitude and duty, drawing after it all essential corruption and actual transgressions.

THE UNFULFILLED MISSION OF CHRISTIANITY:

A LETTER TO THE READER.

WASHINGTON CITY, May 4, 1842.

* * * IT was but yesterday, that I stood in the great Commercial Emporium, and listened pensively to the rustling tread of its hurrying thousands. Here passed the slave of commerce, the devotee of gain, with vacant gaze and introverted perception, his brow working unconsciously as he plodded over the thousands he hoped to win yet dreaded to lose by some casual turn of the wheel of fortune ; scanning, perchance, the sky, to note what prospect of tempest or favoring gale awaited his vessel now approaching the coast, hurrying to the bulletin for news, or to the price current to learn the chance of profit or loss on his ventures. Beside him trudged unheededly the laborer, with his swart

brow and stooping frame, toiling on sturdily, though wearily, through the rugged day, with thoughts of the wife and little ones whose narrow domicil and scanty comforts his arduous, unremitted exertions barely suffice to provide, and thinking sadly, shudderingly, of the period just at hand when his present enployment shall cease, to be succeeded, he knows not how or whence. And now, there pass me the lawyer and the broker, each weaving in his brain the spider-web in which some poor unfortunate shall soon be enclosed, and gloating joyously over the anticipated triumph which to another shall be ruin. Bu' list! a longer stride, a more heedless air: here rushes by a reckless, half-intoxicated sailor, just landed from a voyage around Cape Horn, and hastening to spend, in a few days' riot and debauchery, the hard-won earnings of as many years, and then return to his monotonous round as penniless as ever, and one degree more debased and brutal than before. There prances knavish Bankruptcy in its chariot, spattering the thread-bare garb of some ruined creditor, who goes before on foot; here trips Fashion in lace; there hobbles Beggary in rags, as, with counterfeited limp and loathsome travesty of the human form, it whines out its petition for alms. * * * And now 'tis evening, and the great avenues blaze with light, as the windows of the palaces of Traffic flash with gems and are radiant with the display of costly fabrics. The entrances to the haunts of dissipation are luminous and inviting to their victims, and, from the dark purlieus where they have shunned the glare of day, the votaries of sin come forth to flaunt their little season. In the narrower and less frequented paths, darkness holds partial dominion, and riot, crime, dissipation, and fierce contention, have recommenced their reign, destined, it may be, to outwear the night. Such is a rude and hasty presentment of the moral aspects of a day in *Christian* New-York, where thousands are assembled (very properly and laudably, I doubt not) to devise the ways, and contribute the means, to carry the GOSPEL and its attendant blessings into all parts of the globe.

And now I sit in Washington, where the great and the honorable of the land are assembled to shape its destinies. Their voices reach me in my narrow chamber; the rattle of their wheels is borne freshly to my ear, as they roll over the broad avenue.

The commanding might of Mind is here. The orator, whose fervid utterance in the senate has reverberated through the vast extent of our country, rocking the hearts of millions from the Aroostook to the Sabine, is here. The demagogue, base idol of a multitude's thoughtless hosannas, flatterer and flattered, corrupter and corrupted, is here—the enchantment lent by distance, dispelled by contact—his essential nothingness and selfish aims gleaming out abundantly through the paint and patchwork of counterfeit patriotism, in which he has arrayed himself. The gaudy blazonry of military pomp, of naval prowess, is here. Here the sleek and satisfied official jostles the shrinking and cringing office-hunter from the walk. Still, as ever, amid the shows of luxury and waste, stalks the gaunt form of penury and want, pining for a crust, as it gazes through blazing windows upon the superfluous banquet on which thousands have been squandered. Gliding through, checkering all, are the dark figures of the low-browed children of Cain, bearing ever their unmistakable badge of servitude and degradation. Here, the gambler and the debauchee—honorable and eminent, it may be—are preparing to waste the midnight hours in orgies whereof the speedy issue is shame, debasement, and death. Such is the spectacle presented by the enlightened metropolis of this *Christian* land, whence missionaries are radiating to every corner of the world, in this nineteenth century since the advent of the Savior. In the long interval, the Christian faith and worship have widely diffused themselves, but where is the CHRISTIAN IDEA? Where lingers the kingdom of universal holiness and love which Jesus came to establish ON EARTH?

Where is it? I see around me the stately and costly edifices in which Herod and Dives proceed weekly, with scrupulous punctuality, to worship God in pomp and luxury, as followers of the carpenter of Nazareth, the fishermen of Galilee. Christian forms and observances are thick around me: where is the Christian spirit? I recognize it not in that lordly pile; not within the folds of that ample surplice; not within those richly-cushioned pews, which an humble, threadbare stranger may not enter without encountering a frown, nor an African without provoking a curse on his amazing presumption. Yet, possibly, in that poor Ethiop's heart the divine emotion has found unsuspected welcome; it may glow there as he shrinks tremblingly into some obscure corner of the edifice, and listens rapturously to truths which not even the preacher comprehends. Perhaps, in some dingy conventicle, its material utterance drowned beneath discordant ejaculations of folly and frenzy, of fanaticism and absurdity, the incense of a genuine devotion is ascending, unmarked, to the throne of the everlasting Father. But is this the fullness of the kingdom which Christ came to establish? Shall such occasional and solitary instances be held to overbear and set at naught the sad reality of a world lying in wickedness? Do we not know that evil and anguish, oppression and wretchedness, wrong and despair, are abundant, nearly as ever, among the children of men? And is not the world yet prepared to realize that, in the fullness of the Christian dispensation is contained the remedy for *all* evil—for all that is not incident to our mortality, even here? How long shall it be practically regarded as a form of worship and a code of difficult observances? Why not rather accept it as a divinely appointed means of entire and immediate emancipation from the ills of our earthly condition? Let not the idea be hastily condemned as extravagant; let us soberly consider it.

When Christ directed the inquirer to sell all his goods, and give the avails to the poor — when He declared that the rich should with extreme difficulty enter the kingdom of heaven — when he related the parable of the pearl of great price, &c. did he merely utter extravagant hyperboles? The disciples did not so understand him, as we learn by their having 'all things in common,' even after his death. Did he propound these rules in exclusive reference to some imminent exigency? So it does not appear; nor can it, unless the command to love our neighbor as ourself be understood to have a like limited and now lifeless significance. Why, then, should the Church, or assemblage of believers, prefer the interpretation of Ananias and Sapphira to that of Peter and Paul? Why should Christians famish — nay, why should *men* perish for lack of food, while in Christendom is abundance? Why should believers be driven to solicit and subsist on the freezing charity of our political Organizations, while within the Church is ample wealth? This, surely, is directly contrary to the precept and example of the Apostolic age. I have not traced the history minutely, yet I am confident that the first idea of a universal and permanent provision for the poor and destitute originated in that age, with Christ and His apostles; that it continued a work of the Church, and not at all of the State, down to a comparatively recent period; and that it lapsed into the hands of the latter through the increase of temporal knowledge and wisdom, and the decline of Christianity as a distinct and substantive power over the hearts and actions of men. If so, what is the obvious deduction?

But a mere provision for the destitute is not all that is contemplated by the idea of Christianity. In that idea I clearly recognize the germ of a great Social renovation. In teaching mankind no longer to hate, distrust, and destroy, but to love and cherish each other as themselves, a stupendously beneficent revolution was involved. Alms-houses for the destitute go but a short way toward the fulfilment of the great law of love. Mot merely insurance against extremest misery, but provision for positive and essentially equal happiness, is implied. And why may not this be realized? Why should not the Christian dispensation become the basis of a new and benignant Social Order, from which want and wo, fraud and wrong, discord and antagonism, shall be banished, and the highest attainable good of each member be striven for and secured? Why may not such an order be formed, which shall secure to each individual not only abundant food, and clothing, and shelter, but education, also—intellectual development, and all the means of rationa enjoyment—requiring of him, in turn, that equal and just contribution of his efforts toward the general weal, which the community or church shall require, and which his own capacities and preference (very rarely, if unperverted, at variance) shall indicate? And why may not our race thus emancipate themselves from the bondage of constraint, and privation, and suffering, in which they so long have labored and groaned; and, guided and upheld by the law of universal love, rise speedily and surely to the primal condition, while the long scourged and desolated earth shall grow verdant and beauteous again?

This is a vast and inspiring theme. I should not venture to speak so confidently on the hopeful side of it, had not loftier and serener spirits sounded its depths, and vanquished its difficulties. These have shown that the renovation of society on the basis of the Christian idea is not visionary, is not fantastic, is not impracticable. Nay, undoubted EXPERIENCE, not merely in the repeated and enduring instances of the Shakers and other ascetic communities, but in those of many of larger faith and clearer knowledge, has demonstrated this cheering truth. There is no longer a necessity, there is hardly an excuse for social evil and degradation. The means of avoiding or vanquishing them are within the reach of nearly all. The system of ASSOCIATION, or sharehold property, blended with Attractive Industry, promulgated by FOURIER, does away the last objection, that a Social Order adverse to the present must generate improvidence and idleness, and so perish through human infirmity. Its vast economies will bring wealth within the reach of all, while affording them the amplest means and opportunities for intellectual, moral, and social elevation and enjoyment.

Carlyle casually remarks, that 'a man, able and willing to work, yet unable to find employment, and thence lacking the means of subsistence, is the saddest sight under the sun.' What shall we say of a Christian famishing in a land of Christian affluence, because the means of earning bread is not afforded him in our chaotic and warring social order? Surely the soul of such a one must appear as an accusing angel at the bar of Eternal Justice against the community in which such a tragedy was enacted. Yet such a calamity has taken place, even in this country. Let us hope that the time when it *could* be is nearly at an end, and that the knowledge of its possibility will soon linger only as a fearful tradition in the homes of the children of men.

THE CHURCH AND THE AGE.

I HAVE as little taste as faculty for fine writing; as little appetite as aptitude for mere sentimentality: if I were to attempt even a love-story, I have no doubt it would insensibly grow into a socialist harangue or a dissertation on the causes and cure of human destitution. This life on which we have been lanched, seems a problem so grave and earnest as to afford little time or thought for idyls or madrigals. We awake in it to find ourselves members of the great body of Humanity—and in what condition is that body with which we are so indissolubly blended? Of the one thousand millions of human beings on earth, how large a proportion—certainly more than half—pass through life sufferers from want;—want of opportunity, of education, of shelter, and of food! Millions annually perish prematurely, through ignorance and the resulting evils—victims of famine, of excess, of evil habits, unfit aliment, or lawless passions, from which a better training, a juster idea of the laws of the universe, would have saved them. 'The people perish for lack of vision,' and so have done from the first. Ignorance of the inexorable laws of cause and effect which bind together virtue and happiness, vice and misery, has ever been a chief source of the woes under which 'the whole creation groaneth and travaileth together in pain until now.'

Into the midst of this lazar-house of sin and sorrow, comes the angel Religion—and for what? Even granting that the paramount object of the Savior's mission and the Christian dispensation is salvation beyond the grave, is not the parallel design to mitigate the sufferings and rectify the errors of this present life still obvious, undeniable? The evils and woes over which Christ sorrowed were plainly temporal—the tender concern manifested by the Gospel for the destitute and desolate, is not confined to the future life. I have erringly read the Scriptures, if the solicitude therein expressed for the well-being of our race is at all confined to their condition in the world beyond the grave.

Providence has cast our lot in an age of intense intellectual activity and progress. The proportion of the human family who read and think has been doubled within half a century, and is still rapidly increasing, And parallel, with the diffusion of knowledge, speeds the consciousness of

Brotherhood, the sentiment of love for all who breathe, of sympathy for all who suffer. All over the civilized, the Christian world, novel agencies and efforts of benevolence attest the truth that rivers and mountains no more suffice to make enemies of the nations separated by them, and that the aspiration for universal beneficence is rapidly rising to its proper place of guiding impulse to mankind.

And how does the Christian Church, — using that term to comprehend and designate the whole body of believers in Christ, — regard the advancing spirit? Does she joyfully recognize and tenderly treat it as her own child and servitor? Does she cheerfully submit to be quickened and admonished by it, in case the fire kindled at her altar burns brightly on the new hearth while it has become dim on hers? Does she evince a cordial and thankful willingness to see the good for which she has not time nor means wrought out by other and humbler agencies? In short, does the Church recognize in every instrumentality of good to man a coworker with herself in her glorious mission, and rejoice that its consummation is thus visibly hastened? If so, it is well with her and with our kind.

But let the Church countenance the assumption that Religion is one thing and Philanthropy quite another — let her insist that her concern is chiefly with the things of another world, and at the same time frown upon the efforts of thoughtful, loving men to meliorate the condition of the less fortunate classes in this — let her ministers and oracles, themselves amply fed and cared for, speak slightingly of efforts to secure honestly-earned bread to the needy, and hold it a light thing that so many writhe in penury on this dim, fleeting earth, — and it will be very unfortunate for Philanthropy, and not well for organized Christianity.

Ours is an age of rugged realities, yet of boundless hopes. On every side men are awaking to the calls of duty and of benevolence, and asking 'What shall we do for our afflicted or downcast brethren? By what means may we do most, 'in the little span allotted to us, to diminish the wrongs and 'the woes endured by so many millions of mankind?' These are questions which the Christian Church should prepare herself to answer conclusively. Her answer should be something more than an opiate for the consciences of her wealthier devotees. To say that if every one would serve God and work righteousness all would be prosperous and happy, is not to meet the practical case at all. We do know, beyond doubt, that *all* will *not* act thus wisely and holily, and the essential question will not thus be evaded. It still recurs to demand of the fortunate and powerful what they as Christians or as men propose to do, feel bound to do, in the actual condition of things. Here are a Christian wife and her young children, the victims of a reprobate, drunken husband and father. Are the dictates of Christian duty satisfied by the cold assertion that if he who should be their protector would but refrain from being their tormentor, they might enjoy comparative happiness? What is that worth to the meek, despairing sufferers? How does it excuse those who should be their neighbors? Does not the question inevitably recur in this form: What can we do for them, *in spite of* the great misfortune which has befallen them? Admit that he who should support and cherish will persist in robbing and torturing them, is there nothing which can yet be done to alleviate their miseries? Answer this question in the affirmative, as you must, and the original line of defense of Christian selfishness is turned completely. We are brought face to face with the primary question, modified (or rather, fortified) as follows: Since evil exists, and *will* exist, what can we do to limit its blighting influences? Admit that the transgressor is irreclaimable, or that no benevolence can render him less wretched until he abandons his vicious courses, and still it may be quite feasible to mitigate the sufferings of those he has dragged down with him to perdition. Nay, more! We might, by patient, loving inquiry into his past history and circumstances, discover causes of his aberration, as yet unsuspected, which would serve to soften the abhorrence with which we have learned to regard him. We might bring to light facts showing that his infatuation is not so wanton as we have deemed it, but that influences preceding his birth, and by no means confined to his own narrow family circle, have powerfully aided to make him what he is. Having been drawn thus far in exploring the individual case, we may see before us a broad ocean of inquiry, stretching away to an unexplored continent of duty. We may now be impelled to consider how far the external influences which have conspired to make some men drunkards or outcasts, and others felons, are controllable, and whether it be not practicable to place even the less fortunate in such relations, and train them under such influences, as will assuredly preserve them from the contaminations and perversions of which the fruits are so deadly. We know that the children trained beneath the eye of wise and Christian parents, amid a virtuous, intelligent community, shielded alike from the temptations of affluent grandeur and those of squalid misery, are morally certain to be, as a class, better than those who first open their eyes in castles of indolence or hovels of despair;—and why shall not this knowledge teach us? Why shall not the preservation of the unborn from the depressing and debasing circumstances which have impelled and are still dooming so many millions all around us to perdition, become the paramount idea of the Christian, no less than of the philanthropist? Do you demur that saving men's souls from corruption in the present, or from perdition in the future life, is the chief end of the Gospel? Admit this, and still the question recurs, Can you hope to save the souls immured in bodies subjected to every debasing influence, without removing or counteracting those influences? How shall you hope to regenerate the denizens of the darker haunts of depravity and wretchedness in all our great cities, without removing them to purer homes and enabling them to eat the bread of useful industry and virtuous independence?

It is not long since the thieves of London — that is, a very large number of them — were called together by a philanthropist who had obtained a clew to their haunts and the means of commanding their attention and confidence. Treating them in all things as erring, misguided, unfortunate, sinful brethren, he addressed them on the flagrant iniquity of their lives, the more palpable ruin to which such courses inevitably tended, and closed by exhorting them to instant, thorough reformation. All were affected; many melted to tears. At last one found words to express the general perplexity, substantially thus: 'Good sir, what shall we do? As thieves, we have employment and obtain some sort of a livelihood; as thieves, we have companions, friends, homes. *Will you insure us these as honest men?* We ask no reward for becoming honest and useful; but we can not consent to starve. Show us how to live honestly and avoid starvation, and we will instantly abandon our wretched vocation. But your reputable tradesmen will not hire us; your reputable workmen will not tolerate our presence in the same shop with them; the naked choice afforded us is to steal or starve.' And thus the conference ended, the good Samaritan baffled, puzzled, discouraged. He could of himself do nothing, and the Church was too busy decorating the palaces of its bishops, sending dissenters to prison for non-payment of tithes, and punishing its own ministers for preaching in heretical chapels, to trouble itself with so vulgar a novelty as the reformation of whole battalions of thieves, by enabling them to earn honest bread.

But what is the Church to do? What duties are incumbent on her which for ages have lain unrecognized and neglected? I answer, Many; but this first of all—To shield at least her own members from the temptations and woes which are inseparable from unwilling idleness and consequent destitution. Every church or society of believers should be, to its own members at least, as beneficent as an Odd-Fellow's Lodge or Temperance League. It should, at least, so remotely, faintly approximate the first church* at Jerusalem as to say, 'So long as it shall be within our ability to prevent it, no member of this body shall be idle or destitute, who is willing to work cheerfully and faithfully at whatever innocent employment may be offered him, and which will afford him a subsistence. To this extent, at least, the idea of brotherhood shall be actualized in our relation as fellow Christians.' This would be found in practice a prodigious step in the right path, leading on to others. Let it once be established, as the common law of Christendom, that no believer may stand idle and famishing amid a Christian community, including many who possess, in ample measure, the means of employing and rewarding the needy, and a broad foundation will be laid for a gradual and enduring reform in the relations of wealth to want, of capital to labor. What the world pressingly needs is, not mere alms-giving, but less necessity therefor; not bread in idleness, but opportunity and just recompense for industry secured systematically to all. If political economy and the advancing tide of democracy can secure or promote these, so be it; let us welcome any helps or hints that the progress of knowledge or invention may afford us; but let not the Church seek to excuse herself from her proper responsibility. In the spirit of that divine appeal, 'Lead me not into temptation,' she is bound to take care that her members are not subjected to the trial of Esau, but that each one of them is secured against

* Acts ii. 44, 45.

vagrancy and famine, not in the world's cold, degrading poor-house, but under the paternal guardianship of Christian love. When she shall have risen to the altitude of this duty, she will be fitted to contemplate, without disrelish or dismay, the broader horizon of paternal obligation that stretches away beyond it. Heaven grant her wisdom early to apprehend and joyfully to accept her benignant destiny!

THE IDEAL OF A TRUE LIFE.

A FRAGMENT.

There is, even on this side the grave, a haven where the storms of life break not, or are felt but in gentle undulations of the unrippled and mirroring waters—an oasis, not *in* the desert, but beyond it—a rest, profound and blissful as that of the soldier returned for ever from the dangers, the hardships and turmoil of War, to the bosom of that dear domestic circle, whose blessings he never prized at half their worth till he lost them.

This haven, this oasis, this rest, is a serene and hale Old Age. The tired traveler has abandoned the dusty, crowded, and jostling highway of life, for one of its shadiest and least noted by-lanes. The din of traffic and of worldly strife has no longer magic for his ear—the myriad footfall on the city's stony walks is but noise or nothing to him now. He has run his race of toil, or trade, or ambition. His day's work is accomplished, and he has come home to enjoy, tranquil and unharassed, the splendor of the sunset, the milder glories of late evening. Ask not whether he has or has not been successful, according to the vulgar standard of success. What matters it now whether the multitude has dragged his chariot, rending the air with idolizing acclamations, or howled like wolves on his track, as he fled by night from the fury of those he had wasted his vigor to serve? What avails it that broad lands have rewarded his toil, or that all has, at the last moment, been stricken from his grasp? Ask not whether he brings into retirement the wealth of the Indies or the poverty of a bankrupt—whether his couch be of down or of rushes—his dwelling a hut or a mansion. He has lived to little purpose indeed, if he has not long since realized that Wealth and Renown are not the true ends of exertion, nor their absence the conclusive proof of ill-fortune. Whoever seeks to know if his career has been prosperous and brightening from its outset to its close—if the evening of his days shall be genial and blissful—should ask not for broad acres, nor towering edifices, nor laden coffers. Perverted Old Age may grasp these with the unyielding clutch of insanity; but they add to his cares and anxieties, not to his enjoyments. Ask rather—Has he mastered and harmonized his erring Passions?—Has he lived a True Life?

A True Life!—of how many lives does each hour knell the conclusion! and how few of them are true ones! The poor child of shame, and sin, and crime, who terminates her earthly being in the clouded morning of her scarce budded yet blighted existence—the desperate felon, whose blood is shed by the community, as the dread penalty of its violated law—the miserable debauchee, who totters down to his loathsome grave in the spring-time of his years, but the fullness of his festering iniquities—these, the world valiantly affirms, have not lived true lives! Fearless and righteous world! how profound, how discriminating are thy judgments! But the base idolater of self, who devotes all his moments, his energies, his thoughts, to schemes which begin and end in personal advantage—the grasper of gold, and lands, and tenements—the devotee of pleasure—the man of ignoble and sinister ambition—the woman of frivolity, extravagance and fashion—the idler, the gambler, the voluptuary—on all these and their myriad compeers, while borne on the crest of the advancing billow, how gentle is the reproof, how charitable the judgment, of the world! Nay—is not even our dead Christianity, which picks its way so daintily, cautiously, and inoffensively through the midst of slaveholding, and drunkard-making, and National faith-breaking—which regards with gentle rebuke, and is regarded with amiable toleration by some of the foremost vices of the times—is it not too often oblivious of its paramount duty to teach men how to live worthily and nobly? Are there not thousands to whom its inculcations, so far as duties to Man are concerned, are substantially negative in their character?—who are fortified, by its teachings, in the belief that to do good is a casualty and not a frame of being—who are taught by it to feed the hungry and clothe the naked when they thrust themselves upon the charity of portly affluence, but as an irksome duty, for which they should be rewarded, rather than a blessed privilege for which they should be profoundly grateful? Of the millions weekly listening to the ministrations of the Christian pulpit, how many are clearly, vividly impressed with the great truth, that each, in his own sphere, should live for Mankind, as Christ did, for the redemption, instruction, and exaltation of the race—and, that the power to do this, in his proper place, abides equally with the humblest as the highest? How many centuries more will be required to teach, even the religious world, so called, the full meaning of the term CHRISTIAN?

A true life must be simple in all its elements. Animated by one grand and ennobling impulse, all lesser aspirations find their proper places in harmonious subservience. Simplicity in taste, in appetite, in habits of life, with a corresponding indifference to worldly honors and aggrandizement, is the natural result of the predominance of a divine and unselfish idea. Under the guidance of such a sentiment,

Virtue is not an effort, but a law of nature, like gravitation. It is Vice alone that seems unaccountable—monstrous—well nigh miraculous. Purity is felt to be as necessary to the mind as health to the body, and its absence alike the inevitable source of pain.

A true life must be calm. A life imperfectly directed, is made wretched through distraction. We give up our youth to excitement, and wonder that a decrepit old age steals upon us so soon. We wear out our energies in strife for gold or fame, and then wonder alike at the cost and the worthlessness of the meed. 'Is not the life more than meat?' Ay, truly! but how few have practically, consistently, so regarded it? And little as it is regarded by the imperfectly virtuous, how much less by the vicious and the worldling! What a chaos of struggling emotions is exhibited by the lives of the multitude? How like to the wars of the infuriated animalculæ in a magnified drop of water, is the strife constantly waged in each little mind! How Sloth is jostled by Gluttony, and Pride wrestled with by Avarice, and Ostentation bearded by Meanness! The soul which is not large enough for the indwelling of one virtue, affords lodgment, and scope, and arena for a hundred vices. But their warfare can not be indulged with impunity. Agitation and wretchedness are the inevitable consequences, in the midst of which the flame of life burns flaringly and swiftly to its close.

A true life must be genial and joyous. Tell me not, pale anchorite, of your ceaseless vigils, your fastings, your scourgings. These are fit offerings to Moloch, not to Our Father. The man who is not happy in the path he has chosen, may be very sure he has chosen amiss, or is self-deceived. But not merely happier—he should be kinder, gentler, and more elastic in spirits, as well as firmer and truer. 'I love God and little children,' says a German poet. The good are ever attracted and made happier by the presence of the innocent and lovely. And he who finds his religion adverse to, or a restraint upon, the truly innocent pleasures and gaieties of life, so that the latter do not interfere with and jar upon its sublimer objects—may well doubt whether he has indeed 'learned of Jesus.'

HUMANITY.

THE watchword of the Nineteenth Century is BROTHERHOOD. Rapid and wonderful as is the progress of Physical Science—valuable to Man as are the Steamboat, the Railroad, the Magnetic Telegraph—mighty as are the results attained, mightier the hopes excited and justified, by the march of discovery and invention—the great discovery being made, and to be made, by the children of men, is that of their community of origin, of interests, of aspirations. 'God hath made of one blood all people,' is its essence, proclaimed many years ago; the new truth is but the old realized and made practical. Humanity refuses longer to be separated and arrayed against itself. Whoever oppresses or injures any human being, however abject or culpable, wrongs and tramples all men, himself included.

A grave, momentous truth—let it be heard and heeded. Hear it, grim and ruthless warrior! eager to rush over myriads of gashed and writhing bodies to coveted fame and power! These thou wouldst so readily trample into the earth are not really enemies, not merely victims—not something which may be separated from thee and thine: they are thy fellows, kinsmen, brethren—with thee, 'members of one another!' and of Humanity. The sword which hews them down, maims thee: the hoof that tramples them, wounds thee. No armor ever devised by cunning or selfishness can prevent this: no walls of stone or living men can ward off the blow. As surely as the verdant tree must mark its shadow in the sunshine—as surely as the stone projected upward will not rest in mid-air, but descend—so surely falls the evil on him by whom evil is done or meditated.

Miser! heaping up fresh hoards of yellow dross! thou art starving, not others only, but thyself! Bread may fill thy garners, and thy vaults be stored with ruddy wines; but Plenty can not come where dwells the insatiable thirst for more; and baleful are the possessions which contract the brow and harden the heart; speedy and sure is the judgment which avenges the woes of thy pale, hollow-cheeked victims!

Libertine! believe not that the anguish thou so recklessly invokest on others shall leave thee unscathed! The contrary is written in the law whose date is Eternity, whose sphere the Universe. Fleeting and hollow are the guilty joys thou seekest, while the crimes by which they are compassed shall darken thy soul and embitter thy thoughts for ever!

And thou, humble, self-denying votary of the highest good—the good of thy brethren, thy fellow-beings—vainly shalt thou strive to sacrifice thy own happiness to brighten the dark pathway of the needy, the wretched: the kindly fates will not permit it; Heaven will persist in promptly repaying thee more and better than thou hast given. Give all thou hast to lighten the burdens of others to-day, and the bounteous reward will not wait for to-morrow's sun. It will insist on making thee richer, in thy hunger and nakedness, than the king amid his pomp, the banker amid his treasures. Thy riches are safe from every device of villainy, from every access of calamity; they can not be separated from nor made unavailable to thee. While thou art, they shall be to thee a chastened gladness, a tranquil rapture for ever!

And thou, saintly devotee, and shrine of all virtues! look not down in loathing, but in pity, on the ruined votary of vice and crime. He is here to teach thee not pride, but humility. The corrupt, revolting thing he is, tells thee what thou mightest easily have been, had not Divine Goodness, for its own high ends, not *thine*, willed otherwise. The drunkard's maudlin leer—the lecher's marred and hideous visage—the thief's cat-like tread and greedy eyes—even the murderer's stony heart and reeking hand—all these, rightly viewed, are but indications of the possibilities of thy own nature, commanding gratitude to God, and compassion for all human errors.

Ay, 'we are members together of one body' of Humanity. Whether blackened by the fervid sun of tropical deserts, or bleached by the fogs of a colder clime—whether worshiping God or the Grand Lama, erecting Christian altars in the savage wilderness or falling in frenzy beneath the wheels of Juggernaut—whether acting the part of a Washington or a Nicholas, a Howard or a Thug—the same red current courses through all our veins—the same essential nature reveals itself through all. The slave in his coffle, the overseer brandishing his whip, the abolitionist denouncing oppression—who shall say that any one of these might not have been trained to do the deeds and think the thoughts of any other? Who shall say that the red-handed savage of the wilds might not have been the meek, benign village pastor, blessing and blest by all around him, if his lot had been cast in Vermont instead of Oregon? Who shall say how far his crimes are treasured up against him in the great account, and how far they are charged to the perverting, darkening force of Christian rapacity and fraud, or esteemed the result of a Christian indifference and lethargy only less culpable?

Away, then, from human sight with the hideous implements of human butchery and destruction! Break the sword in its scabbard, bury the cannon in the earth, sink the bombs in the ocean! What business have these to disturb by their hateful presence the visible harmony of God's universe? How dare men go out into the balmy air and bright sunshine, and there, in the full view of Heaven, essay to maim amd massacre each other? How would their wretched babblement of National interests or National honor sound, if addressed directly to the All-Ruling, as an apology for wholesale slaughter? Who would dare be their mouthpiece in proffering an excuse so pitiful? And do not the abettors of War realize that their vile appeals to the baser passions of our nature resound in the ears of the Recording Angel?

But not War alone, the grossest form of human antagonism, but every form, is destined to a speedy extinction. The celestial voice that asked of old the terrific question, "Where is thy brother Abel?" shall yet be heard and responded to by every one who would win profit or enjoyment from that which oppresses or degrades a single human being. The oppressor, the dram-seller, the gamester, are already beginning to listen, perforce, to its searching appeal—listen, at first, perhaps, with frowns, and sneers, and curses? but even these are symptoms of the inward convulsion—first mutterings of the mighty earthquake at hand.

In the day of light now dawning, no relation so palpably vicious as theirs can possibly abide. But theirs are the rude, salient outworks, which cover, while they stand, the smoother, ampler, sturdier citadel of error. That all-pervading selfishness, which forgets or disregards the general well-being, is yet to be tracked to its most secret recesses, and extirpated.

The avocations of Life, the usages and structure of Society, the relations of Power to Humility, of Wealth to Poverty, of served and servant, must all be fused in the crucible of Human Brotherhood, and whatever abides not the test, rejected. Vainly will any seek to avert or escape the ordeal—idly will any hope to preserve from it some darling lust or pampered luxury or vanity. Onward, upward, irresistibly, shall move the Spirit of Reform, abasing the proud, exalting the lowly, until Sloth and Selfishness, Tyranny and Slavery, Waste and Want, Ignorance and Corruption, shall be swept from the face of the earth, and a golden age of Knowledge, of Virtue, of Plenty, and Happiness, shall dawn upon our sinning and suffering Race. Heaven speed its glorious coming and prepare us to welcome and enjoy it!

APPENDIX.

THE

CRYSTAL PALACE AND ITS LESSONS.

EACH age, each race, inscribes itself, with more or less distinctness, on History's dial. Nineveh, almost faded from our traditions of the world's infancy, revisits us in her freshly-exhumed sculptures, and in the vivid narrations of Layard. The Egypt of Sesostris and the Pharaohs survives no less in her pyramids and obelisks, than in the ever-enduring records of Moses and Manetho. Jerusalem, in her lonely humiliation, best typifies the Hebrew state and race. Ancient Rome lives for us in the Capitol and the Coliseum, as does her mediæval and sacerdotal offspring and namesake in St. Peter's and the Vatican. Royal and feudal France, the France of Richelieu and Louis le Grand, still lingers in the boundless magnificence and prodigality, the showy sieges and battle-pieces of Versailles. The England of the last three centuries confronts us in the Bank—not a very stately nor graceful edifice, it must be allowed; but very substantial and well furnished—the fit heart's core of a trading, money-getting people. So we Americans of the Nineteenth Century will be found in due time to have inscribed ourselves most legibly, though all unconsciously, on the earth's unfading records—how, or in what, time alone can tell. Perhaps a railroad over the Rocky Mountains, a telegraph across the Atlantic, a towering observatory, wherein all the storms and calms at any moment prevailing within the earth's atmosphere shall be portrayed on a common dial-plate, and the storms which *shall* take place at any point during the next day or week, with their several directions and intensities—perhaps something very different from any of these. Essential History still insists on writing itself, and will not be controlled nor anticipated.

34*

The CRYSTAL PALACE, with its contents and purposes, was the clearest expression yet given to the spirit and aspirations of our time—aspirations not wholly utterable, nor even comprehensible as yet, but sufficiently so to demand and reward our deepest attention. That Palace was the first edifice ever built for and consecrated to the uses of Universal Industry. It was the first structure ever devoted to the advancement and diffusion of the Useful Arts throughout the world—the first in which, to the greatest extent consistent with individual selfishness, the arcana of skill and production were thrown open to all mankind, with an express invitation, "Come hither, and see how the most successful workers accomplish their ends, and learn to rival or excel them if you can." Herein was assembled the first general convention or council of Captains of Industry—the first practical Peace Congress ever held. Magnificent in conception, and most triumphant in execution, this grand and fruitful enterprise deserves something more than the journalist's fleeting paragraph. We can not waste the time that we devote to its contemplation, even though the speaker should succeed no farther than in drawing your attention to the subject, leaving it to be pondered unaided, unembarrassed, by his crude and hasty suggestions.

Who first proposed a grand Exposition of the Industry of all Nations at London, it were hardly worth while to inquire. The suggestion might have presented itself to any mind, and in fact probably *did* present itself simultaneously, or at least independently, to several. It was a natural sequence of the profound peace everywhere prevailing—of the all-pervading spirit of Enterprise generated by Commerce—of the rapid march of Discovery and Invention—of the steady growth and at length realized importance of the Useful Arts. Good ideas are rather abundant in our day—too plentiful to obtain much credit from a busy, practical, work-day generation. In this instance, however, the seed fell on good ground, and the result was an immense, though not yet fully gathered harvest. Much credit is due to those who first gave the idea hospitality and nurture until it expanded in the warm sunshine of Royal favor, into the benignant reality whereto the nations were gathered. And perhaps the most influential among the early and steadfast friends of the World's Exhibition, was Albert, consort of Queen Victoria, and one of the most constant and discriminating among the patrons and visitors of the great undertaking. In an age when princes are plainly falling into discredit and disuse, let us remember the good which this one powerfully aided to do, and not suffer our republican prejudices to blind us to the moral. Hereditary legislators, and hereditary rulers are plainly absurd; but hereditary patrons and stimulators of inventive genius and industrial efficiency are not to be disparaged. Let them be remembered in the approaching day of kingly tribulation and aristocratic downfall, There are better uses for even the most obsolete and worthless than hanging them. Royalty and Nobility may be at ever so ruinous a discount, but Humanity is still at par. Kill the monarch, but save alive the man. His purple wrappages have cramped and concealed him; strip them off, and burn them, but respect the glorious image of God, which you have thereby uuswathed and liberated.

Nor is it worth while to attempt adjusting the measure of credit due respectively to Paxton and to others, for the idea of the Crystal Palace and its consummation. A solid, rather heavy, North-of-England horticulturist, employed in overseeing the Duke of Devonshire's extensive gardens and conservatories, has a new tropical plant confided to his charge, which, by a perfect knowledge of his art, and an unbounded command of means, he induces to vegetate and flourish in that high latitude—of course, in an artificially fervid soil, and under shielding glass. Here it grows and aspires with unimagined rapidity to an unprecedented height, threatening to shiver its frail covering in its upward career. Necessity, mother of invention, pricks on the unideal gardener to enlarge, and still enlarge, his glass shelter, which this aspiring rival of Jack's Bean-stalk threatens to put his head and arms through, in quest of altitude and sunshine; so he elevates and expands his crystal encasement, until, little by little, step by step, a stately glass house has been erected; and this becomes the model of the hitherto unsuggested Crystal Palace. The gardener had no premonition of this, no idea of any thing beyond sheltering his delicate though gigantic plant, and saving its artificial Timbuctoo from destruction:

"He builded wiser than he knew."

But when plans and designs for the immense edifice required to hold the contributions of all nations to the grand Exposition were advertised for, he was prepared to compete for the proffered reward; and his plan, dictated to him by Nature herself, was found the best of all, adopted, and, with some necessary modifications of detail, carried into effect. The result was the Crystal Palace, the most capacious, convenient, economical, healthful, and admirable structure ever devised for any kindred purpose. Earth was ransacked for alluring marvels; Science racked its brains for brilliant combinations; Art exhausted its subtle alchemy in quest of dazzling effects; Labor poured out its sweat like rain to fill the grand receptacle with whatever is beautiful and winning; yet the Crystal Palace remained to the end the crowning triumph of all.

Within the last century, London has expanded rapidly and immensely, but especially toward the West, or up the Thames. Temple Bar, the western boundary of the city proper (or ancient London), is now considerably East, I think, of the center of the Great Metropolis; while the present residences of nearly all the nobility and gentry are built on grounds which were open country since the days of the Plantagenets and Tudors. In the center of this magnificent "West End," between St. James's Palace and Kensington Gardens, though much nearer the latter, stretches HYDE PARK, one of the most spacious and pleasant expanses of sward, and shade, and water, that eye ever feasted on. Boston Common would be somewhat like it, if it were ten times as large, and twenty times as well watered as at present. Hyde Park is the favorite resort of the Aristocracy for equestrian and carriage exercise, and thoroughly justifies their choice. On the southern verge of this noble expanse, some three miles west of the Bank, Exchange, and London Bridge, the Crystal Palace was erected. It was not an imposing edifice. No stately gateway, no frowning turrets, no graceful spire, no lofty tower, marked the capacious structure, from whose roof the flags of all nations rose and floated in perfect amity. Its slender ribs of iron, covered and hidden for some thirty feet from the earth by boards, like any house of wood, were thenceforth visible through the glass which formed the upper siding and roof, like a spider's web on the grass of a dewy morning. Slender iron columns or pillars, rising at intervals, unperceived, from beneath the floor, helped to sustain the weight of the slight yet ponderous roof, through which, though covered with canvas to modify the heat of the few sunny days vouchsafed to an English summer, an abundance of light, not only under the murkiest London skies, but even during the prevalence of the great July eclipse, was at all times received. So immense was the volume of atmosphere inclosed, or so perfect the arrangements for ventilation, that no sense of exhaustion or of breathing vitiated air was at any time experienced; for the building was something more than a third of a mile in length from east to west, some three hundred feet wide, and rather more than a hundred feet from floor to roof, with eight or ten large doors for entrance and exit, hardly ever closed during the day. On a volume of atmosphere thus extended, and constantly changing, the breathings of sixty thousand persons for hours could make no impression. In this vast bazaar, which a few months saw advance from its first conception to its perfect realization, and which yet was barely completed at the day appointed for opening the exhibition, the choice or characteristic products of all nations had already for some weeks been accumulating. Under the mere corner (though of itself covering more than an acre) devoted to machinery, mainly British, water-pipes and adaptations of steam-power had already been conducted, the steam itself being generated outside. An army of carpenters and other artisans had been some weeks at work on the fixtures and decorations of the several departments, so that, when the eagerly expected opening day at length arrived, although the whole visible area had an unmistakable aspect of haste and rawness—an odor born of green boards and fresh paint—and although an infinity of carpenters' work still remained undone, especially in the galleries, or upper story, yet the Exhibition was plainly there, and only needed time to perfect its huge proportions, and stand forth the acknowledged wonder of the world.

The first of May, 1851, was a happy day for London. Her skies had relaxed something of their habitual sullenness to usher in the pageant whereby the Sovereign of the Realm, surrounded by her chief councilors and grandees, was to inaugurate the first grand Exhibition of All Nations' Industry. The rain, which had dripped or pattered almost or quite daily for weeks, held up the evening before, and promised not to return for this whole May-day—a promise which was only broken by a slight shower at noon, too late to mar the interest or pleasure of the festival. At an early morning hour, a strong current of human life set westward from the city proper toward Hyde Park, and long before the doors of the House of Glass were opened, they were surrounded by eager groups, though no admission was purchasable save at the cost of a season ticket—over fifteen dollars. Even thus, some thirty thousand enjoyed and swelled the indoor pageant; while perhaps ten times as many gazed from the parks and streets at the meager procession out-doors which escorted the Queen from her palace of St. James to the airier, richer palace of the working millions, the hall of vastest prophecy. There arrived a robed and jeweled procession of Princes and Embassadors, of noble Ladies and noble Workers, the Duke of Wellington and Mr. Paxton, the Master of the Buckhounds, Groom of the Stole, Gentleman Usher of Sword and State, Gold Stick in Waiting, Silver Stick in Waiting, and other such antediluvian absurdities, attended Her Majesty, along with the Foreign Commissioners, Architects of the edifice, her older children, and some other living verities, on her slow and measured progress from side to side and end to end of the mighty convocation. This strange mingling of the real with the shadowy, the apposite with the obsolete, gave additional piquancy and zest to the spectacle. Had the courtly sýmbols of an outworn, outgrown feudal age appeared by themselves, we might have taken them for some fanciful creation of a mind diseased by reading Froissart and Walter Scott, and watched to see them exhale like ghosts at cock-crowing; but here they are so mixed up and blended with undeniable entities; with the solid and practical Prince Albert; with our own portly and palpable embassador; with that world-known Celestial who accompanies and illustrates the Chinese Junk—himself first of matter-of-fact conservatives—a walking, human Junk—that we can not refuse to credit its total verity, in spite of the glaring anachronisms. Then there was a prosy though proper Address read by Prince Albert, as head of the Royal Commission, to his Royal consort, as head of the kingdom, telling her how the Exhibition was first started, and how it had moved onward till now—rather superfluous, it must be confessed, since they had doubtless talked the matter all over between them a dozen times, when much more at their ease, and in a far more satisfactory manner ; but Queens must endure and take part in some dreary absurdities as well as other people. This speech was through in time, and was very briefly and fittingly responded to. I trust the prayer which the Archbishop of Canterbury sent up in behalf of us all was as graciously received. There was some music, rather out of place, and lost in the vastness of space to all but the few immediately under the transept, and some other performances; but all in perfect order, in due and punctual season, and without a betrayal of awkwardness or conscious incongruity. Between two and three o'clock, the pageant was at an end—the Royal cortege departed, and the Exhibition formally opened. Let me now try to give some general notion of its character by glancing at the more obvious details, so far as I, at this distance of time and space, may be able to recall them.

There are doors on all sides, one or more devoted exclusively to the reception of articles for exhibition; one for Jurors in attendance on the Fair; others for the Police, the Royal visitors, etc.; while the main entrances for paying visitors are upon the south side, into the transept. But we will enter one of the three or four doors at the east end, and find ourselves at once in the excessive space devoted to contributions from the United States, and which thence seems sparsely filled. Before us are large collections of Lake Superior Native Copper, as it was torn from the rock, in pieces from the size of a bean up to one slab of more than a ton, though still but a wart beside some masses which have been wrenched from the earth's bosom, cut into manageable pieces of two to three tons, and thus dispatched to the smelting furnace and a market. New Jersey Zinc, from the ore to the powder, the paint, the solid metal, is creditably represented; and there are specimens of Adirondack Iron and Steel from Northern New York, which attract and reward attention. Passing these and various cabinets or solitary specimens of the Minerals of Maryland and other States, we are confronted by abundant bales of Cotton, barrels of Wheat and of Flour, casks of Rice, etc.; while various clusters of ears of our yellow and white Indian Corn remind the English of one valued staple which our climate abundantly vouchsafes, and theirs habitually denies. The "Bay State" Shawls of Lawrence, the Axes of Maine, the Flint Glass of Brooklyn, the Daguerreotypes of New York and Philadelphia (whose excellence was acknowledged from the first by nearly every critic), next salute us; and near them are the specimens of various Yankee Locks, and in their midst the invincible Hobbs, a small, young, shrewd, quiet-seeming Yankee, but evidently distinguished for penetration, who would have made fewer enemies in England had he proved less potent a master of his calling.

And now we are at the Grand Aisle, across which is the United States Commissioner's office, with that much ridiculed "pasteboard eagle" displayed along its front, and certainly looking as if its appetite would overtax any ordinary powers of digestion. In front of the office are Yankee Stoves, Safes, Light Wagons, Carriages, Plows and other agricultural implements, including the since famous "Virginia Reaper," which was for months a butt of British journalistic waggery, having been described by one Reporter as "a cross between an Astley's chariot, a flying machine, and a treadmill." They spoke of it far more respectfully after it had been set to work, with memorable results; and it must in fairness be confessed that beauty is not its best point, and that, while nothing is more effective in a grain-field, many things would be more comely in a drawing-room.

But let us return to the main aisle, and, starting at its eastern end, proceed westward.

A model Railroad Bridge of wood and iron fills a very large space at the outset, and is not deemed by British critics a brilliant specimen of Yankee invention. (One of them, however, at length candidly confessed that its capacity of endurance and of resistance must be very great, or the weight of ridicule heaped upon it must inevitably have broken it down long before). Upon it is a handsome show of India Rubber fabrics by Goodyear; while beyond it, toward the west, in a chosen locality in the center of the aisle, stands "the Greek Slave" of Powers, one of the sweetest and most popular achievements of the modern chisel, here constantly surrounded by a swarm of admirers; yet I think it not the best of Powers' works—I am half inclined to say, not *among* his best. He has several stronger heads, possessing far more character, in his studio at Florence; and yet I am glad this statue was in the Exhibition, for it enabled the critics of the London press to say some really smart things about Greek and American slaves, and the Slave as a representative and masterpiece of American artistic achievement, which that heavy metropolis could not well have spared. Let us not grudge them a grin, even at our expense; for mirth promotes digestion, and the hit in this instance is certainly a fair one. "The Dying Indian," just beside the Slave, by a younger and less famous American artist, is a work of power and merit, though the delineation of agony and approaching death can hardly be rendered pleasing. Is it not remarkable that a chained and chattelized woman, and a wounded, dying Indian, should be the subjects chosen by American sculptors for their two works, whereby we shall be most widely known in connection with this Exhibition? But we cross the imaginary line which here separates the United States from the nations of Continental Europe, and look westward.

How magnificent the prospect! Far above is the sober sky of canvas-covered glass, through which the abundant light falls gently and mellowly. Spacious and richly-decorated galleries, some sixty feet apart, overhang all the ground floor but the grand aisle, and are themselves the depositories of many of the richest and most tempting fabrics and lighter wares exhibited. The aisle itself, farther than the eye can reach, is studded with works of art; statues in marble, in bronze, in plaster, in zinc; here a gigantic Amazon on horseback, there a raging lion, a classic group, or a pair of magnificent bronze vases, enriched with exquisite representations of scenes from the master-singers of antiquity. Busts, Casts, Medallions, and smaller Bronzes abound; with elegant Clocks, Chandeliers, Cabinets, etc.; for each nation whose department we pass, has arranged its most enticing products in front, so that they shall be seen from the grand aisle, putting its homelier, though in some cases, intrinsically more valuable productions, in the background. Russia's superb tables and slabs of richest Malachite stand just far enough out of the aisle, within her allotted space, to draw thither the wandering gazer to view her imperial structures of gilded Porcelain, colored Glass, and other barbaric marvels. Austria has brought hither and put in order a suit of rooms sumptuously furnished and ornamented according to her highest ideal of taste and luxury. France displays in the foreground her admirable Bronzes, Porcelain, Musical Instruments, etc.; and so Northern Germany, Switzerland, Belgium, and other European States, each "puts its best foot foremost," in a sense hardly metaphorical. Behind these dainty and rare fabrics are ranged others less difficult of achievement—costly Silks and Laces; then Woolens and Muslins; and behind these you often stumble on coils of Rope or Wire, bars of Steel, or pigs of Iron, Saws, Files, and Hammers, Stoves, Grates, and Furnaces, Bedsteads, Chairs, and Lanterns—these, as you pass laterally from the dazzling glories of the center aisle, between the well-filled sub-compartments devoted to fabrics of taste and adornment, will greet you before you reach the outer walls. For the Crystal Palace has its homelier aspects, like any other, and it but follows the general usage in keeping them as much in the background as possible.

But we pass on down the Grand Aisle, to the Transept or cross, where both the height and width of the building are considerably increased, in order, it would seem, to save two stately and beautiful trees (elms), which here stand in apposition some two hundred feet apart. The Transept embraces and covers both, leaving each ample room to grow and flourish; while, half-way between them, in the exact center of the Palace, a spacious and copious Fountain, wholly of glass, throws its sparkling torrent high into the air, whence it descends from crystal cup to cup, each considerably wider than that next above it, until it reaches the lowest and largest, near the ground, thence gliding away unseen. There are few finer effects in the Exhibition than this of the Crystal Fountain, which utterly shames the Koh-i-Noor, or "Mountain of Light," said to be the largest diamond in the world, and computed worth several millions of dollars, which, obviously over-guarded against robbery, rests in its gilded cage beside the fountain. No child, looking from one to the other, ever suspected, until told it, that the Diamond was deemed worth more than the Fountain. Here are displayed full-length portraits of Queen Victoria and her husband—the latter once handsome, now gross-featured and rather heavy, but still a man of fair appearance, good sense, and varied information. The Queen, never beautiful, has sacrificed her youthful freshness to the cares of maternity and the exactions of late hours and luxurious living, so that at thirty-two she looks plain and old—not in this portrait, but in her living self. But uncommon energy, activity, shrewdness, with an earnest desire to please her people, and promote their welfare, still remain to her, and have rendered her the most popular British Sovereign of the Guelphic family.

The Transept is the heart of the Exhibition, to which all currents converge, from which all expeditions, whether of criticism or discovery, take their departure. Here abound Marble Statues, gigantic Brazen Gates, and other works of Art, while around it are located the fabrics of Turkey and of China, of Australia and of British America, which are as interesting and instructive in their rudeness and clumsiness as others in their grace and perfection. You could hardly realize, without seeing them, what wretched contrivances for Candlesticks, Culinary Utensils, Locks and Keys, etc., etc., are still slowly, toilsomely fabricated in Turkey, in Barbary, and in other half-civilized countries. A decent knowledge of the Useful Arts is yet confined to a few nations, and is imperfectly diffused even in these. And here, too, is sad Italy, not allowed to compete in her own name, but sending feeble and timid contributions as "Sardinia," "Tuscany," "Rome," etc., nothing being allowed to come from Naples. The Roman States, in the heart of ancient Civilization, with Three Millions of People yet, fill half a page of the Catalogue, or about one-seventeenth of the space required by the more distant United States; while the beautiful Statuary of the School of Milan, including the Veiled Vestal, one of the most original and admirable works in the Exhibition, is set down to the credit of *Austria!* There is a debtor as well as creditor side to that Austro-Italian account, and settlement can not be refused forever.

Great Britain and her Colonies engross the entire Western half of the Exhibition, and fill it creditably. In the Fine Arts, properly so called, she has probably less than a fourth of what is contributed; but in Iron and its multiform products, she has far more than all the World besides. In Steam-Engines and Force-Pumps, Looms and Anvils, Ores and Castings, Buttons, Steel Pens, etc., all the rest combined could not compare with her. I doubt if the world ever before saw so complete and instructive a collection of Ores and Minerals, as are here brought together, or that Geology was ever studied under auspices more favorable than this collection would afford. Nearly every metal known to man may here be seen, first as ore, and then in every stage up to that of perfect adaptation to our various human needs. So in the department of Machinery. I think no collection so varied and complete of Looms, Presses, Mills, Pumps, Engines, etc., etc., was ever before grouped under one roof.

The immense Manufacturing capacity and aptitude of Great Britain are here abundantly represented. From the unequalled Shawls of Cashmere, to the fabrics woven of reeds or bark by Australian savages; from the Coal of Pictou to the Spices of Ceylon; almost every thing which mankind have agreed to value and consecrate as property, is collected in the western half of the Crystal Palace, under the folds of the meteor flag, and displayed as specimens of the products of Queen Victoria's spacious Realm. Here Manchester unrolls her serviceable fabrics, and Birmingham displays her cheap and varied wares; here Sheffield, Glasgow, Belfast, and other centers of a vast manufacturing activity, solicit your attention to whatever is most showy or most substantial among their multiform productions. Gilded Fire-places of silver, shining steel, or snowy, speckless marble; vessels of Iron, of Clay, or of Tin; Robes and Couches, Cannon and Bibles, Grindstones and Pianos, by turns arrest the gaze in a bewildering medley, which yet is not quite confusion; for most of the articles are roughly classified, and the vast area is divided into an infinity of apartments, or "courts," closed at the sides, which are covered with cards of their proper wares, as is often the end farthest from the center aisle, and sometimes a good part of the front also. Behind each court is an open passage-way, walled in by displays usually of homely wares and fabrics, mainly of iron or brass, and behind these again are other courts, more open and irregular than the former, devoted to Castings, Metals, Ores, and the ruder forms of mineral wealth, occasionally giving place to the Refreshment Saloons wherewith the Palace is abundantly provided—to Committee Rooms, Jury Rooms, and other incidents of the Exhibition. And, thus environed, we move on, westward, until the grand Machinery Room absorbs henceforth the entire space to the north of us, the hum of its innumerable Wheels, Rotary Pumps, Looms, Spinning-Jennys, Flax-Dressers, Printing-Presses, etc., etc., at all times audible from the distant center of the Palace, in spite of well-directed efforts to drown it. At last we reach the western doorway, half obstructed by gigantic Bells and other bulky Manufactures, beyond which is the naked Park, or would be, but for the still huger blocks of Coal, Stone, etc., for which no place could be made within the building, and our journey is at an end.

But no: we have not yet mounted to the upper story, whither four broad and spacious stairways, in different parts of the building, invite us. Here is a new immensity of Silks and Scarfs, of Millinery and costly Furniture, including illustrations of the Spaniard's ideal of sumptuous magnificence; here Belgium has tried her hand at bronzes with indifferent, and at Castings with considerable success; here the finest achievements in Paper-Hanging and Window-Shading adorn the walls for hundreds of feet, some of the spacious curtains scarcely inferior in effect to any but the very best paintings; while the thousand costly trifles born of Parisian art and elegance, vie with London's less graceful but more massive creations in filling the vast amphitheater with wealth beyond the wildest dreams of a Sindbad or Aladden. Such pyramids of Jewelry and Plate were never before collected under one roof. Clusters of Pearls and Diamonds, each a generous fortune, are here lost in the ocean of magnificence; a single firm has One Million Dollars' worth within a moderate compass; while the displays of rivals in pandering to luxury and ostentation, stretch on either hand as far as the vision can reach. The industry and practical genius of Britain are evinced in the Machinery and serviceable Fabrics below, but her unequalled riches and aristocratic pomp are more vividly depicted here.

But the eyes ache, the brain reels, with this never-ending succession of the sumptuous and the gorgeous; one glimpse of sterile heath, bare sand, or beetling crag, would be a sensible relief. Wearily we turn away from this maze of sensual delights, of costly luxuries, and listlessly wander to that part of the gallery nearest the Transept, with its towering Elms, its Crystal Fountain, its gigantic brazen Gates, its Statues, its Royal Portraits, and Caged Diamond; but these we do not care to look upon again. MAN is nobler than the works of his hands; let us pause and observe. Hark! the clock strikes ten; the gates are opened; the crowds which had collected before them begin to move. No tickets are used; no change given; it is a "shilling day," and whoever approaches any of the gates which open to the general public must have his shilling in hand, so as to pay without stopping the procession as he passes in. In twenty minutes, our scattered, straggling band of Jurors, Exhibitors, Policemen, and servitors, will have been swelled by at least ten thousand gazers; within the hour, fifteen thousand more have added themselves to the number; by one o'clock, the visitors have increased to fifty thousand; every corner and nook swarm with them; even the alleys and other standing-room in the gallery are in good part blocked with them; but the wave-like, endless procession which before and below us sweeps up and down the Central Aisle, is the grand spectacle of all. From our elevated and central position almost the entire length of this magnificent promenade is visible—from the pasteboard eagle of America on the east, to the massive bells and other heavy British products, which mark the western door, though the view is somewhat broken by a few towering trophies of artistic skill, to which places have been assigned at intervals in the middle of the aisle, leaving a broad passage-way on either side. Far as the eye can reach, a sea of human heads is presented, denser toward the center just before us, but with scarcely an interruption any where. The individuals who make up this marching array are moving in opposite directions, or turning off to the right or to the left, and so lost to our view in "Austria," "Russia," "Switzerland," or "France;" but the river flows on unchecked, undiminished, though the particular drops we gazed on a minute ago have passed from our view forever. Still, mainly from the south, a steady stream of new comers, fifty to a hundred per minute, is pouring in to join the eager throng, but scarcely suffice to swell it. The machinery room, the galleries, the side-passages, the refreshment saloons, absorb as fast as the in-flowing current can supply; until, about three o'clock, the tide turns, and the departures thence exceed the arrivals. At length the hour of six strikes, and the edifice is quietly, noiselessly vacated and closed.

But this vast tide of life, which ebbs and flows beneath our gaze as we stand in the gallery, near as we may to the Crystal Fount, is not a mere aggregation of human beings. London, herself a mimic world, has sent hither not merely her thousands but her tens. Among that moving mass you may recognize her ablest and her wisest denizens—her De la Beche, her Murchison, her Brewster, and others honorably distinguished in the arduous paths of Science. Here, too, are her Cobden, her Sturge, her Russell, and others eminent in council and in legislative halls. Of the Peers who make her their winter residence, the names of Canning, Granville. Wharncliffe, Argyle, De Mauley, and others, are honorably connected with the Exhibition, to which they give their time as Jurors; and they are among its almost daily visitors, mainly distinguished by their quiet bearing, and simple, unpretending manners. And here, too, may be often seen the age-enfeebled frame of her veteran Wellington, the victor in so many hard-fought fields, and the final vanquisher of the greatest of modern warriors. Though his eye is dim and his step no longer firm, the conqueror of Hindostan, the liberator of the Peninsular, the victor of Waterloo, still emphatically "the Duke," is among the most absorbed and constant visitors of the great Exhibition, carefully scanning the more interesting objects in detail, and gazing by the hour on achievements so different from those of Assaye, Salamanca, and the Chateau of Hougomont. Do those dull ears, though deafened by twenty years' familiarity with the roar of artillery, catch some prophetic premonition of the New Age dawning upon mankind, wherein Carnage and Devastation shall no more secure the world's proudest honors, while Invention and Production sink into unmarked graves? Sees that dim eye, rekindled for a moment by the neighborhood of death, the approach of that glorious era wherein Man the creator and beautifier shall be honored and feted, and Man the destroyer, discrowned? His furrowed brow, his sunken eye, return no answer to our eager question, as he slowly, thoughtfully plods on.

But not London, not England alone; the Civilized World is here strongly represented. America and Russia, France and Austria, Belgium and Spain, have here their Commissioners, their Notables, their *savans*, earnestly studying the Palace and its contents, eager to carry away something which shall be valued and useful at home. A Yankee Manufacturer passes rapidly through the Machinery-room, until his eye rests on a novel combination for weaving certain fabrics, when, after watching it intently for a few minutes, he claps his hands and exclaims in unconscious, irrepressible enthusiasm, "That will pay my expenses for the trip!" On every side sharp eyes are watching, busy brains are treasuring, practical fingers are testing and comparing. Here are shrewd men from the ends of the earth: can it be that they will go home no wiser than they came? Many are here officially, and under pay from their respective governments; some of them sent out of compliment to her Majesty, who specially invited the co-operation of their masters; but there are skillful artificers, and mechanics also, from Paris, from Brussels, and from far Turin, sent here by subscription, expressly that they may study, profit by, and diffuse the Arts here exhibited in perfection. About the pleasantest fellow *I* met in London was a Turkish official, military by profession, born a Frenchman, but naturalized at Stamboul, who spoke good English, and seemed to understand the world very fairly, though (I judge) rather less a Saint than a Philosopher. The noblest and truest man I encountered in Europe was a Belgian Manufacturer and Juror; and though there were doubtless many unworthy persons attracted to London by the novel spectacle, I doubt whether any General Council of the Christian Church has ever convened an assemblage on the whole superior, morally and intellectually, to that summoned to London by the great Exhibition.

So much of the Crystal Palace and its Contents. And now of its Lessons.

I rank first among these that of the practicability and ultimate certainty of Universal Peace. There have been several amateur Peace Congresses, after a fashion; but I esteem this the first satisfactory working model of a Peace Congress. The men of the Sword and their champions tell us that Nations *will not* submit their conflicting claims and jarring interests to the chances of Arbitration; but here they *did* it, and with the most satisfactory results. Individual heartburnings there must ever be; cases of injustice, neglect of merit, and partiality, there probably were; but as a whole, the award of Prizes at the Fair was discriminating and satisfactory. If the representatives of rival nations there assembled had set to fighting for the honor and credit of their several countries, hired all the bravoes and marketable ruffians they could find to help them, run in debt for more than they were worth, and finally burned up the Glass Palace with all its contents in the heat of the fray, who imagines that the result would have been more conclusive and satisfactory than it now is? Yet the contrast between the settlement of National differences by War and by Arbitration, is as favorable to the latter mode as in the parallel case of rival pretensions to superiority in Art and Industry.

But while I hold that Arbitration is the true mode of settling National differences, and War at all times a blunder and a crime on the part of those who wage it refusing to arbitrate, I do *not*, therefore, hold that those who seek only justice should disarm and proclaim their unqualified adhesion to the doctrines of Non-Resistance, and thus invite the despot, the military adventurer, the pirate, to overrun and ravage at their will. I do not believe that peace and justice are in this way attainable, but by quite a different, an almost opposite course. Let the lovers of Freedom and Right repudiate all standing armies, all military conquests, under any conceivable circumstances—all aggressive interference in the domestic concerns of other nations; but let each People be essentially prepared to resist tyranny at home, and repel invasion from abroad, each with its own chosen weapons, when others shall have proved ineffective. Let the just and pacific take up a position which says to the restless and rapacious, "Be quiet, and do not put us to the disagreeable necessity of quieting you, which you see we are perfectly able to do;" then and thus we may hope for peace; but not while the "old man" absolutely relies on driving off the "rude boys" who are "stealing his apples," with "words and grass" only.

Akin to this is my view of the question of regulated or unrestricted Trade between Nations, which worthily holds so prominent a place in the popular discussions of our time. That men should buy and sell precisely as their several interests (real or fancied) shall dictate, without interference therewith or tax thereon by Governments—this is a very natural and popular demand, which clearly harmonizes with a prevailing tendency of our time, whereof the deification of the individual will and pleasure is the end. But, standing amid this labyrinth of British machinery, this wilderness of European fabrics, I can not but ask, how, with totally unregulated trade, is the all but resistless tendency of Manufactures and Commerce to Centralization to be resisted? How, for instance, shall we rationally hope for the rapid, extensive naturalization of new Arts, the establishment of new and difficult branches of Manufacture, requiring large capital, practiced skill, and ample markets to insure their success, in any quarter of the globe but Europe, while that continent remains the focus of the world's commercial activity and thrift? Suppose, for example, an American should be able to produce the richest and most tasteful fabrics of the French or Flemish looms as cheaply as, or even *more* cheaply than, his European rivals, what are his chances for success in the manufacture? Are there ships departing from *our* sea-ports daily to every inhabited portion of the earth, laden with assorted cargoes of ordered and anxiously-expected *American* fabrics? Have we great mercantile houses engaged in buying up such American fabrics for exportation? Nay, do our own Countrywomen stand ready to buy his Bareges or Laces at the prices which they are daily and freely paying for just such goods from Europe? Suppose he *could* fabricate a hundred thousand pieces per annum, at the lowest possible price for which they can be made in Europe, could he sell them as fast as produced? No, he could not; he does not. The producers in immediate proximity to, in intimate relations with the "merchant princes" of Europe, who are the life-long factors of the traders of India, of Australia, of Asia Minor, Africa, and Russia, have an immense advantage over any rivals located on the Western Continent, or at any similar distance from the commercial centers of Western Europe. The rule that "to him who hath shall be given, while from him who hath not shall be taken away even that he hath," is perpetually and powerfully operative to concentrate the Manufactures and Trade of the world upon London, Paris, and their out-of-town workshops, which, for all commercial purposes, are a part of themselves. This Centralization, unchecked, tends to depopulate and barbarize the rest of the earth, to build up a bloated and factitious prosperity in Western Europe—a prosperity whereof the Laboring Millions are instruments, not sharers—a prosperity whereof a few immense fortunes, amassed at the cost of the world's impoverishment, are the sole enduring trophies. The system which, in the name of Free Trade, is calculated to secure a monopoly of Production and Commerce, in all but the ruder Arts and Manufactures, to Great Britain, France, and Germany, tends to tax the food-grower and the artisan half the value of their respective products, for the cost of transporting them to, and exchanging them with, each other, and so keep them in perpetual vassalage and debt to the "merchant princes," instead of rendering them neighbors and direct exchangers, and thus saving the heavy cost of reaching each other across an ocean and a continent. These convictions are not new to me, but they were strengthened by weeks of earnest observation in the Crystal Palace. More and more was I there convinced that Price is not an infallible measure of Cost, and that a foreign fabric is not proved cheaper than a home-made one, because it is purchased in preference, nor even because it is sold at a lower price. If the whole Earth is ever to be truly Civilized, it must be by the diffusion of the Useful Arts and their Machinery, rather than of their finished products. If Universal Labor is ever to be constantly employed and fairly rewarded, it must be through a more direct and intimate relation of laborer with laborer; not through the system of complexity, aggregation, and needless expense, wherein the grain-grower of Illinois hires through half a dozen intermediates, his Iron made in Wales, and sends his grain thither to pay for the work, instead of having it done at the ore-bed in his township, with the coal which underlies the whole County. I know how strong is the current against this view of Labor's true interest, but the world will refuse to be ruled by names and plausibilities forever.

But the Crystal Palace has other lessons for us than those of Political Economy—it has Social suggestions as well. Here are Hollow Brick, destined, I think, to supersede nearly all others, saving half the expense of solid brick for material and transportation; being far more quickly and cheaply burned; far more easily handled and laid; rendering houses entirely free from dampness, less susceptible to Summer's heat and Winter's cold, while proffering new facilities for warming, ventilation, etc. The invention and diffusion of this Brick alone seem to me worth to mankind the cost of the Exhibition. Here, too, is Claussen, with his Flax discoveries and processes, whereby the entire fiber of the plant is separated from the woody matter of the stalk and rendered as soft, fine, white, and tractable as the choicest Sea-Island Cotton, which it greatly resembles; while, by a little change in the mode of preparing it, it is made closely to imitate Linen, Cotton, or Woolen, and to blend freely in the same web with either. The worth of this discovery to mankind can hardly be over-estimated. Here, too, is his Circular Loom, steadily weaving bags without a seam, and capable of infinite varieties of practical application. Here is McCormick with his masterly Reaper, cutting as clean as Death's scythe, and almost as rapidly; so that the field of waving grain, which the eye could scarcely measure in the morning, has been transformed by it into a field of naked stubble before evening. Here is Ericsson, with his new Caloric

Engine, threatening to reduce steam to its primary insignificance, as, indeed, hundreds have *threatened* before, but as yet none have quite accomplished. Let us hope that some of the present noble strivers will be more successful; for, indeed, steam, though it has done the world good service, is a most expensive ally ; the great bulk and weight of fuel and water it requires to have carried along with it have rendered it thus far entirely useless for locomotive purposes, except on a liquid or metallic track ; while the frequent stoppages it exacts, the nicety of management it demands, and the serious disasters its use involves, unite to proclaim that a blessed day in which mankind shall be able to dispense with it. Whether Ericsson, Page, or some other "visionary," shall achieve for us that victory, I dare not predict; but that its achievement is close at hand, I affirm with undoubting confidence.

A kindred improvement is about to be inaugurated in the more extended and diversified employment of GAS. A hundred models of Gas-Stoves, Gas-Burners, Gas Cooking-Ranges, etc., were exhibited at the Fair, each warranted (as usual), to save half the fuel, and render treble the service of any other ; yet I was not able to designate any one of them as particularly meritorious, nor did the Jury on this department award a premium to any. All seems yet crude and infantile in this field of invention. Yet the study of the various models and contrivances for Gas-Burning there presented, fixed me in the novel faith that Gas is ultimately to be not only the main agent of illumination, but the chief fuel also of all cities and villages ; that the time is at hand when the head of a family, the solitary lodger, requiring either heat or light, will simply touch a bell in his own room, and be supplied with the indicated quantity of Gas, whether for culinary purposes, for warmth, for light, or all together ; and that thus the cost, the trouble, the dust of making fires in all parts of a building, carrying fuel thither, and removing ashes therefrom, will be obviated ; and a single fire, constantly maintained, subserve admirably the purpose of them all ; saving the labor and cost of five hundred wasteful kindlings and clearings, besides affording heat at the moment it is wanted, and stopping its consumption the instant the want is satisfied.

This is but one among a thousand noiseless agencies constantly preaching the advantages and economies of COMBINATION, and indicating the certainty that through Co-operation lies the way whereby Labor is to emerge from bondage, anxiety, and need, into liberty and assured competence. This truth, long apparent to the eye of Reason, threatens to be made palpable even to stolidity and stagnation, by the sharp spur of Necessity. Rude, rugged Labor must organize itself for its appointed task of production, or it will soon have nothing to do. It must concentrate its energies for the creation of commodious and economical homes, or it will have no home but the Union Work-house. It must save and combine its earnings, for the purchase and command of Machinery; or Machinery, owned by and working for Capital alone, will reduce it to insignificance, want, and despair.

On every side the onward march of Invention is constant, rapid, inexorable. The human Reaper of thirty years ago, finds to-day a machine cutting grain twenty times as fast as ever he could; he gets three days' work as its waiter where he formerly had three weeks' steady harvesting; the work is as well done as of old, and far cheaper; but his share of the product is sadly diminished. The Planing-Machine does the work of two hundred men admirably, and pays moderate wages to three or four; the Sewing-Machine, of moderate cost, performs easily and cheaply the labors of forty seamstresses; but all the seamstresses in the world probably do not own the first machine. And so muscular force, or *mere* Labor, becomes daily more and more a drug in the market, shivers at the approach of winter, cringes lower and lower at the glance of a machine-lord or landlord, and vainly paces street after street, with weary limbs and sinking heart, in quest of "something to do."

The only effectual remedy for this deplorable state, and still more deplorable tendency, is found, not in Destruction, but in Construction—not in Anarchy and war on the rights of Property, but in Order and the creation of more property by and for the Poor—not in envy and hatred of the Rich, but in general study and imitation of the forecast and frugality by which they were made rich, which are as potent this hour as they ever were, and which wise Co-operation will render effective for the Poor of to-day. In this country, where so much land is still unappropriated, and the legal right of Association is absolute and universal, the Laboring Classes are masters of their own destiny, and that of their brethren throughout the world. A thousand young men, inured to labor, and as yet unburdened with families, can save at least one hundred dollars each in the space of two years if they will; and by wisely and legally combining this in a capital of $100,000, investing it judiciously in Land, Machinery, and Buildings, under the direction of their ablest and most responsible members, they may be morally certain henceforth of constant employment for each, under circumstances which will insure them the utmost efficiency and the full reward of their labor. To Woman, whose work is still more depressed and still more meagerly rewarded, the means of securing emancipation and just recompense are substantially the same. The workers, in every department of industry, may secure and own the Machinery best calculated to give efficiency to their labor, if they will but unitedly, persistently try. Through the scientific Association of Labor and Capital, three fourths of them may within five years accomplish this, while by heedlessness and isolated competition they are sure to miss it, and see their condition grow gradually worse and worse. Labor working *against* Machinery is inevitably doomed, as the present condition of the hand-loom weavers all over the globe sufficiently attests; labor working *for* Machinery, in which it has no interest, can obtain in the average but a scanty, precarious, and diminishing subsistence; while to Labor working *with* Machinery, which it owns and directs, there are ample recompense, steady employment, and the prospect of gradual improvement. Such is one of the great truths confirmed by the lessons of the Crystal Palace.

Another truth forcibly taught there is that of the steadiness of the march of Invention, and the infinite capacity of the laws and forces of Nature to minister more and more readily and amply to the sustenance and comfort of Man. We are obviously as yet on the bare threshold of chemical discovery and mechanical contrivance for the benefit of Man. The inventor of the Steam-Engine still lived within the memory of many of us; yet even he never dreamed of the stupendous improvements already made on his invention, and the infinite adaptations to human wants of which it is fully proved susceptible. A first-class North River or Sound Steamboat, much more an Atlantic Steamship, would have astonished even *him*. But, though the capacities of Steam are not half exhausted, we grow dissatisfied with its performance, and impatient of its conditions; we demand its power without its weight, its bulk, its cost, its explosive tendencies, or rather those of the elements from which it is evolved—and Electricity, Air, Gunpowder, and other potencies, are analyzed and interrogated in quest of the most advantageous substitute—a search which will ultimately achieve success. The only question is one of time. So in every department of mechanics and manufactures; the victory of to-day opens the path to grander and more beneficent victories to-morrow. There never was a single mind capable of conceiving and working out the idea of the Power Printing-Press of to-day, nor that of the best Carpet-Looms and Paper-Mills in use; each has been produced by gradual, step-by-step improvement; the goal of one inventor serving as the starting-point of his successor; and often an invention which failed to subserve its intended purpose has been found eminently useful in a very different sphere and connection; or, after having been cast aside as worthless, has supplied the necessary hint to another inventor, who has been guided by it to a new achievement of signal beneficence. No real penetration into the arcana of Nature's forces was ever fruitless or unsuggestive. The unpractical side of a newly-discovered scientific truth indicates the position and nature of the practical side as well. To my mind, nothing is clearer than this—the immense strides and vast scope of invention and discovery during the last age, render morally certain the achievement of far more and greater triumphs during the like period just before us. The Railway and its train are by no means the utmost possibilities of overland locomotion; the Telegraph is not the last word of electricity; the Steamship is not the acme of Ocean navigation. These ennobling triumphs herald others which shall swiftly succeed them; and so in all the departments of applied science. And among the agencies which aided and accelerated the march of Invention, which impelled the car of Industrial Progress, I doubt not that our children, looking back on that progress from heights whereof we can but vaguely dream, will honorably distinguish the World's Exhibition of 1851.

Nor can we hesitate to class among the lasting benefits of this Exhibition the wider and deeper appreciation of Labor as a chief source of human enjoyment and a ground of respect and honor for its votaries. I know how little sincerity or depth there is in the usual Fourth-of-July declamation in behalf of the dignity of Labor, the nobleness of Labor, and the like, by men who never did a *bona fide* day's work with their hands unless absolutely driven to it, and who would be ashamed of being caught wheeling a barrow or wielding a spade, unless obviously for exercise or pastime; yet, since "Hypocrisy is the homage which Vice pays to Virtue," even this empty glorification of Labor has some value as a demonstration if not of what the fortunate think, at least of what they think they ought to think. But the tribute paid to Labor in the Great Exhibition was far deeper and higher than this. Here were tens of thousands gathered daily to study and admire the chosen products of the loom, the forge, the shop, the studio, nine tenths of them from no other impulse than that afforded by the pleasure and instruction found therein. Can all this sink into the ground and be forgotten? Shall not we, for instance, who presume ourselves better appreciators of labor than the gilded aristocracies and squalid peasantries of Europe, think more of Industrial capacity since we feel that our country was saved from disgrace at this grand tournament of Industry by the genius of Hobbs, of Steers, of Dick, of M'Cormick? And shall not the Dukes, the Lords, the Generals, the Honorables, who met from day to day to inspect, scrutinize, compare, and judge the rival products of England, France, Germany, and America, in order to award the palm of excellence to the worthiest in each department—who severally felt a thrill of pleasure when a countryman bore off the palm, and a pang of disappointment and chagrin when none such was found entitled to commendation—shall they not henceforth hold in juster esteem the sphere of Creative Art wherein such trophies were lost or won? I can not doubt the beneficent influence of this Exhibition, both in inspiring workers with a clearer consciousness of the quiet dignity of their own sphere, and in diffusing, deepening a corresponding appreciation in the minds of others. If so, who shall say that the Great Exhibition was held in vain?

Yet one more lesson. The "World's Fair" shall teach us the cheering truth that there is rightfully no such thing as "Over-Production," or a glut in the Labor market. There may be misdirected, wasted, useless, or worse than useless Industry, like that devoted to the fabrication of implements of Gaming or Intoxicating Beverages; but of the Labor and Skill devoted to the production of whatever is needful, is tributary to Man's physical sustenance, intellectual and moral culture, or material comfort, there are not and can not be too much. If all were to insist on being employed and subsisted in the fabrication of Hats or of Chintzes, of Pianos or Wall-paper, there would of course be a glut in that particular department, but a corresponding deficiency in others. Not until every family shall be provided with a commodious and comfortable habitation, and that habitation amply supplied with Food and Fuel not only, but with Clothing, Furniture, Books, Maps, Charts, Globes, Musical Instruments, and every other auxiliary to Moral and Intellectual growth, as well as to Physical comfort, can we rationally talk of excessive Production. There is no such thing as general Over-Production, and can be none. Immense as the collection of useful products which the Crystal Palace infolds, it is yet but a drop in the bucket when compared with the far vaster aggregate required to satisfy the legitimate wants even of Europe alone, though that is by far the best supplied of the four quarters of the globe. If each dwelling in wealthy and profusely manufacturing England alone were to be fitly and adequately furnished from the existing stores, the undertaking would very soon dismantle not merely the Crystal Palace, but nearly all the shops and warehouses in the Kingdom. There is at no time a lack of employment because no more needed work remains undone, but only because the machinery of Production has not yet been so adjusted and perfected as to bring the Work and the Workers into their rightful and fruitful relation. Up and down the streets of every great city wander thousands after thousands, seeking work from day to day, and seeking it in vain, when they themselves would reciprocally afford a demand for each other's labor, a market for each other's products, if they could but be placed where they truly belong. Several know how to spin Cotton, Flax, or Wool; others to weave them all into fabrics; and still others to fashion them into the garments whereof the unemployed nearly all stand in need; while other thousands of this hungry multitude know how to grow the grain, and dig or cut the fuel, and make the bread, which are essential to them all. Then why roam this haggard legion from day to day, from week to week, from month to month, idle, anxious, famished, tattered, miserable, and despairing? Do you answer that they lack Industrial training, and thence productive efficiency? Then, I tell you, the greater shame to us, practical workers, or in some sense capitalists, who, realizing their defect, and how it crushes them to the earth—realizing, at least, that they must live somehow, and that, so long as they may remain idle, their sustenance must come out of our earnings or our hoards—still look vacantly, stupidly on, and see them flounder ever in this tantalizing and ultimately devouring whirlpool, without stretching forth a hand to rescue and save them. As individuals, the few can do little or nothing; but as the State, the whole might do much—every thing—for these poor, perishing strugglers. As I look out upon their ill-directed, incoherent, ineffective efforts to find work and bread, they picture themselves on my mind's eye as disjointed fragments and wrecks of Humanity—mere heads, or trunks, or limbs—oftener "hands"—torn apart by some inscrutable Providence, and anxiously, dumbly awaiting the creative word, the electric flash, which can alone recombine and restore them to their proper integrity and practical efficiency. That word no individual has power to speak; but Society, the State, the COMMONWEALTH, may readily pronounce it. Let the State but decree—"There shall be work for every one who will do it; but no subsistence in pauper idleness for any save the incapable of working"—and all will be transformed. Take the orphan from the cellar, the beggar from the street, the petty filcher from the crowded wharves, and place them all where they must earn their bread, and in earning it acquire the capacity to labor efficiently for themselves—this is a primary dictate of Public Economy, no less than of enlightened Philanthropy. Palaces vaster and more commodious than Paxton ever dreamed of might be built and furnished by the labor which now wears itself out in vain attempts to find employment, by the application of faculties now undeveloped or perverted to evil ends. Only let Society recognize and accept its duty to find work for all who can find none for themselves, and the realm of Misery and Despair will be three fourths conquered at a blow by Industry, Thrift, and Content.

But it is time the World's Fair were closed, or at least this meager account of it. The year 1852 has sterner work in hand, in presence of which this wondrous bazaar would seem out of place and incongruous. Haul down, then, those myriad banners, now streaming so peacefully from its roof in the common breeze, and flapping each other so lovingly; they shall full soon be confronted in the red field where the destinies of Mankind must be decided, the liberties of Nations lost and won. Roll out these lumbering cannon, sleeping here side by side so quietly, uncharged, unmounted, the play-things of idle boys and the gazing-stock of country clowns, who wonder what they mean; their iron throats shall tell a fearful tale amid the steadfast ranks and charging columns of the Battle Summer before us. Gray veterans from many lands, leaning on your rusty swords, and stirring each other's recollections of Badajoz, Austerlitz, Leipsic, and Quatre Bras—shake hands once more and part, for the skies are red with the gathering wrath of nations, and air-borne whispers that KOSSUTH is once more free, are troubling the sleep of tyrants. Ho! Royal butcher of Naples! you would not let your subjects visit or enjoy the Exhibition of 1851; rest assured that they will bear a part, and you with them, in the grander, vaster exhibition of 1852. False juggler of the Elysée Bourbon! beware the ides of May, and learn, while not too late, that Republican France has other uses for her armed sons than that of holding sacerdotal despots on their detested thrones. Kingly perjurer of Prussia! you have sworn and broken the last oath to observe and maintain a liberal constitution to which your abused and betrayed people will ever hearken from your lips. Prepare for a reckoning in which perfidy shall no more avail you! Grim Autocrat of the icy North! the coming summer has work in store for *your* relentless legions, not alone this time on the Danube, but on the Rhine, the Oder, the Vistula, as well. Tear down, then, this fragile structure of glass and lath! too slight to breast the rugged shocks of the whirlwind year before us. Ere we meet again as workers to test the fineness of our rival fabrics, the strength of our metals, the draft of our plows, we must vindicate by the mailed hail our right as men to speak, and think, and be. Before us lowers the last decisive struggle of the Millions of Europe for Justice, Opportunity, and Freedom; let not its iron hail appal, its crimson torrents revolt us; for the Bow of Promise gleams through its lurid cloud, and the dove of Peace shall soon be seen hovering over the assuaging waters, fit harbinger of a new and more auspicious era for Freedom and enduring Concord, for Industry and Man!

New York, *November*, 1851

www.ingramcontent.com/pod-product-compliance
Lightning Source LLC
LaVergne TN
LVHW011148110826
845150LV00006B/1187
9781425546359